RENEWALS
DATE DUE

**WITHDRAWN
UTSA LIBRARIES**

Multinationals in their Communities

Also by Ian W. Jones and Michael Pollitt

THE ROLE OF BUSINESS ETHICS IN ECONOMIC PERFORMANCE (*editors*)

UNDERSTANDING HOW ISSUES IN BUSINESS ETHICS DEVELOP (*editors*)

Multinationals in their Communities
A Social Capital Approach to Corporate Citizenship Projects

Ian W. Jones
Lecturer in Management, Somerville College, University of Oxford, UK

Michael G. Pollitt
Reader, Judge Business School, University of Cambridge, UK

David Bek
Research Associate, Centre for Business Research, University of Cambridge, UK

© Ian W. Jones, Michael G. Pollitt and David Bek 2007

All rights reserved. No reproduction, copy or transmission of this publication may be made without written permission.

No paragraph of this publication may be reproduced, copied or transmitted save with written permission or in accordance with the provisions of the Copyright, Designs and Patents Act 1988, or under the terms of any licence permitting limited copying issued by the Copyright Licensing Agency, 90 Tottenham Court Road, London W1T 4LP.

Any person who does any unauthorized act in relation to this publication may be liable to criminal prosecution and civil claims for damages.

The authors have asserted their rights to be identified as the authors of this work in accordance with the Copyright, Designs and Patents Act 1988.

First published 2007 by
PALGRAVE MACMILLAN
Houndmills, Basingstoke, Hampshire RG21 6XS and
175 Fifth Avenue, New York, N.Y. 10010
Companies and representatives throughout the world

PALGRAVE MACMILLAN is the global academic imprint of the Palgrave Macmillan division of St. Martin's Press, LLC and of Palgrave Macmillan Ltd. Macmillan® is a registered trademark in the United States, United Kingdom and other countries. Palgrave is a registered trademark in the European Union and other countries.

ISBN 13: 978–0–230–54568–7   hardback
ISBN 10: 0–230–54568–8   hardback

This book is printed on paper suitable for recycling and made from fully managed and sustained forest sources. Logging, pulping and manufacturing processes are expected to conform to the environmental regulations of the country of origin.

A catalogue record for this book is available from the British Library.

A catalogue record for this book is available from the Library of Congress.

10 9 8 7 6 5 4 3 2 1
16 15 14 13 12 11 10 09 08 07

Printed and bound in Great Britain by
Antony Rowe Ltd, Chippenham and Eastbourne

Library
University of Texas
at San Antonio

Contents

List of Figures	vi
List of Tables	vii
List of Abbreviations	x
Preface and Acknowledgements	xiv
Chapter 1 Multinationals in Their Communities: A Social Capital Approach to Corporate Citizenship Projects	1
Chapter 2 Corporate Citizenship: Definitions and Expenditure	20
Chapter 3 Key Players in the Corporate Citizenship Debate: CSR's Rapidly Evolving Institutional Matrix	49
Chapter 4 Social Capital and Multinationals	90
Chapter 5 Multinationals and Community Engagement in South Africa and Mexico	129
Chapter 6 Multinationals and Community Engagement in Poland	174
Chapter 7 Diageo and its Corporate Citizenship Programme	199
Chapter 8 Anglo American and its Corporate Citizenship Programme	227
Chapter 9 GlaxoSmithKline and its Corporate Citizenship Programme	260
Chapter 10 Vodafone Group and its Corporate Citizenship Programme	282
Chapter 11 What Makes for Good Corporate Citizenship Projects and Programmes?	305
Chapter 12 Learning the Lessons: What Directions should Corporate Citizenship Programmes Take in the Future?	333
Index	347

List of Figures

1.1 The Ethical Issue Life Cycle 6
3.1 The LBG Model 76

List of Tables

2.1	Cross-section of Diageo's community projects	29
2.2	Top US foundations by asset size	38
2.3	Annual corporate donations reported to the PerCent Club 1999–2004	41
2.4	FTSE100 Giving List 2005	41
2.5	Top 20 UK corporate cash givers 2004	42
2.6	Top 20 US corporate cash givers 2004	43
2.7	Top 20 UK corporate in-kind givers 2004	44
2.8	Top 20 US corporate in-kind givers 2004	45
3.1	Comparison of levels of corporate citizenship activity exhibited in selected countries	68
3.2	Comparative economic and social data	74
3.3	Diageo's community investment in £ Sterling by LBG category	77
3.4	CRI performance, 2002–2006	80
3.5	The global spread of the GRI	82
3.6	Involvement in LBG, CRI and GRI of our case study companies	84
4.1	Summarising social capital aspects of CC projects	99
5.1	Rose's (1996) social capital measures	132
5.2	Knack and Keefer's (1997) measures	133
5.3	Narayan and Pritchett's social capital measures (1997)	134
5.4	MHM's (2000) social capital measures	135
5.5	Grootaert's (1999) social capital measures	136
5.6.1	Putnam's (1993) social capital measures	137
5.6.2	Putnam's (2000) SCI variables	137
5.7	Project issue/focus definitions	139
5.8	Regional level institutions: definitions	139
5.9	Scoring system for engagements in a project	140
5.10	Minnesota principles	143
5.11	Network maps: UK firms in South Africa	146
5.12	Norms by industry grouping: UK firms in South Africa	149
5.13	Issue popularity by sector: UK sample	151
5.14	Sectoral engagement by level percentage: UK sample	151
5.15	Sectoral engagement by level: UK sample	151

5.16	Engagement scores and Johannesburg Stock Exchange listing: Industrial and extractive sector firms	152
5.17	Network maps: US firms in Mexico	154
5.18	Norms by industry grouping: US firms in Mexico	161
5.19	Issue popularity by sector: US sample	164
5.20	Sectoral engagements by level percentage: US sample	165
5.21	Sectoral engagement by level: US sample	165
5.22	Summary engagements for US sample	166
5.23	Explaining South African network engagement scores	167
5.24	Explaining Mexican network engagement scores	169
6.1	Number of projects funded, by nation	176
6.2	Breakdown of investment by issue: development gateway categories	177
6.3	Groupings of EU MNC focus	180
6.4	Constituent criteria of the norm index	181
6.5	Scores broken down by industry (NACE) and country of origin	183
6.6	Definitions of the relevant NACE codes	184
6.7	MNC initiatives in Poland – breakdown by issue	185
6.8	Number of engagements by focus and level	186
6.9	Pattern of engagement by focus and level weighted by depth of engagement	186
6.10	Average depth of engagement (Table 6.9/Table 6.8)	186
6.11	Number of engagements, categorised by partner organisation and geographical level	187
6.12	Issue popularity by sector: Poland	188
6.13	Sectoral engagements by level percentage: Poland	189
6.14	Sectoral engagement by level: Poland	189
6.15	Average scores for network maps and norm indices, organised by country	190
6.16	Average number of projects undertaken	191
6.17	Relative preference for projects	191
6.18	Numbers, locations and foci of projects, arranged by MNC nationality	192
6.19	Explaining Poland network engagement scores	193
6.20	Explaining worldwide network map scores	196
7.1	Regional data for Diageo 2004	200
7.2	Community investment performance (£) according to the Annual Giving List	202
7.3	Community investment in £thousand Sterling by LBG category	203

7.4	Community Investment in £ Sterling by focus area 2001–2005	204
7.5	Geographical distribution of environmental champions 2003–2004	214
7.6	Selection of Earthwatch field projects attended by Diageo's champions	214
7.7	Diageo case studies – summary assessment of social capital impacts	224
8.1	Regional data for Anglo American plc 2004	229
8.2	Community investment performance (£m) according to the Annual Giving List	232
8.3	Overall corporate social investment by sector 2004	232
8.4	Sectoral giving through the Anglo Chairman's Fund 2003	234
8.5	Chairman's Fund – number and value of projects 1999–2003	234
8.6	Anglo American case studies – summary assessment of social capital impacts	254
9.1	Regional data for GSK plc 2004	261
9.2	Community investment performance (£m) according to the Annual Giving List	263
9.3	Overall community investment by sector	264
9.4	GSK case studies – summary assessment of social capital impacts	278
10.1	Regional data for Vodafone plc 2004/5	283
10.2	Community investment performance (£m) according to the Annual Giving List	287
10.3	Overall community investment by sector 2003/4	287
10.4	Vodafone case studies – summary assessment of social capital impacts	301
11.1	A comparison of the social capital impact of four projects	306
11.2	Reconciling the pragmatic model and the theoretical basis of social capital	312
11.3	Classification of community engagement projects	317
11.4	Summary of success factors and limitations of main project categories	327

List of Abbreviations

AIDS	Acquired Immune Deficiency Syndrome
ANC	African National Congress
ART	Anti-Retroviral Treatment
BAT	British American Tobacco
BEE	Black Economic Empowerment
BITC	Business in the Community
BPD	Business Partners for Development
BT	British Telecom
CBR	Centre for Business Research, University of Cambridge
CC	Corporate Citizenship
CCC	Corporate Citizenship Company
CCI	Corporate Community Investment
CECP	Committee to Encourage Corporate Philanthropy
CEFTA	Central European Free Trade Area
CEO	Chief Executive Officer
CEP	Code of Ethical Purchasing
CERES	Coalition for Environmentally Responsible Economies
CERG	Corporate Environmental Research Group
CFP	Corporate Financial Performance
CHF	Children's Health Fund
CORE	Corporate Responsibility Coalition
CR	Corporate Responsibility
CRI	Corporate Responsibility Index
CSI	Corporate Social Investment
CSR	Corporate Social Responsibility
DFID	Department for International Development
DTI	Department of Trade and Industry
EITI	Extractive Industries Transparency Initiative
EPA	Environmental Protection Agency
ERM	Environmental Resources Management
ESRC	Economic and Social Research Council
ETI	Ethical Trading Initiative
EU	European Union
FAQs	Frequently Asked Questions
FDI	Foreign Direct Investment
FSC	Forestry Stewardship Council

FSG	Farmer Support Group
FTSE	Financial Times and London Stock Exchange
GAELF	Global Alliance to Eliminate Lymphatic Filariasis
GAO	Government Accountability Office
GATT	General Agreement on Tariffs and Trade
GDP	Gross Domestic Product
GMO	Genetically Modified Organism
GRI	Global Reporting Initiative
GRSP	Global Road Safety Partnership
GSK	GlaxoSmithKline
HIV	Human immunodeficiency virus
HR	Human Resources
HVE	Hippo Valley Estates
IAF	Inter-American Foundation
IBLF	International Business Leaders Forum
IKD	InKind Direct
ILO	International Labour Office
IMF	International Monetary Fund
ISPCC	Irish Society for the Prevention of Cruelty to Children
IT	Information Technology
JSE	Johannesburg Stock Exchange
JV	Joint ventures
KPI	Key Performance Indicator
KRG	Knowledge Resource Group
LAP	Local Action Plan
LBG	London Benchmarking Group
LDC	Less Developed Country
LF	Lymphatic Filariasis
LSE	London Stock Exchange
MBP	Mondi Business Paper
MDG	Millennium Development Goal
MHM	Maluccio, Haddad and May
MIS	Management Information Systems
MNC	Multinational Corporation
MNE	Multinational Enterprise
MP	Member of Parliament
NACE	Statistical Classification of Economic Activities in the European Community
NAFTA	North American Free Trade Agreement
NCP	National Contact Point
NDC	New Denmark Colliery

NEPAD	New Partnership for Africa's Development
NGO	Non-Governmental Organisation
NYCHP	New York Children's Health Project
NYSE	New York Stock Exchange
OECD	Organisation for Economic Co-operation and Development
OI	Opportunity International
OPIC	Overseas Private Investment Corporation
PAN	National Action Party
PCA	Principal Component Analysis
PDA	Personal Digital Assistants
PDF	Portable Document Format
PhRMA	Pharmaceutical Research and Manufacturers of America
PPP	Purchasing Price Parity
PR	Public Relations
PRI	Institutional Revolutionary Party
R&D	Research and Development
RBU	Richmond Business Unit
RMI	Referral Management Initiative
S&P	Standard and Poor's
SB	SmithKline Beecham
SCI	Social Capital Index
SDM	Social Development Manager
SEAT	Socio-Economic Assessment Toolbox
SEED	Schlumberger Excellence in Educational Development
SEF	Small Enterprise Foundation
SENAC	Servicio Nacional de Aprendizaje Comercial
SHE	Safety, Health and Environment
SME	Small and Medium Enterprises
SMME	Small, Medium and Micro Enterprises
SRI	Sustainable and Responsible Development
TB	tuberculosis
TNC	Transnational Corporation
TNI	Transnationality Index
TP	Tomorrow's People
TSF	Télécoms Sans Frontières
TSI	Tshikululu Social Investments
UK	United Kingdom
UN	United Nations
UNCTAD	United Nations Conference on Trade and Development
UNEP	United Nations Environment Programme

UNEP DTIE	United Nations Environment Programme Division of Technology, Industry, and Economics
UNFPA	United Nations Population Fund
US	United States
USAID	United States Agency for International Development
VAT	Value Added Tax
WBCSD	World Business Council for Sustainable Development
WHO	World Health Organisation
WSSD	World Summit on Sustainable Development
WTO	World Trade Organisation
WVS	World Values Survey
WWF	World Wild Life Fund
YBI	Youth Business Initiative
YDB	Youth Development Bond
YEN	Youth Employment Network

Preface and Acknowledgements

This book is based on the results of a six-year research programme at the Centre for Business Research (CBR), University of Cambridge. The work was carried out as part of the Ethics, Globalisation and Regulation project at the CBR. It forms part of the Centre's Corporate Governance, Contracts and Incentives research programme led by Professor Simon Deakin. The support of the Centre, in general, and of Simon Deakin, in particular, is gratefully acknowledged. Much of the work has been financed by the Economic and Social Research Council (ESRC), whose support is appreciated. We also wish to thank Diageo, Anglo American, GSK and Vodafone for their help with the case studies in Chapters 7 to 10.

The authors would like to particularly highlight the contribution to the book of Chris Nyland. Chris was responsible for much of the work behind Chapters 5 and 6, which formed the original inspiration for the book. His work in designing the methodology of social capital measurement in these chapters is very significant. He began this work while a graduate student at the Judge Business School and co-authored three working papers and a journal article over the period 2001–2004. The authors wish you continued success in your career as a lawyer. We also wish to thank Mark Johnson, who provided very excellent help with the regression analysis in Chapters 5 and 6 in the summer of 2006.

The authors also acknowledge the ongoing support of our publishers Palgrave/Macmillan, who published Ian Jones and Michael Pollitt's two previous books in this area: The Role of Business Ethics in Economic Performance (1998) and Understanding How Issues in Business Ethics Develop (2002).

Finally, the authors want to thank their families for their support during the period of 2005–2006 when the book was written up. We especially acknowledge the ongoing support of Sara, Yvonne and Karen. Thank you for your love and patience!

Ian W. Jones
Michael G. Pollitt
David Bek

1
Multinationals in their Communities: A Social Capital Approach to Corporate Citizenship Projects

Introduction

A United Kingdom (UK)-based mining company funds a venture capital fund for black entrepreneurs in South Africa, a US oil-exploration firm funds an Information Technology (IT) training scheme in a Mexican town and a French food producer funds a conference for experts on child nutrition in Poland.[1] These are examples of multinationals engaging in building up the social fabric of developing countries in which they operate. For the firm they represent examples of corporate citizenship projects and form part of their community engagement strategy. They are reported in their annual Corporate Social Responsibility (CSR) reports.

These projects are significant and increasing. In 1994 UK listed firms spent around 0.25% of their profits or around £200 million on corporate citizenship (or corporate social responsibility or corporate social investment) projects.[2] In 2004 the figure was approximately £600 million for FTSE100 companies, increasing to £950 million (or 0.9% of profits) once donations in kind and management time was included.[3] In the US the figure for all US corporations in 2004 was estimated to be $15 billion (or 1.3% of profits),[4] up from $7 billion in 1994.[5] Many of the leading firms included in this figure are multinationals.

The sums of money involved in corporate citizenship projects are significant. Corporate giving in the UK is around 20% of the government overseas aid budget,[6] while in the US it is nearer 50%.[7] In the US corporate giving is 6% of all giving.[8] Around 20% of all US corporate profits are generated abroad, compared to 25% in the UK,[9] suggesting that if this corporate citizenship were carried out overseas in proportion to profits the sums involved would be material. In fact only

8% of US corporate giving was spent overseas in 2004. A significant proportion of corporate giving originates from the firms that operate in the most socially and environmentally sensitive industries, though this share is declining.[10] Some of the money has undoubtedly been wasted: e.g. by the oil major that built three hospitals in Nigeria that never opened.[11] Some corporate giving is undoubtedly aimed at distracting attention from the social and environmental consequences of some companies' production and products – so called 'greenwash' (oil and mining companies spend large amounts).[12] Some companies may be inconsistent spending money on environmental projects while resisting pressure to clean up operations[13] or supporting community healthcare while opposing extension of state provision.[14]

The importance of corporate citizenship expenditure is not just in terms of direct financial support. For pharmaceutical firms there is very significant product donation and distribution (indeed over 25% of headline US corporate giving is product donation by such firms).[15] There are significant inputs of managerial expertise leading to innovative projects which break new ground (such as the phone company that funded local phone shops which allowed poor people to access telecom services).[16] There is a substantial multiplier effect where company involvement occurs in partnership with non-governmental organisations (NGOs), governments, international agencies and hence allows projects to achieve disproportionately more than if the company were not involved (such as the mining company that teamed up with an NGO to tackle AIDS among its workforce).[17]

The world's aspirations for development to 2015 are summed up in the UN's Millennium Development Goals (MDGs).[18] Goal 8 calls for the creation of 'a global partnership for development'. This involves increasing cooperation between traditional development organisations and the private sector. Multinationals are an important part of this partnership for development. This book seeks to assess how it is that multinationals can be more effective in contributing to economic development, particularly in developing countries, via their corporate citizenship programmes.

Why multinationals, why Corporate Citizenship (CC)?

Multinational corporations (MNCs) are increasingly important actors in economic development. They currently account for 33% of world exports and 10% of world GDP (UNCTAD, 2005). Foreign affiliates of multinationals are extremely significant agents of productivity growth with 16% of global private sector R&D (UNCTAD, 2005). These numbers are increasing over time. Developing countries that display greater openness to multinationals have higher rates of economic growth. The significance of multinationals is magnified by their presence as key purchasers of local inputs, agents of globalisation and their high international transparency and accountability to home governments, shareholders and consumers.

Multinationals are mainly headquartered in developed countries. Given their share of world GDP they are responsible for more inputs in developing countries than the development agencies of developed countries. For example a single UK multinational, Unilever, contributed taxes (not including sales taxes) of $170 million to the Indonesian economy in 2003,[19] while total UK development aid to Indonesia was significantly less than $100 million.[20] Multinationals often operate in challenging environments geographically and socially and have the capacity to invest heavily in underdeveloped communities if there is a business case for doing so. As such they are in a position to be a part of the solution to chronic economic underdevelopment such as in sub-Saharan Africa.[21] Multinationals are also increasingly accountable organisations, producing a wealth of information on their community activities in developing countries. Indeed empirical evidence has indicated the importance of public visibility as a driver of both reporting and giving by firms.[22] Thus anyone from the developed world interested in promoting socio-economic development in the developing world should pay attention to the behaviour of these key agents of global development.

Corporate citizenship relates to how companies would like to act towards wider society. An example of a definition used by a leading proponent of corporate citizenship is that used by the international alcoholic drinks firm, Diageo: 'For Diageo, corporate citizenship means acting responsibly in everything we do – where our business impacts on society and the environment, how we govern our company and conduct ourselves in business. As with individual citizenship we believe such responsibility confers rights – to trade freely and be treated fairly. Clearly, this balance is essential to the sustainability of our business.'[23]

Corporate citizenship (CC) has emerged from corporate social responsibility (CSR). However it is subtly different from it. The dropping of the term 'responsibility' is significant, particularly for many companies with significant negative environmental or social impacts.

Such companies want to be seen to be good citizens but not necessarily held fully accountable for all of the consequences of either the production or consumption of their products. Corporate citizenship is also rather different from corporate philanthropy where companies simply wish to give money to good causes with little regard for the benefits to the company of such giving. Rather it is, as the definition from Diageo suggests, about being accepted by society such that the company can trade sustainably.

Corporate citizenship projects are a major part of a wider corporate citizenship strategy that often includes health and safety and environmental issues. Indeed the central rationale for having a separate CSR report is to report on giving to community projects. Indeed mining firm, Anglo American, offers the following definition of corporate citizenship explaining the link between communities' projects and corporate citizenship: 'We respect human dignity and the rights of individuals and of the communities associated with our operations. We seek to make a contribution to the economic, social and educational well-being of these communities, including through local business development and providing opportunities for workers from disadvantaged backgrounds.'[24]

A social capital approach?

Corporate citizenship projects are very diverse, both in terms of the form that they take and the outputs that they produce. In order to compare them within companies, between companies and across countries we need an analytical approach that enables characterisation and measurement. For this we turn to the concept of social capital. A social capital approach is tailor-made for understanding the developmental outcomes and aims that characterise firm engagements in host countries, given that the two dominant analyses of the concept (both of which are outside management literature) are provided by the political scientist Robert Putnam's analyses of engagement in the civic sphere (Putnam, 2000) and the development social scientist Michael Woolcock's critiques of development policy (Woolcock, 1998; 2000).

Social capital can be defined as those 'features of social organisation, such as trust, norms and networks, that can improve the efficiency of society by facilitating co-ordinated actions.' (Putnam, 1993, p.167)

Social capital is an extremely useful analytical concept because it can be used to explain the efficacy for economic activity of different social relations. This immediately suggests why corporate citizenship programmes – as deliberate attempts to improve the social relations enjoyed by a company – might have direct and indirect economic and social benefits. It is also a bridging concept between sociology, political science and economics that allows these disciplines to understand phenomena of mutual interest in language that resonates within each discipline.

Many authors, working within several disciplines, have developed the theory of social capital. Social capital seems to work by improving societal trust (especially outside one's family and ethnic group), reinforcing good norms of behaviour (such as honesty, work ethic and pro-enterprise) and via improved networking between individuals (especially with the influential or well informed). Economists have seen clear links between social capital and the game theory of co-operation and trust (e.g. Dasgupta, 2000). Others might see that social capital is linked clearly to issues of social inclusion.

In this volume we make use of the analytical components of social capital in our case studies of individual multinational corporate citizenship projects. However we also build on some of the empirical social capital literature, which attempts to measure social capital in different contexts in order to test various hypotheses about economic and social development. This is an important task, as it has proved difficult to measure phenomena in CC and CSR, especially to allow inter-company or cross-country comparison. This has the effect of limiting the amount of statistical hypothesis testing that can be applied in this area. By contrast the concept of social capital has now developed to the point where measures of social capital do lend themselves to hypothesis testing.[25]

This volume therefore incorporates an attempt to contribute to the debate about the CSR/CC impact of multinationals, in the light of developments in the empirical social capital literature. The empirical social capital literature has itself focussed on measurement at the level of the country (e.g. Knack and Keefer, 1997) or the region (e.g. Putnam, 2000) rather than at the level of the company, as in this book. The sort of quantification that we suggest may prove useful to concerned companies seeking to benchmark themselves against others, and to development agencies seeking to improve the image and impact of multinationals in host countries.

Understanding CC projects and programmes

Corporate citizenship is closely related to issues of business ethics. Indeed the development of corporate citizenship can be seen as a response to public attitudes to business ethics.[26] Jones and Pollitt

(2002) highlighted the importance to companies of understanding where issues in business ethics came from. They suggested that there existed an ethical issue life cycle. Individual ethical issues existed across a spectrum of seriousness as in Figure 1.1 that ran from voluntary best practice response through to voluntary group response to mandatory response, with issues making progress along the spectrum as public pressure for action on the issue increased. Voluntary best practice involved visionary companies unilaterally taking action on particular issues; where trade associations took coordinated action this was a voluntary group response. A mandatory response involved legal enforcement of corporate actions to deal with the issue. Multinationals' role in economic development has been making progress from left to right along this spectrum. Individual firms, as we shall see, are taking innovative approaches to development. However there have been particular group responses to 'third world suppliers' such as the Ethical Trading Initiative (supported by supermarkets purchasing food and other goods sourced from developing countries).[27] Some issues such as bribery of foreign government officials by multinationals has become mandatory via the pressure of the OECD Anti-bribery Convention which passed into law in the UK in 2002 (modelled on the US Foreign Corrupt Practices Act of 1977).[28]

A desire to understand the issue of how multinationals might be contributing to development in the third world is what has led us to

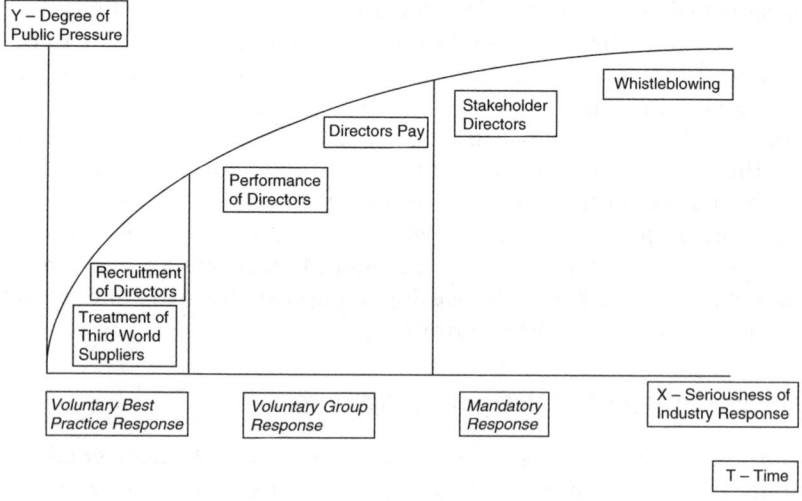

Figure 1.1   The Ethical Issue Life Cycle (Jones and Pollitt, 1999b)

this current volume. Such a starting point brings together the three themes of ethics, regulation and globalisation, which together form the focus of our research project into Business Ethics at the Centre for Business Research in the University of Cambridge, which has been running since 1995.[29]

The research for this book has been conducted over a six-year period and the results contained in the book extend previous published analyses. The work began in 2001 with a study of the corporate citizenship projects of UK multinationals in South Africa (Jones, Nyland and Pollitt, 2001; 2004a). This involved the application of social capital concepts to the empirical scoring of individual firms' projects. In order to extend this work and to test the importance of country of origin and host country effects we conducted a follow up study in 2002 of the corporate citizenship projects of US multinationals in Mexico (Jones, Nyland and Pollitt, 2002). A third study of EU multinationals in Poland was conducted in 2003, allowing us to control for host country effect while still investigating country of origin effects (Jones, Nyland and Pollitt, 2004b). These empirical studies allowed us to map and compare statistically the social capital contributions of corporate citizenship projects. However they raised questions about the exact nature of corporate citizenship programmes, how the effectiveness of individual projects might be measured and how companies chose the projects that they undertook. This led us to conduct a detailed case study of the corporate citizenship strategy of one multinational – the UK alcoholic drinks firm, Diageo, in 2004 (Bek, Jones and Pollitt, 2005). In order to provide comparative information on the details of corporate citizenship programmes, we conducted three follow-up cases in 2005 on companies drawn from the FTSE100 who have received wider recognition for the quality of their CC activities, namely – Anglo American, GlaxoSmithKline (GSK) and Vodafone. These firms were chosen as representing good practice in CSR, to represent a range of industries, and for ease of research access. In each of these cases we engaged in dialogue with each firm about which projects we should evaluate. In some cases they advised us which projects in their view best fitted our research criteria whilst, with their agreement, we also examined other projects to ensure that we covered a sectoral and geographical range. This provides us with a sample of 13 projects including several judged by the companies to exemplify best practice.

Our initial work in South Africa, Mexico and Poland involved desk-based research mainly involving Internet searching of company websites. The case studies involved detailed cooperation from the four case study companies and external verification via interview and correspondence with a number of external participants and NGOs. In this volume we extend the initial work with new econometric analysis of the original data and we publish much of the case study data for the first time. We also aim to draw together the significant insights from this programme of work.

We now summarise the specific questions that we seek to address in this volume.

What are CC programmes and how have they evolved?

Corporate citizenship is a voluntary activity of private companies. As such it is self-defined. Each company is free to make up its own definition of what it means by corporate citizenship and to define the activities which we class as corporate citizenship as corporate giving, corporate philanthropy, corporate social investment, corporate social responsibility, societal engagement, etc. We focus specifically on the budgeted giving of multinationals and what this is spent on. We seek to explain what it is that firms are doing under this general term and explain how this activity has evolved over time. We will do this by looking at the aggregate picture in the US and the UK and by examination of empirical evidence from samples of companies in particular countries and by specific case studies of company programmes and their constituent individual projects.

Who are the principal actors in shaping the CC debate?

By definition, corporate citizenship must involve engagement with parties external to the firm. External interaction opens the firm up to external influence. In line with our previous work on the sources of influence in the development of ethical issues we identify who the key players in the CC debate are. These consist of consultancies, campaigning NGOs, industry groupings and governments in home and host countries. Within the individual projects that we discuss many of these actors play significant roles and hence we discuss them up front (in Chapter 3).

How can we use social capital concepts to better understand CC projects?

Social capital is a concept that allows us to score the value of an individual project, and hence a company's whole CC programme in terms of the social networking involved. We can also score the social norms exhibited by the firm in the quality of its CC reporting. These measures allow companies who have very different projects to be compared. Such numerical comparisons allow the role of industry, size and other factors to be investigated in attempting to explain the differences in CC programmes between firms. We can also use the social capital concept to effect qualitative comparisons between the detailed case studies of individual projects we undertake for our four case study firms. We do this by breaking down the nature of the projects examined into their social capital components. This facilitates comparison of the development nature, mode of functioning and firm and societal outputs of our case study projects.

What do CC programmes look like and do they have a defensible rationale?

Once we have described the societal impact of programmes and projects, it is logical to take the next step of asking to what extent programmes and their constituent projects make sense. For instance, we might suggest that particular sorts of firms are better suited to particular projects, e.g. pharmaceutical firms might be best suited to health-related projects. However CC programmes may either support poorly thought out projects with low social value (minimal social capital impacts) or projects that reflect a history of the firm in its home country. Developing countries might be concerned that MNCs follow first world agendas or neglect social capital building in developing countries because this is where the majority of shareholders, customers and NGO pressure is focussed. We wish to explore where ideas for projects come from, what thought goes in to what the company is doing in this area and can it be rationalised in a way that allows the company to claim credit for being a good corporate citizen. It is of course possible to have a CC programme which makes perfect sense in business terms but which does not represent CSR in the community building way that the company claims for it. Indeed many CC projects have a direct business rationale and these benefits need to be clearly distinguished from claims that they represent corporate philanthropy.

What lessons can be drawn from specific examples of good practice in CC projects?

Our empirical research shows that many businesses undertake little or no CC projects in the countries in which they operate and that there is a large range of variation between the best and the worst performing companies in this area. However there are many examples of excellent projects within excellent CC programmes. Our company case studies cover four MNCs with much to teach others about good practice in this area. The projects we examine were largely the choice of the company concerned and hence represent a corporate view of what best practice projects look like. However they do provide examples of the very best projects in terms of their contribution to social capital and projects, which although the company may value them, are of less value in social capital terms. Our aim in discussing each of the projects is to draw out what made them operate effectively and what areas for improvement within the project can be identified, both in terms of how the project was run and in terms of choosing other projects over the ones selected. We also aim to provide details of how our case study companies organised their overall CC programme in order to develop and choose effective projects.

How can CC programmes contribute more effectively to development?

CC programmes are vehicles for delivering community development. For MNCs this is significantly focussed on developing countries. The issue is how they can be made to deliver development goals more effectively. MDG 8 specifically refers to pharmaceutical and information technology companies as partners in development. It also refers to partnerships to reduce youth unemployment. MDG 5 refers to combating HIV/AIDS. All four of our case study companies highlight at least one major project that directly addresses one of these MDGs. Many other multinationals are also involved with local, national and international projects that address these and other MDGs.[30] The issue is how can CC programmes do more to contribute to development, even within their existing budgets. In discussing this we recognise that there are limits on the role of companies in development both in terms of resources, focus and geographical location. We conclude the volume with lessons for companies and for governments and NGOs in how to more effectively focus CC programmes on building forms of social capital which address the most pressing development problems.

An overview of the chapters

In Chapter 2 we address the issue of what corporate citizenship is. We begin by looking at the term in its global context, relating it to the

OECD Guidelines for Multinational Enterprises, the UN Global Compact and the activities of Business Partners for Development. These three mechanisms have sought to define the responsibilities of multinationals and to encourage their partnership in development and the generation of innovative community engagement projects. We then go on to examine how firms themselves define corporate citizenship and why firms voluntarily undertake corporate citizenship projects. Next we review the body of academic literature which analyses the extent of philanthropy amongst leading firms and the ways in which donation patterns vary between firms of different types. We further develop this literature by examining the value of corporate giving in the US and in the UK, highlighting how this is measured and what information is publicly available on the distribution of such giving. In passing we might note that the trend in corporate giving is up in the UK as more companies subscribe to the PerCent Club[31] standard of giving 1% of their pre-tax profits, while the trend is down in the US where giving has fallen back towards 1% of pre-tax profits from a level above 2% in the mid-1980s.[32]

Chapter 3 focusses on the key players shaping the corporate governance debate: CSR promoting institutions, governments and business grouping initiatives. This is an important discussion in itself but also because many of the players we introduce here re-appear in later chapters.

We begin with specifically CSR promoting institutions. We do this by dividing the players into broad groupings and highlighting the role of some of the leading players within these groupings. We begin with consultancies that provide services for businesses in measurement and assessment of ethical conduct. Here we profile: Accountability and the Corporate Citizenship Group. Next we examine information providers and opinion formers, highlighting the SRI World Group, Mallen Baker and Ethical Corporation as they provide analysis of CSR trends. Then we look at the role of financial indices focussing on the FTSE4Good and the Dow Jones Sustainability Index that encourage firms to attain higher levels of social/environmental standards than the financial market as a whole. A final grouping would be advocacy institutions who represent civil society more broadly and who periodically target MNCs as part of larger social and environmental agendas. One example we look at is the UK NGO Christian Aid, who have authored several significant critiques of MNCs' records on CSR.

Although our research is focussed on a social capital approach to the CC activities of private MNCs, it is clear that development policy is primarily a responsibility of national governments. We discuss the attitudes of the US and UK governments to the role of companies in development and to CSR. We also note the attitude of three host country governments – South Africa, Mexico and Poland – as these three countries are the subject of our empirical work in Chapters 5 and 6. We note the important differences in attitude between governments.

We conclude this chapter by focussing on some of the group responses of companies to CSR. Various systems and methodologies for assessing and encouraging CC have emerged. We profile the London Benchmarking Group's model and the Business in the Community Corporate Responsibility Index which assess the amount of a corporation's CC activity and the Global Reporting Initiative which encourages standardisation of best practice reporting of CC activity.

Chapter 4 relates developments in the theory and measurement of social capital to multinationals community engagement or CC activity. The literature on social capital is extensive, as this chapter makes clear, but what we seek to do is to draw out the facets that allow us to generate observable and measurable social capital features of CC projects. The theoretical elements of social capital can be summarised under scope, form and channel.[33] *Scope* refers to which sorts of actors are involved (e.g. a company official and a local inhabitant). *Form* refers to the method by which social capital is created (e.g. via creating a forum for interaction, such as a committee). *Channel* refers to the way in which improved social relations translates into positive outcomes (e.g. collective action to address a social problem). Social capital has been substantially developed as a tool to compare communities and countries and to relate their levels of civic engagement to economic and social outputs. It has also been used by a small number of writers to analyse the internal operation of companies with a view to suggesting how better social networking, norms and trust within firms could improve their performance.[34] However it has rarely been used in the way we suggest to measure the impact of companies on their host communities. We discuss the literature with this extension in mind and also briefly review the social capital background to South Africa, Mexico and Poland ahead of our empirical work.

Chapters 5 and 6 summarise and extend our previous papers looking at samples of MNCs within particular host countries, drawing on Internet reported engagements. This work provides a broad context for looking at CC activity and comparing it across firms and countries. Drawing on the ideas from the social capital literature we are able to generate two scores for each firm. A *network map score* is a score for the total amount of CC activity. The total score reflects three dimensions: number of projects, the depth of engagement in each project (on a scale of 1 to 5) and the number of levels of engagement (involving four different types of organisation at the local, national and transnational levels). We present this information by type of project (e.g. health or employment). This weighting reflects the social capital value of multiple network linkages at different horizontal and vertical levels. A *norm score* reflects the quality of a company's reporting of its CC activity, its ease of access to information about its community funding and also a measure of participation in the FTSE4Good index or the Global Reporting Initiative where this is relevant. Reducing the multi-dimensional concept of social capital to these easily comparable measures is a core strength of the empirical analysis of social capital. It allows us to extend our analysis by econometric testing of hypotheses about the determinants of the level of CC activity.

Chapter 5 begins this analysis by discussion of the results of two surveys. The first is a survey of 37 UK multinationals in South Africa in 2001. The second is a survey of 73 US multinationals in Mexico in 2002. We outline the measurement methodology and report the firm level network map and norm scores in each case. The results show considerable variation between firms with each sample. Some firms have very significant projects (in terms of social capital), but many firms exhibit a zero network map score. For each sample we seek to explore the drivers behind this econometrically. For both sets of firms we have data on industry of activity, on global and host country size of the firms and the presence of a joint venture. We can also relate norm and network map scores. For UK firms we additionally have information on the existence of a listing on the Johannesburg Stock Exchange and the global CSR spend. For US firms we have information on the age of the Mexican subsidiary. We find substantial industry effects on social capital building activity but a surprisingly small subsidiary size effect. This suggests that while there are some obvious drivers of CC activity, the amount of CC activity is difficult to explain systematically.

Chapter 6 uses the same method of calculating network map and norm scores to examine a sample of 49 EU-based multinationals operating in Poland in 2003. This allows us to examine country of origin effects on CC activity, as we have MNCs originating from the UK, Netherlands, France, Germany, Sweden and Italy in our sample. Network map and norm scores are only weakly correlated indicating a gap between rhetoric and CC activity. As for the earlier samples we are able to undertake econometric analysis in order to examine the network map score using data on industry of activity, on global and host country size of firms, the age of the subsidiary and the presence of a joint venture. However we have also collected data on the absolute number of global corporate citizenship projects broken down by location in home country, Poland or rest of the world. This allows us to investigate the presence of home country bias and relate global social capital projects to industry and size. We find a weak relationship between size in Poland and social capital score and a strong relationship between the level of worldwide CC activity and activity in Poland. We also suggest that firms that are good at CC are good everywhere, regardless of the size of their individual subsidiaries.

Chapters 7, 8, 9 and 10 contain our company case studies in turn. The case studies allow us to go beyond the network map and norm scores and to understand the development of both the whole CC programme in a company and some of the best individual projects. It allows us to address the question of what makes for a successful project in terms of building social capital. For each of our case study companies we begin with a discussion of the company, the ethical issues that it faces and the organisation and scale of its CC activity. We then discuss three or four projects in detail. In each case we examine the origin of the project, the nature of company involvement and discuss what made the project successful (all the projects were regarded as successful by the company concerned). We conclude by providing a detailed comparative analysis of the social capital impact of each project drawing on the categorisation of the scope, form and channel of social capital in Chapter 4. All of the firms that we focus on are genuinely multinational with 60–85% of their operations outside their home country of the UK.[35]

Chapter 7 is a case study of the UK alcoholic drinks firm Diageo. For this firm we discuss four projects, allowing ourselves one more than in the other case study chapters, due to the amount information that we have on this company. The first two projects are *Tomorrow's People* (TP) and *Youth Business International* (YBI) which support youth employment respectively in the UK and internationally. The third project is *Earthwatch*, which is an environmentally-based project that trains local environmental champions within the firm. The final project is *Projeto Bartender* that trains responsible bartenders in Brazil from poor backgrounds, partly to address concerns about socially irresponsible drinking.

Chapter 8 contains a case study of the UK headquartered but South Africa listed mining and resources firm, Anglo American. We discuss three very different projects. *Anglo Zimele* is a venture capital fund for black entrepreneurs setting up small and medium sized businesses. *loveLife* is a project with an NGO to combat AIDS among mining communities. *RBU* (Richmond Business Unit) is a project that involves an engagement strategy with a disaffected local community aimed at reducing attacks on Anglo American forestry assets. This project is an example of the implementation of the company's Socio-Economic Assessment Toolbox (SEAT) used in engaging with local communities.

Chapter 9 looks at the CC policies of the UK–US multinational pharmaceutical company GSK. We look at three projects, all health-related. *Barretstown* is a residential centre providing family holidays with treatment for European children with cancer. *LF* (Lymphatic Filariasis) is an international free drug distribution programme to eliminate Elephantiasis in developing countries. *RMI* (Referral Management Initiative) provides free healthcare to disadvantaged children in the US.

Chapter 10 concludes the case studies with a discussion of the UK-based telecoms multinational Vodafone. Vodafone's three example projects are all technology-related. *Community phone shops* provides subsidies to South African entrepreneurs setting up local phone shops to sell calls to customers too poor to own their own phone. *Opportunity International* provided financial support to a micro-finance NGO operating in Albania and Romania to buy Personal Digital Assistants (PDAs) for its loan officers. *TSF* (Télécoms Sans Frontières) provides support to an NGO that provides telecommunications services in the aftermath of natural disasters.

The 13 cases, taken together, cover a wide range of best practice projects and locations. In terms of geographic scope, ten involve developing countries, of these four are in South Africa, one in Europe, one in South America and four are international. In terms of project type, four are health-related, three involve youth employment, three support entrepreneurship, one is environmental, one involves community relations and one addresses disaster relief.

Chapter 11 discusses what makes for good corporate citizenship projects. It does this by comparing the case study projects and their success in building social capital.

We begin by a comparison of the social capital outcomes of four of the projects, two of which might be thought as superlative examples of how to do projects and two of which are problematic in terms of their social capital impact. We go on to characterise all 13 projects within a framework that examines the types of social networks involved, how these networks worked within the project and what the ultimate outputs for society and for the firm were. We highlight issues which projects address for the firm such as public sensitivities to the misuse of company products or public concern about production methods. We point out which MDGs are impacted by each project.

Next we delve deeper into how individual projects can be made to work effectively. We identify three generic types of project: discrete projects with high profile results (e.g. LF), projects responding to a specific operational business relationship problem (e.g. RBU) and projects which respond to specific relationship problems which are not strictly operational (e.g. Projeto Bartender). In each case we discuss what makes for a successful project of this type, what the limitations on company involvement in this type of project are and the nature of successful management of these projects.

We conclude our lessons from the case studies by focussing on the design of a CC programme, as opposed to just an individual project. These lessons include understanding the strategic nature of the industry of operation in the choice of social capital building projects, the importance of networking for its own sake for corporate reputation, the need for due management process to be followed in allocating and assessing projects, the importance of appropriate partners and the necessity of establishing that company involvement in CC has added value through multiplier and innovation effects.

Taken together we hope the chapters have much to say about the nature of effective corporate citizenship programmes and projects. Our contention is that by applying well established concepts of social capital we can focus attention on how the considerable resources devoted to CC by companies can be leveraged to produce a more positive impact on society. Such effective CC programmes promote economic development, solve social problems and provide positive reasons to support the presence of multinationals in host countries.

Notes

1. Mining company Anglo American's Zimele project is discussed in Chapter 8; Oil exploration firm Schlumberger's SEED programme is discussed in Chapter 5; and food producer Danone's nutrition programme is discussed in Chapter 8.
2. Cash contributions only, *source*: Campbell, Moore and Metzger (2002, p.37). See also Brammer and Millington (2003) for a discussion of trends.
3. *Source: The Guardian*, Giving List 2005 at www.guardian.co.uk
4. The Corporate Giving Standard at www.givingstandard.com
5. See Weedon (1998, pp.5, 6).

Multinationals in their Communities 17

6   This was £3.8billion in 2004–05 increasing to £5.3 billion in 2007–08. *Source*: HM Treasury at http://www.hm-treasury.gov.uk/spending_review/spend_sr04/press/spend_sr04_press09.cfm
7   US Official Development Assistance was $27.5bn in 2005, source: http://www.globalissues.org/TradeRelated/Debt/USAid.asp
8   *Source*: Fulton and Blau (2005, p.7).
9   These are not straightforward to calculate. Total corporate profits in the US were $1183 billion in 2004. Net overseas profits were $176 billion. However US multinationals are part of the gross figure of $330 billion (*Source*: US Bureau of Economic Analysis, www.bea.gov). This suggests that the overseas share is less than 330 / 1183 (because $1183 billion is itself a net figure) but greater than 176/1183. Comparable overseas profit share figures for the UK in 2004 are between 75 / 198 and 37 / 198 (*Source*: UK National Accounts, 2006). We take the mid figure of the two ratios in each case.
10 Brammer and Millington (2003) estimated their share to be 30% of total corporate giving in the UK in 1999, but this had declined from 44% in 1989.
11 See the discussion of Shell in Nigeria in Chapter 4.
12 See Fig (2005) for this perspective on multinational CSR in South Africa.
13 In Chapter 4 we note Anglo American's Mondi subsidiary problems, while in Chapter 8 we have a positive example of a CC project from the same subsidiary.
14 GSK (as SmithKline Beecham) was among a group of pharmaceutical companies resisting Hilary Clinton's attempts in 1993 and 1994 to extend state healthcare provision in the US (see Jones and Pollitt, 1999a), while in chapter 9 we report on a project helping the uninsured to obtain healthcare in the US.
15 *Source*: Corporate Giving Standard, www.givingstandard.com
16 See Vodafone's Community Phone Shops project in Chapter 10.
17 See Anglo American's loveLife project in Chapter 8.
18 See UN (2006).
19 *Source*: Clay (2005, p.40).
20 *Source*: DFID (2006, p.224).
21 See www.BusinessActionforAfrica.org
22 See Campbell and Slack (2006) for UK evidence on this.
23 Lord Blyth of Rowington and Paul S. Walsh (Diageo, Corporate Citizenship Report 2005, p.1)
24 Anglo American (2004, p.3).
25 For examples: see Knack and Keefer, 1997 and Putnam, 2000 who link low social capital to poor economic performance.
26 See Jenkins (2005, pp.526–528).
27 See www.ethicaltrade.org
28 See Rodmell (2002).
29 See www.cbr.cam.ac.uk
30 See World Business Council for Sustainable Development (2005).
31 See http://www.bitc.org.uk
32 See the trend data in Campbell, Moore and Metzger (2002).
33 Following Grootaert and Bastelear (2002).
34 E.g. Cohen and Prusak (2001).
35 Using the Transnationality Index (TNI) reported in UNCTAD (2004, 2005).

References

Anglo American (2004), *Good Citizenship: Our Business Principles*, London: Anglo American.
Bek, D., Jones, I.W. and Pollitt, M.G. (2005), *How do multinationals build social capital? Diageo's Corporate Citizenship Programme*, Centre for Business Research Working Paper, No.285.
Brammer, S. and Millington, A. (2003), 'The evolution of corporate charitable contributions in the UK between 1989 and 1999', *Business Ethics: A European Review*, Vol.12, No.3, pp.216–228.
Campbell, D., Moore, G. and Metzger, M. (2002), 'Corporate Philanthropy in the UK, 1985–2000: Some Empirical Findings', *Journal of Business Ethics*, Vol.39, pp.29–41.
Campbell, D. and Slack, R. (2006), 'Public visibility as a determinant of the rate of corporate charitable donations', *Business Ethics: A European Review*, Vol.15, No.1, pp.19–28.
Clay, J. (2005), *Exploring the Links Between International Business and Poverty Reduction: A Case Study of Unilever in Indonesia*, Oxford: Oxfam GB, Novib Oxfam Netherlands and Unilever.
Cohen, D. and Prusak, L. (2001), *In Good Company – How Social Capital Makes Organizations Work*, Cambridge, Mass: Harvard Business School Press.
Dasgupta, P. (2000), 'Economic progress and the idea of social capital', In Dasgupta, P. and Serageldin, I. (eds), *Social Capital: A multifaceted perspective*, Washington, D.C.: World Bank, pp.325–424.
DFID (2006), *Departmental Report 2006*, CM6824, London: Department for International Development.
Fig, D. (2005), 'Manufacturing Amnesia: Corporate Social Responsibility in South Africa', *International Affairs*, Vol.81 (3), pp.599–617.
Fulton, K. and Blau, A. (2005), *Looking Out for the Future: An Orientation for Twenty-First Century Philanthropists*, Monitor Group.
Grootaert, C. and Van Bastelear, T. (eds) (2002), *Understanding and Measuring Social Capital: A Multi-Disciplinary Tool for Practitioners*, Washington, D.C.: World Bank.
Jenkins, R. (2005), 'Globalisation, Corporate Social Responsibility and poverty', *International Affairs*, Vol.81 (3), pp.525–540.
Jones, I.W., Nyland, C.M. and Pollitt, M.G. (2001), *How do multinationals build social capital? Evidence from South Africa*, December, CBR Working Paper, No.220.
Jones, I.W., Nyland, C.M. and Pollitt, M.G. (2002), *How do multinationals build social capital? Evidence from Mexico*, December, CBR Working Paper, No.249.
Jones, I.W., Nyland, C.M. and Pollitt, M.G. (2004a), 'Multinationals in Developing Communities: How UK Multinationals Build Social Capital in South Africa', *New Academy Review*, Vol.3, No.2, pp.70–91.
Jones, I.W., Nyland, C.M. and Pollitt, M.G. (2004b), *Multinationals in Developing Communities: How EU Multinationals Build Social Capital in Poland*, March, CBR Working Paper, No.285.
Jones, I.W. and Pollitt, M.G. (1999a), 'From Promise to Compliance: the development of "Integrity" at SmithKline Beecham', *Long Range Planning*, Vol.32, No.2, pp.190–198.

Jones, I.W. and Pollitt, M.G. (1999b), *The Development of Ethical Issues facing Boards of Directors: A model with implications*, ESRC Centre for Business Research Working Paper No.151.

Jones, I.W. and Pollitt, M.G. (2002) (eds), *Understanding How Issues in Business Ethics Develop*, Basingstoke: Palgrave.

Knack, S. and Keefer, P. (1997), 'Does Social Capital Have an Economic Payoff? A Cross Country Investigation', *Quarterly Journal of Economics*, Vol.112, pp.1251–1288.

Putnam, R. (1993), *Making Democracy Work: Civic Traditions in Modern Italy*, Princeton, NJ: Princeton University Press.

Putnam, R. (2000), *Bowling Alone. The Collapse and Revival of the American Community*, New York: Simon and Schuster.

Rodmell, G. (2002), 'The OECD's Anti-Bribery Convention', in I.W. Jones and M.G. Pollitt (eds), *Understanding How Issues in Business Ethics Develop*, Basingstoke: Palgrave, pp.135–141.

UN (2006), *The Millennium Development Goals Report 2006*, New York: United Nations.

UNCTAD (2004), *World Investment Report 2004*, Geneva: UNCTAD.

UNCTAD (2005), *World Investment Report 2005*, Geneva: UNCTAD.

Weedon, C. (1998), *Corporate Social Investing*, San Francisco: Berrett-Koehler Publishers.

Woolcock, M. (1998), 'Social Capital and Economic Development: Toward a Theoretical Synthesis and Policy Framework,' *Theory and Society*, 27/1 (1998): pp.151–208.

Woolcock, M. (2000), 'Social Capital in Theory and Practice – Where do we Stand?', In J. Isham, T. Kelly and S. Ramaswamy (eds), *Social capital and economic development: well being in developing countries*, Aldershot: Edward Elgar, pp.18–39.

World Business Council for Sustainable Development (2005), *Business for Development: Business solutions in support of the Millennium Development Goals*, Geneva: WBCSD.

2
Corporate Citizenship: Definitions and Expenditure

Introduction

In recent years several significant global scale corporate citizenship initiatives have emerged via the operations of major international bodies such as the OECD, the UN and the World Bank. The first section of this chapter outlines key guidelines and protocols emanating from each of these globally influential bodies. The reality that such initiatives are being supported at a multilateral level is suggestive of the extent to which notions of corporate citizenship are entering mainstream thinking concerning the role of multinational corporations (MNCs) in the present phase of globalisation. The chapter continues by examining one aspect of corporate citizenship, philanthropy (or giving), which has a long-standing tradition in the USA and we continue our comparative analysis through an examination of current trends in philanthropic activity in the UK and the USA. The corporate citizenship projects, which form the core focus of this book, are the major part of the objects of corporate giving.

Global instruments supporting corporate citizenship

Within the last decade internationally influential organisations have engaged in considerable activity in the area of corporate responsibility. A range of codes of conduct and standards, 'global instruments' (OECD, 2001), have been issued providing guidance to MNCs regarding their non-financial performance and practices. Such instruments are of value to companies in helping them to evaluate their broader responsibilities and to formulate public commitments related to elements of their business conduct. These instruments are quite different in their scope, some focus on very specific areas of business activity; whilst others cover a wide range of applicable issue areas, some identify broad principles whilst others make specific recommendations. Highly influential instruments include (OECD, 2001): the Caux Principles for Business, the Global Reporting Initiative, the Global Sullivan Principles, the OECD Guidelines for MNEs, Principles for Global Corporate Responsibility, Social Accountability 8000 and the UN Compact. Here we examine three of the most influential instruments emanating from the OECD, the UN and the World Bank.

Organisation for Economic Co-operation and Development (OECD) Guidelines for multinational enterprises[1]

The OECD promotes the development of democratic government and market economies. Thirty countries are represented amongst its membership, whilst 70 other countries engage in active relationships with the organisation. The OECD produces internationally agreed instruments and recommendations in order to support the development of good governance in public services and corporate activity. The Guidelines are one part of the OECD declaration on International Investment and Multinational Enterprises adopted by OECD governments in 1976 to facilitate foreign direct investment (FDI) amongst OECD members. The Guidelines set out voluntary principles and standards for regulating business conduct in areas such as employment and industrial relations, human rights, environment, information disclosure, competition, taxation, science and technology. The Guidelines are being applied in the 30 OECD member countries as well as Argentina, Brazil, Chile, Estonia, Israel, Latvia, Lithuania, Romania and Slovenia. The Guidelines seek to promote the constructive role that multinational enterprises (MNEs) can make towards economic, environmental and social progress. Importantly, the Guidelines are the only multilaterally endorsed code that governments are committed to supporting. The Guidelines do not support regulation of MNE activity but instead cultivate an approach built around dialogue and agreement between business, labour and governments. The Guidelines reinforce other endeavours seeking to improve MNE's policies, management and reporting related to the triple bottom line. The Guidelines are promoted via National Contact Points (NCP), the Business and Industry Advisory Committee and the Trade Union Advisory Committee. The NCPs play an integral role in the application of the guidelines. The NCPs promote the guidelines in various ways and seek to provide prospective investors with information about the Guidelines.

The NCPs work with a wide range of organisations including the business community, employee organisations, NGOs and civil society.

The UN Global Compact[2]

A direct initiative of the then UN Secretary General, Kofi Annan, the Global Compact was first announced at the World Economic Forum on 31st January 1999. The central driving force of the Global Compact is the notion that companies, UN agencies, labour and civil society can work together to support and implement universal environmental and social principles. Alternatively, the Compact engages the world's leading companies in 'voluntary programmes that combine CSR with a new level of rigour in global risk management'. Through the evolution of the Compact it is intended that business can be part of the solution to the challenge of globalisation. Communication is integral to the Compact dynamic; thus chief executive officers (CEOs) shall make their commitment explicit to external and internal stakeholders; companies shall communicate 'good stories' of best practice and companies should report on the four areas of concern to the Compact: human rights, workplace issues, environment and anti-corruption. Companies are encouraged to devise performance indicators and/or to utilise the tools provided through the Global Reporting Initiative (GRI).

Objectives and principles

There are two fundamental objectives:

1. Mainstream the ten principles in business activities around the world.
2. Catalyse actions that target UN goals.

The Global Compact's principles are derived from: The Universal Declaration of Human Rights, The International Labour Organization's Declaration on Fundamental Principles and Rights at Work, The Rio Declaration on Environment and Development and The United Nations Convention Against Corruption.

The Principles state that businesses should:

1. support and respect the protection of internationally proclaimed human rights;
2. make sure that they are not complicit in human rights abuses;

3. uphold the freedom of association and the effective recognition of the right to collective bargaining;
4. support the elimination of all forms of forced and compulsory labour;
5. ensure the effective abolition of child labour;
6. ensure the elimination of discrimination in respect of employment and occupation;
7. support a precautionary approach to environmental challenges;
8. undertake initiatives to promote greater environmental responsibility;
9. encourage the development and diffusion of environmentally friendly technologies; and
10. work against all forms of corruption, including extortion and bribery.

Benefits of the Global Compact

Stated benefits of involvement in the Compact include:

- Risk management, as adherence to the Compact principles effectively negates a number of risks currently confronted by corporations.
- Improving corporate management and raising employee morale.
- Leveraging the UN's global reach and convening power with key stakeholders such as government, business and civil society.
- Access to a multi-stakeholder context that facilitates the implementation of solutions to challenges imposed by globalisation, sustainable development and Corporate Social Responsibility (CSR).

Progress[3]

By May 2005 more than 2,000 companies from across the world had made a commitment to the principles of the Compact. These companies include: Accor, Anglo American plc, BP, BT Group Ltd, Diageo, Lafarge, Nestle SA, Nike, Nokia, Pfizer, Volvo AB and Westpac Banking Corporation. The Compact is credited with raising awareness of CSR throughout the global business community. For example, in India more than 90 companies are engaging with the Compact along with other industry and employer bodies. The Compact is not an enforcement mechanism, nor does it benchmark the activities of those involved. It operates according to the principles of 'learning dialogues' and the benefits of constructive networking, thus companies can utilise the Compact as a mechanism for understanding how to implement human rights in the workplace or how to measure environmental performance. There are more than 40 networks now operating globally, these are organised according to geographic and/or sectoral lines.

Critics of the Compact fall into two broad camps. On the one hand, business lobbyists comment that the mechanisms espoused by the Compact can act as a drag upon more fundamental business objectives, whilst socially-oriented critics believe that the agenda is too business oriented and that the voluntary nature of the scheme renders it relatively toothless. Several specific criticisms have been levelled at the Compact by the latter group. Amongst these are (i) concerns that firms with questionable business practices are able to freely participate in the Compact, whilst benefiting from 'bluewash' whereby companies are able to claim that their business activities are approved by the UN; (ii) the way that the Compact operates allows larger companies to compound their power within the global economy; (iii) the Compact's agenda is being shaped by business rather than other stakeholders; (iv) fundamental questions of political economy and macro-economic policy are being sidelined by a focus upon 'the technicalities of specific interventions' (Utting, 2003 in Bendell, 2004, p.19). Thus, the underlying causes of problems relating to poverty and inequality are being neglected.

Business Partners for Development (BPD)[4]

The BPD was set up in 1998 with the aim of generating innovative projects of benefit to communities through partnerships between business, civil society and government. The World Bank Group acted as a facilitating partner during the BPD programme. Three core hypotheses framed the BPD's activities:

- Business partnerships for development can provide win-win benefits for all three partners.
- Partnerships can be used more widely throughout the world.
- Partnerships can be scaled up to national and regional levels.

BPD partners worked on 30 pilot projects in 20 countries over a period of three years. These projects were grouped into four clusters of activity, each supported by co-convenors drawn from differing institutional backgrounds. The clusters were as follows:

Natural Resources (oil, gas and mining companies) which aimed to improve systems for interacting with local communities via tri-sector partnerships. Co-convenors: BP Amoco, WMC Resources Ltd, Care International and the World Bank Group. Projects included: Rio

Tinto's closure of Kelian Gold/Silver mine (Kalimantan) Indonesia and Shell Petroleum Development Company of Nigeria's improvements to their Environmental Impact Assessments.

Water and Sanitation which aimed to learn from existing projects how best to provide appropriate water services for the urban poor. Co-convenors: Vivendi, WaterAid and the World Bank Group. Projects included: Vivendi and Mvula Trust's Management of Water Services in Peri-Urban Areas of South Africa and Lyonnaise des Eaux Innovative Water Solutions for Underprivileged Districts of Buenos Aires, Argentina.

Global Partnership for Youth Development aimed to utilise existing infrastructures in order to mobilise resources to strengthen and scale up best practice in youth development. Co-convenors: Kellogg's, the International Youth Federation and the World Bank Group. Projects included: the Global Alliance for Workers and Communities (Nike and The Gap), China, Vietnam, Indonesia, Thailand and American Express' Travel and Tourism Programmes in Brazil.

Global Road Safety Partnership (GRSP) which aimed to reduce deaths and injuries through collaboration between national and regional authorities. Co-convenors include: the International Federation of the Red Cross and Red Crescent Societies and the World Bank Group. GRSP is active in ten focus countries, including Thailand, Vietnam, Poland, Romania, South Africa and Brazil.

In addition, a Knowledge Resource Group (KRG) was initiated to connect and collect lessons learned on tri-sector partnerships across the four clusters. The KRG was co-convened by the Prince of Wales Business Leaders Forum, CIVICUS and the World Bank Group.

The initial three years of the BPD was considered to be successful as it demonstrated the value of tri-sector partnerships for all stakeholders. Furthermore, it became clear that the principles of collaboration could be rolled out into other arenas. The BPD formally ended in 2001 although the Water and Sanitation and Global Road Safety clusters are still operational.

It is clear that the corporate citizenship agenda has permeated the very highest levels of some of the world's most important organisations and institutions. Clear positions regarding the importance of corporate responsibility and citizenship have been staked out.

Corporations and corporate citizenship

Given the intensity of activity generated by the organisations outlined within the previous section it is only logical that there will have been an appreciable impact upon corporations' activities. It is certainly true to say that shifts in the organisational behaviour of many of the world's leading companies indicate that corporate citizenship is fast gaining currency as a core business practice. As Zadek observes (2001, p.7), 'the last decade has certainly witnessed a renaissance in corporate citizenship'. Indeed, the vast majority of the UK's FTSE100 group of companies claim to be adherents to the corporate citizenship agenda with many having dedicated CSR departments or at least departments, often external affairs, whose remit involves CSR. However, what is it that they are subscribing to? In other words, exactly what constitutes corporate citizenship? The contemporary business lexicon is replete with terms such as Corporate Social Responsibility, Corporate Responsibility, Corporate Citizenship, Sustainable Development, Social Responsibility, Social Investment, Community Investment, and the Triple Bottom Line. To a greater or lesser extent these terms are often deployed almost interchangeably, particularly in more populist literatures. Businesses for their part are able to select terminologies that best encapsulate the philosophy that represents their practice to their internal and external communities at any given point in time. Here we will provide and briefly review some definitions of corporate citizenship, and its sister concept CSR, in order to illustrate the types of corporate behaviour being encouraged.

According to AccountAbility's Simon Zadek, 'Corporate citizenship is about business taking greater account of its social and environmental – as well as its financial – footprints'.[5]

Whilst at the World Economic Forum corporate citizenship was defined as, 'the contribution that a company makes to society through its core business activities, its social investment and philanthropy programmes and its engagement in public policy. It is determined by the manner in which a company manages its economic, social and environmental impacts and good relationships with different stakeholders, in particular, investors, employees, customers, business partners, governments and communities'.[6]

The European Union (EU) has defined CSR as, 'a concept whereby companies integrate social and environmental concerns in their business operations and in their interaction with their stakeholders on a voluntary basis (...) not only fulfilling legal expectations, but also going beyond compliance'.[7]

Business in the Community defines corporate responsibility as the management of: 'a company's positive impact on society and the environment through its operations, products or services and through its interaction with key stakeholders such as employees, customers, investors, communities and suppliers'.[8]

It is clear what is being referred to, at least in broad terms, although the conceptual overlaps between these different definitions are self-evident. These definitions incorporate many of the buzz phrases that frequent corporate citizenship literatures: ethics, sustainability, philanthropy, stakeholders, social, environmental.

Individual companies decide to headline their activities under a single banner, often CSR, sometimes Corporate Citizenship and occasionally Sustainability. Indeed, the chosen headline is very important to the company in terms of the meanings that are conveyed to different audiences. At times the whole image of the company can be at stake. For example, alcoholic beverages company Diageo faces many external affairs challenges owing to concerns over the impact of alcohol on society, especially in the UK. Thus, its decision to focus upon corporate citizenship is extremely important as it infers that Diageo views itself as *citizen* with all the responsibilities that citizenship entails. Anglo American's external affairs concerns have a different focus as the firm's primary impacts are environmental. Thus, developing a stance which seemingly connects the firm to the broader sustainability agenda is highly logical. Despite the differences in the choice of overarching terms there are many similarities in the types of activity being undertaken in the name of corporate citizenship on the one hand and sustainability on the other. Thus, within their respective non-financial reports and website sections Diageo and Anglo American refer to their company's policies and impacts in relation to local and national economies, the environment, their employees and the broader community. In essence, the contemporary corporate citizenship agenda encourages firms to explicitly focus upon their impacts within these areas, to identify, and where necessary, consult with the stakeholders involved and devise appropriate policies. In order to elucidate the ways in which corporate citizenship is practised we include below a brief analysis of the ways that Diageo's 2003 Corporate Citizenship Report (Diageo, 2003) describes and evaluates the firm's corporate citizenship programme.

Diageo categorises its citizenship impacts within the following three impact areas: social, environmental and economic.

Social incorporates the company's responsibilities towards and impact upon the firm's internal community and society at large. Thus, the issue of 'responsible drinking' and the firm's response is discussed. The needs of the firm's employees are considered in some detail and finally the firm's interactions with local communities, particularly through philanthropic and social investment ventures are outlined.

The *Economic* section details the contributions that Diageo makes to its shareholders, suppliers and host governments and their citizens through the payment of taxes and general employment creation in different geographical regions. In addition, the value gained by shareholders, the impacts of the firm's pension scheme and the distribution of value added are outlined.

Environmental outlines the various ways that the firm's operations, especially its manufacturing processes impact upon the natural environment and the steps the firm have taken to reduce these impacts. Recycling and use of energy and water are particular focus areas. In addition, activities to promote biodiversity that are not related to core business are also mentioned.

In addition the report outlines: the firm's approach to corporate governance, especially in relation to corporate citizenship; the systems utilised for measuring and reporting; the firm's status within external indices; and concludes with an Assurance Statement provided by the Corporate Citizenship Company.

The structure outlined above is fairly typical of many company's reports and thus reflects the ways in which corporate citizenship is interpreted at a practical level. Contained within the social impact section is a discussion of Diageo's impacts at a community level. Specific investments into community-focussed projects of one form or another are detailed. Two pages within the 32-page report are specifically dedicated to this aspect of corporate citizenship, although brief references are made to projects in other sections where applicable. Thus, corporate citizenship must be understood as a broad concept within which philanthropy and social investment play only a relatively small part. The majority of citizenship activities are related to the conduct of the business, whether it is related to human resource development, managing the firm's environmental impacts or managing the impact of the firm's product upon wider society. This contradicts a still widely held misconception that corporate citizenship is largely a distraction from the 'business of business' which involves giving away shareholders' money. Much activity in fact supports the business by improving internal governance, ensuring that employees are well trained and motivated, improving the brand image, ensuring compliance with laws and regulations and in some cases preparing for potential future regulation. As we will show in later chapters, even the majority of philanthropic/social investment elements generate important 'business-case' dividends.

It is the philanthropic/social investment element which primarily seeks to benefit local, national and even global scale communities through actions that go beyond the demands of the core business. As we will demonstrate in chapters 5–10, such activities can take one of several forms ranging from a single financial donation to a good cause to a long term financial and institutional investment in a multi-partner initiative on a global scale. For some firms this aspect of citizenship is an integral component of a firm's identity, for others it is more marginal. The vast majority of top MNCs engage in such activities to some extent. It is usually the case that firms' project portfolios tend to comprise a range of activities that are qualitatively very different. There is almost invariably a link between the core business of the firm and the types of social project that the firm chooses to invest in. Broadly speaking firms tend to engage in the following types of projects and programmes: education, health, local economic development, regeneration, environment and disaster relief. The table below illustrates a small cross-section of recent community projects involving Diageo. This demonstrates the range of projects Diageo becomes involved with and the ways that Diageo contributes to these projects.

Table 2.1 Cross-section of Diageo's community projects

Project	Contribution from Diageo
Tomorrow's People	Ongoing 20-year commitment during which £20 million in funding has been provided. Considerable involvement from Diageo personnel at all levels.
Thalidomide Trust	Ongoing 30-year commitment to provide funds to the Thalidomide Trust.
Micro-hydro Training, Peru	£20,000 donated to the Intermediate Technology Development Group to be spent on training and dissemination.
Community Connect Challenge	14 employees from a business department painted and decorated a primary school classroom in Hackney.
Twinning Leaders from Private and Public Sectors	Senior executives and managers twinned with their equivalents in the voluntary sector. Six to eight meetings held over the course of a year to facilitate exchange of skills.
Disaster Relief in Colombia	US$200,000 provided for relief efforts following an earthquake.

Firms' involvement in a project can take a number of forms. The vast majority of projects involve the donation of financial resources, often disbursed via a Foundation. These funds support the activities of a third party, often a charity or NGO. Firms may also donate non-financial resources of one form or another to support the endeavours of their recipient or partner organisation. Such resources can include free or subsidised use of a company's facilities, such as meeting rooms, obsolete equipment or company products. Human resources are also donated, often through employee volunteering programmes. The nature of these latter forms of donation is of particular interest in the context of evaluations of social capital impacts. In some cases a deep form of engagement is facilitated whereby corporate employees become profoundly involved in a partner organisation's work, for example the secondment of a marketing manager to an NGO in order to set up marketing systems and train their staff. Alternatively, the involvement of senior figures in corporations can enable their partners to become part of new influential networks. In these cases corporations can directly stimulate the development of beneficial forms of social capital (see chapter 4). Donating financial resources can bring similar *indirect* benefits, whereby recipient organisations are able to buy-in training, attend conferences or otherwise engage in activities that enable them to develop organisationally. Furthermore, the very fact that an NGO is receiving support from, and publicity via, a major company can be important for profile raising. From a social capital building perspective the most effective forms of engagement occur when companies become more directly involved in the inception and delivery of a partner organisation's project or programme. Furthermore, the business environment is said to foster innovative skills, have a lack of respect for red tape and a 'can-do' attitude. The transfer of such business skills, knowledge and access to networks can add particular value to projects, indeed it can be argued that this is the single most important impact that community-oriented programmes can make. The dissemination of these competencies, sometimes referred to as the 'DNA of business' (Ward, 2005), can reap immense dividends for society more broadly. However, some observers believe that this crucial aspect of corporations' contributions is all too often neglected and that firms tend to engage in relatively superficial ways, which do not maximise their potential impact.

There are a number of reasons why firms engage in corporate citizenship activities:

Firstly, there are internal pressures. It is increasingly being recognised that a firm with a good ethical reputation will succeed in attracting better quality recruits, retaining them and motivating them. According to surveys more than 75% of undergraduates consider a firm's ethical reputation when making job applications (Jones, 2005). This is a particularly important consideration for leading MNCs. Shell's experiences in Nigeria in the late 1990s are reported to have had a negative impact upon the firm's retention rates and graduate recruitment was severely hit in the immediate aftermath.

Secondly, the onset of the new wave of corporate citizenship has certainly been driven by external forces. Civil society generally has come to expect more from corporations than employment and shareholder value. Increasing concerns over corporate conduct – sweatshops, prices paid to third world farmers, executive pay, pollution, support for corrupt regimes and general corporate governance issues have all been propagated within the public domain. As a result there has been pressure on companies to respond positively, not only to mitigate the negative impacts of their actions but also to make explicit contributions to wider society beyond their core business. Many are so doing via their corporate citizenship programmes. Further incentives have come from government and multilateral agencies who wish to tap into 'business DNA' and financial resources in order to overcome some of the more seemingly intractable social and economic ills facing national and global society.

Thirdly, firms are increasingly concerned about their brand image. Corporate citizenship programmes are particularly important to big companies with strong brand images. The direct association between their products and the company leaves firms such as Shell, Starbucks and Nike vulnerable to consumer actions. Such firms have a vested interest in developing well publicised corporate citizenship programmes which can help to deflect criticism. Partner organisations, such as NGOs, may also be willing to stand up for their corporate partners should there be criticism of some aspect of the firm's activities.

Fourthly, some corporate citizenship programmes enable firms to improve their own social capital. This particularly applies in programmes involving a multi-stakeholder, coalition building approach where other big firms, governmental actors and global institutions are involved. The opportunities in these cases for making important contacts and 'gaining the ear' of key policy makers can be immense.

Fifthly, the rise of socially responsible investment indices and products also acts as a stimulus for firms to engage in various elements of corporate citizenship. Inclusion in such indices is perceived as important for two reasons. Firstly, to maximise the quantity of investment directed to the firm. Secondly, firms with clearly defined corporate citizenship strategies that stand up to the scrutiny of the indices are perceived to be firms that are generally well managed. In this sense corporate citizenship acts as proxy for broader corporate governance sending important signals to the wider investment community. Furthermore, firms that are implementing thorough corporate citizenship strategies are more likely to be acting to negate actions that may affect future profits. In this sense corporate citizenship has a direct risk management aspect.

Corporate philanthropy trends

In the last decade or so corporate philanthropy has been subject to an increasing amount of scrutiny by academics based in UK and US business schools. We begin this section by reviewing the literature that has emanated from such research. Such research has examined the extent of philanthropy amongst leading firms as well as analysing the ways in which donation patterns vary between firms of different types. Through such analysis it is possible to identify trends which may be driving the donation process. We proceed by comparing giving trends in the USA and the UK and in the process update analysis of some of the trends identified in the review of the corporate philanthropy literature.

Corporate donations in the UK rose by as much as 146% in real terms during the 1990s. During this time the mean contribution as a percentage of pre-tax profit increased from 0.25 to 0.75% (Brammer and Millington, 2004). However, overall corporate giving is highly concentrated with 50 of the firms listed on the London Stock Exchange (LSE) contributing 92% of all listed company donations. During the 1990s the sensitivity of donation levels to profit variations declined, reflecting perhaps an increase in the strategic value of donations. Interestingly, donation patterns noted in the UK context can be contrasted with sharp declines in the US, where donations dropped from 2.3% to 1.3% of pre-tax profits between 1986 and 1996 as giving managers came under increasing pressure to justify philanthropy in terms of impacts upon the financial bottom line (Buchholtz et al., 1999). Brammer and Millington (2003) note that despite considerable exhortation and some incentivisation the total sum of corporate giving in the UK remains comparatively small, representing less than 5% of the total income of the voluntary sector.

The personal values of CEOs and top level management are thought to play an important role in determining donation patterns (Buchholtz et al., 1999). Such influences are increasingly being mediated by a desire to use philanthropic donations as a means to manage firms' internal and external stakeholders. The upshot is that in many cases corporate philanthropy programmes are being increasingly professionally managed (Brammer et al., 2006) in order to ensure that benefits to the community are maximised whilst 'helping to better position the firm' (Saiia et al., 2003, p.186).

Brammer and Millington (2003; 2004) have uncovered interesting differences in donation patterns according to productive sector. UK-based manufacturing and finance companies tend to be substantially more generous that service companies. Pharmaceutical companies in particular make disproportionately large donations. The existence of such donation patterns has led many analysts to view 'these contributions as a form of investment rather than classic philanthropy'.[9] Various pieces of research suggest that such donation patterns are linked to processes of stakeholder management by firms (Brammer and Millington, 2003; Brammer and Millington, 2004; Brammer et al., 2006; Buchholtz et al., 1999; Campbell and Slack, 2006). Firms with high public visibility, partly measured in terms of size but more associated with strong brand recognition, tend to be substantially more generous (Brammer and Millington, 2004). This is particularly true of firms whose activities are associated with generating negative impacts upon society and the environment. Contributions made by such firms increased disproportionately in comparison to other firms during the 1990s. As Brammer and Millington[10] state, 'corporate charitable contributions are concentrated in a subset of industries that are characterised by significant stakeholder pressure.' Thus, it may well be the case that these companies utilise strategic donations as a means to deflect criticism and reduce the likelihood of regulatory action that may negatively affect the financial bottom line. Indeed, pharmaceutical firms, who have faced an array of criticism related to drug access and animal rights issues, accounted for 17% of aggregate corporate charitable donations in 1999 whilst only being responsible for 3% of aggregate turnover (Brammer and Millington, 2003).

Thus, philanthropy is increasingly strategic in its orientation – an observation backed up by research on US-based firms (Buchholtz et al., 1999). The term 'strategic philanthropy' may appear to be an oxymoron, however firms are clearly conducting an activity dubbed (particularly by donors) 'philanthropy' which is increasingly strategic in the way that it is carried out. In other words the needs of the core business are clearly linked to the outcomes of the act of donation. This linkage causes some observers to believe that the 'ethical basis through which...donations are acquired',[11] is open to question.

Corporate giving in the USA

Publicly available data on corporate philanthropy in the USA is limited. There is no requirement that companies should publicly report levels of spending. Even in cases where they chose to do so there is much variability in the quality and scope of the data provided.[12] This is due to a lack of consistent standards for valuing gifts, particularly in-kind goods and services. However, since 2000 a handful of published surveys have been developed that investigate and, to varying degrees, report upon the extent of giving by US corporations. Here we outline the Giving Standard, administered by the Committee to Encourage Corporate Philanthropy and the annual Business Week survey. The respective methodologies and donation patterns exhibited by these surveys are outlined below.

The Committee to Encourage Corporate Philanthropy's (CECP)[13] Giving Standard

The CECP was founded in 1998 and is the only national philanthropy-focussed forum formed by business CEOs and chairpersons. The Board of Directors includes Paul Newman and GSK's J.P. Garnier. Corporate membership levels now exceed 100. The CECP seek to promote the notion that corporate philanthropy is an important part of a corporation's broader social responsibility and that it is also a sound business practice. The CECP advocates and facilitates the development of increased corporate philanthropy. Excellence Awards are conducted each year, a Corporate Philanthropy Day has been designated, a quarterly newsletter entitled New Century Philanthropy is distributed and an annual survey is conducted in order to produce the Corporate Giving Standard.

Data for the Giving Standard is collected by the CECP using a thorough and systematic methodology devised with the support of the American Productivity and Quality Centre, The Centre for Corporate Citizenship at Boston College and the Corporate Citizenship Company. The Corporate Giving Standard questionnaire requests information on the following:[14]

- Levels of direct and foundation cash grants.
- Non-cash contributions.

- Management and programme costs.
- Volunteer costs and hours.
- End recipients of giving by programme type, geographical, ethnicity and gender.
- Giving by motivation and corporate cost centre.

The Corporate Giving Standard reporting software allows participating companies to view a variety of data reports, facilitates internal year on year comparisons and benchmarking against peer corporations. The number of companies participating in the survey has grown steadily from 17 in 2001 to 71 in 2004, including 30 of the Fortune Magazine's top 100. Whilst the survey collects extremely detailed data, this can only be accessed by the companies who subscribe to the system. Universities, NGOs and the media are not permitted access to the specific corporate level information held within the database.

Key findings from the 2003 and 2004 surveys:

- It is estimated that total giving by US corporations was $13.5 billion in 2003.
- The total giving figure captured by the 2004 survey (estimated to represent 45% of total US corporate giving) of $7.56 billion comprised direct cash donations of $1.48 billion, further cash donations of $1.06 billion and non-cash-donations of $5.02 billion. In addition, corporate sponsored volunteerism was valued at $51 million.
- Median giving as percentage of pre-tax profits was 1.3% in 2004, an increase over the 0.9% reported in 2002 and 1.1% in 2003.
- The ratio of cash to non-cash donations in the overall figures is skewed by the hefty in-kind donations made by the pharmaceutical companies. According to the 2003 survey the average corporation made 75% of their donations as cash and the remaining 25% as in-kind gifts.
- Thirty-one percent of giving was sourced from corporate foundations, 38% from corporate community office departments and 30% from other sources, including individual business units.
- Donations classified as 'charitable' represent 49% of all giving, 'strategic' gifts 36% and 'commercially oriented' gifts 15%.
- The largest programme sector receiving funds was Health and Social Services (36%), followed by Higher Education (15.3%), School Education (11.6%), Community and Economic Development (10.6%), Civic and Public Affairs (6.4%), Arts and Culture (5.7%), the Environment (3.1%), with 10.5% going to other miscellaneous causes.

The Business Week survey[15]

Since 2003 the US journal Business Week has conducted annual surveys of companies' philanthropic spending. Charles Moore from the CECP has lent support to the development of an appropriate methodology. All of the firms in the Standard and Poor's (S&P) 500 Index are sent surveys asking about their cash and in-kind donations. In the first survey 47% of companies responded with some form of data. The survey published in 2004 captured total corporate giving to the value of $3.26 billion. The top five companies in terms of total donations were: Wal Mart ($176 million), Ford Motor Company ($120 million), Altria ($119 million), Johnson and Johnson ($99 million) and Exxon Mobil ($92 million). The Business Week survey makes the best use of the information provided to rank the top 15 monetary and in-kind donors (see tables below). The two rankings are kept separate due to problems in producing accurate, statistically comparable data for in-kind donations. The rankings are based upon the total sum donated in each category and comparability between firms of different sizes is permitted by expressing the sum donated as a percentage of total revenue. An alternative source of US data on corporate giving is provided by Forbes magazine, which publishes selected data taken from the Chronicle of Philanthropy (Moyer, 2005).

Patterns and trends

Only 25% of the companies surveyed contribute to international giving programmes. Yet, at least 22% of corporate revenue is earned overseas. However, the 2004 survey detected a trend towards significant increases in international donations. It is estimated that 16% of US corporate donations are now directed abroad. Examples of specific interventions by US companies include General Electric's commitment to build 11 hospitals in Ghana via donations of $20 million and Intel's provision of facilities in 32 countries providing Internet access and IT training for children. Nike has almost doubled their foreign community involvement, to 39% of all giving, since 2000. Citigroup and IBM both donate almost 30% of their total community spend to programmes in other countries. Thus, some firms are beginning to match the geographical patterns of their revenue sources and their donation distributions. The reasons why increased levels of donations are being disbursed abroad include: overseas markets represent an increasing component of revenue streams; activist pressure relating to perceived social and environmental abuses can be negated to some degree and the increase in anti-American sentiment needs to be combated. A

Gap Foundation Vice President notes, 'our backyard is increasingly larger'.[16]

The authors of the Business Week survey note that an important adjunct to straightforward giving is emerging in the USA – namely the 'core competency movement', whereby companies are working directly with partner organisations in order to share ideas and good practice. Hempel et al. (2004) record, 'businesses are attempting to solve large scale community issues through strategic planning, prudent budgets and in many instances, the same accountability measures they use to evaluate their own business'. Bain and Co., for example, have created an NGO providing charities with cheap consultancy advice to assist them with the day-to-day management of their organisation. This move towards building human and social capitals is strongly supported by James Austin, Chair of the Initiative on Social Enterprise at Harvard Business School, who states, 'by just writing cheques, you are really undermining the full potential of the social potential of the social value you can produce,' (Hempel et al., 2004). Furthermore, such inputs from firms ensure that the full value of their final inputs are maximised, as charities become better equipped to utilise funds efficiently and effectively.

Foundations and individual donations

An interesting facet of US corporate giving is the donation pattern exhibited by individuals whose business activities have netted them large fortunes. Individual giving is a distinctive and well-established feature of American corporate society with a handful of individuals seeking to ultimately invest their entire fortunes into social ventures. During 2003 several immense one-off donations were made: Bill and Melinda Gates donated all $3 billion of their dividends from Microsoft to their Foundation (this compares rather well with the total of $5.76 billion donated by all the companies contributing to the Business Week survey). Whilst Susie Buffett, wife of financial investor Warren Buffett, bequeathed approximately $2.5 billion to their charitable Foundation. Vast individual sums are increasingly being donated to specific programmes in order to kick-start success. As Paul Jansen, director of McKinsey and Co's non-profit practice explains, 'the realisation is that it takes that much money to move the dial'. Thus, seven figure donations are becoming increasingly popular. For example, Alfred Mann whose fortune emanates from medical device development gave $200 million to medical research institutes in Israel and Johns Hopkins University, whilst Sidney Frank donated $100 million

Table 2.2   Top US foundations by asset size

Bill and Melinda Gates Foundation	$29,153,508,000	31/12/05
The Ford Foundation	$11,570,213,000	30/09/05
J. Paul Getty Trust	$9,642,414,092	30/06/04
The Robert Wood Johnson Foundation	$8,991,086,132	31/12/04
Lily Endowment Inc	$8,360,760,584	31/12/05

N.B.: Forty-seven foundations possess assets worth in excess of $1 billion.
Source: http://foundationcenter.org/findfunders/topfunders/top100assets.html

to Brown University to fund scholarships for students from underprivileged backgrounds. In total the top 50 donors identified by Business Week have invested $65 billion into charitable endeavours during their lifetimes. Large targeted donations from individuals are increasingly seen as an important mechanism for stimulating change. In contrast there has been much criticism of Foundations which often only dispense 5% of their assets each year. Whilst this approach enables their beneficial impacts to continue well into the foreseeable future it limits their short term impact and ultimately significantly reduces their buying power. Foundations managed on behalf of individuals are sometimes associated with innovative approaches to problem solving as individuals are often in position to take riskier decisions than corporations who have to consider the reactions of diverse stakeholders when implementing investment strategies. The Gates Foundation, for example, is credited with breaking the mould on approaches to research into developing world diseases, which have been neglected by conventional research programmes. The private sector is being influenced by the leadership being provided in this regard and increasing levels of resources are starting to be directed towards this area.

Corporate giving in the UK

In the UK data on corporate giving is collected as part of the PerCent Standard benchmarking process. The methodology of this index is outlined below and recent results outlined and analysed. In contrast to publication practices in the US this information is published in full on an annual basis in the Guardian newspaper.

The PerCent Standard

The PerCent Standard is a voluntary benchmark administered by Business in the Community (BITC – see profile in Chapter 3). The Index was launched in 1986 by the Prince of Wales. Companies' community contributions via cash, gifts in kind and staff and management time are quantified using an agreed set of guidelines and formulae. The objective of the PerCent Standard is to encourage companies to donate a minimum of 1% of pre-tax profits each year (BITC, 2005b). The guidance notes issued by BITC record that the equivalent statistic in the USA is 2% (BITC, 2005a). Companies who succeed in meeting this objective are awarded a certificate and are allowed to use the PerCent Club logo on their corporate materials. All companies who submit details of their donations are listed in the PerCent Club index. Submissions are included in the Giving List which is published in the Guardian newspaper each November. The PerCent Standard guidance notes outline the methodology for producing reviews of Community Investment programmes. It is recognised that some activities are difficult to quantify and it is suggested that these are detailed in qualitative formats within corporate reporting. The PerCent Standard methodology also states that the intent driving a particular activity should be considered carefully. Thus, activities whose primary purpose relates to core-business goals may not be considered suitable for classification within the community spend figures. For example, sponsorship of major events should be excluded, except for specific components that produce a direct community benefit. Local events may, however, be included provided the corporate publicity gained is 'low key' and the event 'is largely in aid of a charity or local community' (BITC, 2005a, p.3). The Giving List records whether firms are members of InKind Direct (IKD), an organisation that coordinates the distribution of companies' surplus stock to good causes (InKindDirect, 2003; InKindDirect, 2005a; InKindDirect, 2005b). Goods that are donated include: end of lines, seasonal items, samples, customer returns and products with slight defects. The London Benchmarking Group (LBG) and the PerCent Standard provide mechanisms for valuing goods passed on to IKD.

Key points from the BITC guidelines:

- The Index is primarily concerned with UK investment but accepts global data for MNCs.
- Investment values should include: (i) financial contributions (cash donations and sponsorships); (ii) staff time; (iii) provision of professional services; (iv) gifts in kind; (v) use of facilities; (vi) loans of assets.
- Benefits should be experienced by the following groups – charities, not-for-profit organisations, schools and youth organisations, envi-

ronmental, development and cultural groups, organisations that aid social economic regeneration, social enterprises.

Guidance on calculating costs:

- Funds raised by staff, the community and customers should not be included, although associated administration costs and matched funding should be.
- Only paid time-off and direct employee costs should be included in valuing staff time.
- Great care must be taken in costing Cause Related Marketing Programmes. Commercial management aspects should be excluded.

It is recognised that contributions consisting of time and expertise are difficult to quantify, yet they represent a particularly important form of corporate contribution. Outward and inward secondments are popular forms of interaction with external organisations and are, indeed, crucial channels for social capital building. However, such secondments can produce significant dividends for the company, in such cases only a proportion of the costs should be included as community involvement. Qualitative reporting of activities that are difficult to cost is encouraged. Such activities include corporate fund raising, partnership sourcing (procuring goods and services from small local suppliers), locating business sites in economically depressed areas, costs of employee payroll giving and special appeals. Companies often offer considerable support to the education sector. These can include provision of research grants, funding of lectureships and Chairs, provision of educational aids and materials, provision of work experience and shadowing for students and teachers, donations of equipment. These forms of support should all be carefully costed. However, activities such as out-of-hours voluntary involvement of individual staff members within education, such as being school governors, should be excluded from quantifiable assessment but may be referred to in qualitative reporting.

PerCent Standard results 2004 (BITC, 2004a)

Submissions were sought from members of the FTSE250 and BITC's own membership. In 2004, 152 companies reported on their community investment. Of these companies 109 are members of BITC, 56 are members of the FTSE100 and 58 are members of the LBG. One hundred and sixteen companies achieved the 1% standard. Total reported community investment was £934,327,608. Total donations have risen steadily year-on-year. Part of the increase is due to better measurement and reporting. The table below illustrates the breakdown of this investment:

Table 2.3 Annual corporate donations reported to the PerCent Club 1999–2004 (£)

	Cash contribution	Employee time	Gifts in kind	Management costs	Total
2004	604,509,460	60,618,041	195,848,025	73,351,282	934,326,808
2003	496,623,319	44,819,158	263,204,495	50,086,509	854,733,481
2000	244,126,127	28,754,690	41,798,114	28,777,488	343,456,419
1999	200,755,733	25,500,729	35,032,923	22,332,603	283,621,988

Sources: http://image.guardian.co.uk/sys-files/Society/documents/2004/11/08/giving.pdf
http://image.guardian.co.uk/sys-files/Guardian/documents/2004/04/28/2003am endedtable.pdf
http://society.guardian.co.uk/givinglist/tables/0,10999,848892,00.html
http://image.guardian.co.uk/sysfiles/Society/documents/2005/11/28/GivingList_paper_281105.pdf

The PerCent Club have been working increasingly closely with the LBG in order to ensure consistency of reporting, accuracy of measurement and completeness of submissions. LBG members are encouraged

Table 2.4 FTSE100 Giving List 2005

	% of pre-tax profits	Cash donation (£m)	Staff/management costs (£m)	Gifts in kind (£m)	Total donation (£m)	Rank 2004	Members of
ITV	10.8	2.86	0.07	19.18	22.37	1	% IKD
J Sainsbury	2.7	2.34	0.3	4.12	6.76	5	LBG
GlaxoSmithkline	2.0	48.4	17.7	56.8	122.9	10	%, LBG
Anglo American	1.2	23.26	2.49	0.6	26.35	19	LBG
Diageo	1.2	20.13	1.22	1.27	22.62	18	%, LBG
Vodafone in the UK	0.5	7.65	0.53	0.11	8.29	56	LBG

Source: Giving List 2005, http://image.guardian.co.uk/sys-files/Society/documents/2005/11/28/GivingList_paper_281105.pdf

'to submit data for assessment against the PerCent Standard and PerCent Club members to embrace the work of the LBG' (BITC, 2004b).

Comparison of US and UK corporate giving 2004

The tables below facilitate the drawing of comparisons between the cash and in-kind donations made by the top UK companies and their US counterparts during 2004. The data provided in the tables above is drawn from the Giving List, which focusses upon the philanthropic performance of the members of the FTSE100 Index. The US data is published by Business Week magazine based upon a survey of the members of the S&P500. In 2005, 204 companies provided data for the survey. The first pair of tables (2.5 and 2.6) focusses upon total levels of reported cash donations and thus lists the top 20 donors in absolute

Table 2.5   Top 20 UK corporate cash givers 2004

	2004 cash donations (£m)	$m equivalent	% of profits
Rio Tinto	49.63	93.21	2.4
BP	49.19	92.12	0.58
GSK	48.4	90.58	0.78
HSBC	39.11	73.44	0.4
Lloyds TSB	32.24	60.54	0.90
RBS	28.29	53.12	0.43
Unilever	27.59	51.81	1.43
Barclays	27.41	51.47	0.94
BHP Billiton	25.52	47.92	0.79
Anglo American	23.26	43.65	1.06
Diageo	20.13	37.78	1.07
BAT	14.60	26.56	0.8
Tesco	13.51	25.34	0.68
BT Group	13.12	24.61	0.63
AstraZeneca	11.7	21.94	0.4
SAB Miller	9.00	16.87	0.7
HBOS	8.79	16.48	0.27
BAA	8.12	15.22	1.24
Vodafone in the UK	7.65	14.34	0.45
National Grid	7.3	13.68	0.55
Average figures	**23.23**	**43.53**	**0.87**

Source: Giving List 2005, http://image.guardian.co.uk/sys-files/Society/documents/2005/11/28/GivingList_paper_281105.pdf

N.B.: Dollar equivalents calculated on 2nd August 2006 at $1.87 to £1.00.

Table 2.6 Top 20 US corporate cash givers 2004

	2004 Cash donations ($m)	% of profit
Wal-Mart Stores, Inc.	188	1.2
Johnson & Johnson	121.8	0.9
Altria Group, Inc.	113.4	0.8
Citigroup Inc.	111.3	0.5
Ford Motors	109.8	2.3
Bank of America Corp.	108	0.5
Target Corp.	107.8	3.6
Exxon Mobil Corp.	106.5	0.3
Wells Fargo	93	0.9
Wachovia Corp.	81.7	1
General Electric	81.0	0.4
SBC Comms Inc.	81.0	1.1
Intel Corp.	79.4	0.8
Verizon Communications	71.4	0.6
Lilly, Eli	71.3	2.4
Pfizer, Inc.	70.6	0.5
SLM Corp.	41.2	1.6
Coca-Cola Co.	67.2	1.1
Bristol-Myers Squibb	64.4	1.5
Chevron Texaco Corp.	63.8	0.3
Average figures	**91.6**	**1.12**

Source: Business Week Survey – www.businessweek.com/philanthropy/2005/donations.htm

value terms in each country. In order to facilitate cross-company comparisons these are expressed as a percentage of pre-tax profits. The second pair of tables (2.7 and 2.8) compares in-kind donations between the top performers in each country. It is important to treat these data with some care as methodologies for capturing in-kind valuations vary considerably as no international standards have yet been agreed upon. However, the data provided is the best available at the present time and does facilitate the drawing of tentative conclusions.

Observations

The data provided by these sources suggests that there are similarities in the generosity of UK and US firms. In the UK six of the top largest donors give away 1% or more of their profits, whilst in the US seven firms do likewise. On average the top US firms are slightly more generous – donating 1.12% of their profits, whilst in the UK the equivalent figure of 0.87%. In the US the larger firms are more generous in

Table 2.7 Top 20 UK corporate in-kind givers 2004

Company	2004 In-Kind Donations (£m)	$m equivalent	% of profits
GSK	74.5	140.00	1.21
HBOS	23.77	44.50	0.51
ITV	19.51	36.50	9.41
RBS	17.73	33.20	0.27
Unilever	16.69	31.33	0.93
WPP	11.6	21.70	2.54
Tesco Stores	8.24	15.43	0.41
BT Group	7.67	14.39	0.40
BHP Billiton	6.88	12.90	0.21
Marks and Spencer	6.81	12.80	0.90
Cadbury Schweppes	4.14	7.77	0.62
Pearson	3.58	6.71	0.84
Lloyds TSB	3.23	6.06	0.10
Standard Chartered	2.97	5.57	0.24
Rolls Royce	2.59	4.86	0.83
Boots Group	2.23	4.18	0.46
Severn Trent	1.96	3.67	0.84
Reed Elsevier	1.70	3.19	0.41
O2	1.69	3.17	0.41
Whitbread	1.38	2.59	0.52
Average figures	**10.94**	**20.53**	**1.1**

Source: Giving List 2005, http://image.guardian.co.uk/sys-files/Society/documents/2005/11/28/GivingList_paper_281105.pdf

N.B.: Dollar equivalents calculated on 2nd August 2006 at $1.87 to £1.00.

absolute terms with an average donation of $91 million as against $43 million in the UK – a trend exemplified by the top performers in each country – Rio Tinto gave away $93 million compared to Wal Mart's $188 million. Of course the relative size of the companies concerned should be taken into account, which is why the percentage profit figure is a useful comparative indicator. Looking beyond the Top 20 companies in absolute terms it is apparent that US firms are more generous as only a dozen UK firms are listed as donating 1% or more compared to 64 in the Business Week list.

In terms of In-Kind Giving the available data suggests that US companies are more generous – average donations amongst the top 20 are only $20 million compared to $304 million. Only three UK companies exceed the 1% mark compared to 16 US firms. The variations noted

Table 2.8 Top 20 US corporate in-kind givers 2004

Company	2004 in-kind donations ($m)	% of profit
Pfizer, Inc.	1,161.9	8.3
HCA Inc.	926	43.3
Merck & Co.	921	n/a
Bristol-Myers Squibb	601.9	13.6
Johnson & Johnson	407	n/a
Microsoft Corp.	362	2.2
Lilly, Eli	338	11.5
Abbott Laboratories	270	6.5
Halliburton Co.	227	34.9
Oracle Corp.	151	3.7
Time Warner Inc.	135	2.6
International Business Machines	115.5	1
Safeway Inc	100	12.6
Altria Group, Inc.	66.8	0.5
Biogen IDEC Inc.	65	101.4
Yum! Brands, Inc.	54	5.3
PepsiCo, Inc.	50	0.9
Genzyme Corp.	46.2	20.8
Hewlett-Packard	45	1.1
McGraw-Hill Corp.	43.2	3.7
Average figures	**304.3**	**15.3**

Source: www.businessweek.com/philanthropy/2005/inkind.htm

here stem in part from differences in the methodologies employed for calculating levels of such inputs. Furthermore, the US figures are dominated by pharmaceutical companies who are likely to utilise a more generous market value price system for counting the value of drug donations whereas in the UK valuations are tied more closely to the much lower production cost figures. Moyer (2005) notes that Merck and Bristol-Meyer Squibb made donations equivalent to 9% and 11% of profits respectively in 2004 and the majority of all their donations was in the form of pharmaceuticals.

The focus on corporate giving in the analytical literature and in the reporting leaves us with the question of what is the impact of this giving? Exploring this, using data on actual corporate citizenship projects, is the focus of later chapters. The next chapter, however, continues our discussion of the nature of corporate citizenship, providing more detail on the key actors shaping the corporate citizenship agenda.

Notes

1. See OECD (2005a, b, c).
2. See unglobalcompact.org (2005a, b, c).
3. See PriceWaterhouseCoopers (2005).
4. Sources: BPD (2005a, b, c).
5. Zadek, (2001, p.7).
6. www.weforum.org/pdf/GCCI/corpcitizen.pdf.
7. www.weforum.org/file-storage/download/?file_id=29500.
8. http://www.bitc.org.uk/about_bitc/faqs.html.
9. *Source*: Siegfried et al. (1983, pp.87) cited in Adams and Hardwick (1998, p.641).
10. Brammer and Millington (2003, p.224).
11. Brammer and Millington (2003, p.225).
12. See for example Baue (2004 and 2005) and GAO (2005).
13. See corphilanthropy.org (2005).
14. See givingstandard.com (2005a, b, c).
15. See Hempel (2003, 2004) and Hempel et al. (2003).
16. http://www.businessweek.com/magazine/content/04_48/b3910408.htm.

References

Adams, M. and Hardwick, P. (1998), 'An Analysis of Corporate Donations: United Kingdom Evidence', *Journal of Management Studies*, Vol.35: pp.641–654.

Baue, W. (2004), *Report Finds CSR Policies on the Rise in Asia, Europe and North America*. Available at: www.socialfunds.com/news/print.cgi?sfArticleId=1446. Accessed 11/10/2005.

Baue, W. (2005), *GAO Finds Federal Corporate Social Responsibility Programs Widespread but Uncoordinated*. Available at: www.csrwire.com/sfprint.cgi?sfArticleId=1817. Accessed 11/10/2005.

Bendell, J. (2004), *Flags of Inconvenience? The Global Compact and the Future of the United Nations*, International Centre for CSR, Nottingham University, ICCSR Research Paper Series, No. 22.

BITC (2004a), *2004 PerCent Standard Results*. Available at: www.bitc.org.uk/programmes/programme_directory/percent_club/results.html. Accessed 10/05/2005.

BITC (2004b), *Message from the PerCent Club Chairman*. Available at: www.bitc.org.uk/programmes/programme_directory/percent_club/message_from_chairman.html. Accessed 10/05/2005.

BITC (2005a), *The PerCent Club Index – Guidance*. Available at: www.bitc.org.uk/programmes/programme_directory/percent_club. Accessed 09/05/2005.

BITC (2005b), *The PerCent Standard*. Available at: www.bitc.org.uk/programmes/programme/percent_club/index.html. Accessed 09/05/2005.

Brammer, S. and Millington, A. (2003), 'The Evolution of Corporate Contributions in the UK between 1989 and 1999: industry structure and stakeholder influences', *Business Ethics: A European Review*, Vol.12: pp.216–227.

Brammer, S. and Millington, A. (2004), 'The Development of Corporate Charitable Contributions in the UK: A Stakeholder Analysis', *Journal of Management Studies*, Vol.41: pp.1411–1434.

Brammer, S., Millington, A. and Pavelin, S. (2006), 'Is Philanthropy Strategic? An analysis of the management of charitable giving in large UK companies', *Business Ethics: A European Review*, Vol.15: pp.234–245.
Buchholtz, A.K., Amason, A.C. and Rutherford, M.A. (1999), 'Beyond Resources. The Mediating Effect of Top Management Discretion and Values on Corporate Philanthropy', *Business and Society*, Vol.38: pp.167–187.
Business Partners for Development (BPD) (2005a), *Knowledge Resource Group, Focus Projects*. Available at: www.bpdweb.com/projects.htm. Accessed 19/08/2005.
Business Partners for Development (BPD) (2005b), *Knowledge Resource Group, Overview*. Available at: www.bdpweb.com/overview.htm. Accessed 19/08/2005.
Business Partners for Development (BPD) (2005c), *Welcome*. Available at: www.bpdweb.com/index.htm. Accessed 12/08/2005.
Campbell, D. and Slack, R. (2006), 'Public Visibility as a determinant of the rate of corporate charitable donations', *Business Ethics: A European Review*, Vol.15: pp.19–28.
corphilanthropy.org (2005), *About CECP: Overview*. Available at: www.corpphilanthropy.org/cdocs/cecp.html. Accessed 10/08/2005.
Diageo (2003), *Corporate Citizenship Report*, Diageo plc, London.
GAO (2005), *Globalization: Numerous Federal Activities Complement U.S. Business's Global Corporate Social Responsibility Efforts*. Available at: http://www.gao.gov/new.items/d05744.pdf. Accessed 29/09/2005.
givingstandard.com (2005a), *The Corporate Giving Standard*. Available at: www.givingstandard.com/cgsSolution.htm. Accessed 10/08/2005.
givingstandard.com (2005b), *Welcome to the Corporate Giving Standard*. Available at: www.givingstandard.com. Accessed 10/08/2005.
givingstandard.com (2005c), *Who we are*. Available at: www.givingstandard.com/cgsWho.htm. Accessed 10/08/2005.
Hempel, J. (2003), *A Corporate Cornucopia*. Available at: http://www.businessweek.com/cgi-bin/register/archiveSearch.cgi?h=03_48/b3860622.htm. Accessed 10/08/2005.
Hempel, J. (2004), *Linking Companies and Communities; That's what corporate philanthropy does, says expert Cari Parsons, who cites IBM, Novartis, and GE for leading the way*. Available at: http://www.businessweek.com/bwdaily/dnflash/dec2004/nf20041221_2988_db008.htm. Accessed 10/08/2005.
Hempel, J., Conlin, M., Tanzer, J. and Polek, D. (2003), *The Corporate Donors*. Available at: http://www.businessweek.com/cgi-bin/register/archiveSearch.cgi?h=03_48/ b3860616.htm. Accessed 10/08/2005.
Hempel, J., Gard, L., Polek, D. and Tanzer, J. (2004), *The Corporate Givers*. Available at: http://www.businessweek.com/cgi-bin/register/archiveSearch.cgi?h=04_48/b3910408.htm. Accessed 10/08/2005.
InKindDirect (2003), *Annual Review 2003*. Available at: http://www.inkinddirect.org/_uploads/simpleattachments/AnnualReview03.pdf. Accessed 21/05/2005.
InKindDirect (2005a), *About Us*. Available at: www.inkinddirect.org/html/3. Accessed 21/05/2005.
InKindDirect (2005b), *Benefits of Donating*. Available at: www.inkinddirect.org/html/41. Accessed 21/05/05.
Jones, H. (2005), *Is Corporate Social Responsibility Important to You?* Available at: http://www.milkround.com/s4/jobseekers/news/general/editorial_display.asp?newsid=5100&from=1. Accessed 20/08/2005.

Moyer, L. (2005), *The Most Charitable Companies*. Available at: www.forbes.com/ 2005/11/11/charities-corporations-giving-cx_1m_111charity_print.html. Accessed 01/08/2006.

OECD (2001), *The OECD Guidelines and Other Corporate Responsibility Instruments: A Comparison*. Available at: http://www.oecd.org/dataoecd/ 46/36/2075173.pdf. Accessed 04/09/2005.

OECD (2005a), *About OECD*. Available at: www.oecd.org/about/0,2337, en_2649_201185_1_1_1_1_1,00.html. Accessed 05/09/2005.

OECD (2005b), *Guidelines for Multinational Enterprises, About*. Available at: www.oecd.org/about/0,2337,en_2649_34889_1_1_1_1_1,00.html. Accessed 05/09/2005.

OECD (2005c), *The OECD Guidelines for Multinational Enterprises: FAQs*. Available at: www.oecd.org/document?58/0,2340,en_2649_34889_2349370_1_1_1_1,00.html. Accessed 05/09/2005.

PriceWaterhouseCoopers (2005), *The UN Global Compact: Moving to the Business Mainstream*. Available at: http://www.unglobalcompact.org/content/NewsEvents/ ArticlesPapers/pwc_int_2005.pdf. Accessed 09/08/2005.

Saiia, D.H., Carroll, A.B. and Buchholtz, A.K. (2003), 'Philanthropy as Strategy. When Corporate Charity "Begins at Home".' *Business and Society* Vol.42: pp. 169–201.

Siegfried, J.J., McElroy, K.M. and Biernot-Fawkes, D. (1983), 'The Management of Corporate Contributions', *Research in Corporate Performance and Policy* Vol.5: pp.87–102.

unglobalcompact.org (2005a), *About the Global Compact*. Available at: http://www.unglobalcompact.org/Portal/?NavigationTarget=/roles/portal_user /companies/Companies/nf/companySearch. Accessed 08/08/2005.

unglobalcompact.org (2005b), *Frequently Asked Questions*. Available at: http://www.unglobalcompact.org/Portal/?NavigationTarget=/roles/portal_user /companies/Companies/nf/companySearch. Accessed 08/08/2005.

unglobalcompact.org (2005c), *Participant Search*. Available at: http://www.unglobal-compact.org/Portal/?NavigationTarget=/roles/portal_user/companies/Compani es/nf/companySearch. Accessed 08/08/2005.

Utting, P. (2003), *The Global Compact: Why All the Fuss?* Available at: www.un.org/ Pubs/chronicle/2003/issue1/0103p.65.html. Accessed 16/09/2005.

Ward, H. (2005), *Corporate Social Responsibility–a step towards stronger involvement of business in MEA implementation?* Available at: http://www.oecd.org/dataoecd/ 63/46/35173055.pdf. Accessed 17/11/2005.

3
Key Players in the Corporate Citizenship Debate: CSR's Rapidly Evolving Institutional Matrix

Introduction

'Most people...would be amazed if they lifted the stone of contemporary business activity and saw the armies of consultants, experts, charlatans and do-gooders scurrying around inside and outside companies trying to help them become more socially responsible' (Hilton and Gibbon, 2002).[1]

This chapter is intended to provide important contextual information on the forces shaping the development of corporate citizenship. It details some of the key institutions that have shaped the development of corporate citizenship programmes and which are mentioned in our case studies in chapters 7–10.

Since the late 1990s issues surrounding corporate social responsibility (CSR) have moved rapidly into the mainstream of daily business discourse. Integral to this process has been the evolution of a complex network of organisations and actors that feed into, feed off and drive the practice of CSR. Moon (2004, p.15) has referred to the ways in which 'UK CSR has grown and become more institutionalised'. This institutionalisation is reflected in the rapid growth of business organisations, consultancies and information sources whose collective endeavours have a CSR focus. The growth in consultancy services is symptomatic of the extent to which the phenomenon that may be labelled the 'new wave of CSR' in the UK has become institutionalised. Eighty-four organisations who provide CSR consultancy services have been identified in the UK, of these 62% have been formed within the last decade (Fernandez-Young et al., 2004). Whilst business associations with a CSR remit and related member organisations have also emerged and experienced rapid growth. This growth can be associated with an increasingly concern for the management of ethical issues within business practice (Jones and Pollitt, 2002).

In the first section below we provide pen portraits of some of the many organisations which form part of CSR's rapidly evolving institutional matrix. Some are represented here due to their centrality and influence within UK, and even global CSR, whilst others are profiled because they play an important role in one or more of the corporate case studies profiled later in this book. In this sense the array of organisations represented here is not intended to be definitive or even fully representative of the institutional matrix as a whole. However, a snapshot is provided of the types of organisation that are interfacing with corporations and influencing their citizenship strategies in one way or another. By its very nature such an intricate institutional matrix is evidence of social capital development as the key players form part of important and often influential networks of association.

Here we categorise CSR-related organisations into broad groupings, although it should be noted that there are overlaps as some organisations offer a wide variety of services. Thus, in the first section we profile two of the leading firms, AccountAbility and the Corporate Citizenship Group, who provide *consultancy* services for businesses by developing and promoting measurement protocols for assessing ethical conduct of various forms. *Information* and *opinion leading* services such as SRI World Group, Mallen Baker and Ethical Corporation collate and publish various forms of information and analytical accounts concerning global CSR trends. Such accounts are directed towards the needs of a range of stakeholders, most especially those in the corporate and financial worlds. Whilst *financial indices* such as FTSE4Good and the Dow Jones Sustainability Index, provide products ring fenced for corporations deemed to be attaining certain levels of social/environment standards. Whilst the aforementioned organisational types all operate within the mainstream of daily business discourse, other forms of organisation offer an important, alternative outlook via *advocacy*. Here, we profile NGOs such as Christian Aid who claim to represent civil society more broadly and as such are in a position to critique the processes and praxis of corporate citizenship from the perspective of non-financial stakeholders.

During our interviews with corporate representatives it became clear that these various organisations and specific individual actors are collectively very important in driving corporate agendas. Of course firms operate within specific regulatory environments driven by national governments. Here we firstly outline the political and socio-economic status of South Africa, Poland and Mexico in relation to the scope for MNC activity that exists in each country. This information provides an important contextual setting for the analysis that ensues in chapters 5 and 6. Then we briefly examine governmental responses to the corporate citizenship agenda in the USA and the UK. It is clear that this broad agenda has made substantially greater inroads into policy discussions in the UK and Europe than in the USA.

The chapter's second section considers how firms are responding to the apparent imperative to adopt corporate citizenship within their business plans. In particular the ways in which companies are interpreting citizenship are considered in terms of the types of programme being described and implemented. The final section outlines the ways in which companies are responding to the need to measure and report upon their activities. Various systems and methodologies have emerged, which are rapidly becoming industry standards in this regard. Here, the methodologies driving the London Benchmarking Group's (LBG) model and Business in the Community's Corporate Responsibility Index are profiled.

Consultancies

AccountAbility (The Institute of Social and Ethical AccountAbility)

A not-for-profit organisation formed in 1995 that seeks to strengthen the social responsibility and ethical behaviour of the business community and non-profit organisations (AccountAbility.org.uk, 2005). It is international in its scope and draws together a membership from business, civil society and the public sector. AccountAbility develops and disseminates systems of social and ethical accountability, auditing and reporting. AccountAbility have developed and promoted the AA 1000 Series, which enables organisations to record and evaluate their ethical performance and which facilitates inter-organisational comparisons. AccountAbility also undertake research that evaluates ongoing developments within CSR. An annual conference is held each year exploring themes consistent with AccountAbility's remit. Social Reporting Awards are held to recognise the achievements of organisations which are demonstrating good practice in reporting and measuring their social impacts. AccountAbility's CEO (in 2006) is Simon Zadek who is widely recognised as an influential figure in the ongoing evolution of CSR and its associated reporting mechanisms.

The Corporate Citizenship Company (CCC)

The CCC was formed in February 1997 by CSR specialists David Logan and Michael Tuffrey. The company (in 2006) has a team of ten full-time consultants, researchers and support staff based in London and is linked in with a network of specialist associates across the globe. The CCC has three specialisms: issues research, evaluation through measurement and benchmarking and reporting. The company's mission is to 'help companies succeed as commercial entities by being active corporate citizens, so meeting the aspirations of their diverse stakeholders and the wider society of which they are part' (Corporate Citizenship Company, 2005a).

Corporate community involvement is a key area of the CCC's work. Logan and Tuffrey have been at the forefront of the development of the LBG model. Furthermore, they provide advice on the development of corporate citizenship programmes, for example, 'from where (a) company can do the most good, to the form of contribution best suited to (the) firm, through to which "third sector" organisations (a company) should consider partnership with in any given country' (Corporate Citizenship Company, 2005a).

Examples of the CCC's work in different arenas is outlined below (Corporate Citizenship Company, 2005b):

- Production of an in-depth study of the total impact 'footprint' of a single industry in a sub-Saharan country.
- Conducting a ground-breaking study of the impact on Poland of a British drinks company's operations.
- Establishing a forum for companies that are applying the LBG model to their community contributions programmes.
- Undertaking an assessment of the procedures for establishing a corporate foundation for a major European multinational.
- Drafting codes on child labour and human rights in the supply chain in Africa, Asia and the former Soviet Union.
- Facilitating a seminar at the Commonwealth heads of Government Meeting Forum on business and society.
- Carrying out an assessment of the HR benefits of long term corporate volunteering for a major development NGO.

Business-led organisations

Business in the Community (BITC)

Business in the Community was established in 1982 (BITC, 2005b). At this time of high unemployment and urban riots there was recognition amongst BITC's founders that large companies needed to become more involved with their local communities. Its formation can be interpreted as one of the first signs of the ongoing new wave of corporate citizenship in the UK. The Prince of Wales became President of the organisation in 1985 and has subsequently attended over 350-related engagements. BITC is a registered charity whose purpose is to 'create a public benefit by working with companies to improve the positive impact of business in society' (BITC, 2005d). BITC currently has in excess of 700 members (including Anglo American, Diageo, GSK and Vodafone) and a further 1,600 participate in programmes and campaigns. BITC works with 45 global partners and operates in the UK through 98 local business-led partnerships. BITC has 400 employees working in 48 offices within the UK, its headquarters are in Hackney, London. BITC commits its members to, 'manage, measure and integrate responsible business practice throughout their business' (BITC, 2005a; BITC, 2005d).

BITCs activities are diverse. A series of benchmarks have been developed to help companies in the quantification of their non-financial activities. The Business in the Environment Index was initiated in 1998 and is now utilised by 206 companies, including 83 from the FTSE100. Benchmarks and trackers evaluating corporate interventions in the workplace, marketplace and community are also used. The Corporate Responsibility Index (CRI) is one of the newest of their initiatives.

BITC run a broad range of programmes. A selection of these in 2005 is provided below (BITC, 2005c):

- *Business Action on Education* encourages and facilitates business engagement from the 70% of member companies who identify education as their focus for community involvement and inspires the remaining 30% to get involved.
- *Cares* is the main business-led employee volunteering programme in the UK. Employees give their time and skills to the communities in which they live and work.
- The *Cause-Related Marketing Campaign* generates awareness and understanding of cause-related marketing, inspiring a greater quality and extent of programmes by demonstrating the power of brands in partnership with charities and causes to make a positive impact on key social issues.
- The *Corporate Community Investment* campaign is involved in a range of programmes from benchmarking, measuring and evaluating corporate community investment (CCI) to promoting best practice

through regional awards and case studies, from helping companies to get started to leading on corporate social innovation.
- The *CSR Academy* is an initiative supported by the Department of Trade and Industry which aims to promote CSR learning through its CSR competency framework. It is for companies of all sizes as well as for UK educational institutions.

The International Business Leaders Forum (IBLF)

Founded in 1990 as a personal initiative of HRH The Prince of Wales, the not-for-profit forum operates in 60 countries and has a membership of more than 70 MNCs. Diageo, GSK and Vodafone are amongst the IBLF's 16 listed Principal Supporters and Anglo American are amongst the 45 Council Members (IBLF, 2006). The forum aims to promote international leadership in responsible business practices and to work strategically with leaders in business, civil society and the public sector in transition and emerging economies. The Forum operates according to an A, B, C, D of core principles:

- Advocacy of the case for business social responsibility and partnership.
- Brokerage of partners.
- Capacity-building in training managers and partners for leadership and action.
- Dissemination of ideas and good practices.

The IBLF has been ground-breaking in that it has endeavoured to raise and tackle major issues before they enter the mainstream. For example, IBLF challenged corporations to explicitly consider issues such as human rights, social development and business ethics in the early 1990s. The IBLF utilises a network approach in order to maximise its impact. It operates capacity-building programmes in order to disseminate knowledge and encourages self-sustaining action through the formation of business coalitions, such as independent Business Leaders Forums.

Information services

SRI World Group Inc, which was founded in 1999, is a US-based social investment and CSR reporting news, research and consultancy firm that advises clients regarding sustainable development investment issues and corporate responsibility practices. It is the parent company of *CSRwire.com*, a global news service for Corporate Responsibility press releases, *SocialFunds.com* the Web's largest personal finance site devoted to social investment issues and *InstitutionalShareholder.com* which provides an information service about social investment issues tailored to the requirements of institutional shareholders. SocialFunds.com includes a Corporate Social Research centre that provides social and environmental assessments of more than 1,000 US and overseas corporations. Details of specific SRI Funds and articles on a range of current issues are provided by the Group. SRI World Group Inc have recently launched OneReport, an electronic reporting network that facilitates efficient reporting on social, environmental, economic and corporate governance issues to investors, the financial community and other stakeholders. OneReport has been constructed such that it is consistent with GRI guidelines and data assurance can be provided via AA 1000 Assurance standards. AccountAbility's Simon Zadek describes OneReport as 'a crucial piece of the accountability puzzle going forward'.

MallenBaker.net – the personal website of BITC's Development Director. The website reflects 'how companies respond to the agenda for corporate citizenship, the growing need to manage issues that affect their business reputation and to respond to the growing needs and concerns of a range of different stakeholders.' The site examines emerging CSR issues from across the world, with a focus upon the agents driving change in business practice. As well as providing articles drawn from a range of media across the world Baker also writes analytical articles drawing upon his own experience and perspective.

Ethical Corporation, founded in 2001, is financed by and headquartered with First Conferences Ltd an independent privately owned publisher. Ethical Corporation produces a monthly magazine, a website that is updated daily, holds conferences and publishes research informed reports on the practice of business ethics in major companies. Ethical Corporation recently produced a report for the World Bank and the International Finance Corporation entitled 'Race to the Top, Attracting and Enabling Global Sustainable Business'. Their report 'The Business and Human Rights Management Report' claims to be 'the first such in-depth report on the subject' (Ethical Corporation, 2005). Among the companies analysed are BP, Anglo American and BT(British Telecom).

Ethical investment indices

In recent years Socially Responsible Investment (SRI) has been a notable feature within international financial markets. The demand for responsible investments has been associated with the production of specifically tailored investment products and the creation of sustainable investment indices. In the USA, where 11% of investment funds are directed towards SRI, the Dow Jones Sustainability Indexes were launched in 1999 in order to track the financial performance of the world's leading sustainability driven companies. In South Africa in 2004 only 1% of the R1.7 trillion local investment industry is so directed. It is to be hoped that the introduction (in 2004) of the Johannesburg Securities Exchange's Socially Responsible Investment Index will address this imbalance and help to direct investment in ways that will challenge the profound political, economic and social challenges faced within South Africa. In the UK the leading ethical index is administered by the FTSE Group.

FTSE4Good Index series

The FTSE4Good Index series was launched in July 2001 to assist those interested in socially responsible investment. The FTSE4Good selection criteria cover three areas:

- Working towards environmental sustainability.
- Developing positive relationships with stakeholders.
- Upholding and supporting universal human rights.

The FTSE4Good website (FTSE4Good.com, 2005) notes that implementation of effective CSR policies, and thus successful inclusion within the FTSE4Good Indices, can benefit corporations in various ways, for example by mitigating the following risks: reputation damage, reduced access to human capital, litigation, higher security costs, media harassment, critical shareholder action and reduced access to capital. In order to be entered into the indices companies must pass through selection criteria which evaluate their performance and systems in the above three areas. The indices are reviewed every six months. Companies that fail to perform according to acceptable standards can be removed from the Index. Nestle were excluded due to their strategy for marketing breast milk substitutes. The number of companies in the index has increased from 700 to 900 since launch in 2001. In 2002 450 firms failed to meet the necessary criteria. By March 2005 almost 200 of those firms had achieved the required standard, whilst 80 had been deleted and 100 are working towards meeting the criteria. Diageo, GSK and Vodafone have been successful in achieving FTSE4Good listings. FTSE4Good are continually refining their criteria. In 2003 its human rights criteria were reviewed and tightened. Fifty-eight companies responded and were able to meet the criteria, whilst 20 others were deleted. In November 2004 the policy committee approved new, more stringent supply chain labour standards. In this way the bar for entry into the indices is gradually being raised by small but attainable increments. The new labour standards criteria apply only to 'first tier' suppliers – those that corporations have the closest, most direct relationship with. According to Mallen Baker, 'FTSE4Good is biting off what it can chew for the time being, addressing known solvable problems. In the future FTSE4Good will consider adding more teeth to the criteria, for example, applying the criteria down the supply chain to the source or adding audit requirements'.

Advocacy groups

A loose coalition of NGOs and lobbying groups are involved in advocating changes in corporate practices and the broader regulatory environment within which business operates. The organisations involved are largely household names including Oxfam, Save the Children, *ActionAid*, War on Want and Amnesty International. Whilst there is much cooperation between these organisations they can certainly be differentiated in terms of their oppositional emphasis with some, such as War on Want having radical objectives whilst others, such as Oxfam, are more closely aligned with mainstream development thinking. Furthermore, some observers note that some organisations enjoy preferential access to policy makers and the media. Collectively, the work of these bodies has been vital in terms of stimulated debate, uncovering evidence of corporate misdemeanours and in shifting policy agendas. Below, some of these groups (including ones contacted during the course of this research) are briefly profiled and their key research contributions to corporate citizenship debates are identified.

Oxfam

Oxfam was formed in 1942 as a Famine Relief Committee dedicated to persuading the British government to allow essential supplies through the Allies naval blockade, which was causing dire food supply problems for civilians across Europe (Oxfam.co.uk, 2006). Oxfam's objectives evolved in subsequent decades to become one of the world's best-known advocates for the eradication of global poverty. Oxfam's actions in this regard include fund raising, local development projects, policy research and advocacy and pro-poor marketing. In terms of research-based lobbying with implications for corporate activities important reports include, 'Rigged Rules and Double Standards – trade, globalisation and the fight against Poverty' (maketradefair.com, 2002) and 'Beyond Philanthropy – the Pharmaceutical Industry, CSR and the Developing World' (Oxfam et al., 2002) and 'Offside! Labour rights and sportswear production in Asia' (Oxfam International, 2006).

Christian Aid

Christian Aid is a UK and Ireland-based charity that is involved in many projects in developing countries that seek to assist people living in poverty (Christian Aid, 2004a; Christian Aid, 2004b; Christian Aid, 2005a; Christian Aid, 2005b). Christian Aid is also involved in research and advocacy work, which informs its development assistance programmes. Christian Aid specifically aims to tackle the causes of poverty and injustice through its direct project work and through its education and advocacy endeavours (Oxfam.org.uk, 2006). In the mid-1990s Christian Aid produced two ground-breaking reports, which were pivotal in bringing concerns about child labour to wider audiences – 'Pulling the Rug on poverty: Child Labour in India's Carpet Industry' (1994) and 'Sporting Chance. Tackling Child Labour in India's Sports Goods Industry' (1997). Christian Aid's recent contributions to analysis of CSR include: 'BAT (British American Tobacco) in its own words – Behind the mask of corporate social responsibility', a report which shows how BAT fought to resist international health laws to curb smoking (Christian Aid et al., 2004).

'Behind the mask: The real face of corporate social responsibility' (Christian Aid, 2004a), a report which analyses case studies of CSR and concludes that voluntary approaches are proving ineffective and thus calls for laws to make multinational companies meet basic social and environmental standards in poor countries.

Corporate Watch

Corporate Watch is a small, independent not-for-profit advocacy body, which researches and publishes material detailing the social and environmental impacts of large corporations (Corporate Watch, 2005a; Corporate Watch, 2005b). The group's research is used to support the anti-corporate movement's campaigns against perceived corporate excesses. Corporate Watch have conducted research into many aspects of corporate activity including the oil industry, privatisation, toxic chemicals, food production and genetic engineering. Corporate Watch does not accept donations from government or corporations but instead relies upon individuals and independent trusts and foundations to provide support. A website is maintained providing detailed profiles of some of the world's largest corporations and their misdeeds, as well as industrial sector overviews. A similar organisation named Corpwatch operates in the USA.

Action Aid

Action Aid was founded in 1972 as a child sponsorship charity based in the UK (Action Aid, 2006e). During the 1980s Action Aid's size and scope grew rapidly as the organisation's focus shifted to tackling the root causes of poverty rather than just its symptoms. A key aspect of Action Aid's work has been to engage communities such that they might improve their access to resources and achieve political influence (Action Aid, 2006d). More recently Action Aid has sought to actively lobby governments and agencies such as the World Bank. In 2003 Action Aid International, with a head office in South Africa, was launched as a coalition to fight poverty across the world (Action Aid, 2006a). Between 1999 and 2005 Action Aid worked towards the attainment of four strategic goals: 'equal rights for women', 'influence the powerful', 'global action against poverty' and a 'voice for all' (Action Aid, 2006c). Corporate accountability is one of Action Aid's themes for research and advocacy. Recent research contributions in this area include: 'Rotten Fruit: Tesco profits as women workers pay a high price'; 'Under the Influence: exposing undue corporate influence over policy-making at the WTO' and 'Power Hungry: six reasons to regulate global food companies' (Action Aid, 2006b).

Corporate Responsibility Coalition (CORE)

CORE's central objective is to lobby for improved regulation of corporate activities (CORE, 2006a; CORE, 2006b). The underlying premise of CORE's ethos is that the voluntary approach to corporate accountability has failed. Whilst the UK government has claimed that the changing demands of the marketplace will ensure that companies meet their environmental and social obligations, in reality few firms prioritise the triple bottom line in their decision-making. CORE is campaigning for new laws in three areas: Mandatory Sustainability Reporting, Directors' Duties of Care to include community and environment as well as profit-making and Access to Justice whereby UK law has to be made to apply to corporate activities abroad. CORE's steering group includes Amnesty International UK, Action Aid, Christian Aid, Friends of the Earth, Traidcraft, War On Want and WWF (UK). Overall membership is drawn from 130 diverse organisations including the Transport and

General Workers' Union, the Unity Trust Bank and various individuals including political representatives.

Corporate citizenship in the USA – policy and praxis

The policy environment

American companies are 'ambassadors of American values – values like democracy, freedom and respect for human dignity', former US Secretary of State, Colin Powell (Powell, 2003).

The USA hosts more multinationals than any other country, indeed many of the world's largest and most powerful firms are US-based. As Powell asserts such firms can play a pivotal role in highlighting the qualities of their home nation, however if they transgress the rules of good corporate citizenship they can compromise America's image and even undermine its foreign policy interests. Yet in 2006, there is no official US definition of CSR and there has been little effort by the federal government to formulate a coherent strategy to promote CSR strategies amongst the US corporate community. According to Aaronson and Reeves, 'the US (has a patchwork) of poorly coordinated and little known policies' whilst Conley and Williams (2004, p.5) note 'on the legal front it (the CSR movement) has thus far had limited impact in this country (USA)'. In contrast, various indicators show that ethical and social concerns are of significance to key constituents within American society: $1 in $8 in investments such as social funds, mutual funds and foundations are now directed towards socially responsible funds; corporations donate in excess of $15 billion a year to philanthropic and related causes; wealthy individuals direct seven figure investments towards social causes and the public at large increasingly engage in activities such as purchasing fair trade and organic products, supporting environmental and social causes and engaging in consumer activism. It is against this backdrop that a momentum seems to be slowly building such that CSR may gain a more explicit foothold within the federal policy environment.

In 2003 a study entitled 'The Kenan Consensus' was published by the Global Corporate Social Responsibility Policy Project based at the Kenan-Flagler Business School, University of North Carolina. The study was generated through the contributions of a multi-stakeholder group of representatives from business, civil society, government, labour and academia. The group made a series of 18 recommendations outlining ways that the government can give priority, focus and consistency to its efforts to support global CSR. These recommendations can be summarised under the following themes:

- Promote transparency and disclosure practices.
- Encourage adherence to internationally accepted social and environmental standards.
- Offer resources to improve governance institutions worldwide.
- Strengthen US government co-ordination and capacity to promote global CSR.
- Convene multi-stakeholder dialogues to encourage and strengthen global CSR practices.
- Provide incentives and use government procurement policies as tools to promote global CSR.[2]

Amongst the specific recommendations are suggestions that the US State Department should explicitly promote the OECD Guidelines for MNEs, whilst the Department of Labor should promote adherence to the ILO's Tripartite Declaration of Principles concerning MNEs and Social Policy. Furthermore, the government should create a multi-stakeholder forum to promote global institutions such as the GRI, Fair Labour Association, the Ethical Trade Initiative and Social Accountability International.

This study generated much interest, to the extent that three Congressmen requested that the Government Accountability Office (GAO) produce a report establishing the nature of current government policy and praxis in relation to CSR and outline ways that the government can support firms in improving their social and environmental practices. The resultant report entitled 'Numerous Federal Activities Complement US Business's Global Corporate Responsibility Efforts' was published in August 2005.

The report recorded that there is evidence that US firms are involved in many activities that may be classified as CSR-related, although corporate policy often does not make an explicit link to the CSR agenda. Thus, activities in the realms of business ethics, community development, environment, governance, human rights, marketplace and workplace can be identified. A small number of firms utilise reporting systems for environmental, social and economic data beyond that required for formal financial reporting, whilst some firms 'conduct some CSR effort' (GAO 2005, p.10). Sixty-nine firms have registered with the GRI and 71 have signed up to the UN's Global Compact by 2006.

The GAO report conducted a thorough review of current US policy programmes and revealed that there was no federal government led legislation driving the development of CSR. Indeed, few government agencies operate working definitions for CSR. The research conducted to inform the GAO report examined federal policy programmes in great detail. In the process it was revealed that over 50 programmes, policies and activities within 12 agencies can be considered relevant to the promulgation of CSR, although few agencies actively label their activities as supporting CSR. Thus, actions were identified in areas such as labour, environment, human rights and corporate governance. An informal integration initiative was set in motion during 2005 aiming to create a website cataloguing federal CSR initiatives with the intention of providing a platform through which good governance practices can be promoted to business and NGOs. The key players in this initiative are the Inter-American Foundation (IAF), the Department of State, USAID, the Department of Commerce, the Environmental Protection Agency (EPA) and the Overseas Private Investment Corporation (OPIC).

Approaches to CSR vary considerably between departments. For example, the Departments of State and Commerce actively embrace CSR as the core values of CSR resonate with the broader remit of these departments. Conversely, the Department of Labor and the Office of US Trade Representatives undertake activities compatible with CSR but do not feel that they have the authority to explicitly focus on CSR *per se*. USAID and the EPA have not adopted formal positions in relation to CSR but clearly their work involves an inherent focus upon such activities. USAID's Global Development Alliance is reliant upon the successful leveraging of resources from the private sector and other partners in order to fulfil its key objectives of facilitating economic growth, improving healthcare, education and technological capabilities. Between 2002 and 2004 USAID funded 290 public-private initiatives using $1.1 billion of federal input and over $3.7 billion in partner contributions.

The majority of federal CSR activities operate with small budgets and low levels of dedicated personnel. Only four programmes had budgets exceeding $2 million in fiscal year 2003. The best funded federal programmes are located within the Department of Labour ($20 million) and USAID ($30 million). The majority of federal CSR endeavours are staffed by officials with multiple responsibilities, who thus only focus on CSR for a small proportion of the time.

Examples of US government CSR-related activities categorised according to World Bank classifications include:

Endorsement occurs through the provision of awards for CSR activities and references to CSR in public speeches. The Department of State administers an Annual Award for Corporate Excellence focussing upon the role of US companies in advancing good corporate governance and democratic values overseas.

Facilitation occurs in the provision of information, funding and incentives. The Department of Commerce trains commercial service staff on matters relating to the rule of law, human rights and corporate stewardship. These officials are able to pass on their knowledge during their interactions with companies involved in export promotion.

Partnerships between government and corporations can assist companies in advancing CSR objectives. The EPA operates a Climate Leadership Program, which enlists major US companies in setting greenhouse gas emission reduction targets. Voluntary principles on Security and Human Rights have been adopted by the majority of oil and mining companies following a collaborative endeavour between the UK and US governments intending to eliminate human rights abuses by hired security forces in extractive industries.

A number of federal regulatory mechanisms impose *mandatory* forms of CSR. For example, the OPIC, which supports US companies investing in emerging markets, requires companies to comply with certain CSR criteria relating to developmental impact, environmental protection, labour and human rights.

Corporate citizenship in the UK – policy and praxis[3]

The UK government's declared vision is, 'to see UK businesses taking account of their economic, social and environmental impact and acting to address the key sustainable development challenges based on their core competencies wherever they operate – locally, regionally and internationally'.[4]

- Corporate citizenship in various guises has a long tradition in the UK, with Cadbury's and Lever Brothers enjoying iconic status in this regard. During the 20th century corporate citizenship made little impact upon government policy until the inner city riots of the 1980s whence the Thatcher government sought support from business in order to overcome social ills such as unemployment. The current Labour Party administration, elected in 1997, is an enthusiastic proponent of the broad CSR agenda. An increase in public awareness around questions of corporate responsibility has been one of the factors driving the Blair government's interest in corporate citizenship. Furthermore, Moon considers that 'CSR is not seen as a piecemeal supplement to government activity. Rather it is regarded as a more systematic feature of the emerging governance mix'.[5] The Department of Trade and Industry (DTI) has taken the strategic lead in integrating the corporate citizenship agenda into wider policy. The government has adopted the stance that CSR should encourage companies to move beyond legal compliance and should integrate socially responsible behaviour into the core values of their daily operations thus benefiting their own competitive interests and the interests of wider society. CSR is seen as inextricably linked with the broader sustainable development agenda to which the current UK government subscribes. Whilst the government aims to support high and stable levels of economic growth and employment it also wishes to implement a framework that facilitates sustainable growth, ensuring that the price of growth is not environmental decline or social injustice. To this end a series of actions have been taken:

- A Minister for CSR has been appointed, in 2006 this was Nigel Griffiths MP.
- Specific measures adopted in the UK include, the Pensions Act Amendment, the encouragement of CSR reporting and the proposed Operating and Financial Review.
- The government's commitment to integrating CSR into all departments activities is evidenced through the development of a dedicated website (www.csr.gov.uk), which sets out the different ways in which the government is seeking to support CSR.
- The principles of good citizenship are perceived as relevant to the daily activities of governmental organisations, thus since 1999 the government has regularly reported on the ways that their policies and practices contribute to sustainable development. Furthermore, as part of the World Summit on Sustainable Development (WSSD) commitment on sustainable production and consumption the government has pledged to ensure that its procurement of goods and services (worth approximately £130 billion per annum) will be sustainable through the meeting of minimum environmental standards.
- The government seeks to encourage and incentivise the adoption and reporting of CSR through best practice guidance, regulation (where absolutely necessary) and fiscal incentives.[6] A CSR Academy was part of this initiative.

The government has initiated an array of programmes and policies and also supports others emanating from local, regional and global institutions. *Inter alia* these include; Community Development Venture Fund, Fair Trade, Skills for CSR Practice, UN Global Compact, Environmental Reporting, Flexible Environmental Regulation, Ethical Trade Initiative, Extractive Industries Transparency Initiative, ILO declaration of principles governing entrepreneurship and social policy.

Despite the Government's strong advocacy of a pro-CSR agenda critics have noted that there has been more heat than light in terms of outcomes. Perhaps the biggest area of controversy is the emphasis upon voluntarism on the part of the private sector. The Government's approach to the implementation of the OECD Guidelines for MNEs may be seen as emblematic of the structural weaknesses with the voluntary approach. A 2006 study by Amnesty International UK, Christian Aid and Friends of the Earth stated that the UK government has fallen short in its implementation of the Guidelines (Amnesty International UK et al., 2006). For example, awareness raising amongst business and the public has been limited; there has been little engagement with civil society and there is a lack of due process for dealing with complaints about MNC activities. The report shows 'the lack of rigour and credibility in the way the UK's National Contact Office operates, the limitations inherent in the OECD Guidelines themselves and the UK government's reliance on voluntary initiatives to improve corporate behaviour'.[7] This perspective is even reinforced by private sector observers with a source from De Beers stating, 'We think highly of the guidelines, but the problem is implementation and the political will is lacking'.[8] The Department for International Development's (DFID) 2006 White Paper 'Eliminating World Poverty: Making governance work for the poor', recognises some of these shortcomings in the realms of implementation and announced, *inter alia*, that the National Contact Office was to be revamped in autumn 2006 (DFID, 2006).

One of the DTI's more innovative initiatives has been the creation of the Ethical Trading Initiative (ETI), which seeks to improve labour standards within international supply chains. The ETI has utilised a novel methodology which brings the private sector, labour unions and NGOs together to develop mutual understandings and work towards common goals. A pilot initiative based on the South African wine industry led to the creation of the locally managed Wine Industry Ethical Trade Association, which is widely recognised as a world-first multi-stakeholder organisation aiming to improve working conditions within supply chains. The ETI is currently involved in work on gangmasters in UK agriculture, Indian homeworkers, China and the Sri Lankan garment industry (ETI, 2005).

In terms of development the UK government is a strong advocate of the beneficial roles that may be played by the private sector. The government's approach is typified by Prime Minister Tony Blair's comments at the opening of the July 2005 G8 Business Action for African summit in London, attended by African leaders and the heads of some of the world's biggest companies, 'The private sector is the engine for growth in Africa. Growth and development can happen only when governments and business work together. So Business Action for Africa is already fostering the vigorous private sector engagement needed to create wealth, jobs and the momentum for growth' (politics.co.uk, 2005).

CSR clearly plays an integral role within DFID. DFID has been described as 'a pioneer in practising CSR in a development context'.[9] A Socially Responsible Business Unit was created in 1997, later to be superseded by the Multinational Enterprises Engagement Team. The first White Paper on International Development committed the Department to the promotion of ethical business and voluntary codes on core labour standards. The Department subsequently published an 'issues paper' (DFID, 2003) outlining the ways in which the Department believes the private sector can support economic growth and social transformation in the developing world. CSR is believed to be important in building trust in corporations' *modus operandi* such that the full benefits of investment can be observed on the ground. DFID has utilised the CSR agenda as a mechanism for re-evaluating its relationship with, and its expectations of, the private sector within the development arena. Discussions around CSR are perceived to be important in enabling the full potential of international business for sustainable development to be identified.

DFID has been at the forefront of the development of the Extractive Industries Transparency Initiative (EITI), which was announced at the WSSD in Johannesburg in 2002 (DFID, 2004). This scheme seeks to promote transparency regarding financial flows resulting from national resource extraction in developing countries. Whilst revenues such as taxes, royalties and signatory bonuses should be triggers for economic growth the reality is that corruption and conflict have proven more commonplace in resource-rich nations. This multi-stakeholder initiative, supported by private sector, NGO and multilateral organisations, seeks to challenge this depressing situation by encouraging explicit declarations regarding financial flows and expenditures resulting from resource extraction.

An interesting dimension of the initiatives emanating from the UK is the extent to which their success is premised upon the dissemination of progressive forms of social capital (see chapter 4 for more details). Both the EITI and the ETI, for example, seek to promote positive norms of behaviour across various influential networks. Their scale of activity within this regard is particularly interesting as they seek to draw in major institutions whilst also facilitating localised transfers at the individual level. For example, the ETI wine pilot brought together UK supermarkets and representatives from South African wine industry unions, groups who would not normally interface due to the structure of the supply chain concerned. At a local level, workers became better informed as to their rights and employers were better informed as to their obligations with regard to provision of written contracts and health and safety mechanisms. Thus, networks have been strengthened and norms of behaviour, such as producer compliance with health and safety regulations, have been strengthened.

At an international level the UK is recognised as one of CSR's leading advocates. UK delegates have played a key role in the promotion of CSR within the EU. European Conferences on CSR have been held in recent years. On a global scale the government seeks to promote the dissemination of best practice so that business can improve its contribution to sustainable development and endeavours to learn from experience in different countries whilst taking into account the perceptions of different stakeholders. The government supports and seeks to further develop a wide range of initiatives, such as the OECD Guidelines for MNCs, the UN Global Compact and the GRI. A study by Chatham House was commissioned to set out recommendations following the World Summit on Sustainable Development's commitment to CSR. This suggested that existing initiatives such as the OECD Guidelines on MNCs and the Global Compact should be tightened and that the role of the government in promoting CSR requires clarification and strengthening. In March 2005 the Minister for CSR launched the International Strategic Framework into CSR at the Chatham House CSR Conference. As part of this process the government is setting up an advisory group drawn from business, academia and civil society to help implement the framework and measure the impacts business and government can have, thus informing future policy direction. Whilst the government has received many plaudits for the enthusiasm with which it has taken up the CSR baton, some observers have expressed reservations about the scope of the government's commitment. The emphasis upon voluntary adherence to codes and standards rather than regulation in key areas is seen as a particular weakness by some advocacy groups.

Traditions of corporate ethics and philanthropy are firmly rooted in US corporate practice, indeed the USA can justifiably be described as their spiritual home. Yet, it is clear that the US government's stance on CSR is poorly developed and lacks a coherent focus, particularly when compared with the proactive stance adopted in the UK. A report by the University of Hong Kong's Centre for Urban Planning and Environmental Development revealed that levels of CSR are noticeably higher amongst top European companies and that policies promoting two-way dialogue with stakeholders are comparatively rare in North America, lower even than amongst the Asian companies surveyed. Some analysts link the government's reticence in this area with the reality that US corporations as a broad group are lagging behind their European counterparts in terms of practising CSR programmes (see Table 3.1 below). As Dr. Susan Aaronson (Senior Fellow at the National Policy Association, Washington DC) observes, 'in recent years European initiatives have eclipsed the level of American commitment to corporate social responsibility. The US government and American corporations are dragging their feet while the Europeans have sprung ahead and are creating a different corporate environment' (in Baue, 2002).

Table 3.1 Comparison of levels of corporate citizenship activity exhibited in selected countries

Country	Private sector participation	Government advocacy and promotion	General public awareness
Canada	Med-high	Med	Med-high
EU	Med	Med-high	Low-med
France	Med	Med	Med
Germany	Low-med	Med	Low-med
Netherlands	High	High	High
Sweden	Med-high	Med	Low-med
UK	High	High	High
USA	Med	Low-med	Low-med

Low – Difficult to find support or information; minimal promotion; little knowledge or advocacy by public.
Medium – Some involvement by private sector; some government support (i.e. not going beyond minimum standards for OECD Guidelines); some public awareness.
High – Very active; government information is easy to find; corporate citizenship is promoted by government officials; public actively engaged.

Source: www.kenan-flagler.unc.edu/KI/kiWashington/csrpolicies/corporateCitizenship.cfm

Country profiles: the social and economic contexts to MNC activity

Below are brief profiles of South Africa, Mexico and Poland. These profiles (supplemented by those in Chapter 4 focussing on the social capital background in these countries) provide contextual information against which it is possible to make sense of the form and scope of multinational engagements within these countries as outlined in Chapters 5 and 6 and where relevant in the ensuing company case study chapters. Interestingly each of these countries has undergone significant political change within the last 15 years or so and their economies may be described as transitional. Furthermore, all three of these countries are reported to have embraced economic liberalism to the full and sought to draw in MNCs in order to facilitate economic growth and social upliftment. Although CSR issues are becoming increasingly apparent in each of these nations, given the challenges facing the governments concerned, coherent policies on CSR are, not surprisingly, lacking. The South African government have, however, been at the vanguard of innovative attempts to facilitate engagements in this regard. Comparative data on the three countries is given in Table 3.2.

South Africa

South Africa is the economic powerhouse of the African continent, generating a quarter of the continent's GDP. South Africa possesses considerable mineral resources that have fuelled the country's economic development in the last two centuries. Per capita GDP expressed in terms of purchasing power parity (PPP) places the country within the 50 or so wealthiest nations in the world (*Economist*, 2006b; Wikipedia.org, 2006c). However, there are tremendous spatial and racial disparities in wealth such that South Africa is one of the most unequal societies in the world. These inequalities are a legacy of the nation's complex colonial history which culminated in the apartheid (separate development) programme initiated in 1948 by the ruling National Party, which formalised pre-existing restrictions on the rights of the non-white population. In 1994 the country's first free and fair elections were held resulting in the Presidency of Nelson Mandela, leader of the African National Congress (ANC) Party. Overcoming the bitter legacies of apartheid have proven immense challenges for the ANC. Whilst significant achievements have been made, such as the attainment of political and economic stability, socio-economic problems such as unemployment and social deprivation have proven stubborn obstacles.

Once in power the ANC quickly rejected its rhetorical commitment to socialist ideals and adopted macro-economic policies consistent with neoliberalism. In short, it was believed that the attainment of macro-economic stability would create an environment conducive for high levels of private sector investment, especially from overseas transnational corporations (TNCs). Thus, economic growth would be generated leading to a reduction in poverty levels. Barriers to trade and investment were quickly dismantled and privatisation programmes followed. South Africa has been a leading light within the pro-private sector institution, the New Economic Partnership for Africa's Development (NEPAD). However, despite South Africa's embracing of economic orthodoxy there has been no flood of investment by overseas TNCs. Investor confidence is starting to grow and it is hoped that significant investments during 2006 by Barclays Bank and Vodafone may represent a breakpoint in investment trends heralding a brighter future (SouthAfrica.Info, 2006a; Wikipedia.org, 2006c). A number of major South African companies exist especially within the mining and manufacturing sectors. Indeed the Johannesburg Stock Exchange is the tenth largest in the world.

In the post-apartheid era long established companies and overseas investors have been encouraged to make significant contributions to the nation's transformation process through their Corporate Social Investment (CSI) programmes.[10] Mandela has proven particularly adept at persuading CEOs to sponsor programmes. More formally the ANC has implemented a series of policies aiming to increase the participation of black people within the formal economy. In 2004 the Broad-Based Black Economic Empowerment Act was introduced (Alexander, 2006; SouthAfrica.Info, 2006b). The Act encourages firms to use a scorecard system for measuring different facets of their progress towards empowerment including ownership of resources, management representation, human resource development, employment equity and various forms of indirect empowerment including CSI. The implications of the Act are powerful and private companies must apply the associated codes if they wish to do business with any government enterprise. The existence of such legislation certainly increases the necessity for firms to play a pro-active role within the broader development of the society within which they are operating. A further imperative confronting firms in South Africa is the HIV/AIDS crisis. It is estimated that more than 20% of the population are infected. In the absence of concerted action from government major firms have started devising their own responses to the crisis including the implementation of education and treatment programmes.

Mexico

The Latin American state of Mexico, the most populous Spanish speaking country in the world, borders the USA to the north and Guatemala and Belize to the south. The PRI (Institutional Revolutionary Party) governed the country for 71 years until July 2000 when the PAN (National Action Party) led by Vicente Fox achieved electoral success (*Economist*, 2000b; *Economist*, 2003a). For much of the PRI's reign the Mexican economy had followed the broader Latin American model of inward orientation (Gwynne and Kay, 1999). Thus, tariffs, quotas and exchange controls were implemented to protect local industries from foreign competition. During the 1950s–1970s the countries of Latin America enjoyed high economic growth rates. However, inflation was to pose immense challenges leading to the debt crisis of the early 1980s when Mexico declared a moratorium on its debt repayment. The International Monetary Fund (IMF) and World Bank were at the forefront of policies to counter the debt crisis and their lending conditionality included an emphasis on export-led growth and a reduction in government interaction in the economy. Mexico was an early adopter of such measures. As a result transnational actors have been able to play a greater role within the economy, especially in providing necessary expertise in supply chain management. Thus, the Mexican economy has been transformed from being state dominated and protectionist to being one of the most liberalised in Latin America. It is one of the world's largest exporters and the USA's second biggest trading partner (*Economist*, 2000b).

The country faces many challenges with nearly 20% of the population deemed to be living in poverty. There is a massive disparity between the rich and poor, such disparities exhibiting distinct spatial patterns with urban/rural and north/south differences (Wikipedia.org, 2006a). Much of the country's economic activity is in the US border zone where global companies such as Volkswagen have located assembly plants in order to supply the North American market. The signing of the North American Free Trade Agreement (NAFTA) in 1994 exemplifies the extent to which Mexico has embraced outward oriented policies (*Economist*, 2000a). Investment levels tripled and exports doubled within the first six years. Not surprisingly investments from the USA have increased substantially with manufacturing becoming the main source of export earnings, contributing 20% of GDP and 85% of export earnings (*Economist*, 2004). Over reliance on the US is a large problem however. Openness to MNCs is not uniform throughout the economy. The energy sector remains firmly in government control which is posing problems as state owned companies lack the capability to exploit less accessible reserves (*Economist*, 2005).

Philanthropy has enjoyed a long-standing tradition amongst firms in Mexico. The transition from philanthropy to more complex implementations of social investment and CSR is well underway. The Alliance for Corporate Social Responsibility in Mexico was set up following the Third Conference on Business and Social Responsibility in the Americas which was held in Mexico in 2000 (Arango, 2005). The Alliance enjoys participation from six leading business organisations that have a joint membership of 40,000 people. Furthermore, the business journal Expansion includes CSR as one of the criteria for ranking the top companies in Mexico.

Poland

The Republic of Poland is situated in Central Europe bordering, *inter alia*, Germany, the Czech Republic and Russia. Following the Second World War the People's Republic of Poland was formed as a socialistic satellite state of the Soviet Union. Thus, in the years leading up to 1989 the economy was state managed via a centrally planned system. There was a focus on heavy industry with very little efficient consumer oriented manufacturing and an underdeveloped service sector. The governments of the post-socialist era have thus had to contend with an inefficient, investment starved economy. Whilst the country has faced a series of political travails since 1989 it is widely recognised that the economy has undergone a fairly successful transition to a liberalised, open market economy with small and medium-sized state owned companies undergoing privatisation and the private sector undergoing rapid expansion generating more than 75% of GDP (*Economist*, 2006a; Wikipedia.org, 2006b). Recent governments have demonstrated an outward looking approach and sought to attract trade and investment opportunities. Poland is a member of OECD, CEFTA (Central European Free Trade Area) and joined the EU in 2004. Indeed, the government has resisted calls to instigate policies to soften the impacts of liberalisation as all efforts have been made to meet the EU's criteria for full membership. The largest privatisation to date has been the sale of Telekomunikacja Polska to France Telecom and the issuing of 30% shares in the largest domestic bank, PKO BP, on the Polish stock market in 2004 (Wikipedia.org, 2006b).

Not surprisingly political and economic transition has been associated with various socio-economic problems. Unemployment is the highest in the EU (15.7% in July 2006) and from joining the EU in May 2004 to mid-2006 up to one million Poles have migrated to other EU countries in search of better opportunities (*Economist*, 2006c; *Economist*, 2006d; Wikipedia.org, 2006b). Such movements are believed to be circulatory rather than permanent and thus will bring longer term benefits to the Polish economy via remittances and the development of more outward-looking attitudes within the workplace. The structure of the Polish economy has changed significantly and is now more like that of a developed market economy with services contributing about two-thirds of GDP (*Economist*, 2003b). The private sector has grown rapidly, accounting for the bulk of foreign trade. There have been significant inflows of FDI but foreign ownership still plays only a limited role in the overall economy with foreign firms accounting for only 4% of total employment (*Economist*, 2003b; Murgasova, 2005). High taxes and bureaucracy are significant obstacles to private sector activity – according to the World Bank assessment of the competitiveness of the business environment Poland ranks 54th in the world (*Economist*, 2006c).

CSR is undoubtedly becoming more sophisticated in its practice. CSR initiatives are largely being driven from companies outwards as there is a perception that government policy on the promotion of CSR rather lacks clarity (World Bank, 2005). Firms based in Poland feel that there needs to be more national level action to support their activities in the form of regulatory reform and national dialogue with government. Certainly there appears to be space for government initiatives which support corporations in the attainment of European environmental and social standards, which will enable firms to improve their trading position.

Measurement, benchmarking and reporting of corporate community involvement

The new wave of corporate citizenship has been associated with an increasing desire to measure, benchmark and report upon corporate citizenship activities. The data provided through methodologies such as the London Benchmarking Group (LBG) are increasingly being used to provide information that is included in annual CSR reports. The latter have become a feature of the annual reporting cycle in many firms. This section provides an outline of the systems that are used to measure and benchmark corporations' interactions with communities. The most influential systems are: the LBG model, the Corporate

Table 3.2   Comparative economic and social data

	South Africa	Poland	Mexico
Population (2005)[1]	47 million	38 million	106 million
GDP per capita PPP (2005)[1]	$12,161	$10,477	$10,036
Human Development Index (2003) Global ranking[1]	0.658 (120th)	0.858 (36th)	0.814 (53rd)
New FDI projects (2005)[2]	61	270	137
Value of FDI in 2005[2]	$1.58 billion	$9.60 billion	$3.23 billion
Number of Overseas TNC Parent Companies in Country (2004)[3]	85	58	No data
Foreign affiliates in Country (2004)[3]	845	14,469	25,708
Main sources of FDI 2005[2]	UK, USA, Germany, India, Canada	USA, Germany, UK, Sweden, France	USA, Canada, Japan, Spain, Germany
Major recent investors[2]	Vodafone, Barclays, Toyota, Volkswagen, India Hotels	Electrolux, Parkridge CE Developments, LG Electronics	Con-Way Transportation Services, Daimler Chrysler, Electrolux.

Sources:
1 http://en.wikipedia/wiki/Mexico, http://en.wikipedia/wiki/Poland, http://en.wikipedia/wiki/South_africa,
2 http://www.locomonitor.com/index.cfm?page_title=FDI%20By%20Country&child_page=Africa&c=South%20Africa, http://www.locomonitor.com/index.cfm?page_title=FDI%20By%20Country&child_page=Europe%20(Developing)&c=Poland&ShowAll=yes, http://www.locomonitor.com/index.cfm?page_title=FDI%20By%20Country&child_page=Latin%20America%20/%20Caribbean&c=Mexico&ShowAll=yes,
3 http://www.unctad.org/en/docs/wir2005annexes_en.pdf pp. 264–266.

Responsibility Index (CRI) and the PerCent Club, which was profiled in the previous chapter. These models/indices have mostly come into the public domain since 2000. It should be noted that the LBG and PerCent Club models focus upon providing quantifiable data that facilitates comparison via benchmarking of the companies concerned, whilst the CRI assesses the systems that companies are developing for implementing and measuring their CSR activities. It may be fair to say that the emphasis is very much upon CSR from the perspective of the company and as yet there is little evidence of incorporation of detailed assessments of the impacts of companies' interventions from the end users' perspective, i.e. NGOs, communities, etc. In other words, are the interventions actually making a qualitative difference on the ground? Moreover our research indicates that firms rarely undertake thorough impact studies of their projects and programmes, Oxford Economic Forecasting's evaluation of Diageo's Tomorrow's People programme being an exception to the rule (Oxford Economic Forecasting, 2004). In terms of reporting, corporate citizenship reports are a relatively new phenomenon and thus there was much variation in their incarnations in terms of style and content. However, greater consensus is being gained as to what constitutes appropriate content for these documents. The GRI Guidelines outlined here have been crucial in helping to set out appropriate structures.

The London Benchmarking Group (LBG) Model

According to LBG adviser David Logan, the LBG model was devised in response to changes in the dynamics between business and society that emerged in the 1980s and early 1990s (LBG, 2005). Specifically, businesses were facing increasing social and commercial imperatives to engage with communities. The original members of the LBG identified three factors motivating corporations to engage proactively with communities (LBG, 2004c):

- Moral and social responsibility in part driven by increased expectations emanating from society.
- Enlightened self-interest, as companies' long term financial success depends upon a stable community – 'healthy back streets equal healthy high streets'.
- Benefits feedback to business through increased productivity, stronger corporate image, reduced costs, better employee morale and improved customer loyalty.

However, there was a marked absence of appropriate management tools to facilitate this process and companies were facing strategic problems in categorising and quantifying their community engagements. Thus, comparisons between and within firms tended to be highly subjective. In 1994 the LBG was formed based around members drawn from six UK companies, including Diageo. Supported by consultant David Logan they worked upon producing a model for assessing corporate community involvement. The membership expanded to 18 in 1997 as the model was piloted and tested. The model, which emerged in 1997, provided a basis for defining what is, and what is not, community investment. Before this model was developed there was no systematic way for companies to monitor, value and measure their work with communities. In 2000 LBG membership was opened up to all UK companies and the model officially moved into the public domain. Many members use the LBG model to calculate their community spend for inclusion in the Giving List published each year in the Guardian newspaper (Corporate Citizenship Company, 2004; LBG, 2004a). By June 2005 LBG had 92 members with HSBC, SAB Miller and Astra Zeneca amongst the most recent firms to sign up.

Methodology

The model differentiates between different types of corporate donations (see Figure 3.1 and Table 3.3):

- Charitable giving/philanthropy – given with minimal concern for a return to the business – it is seen as the right thing to do.

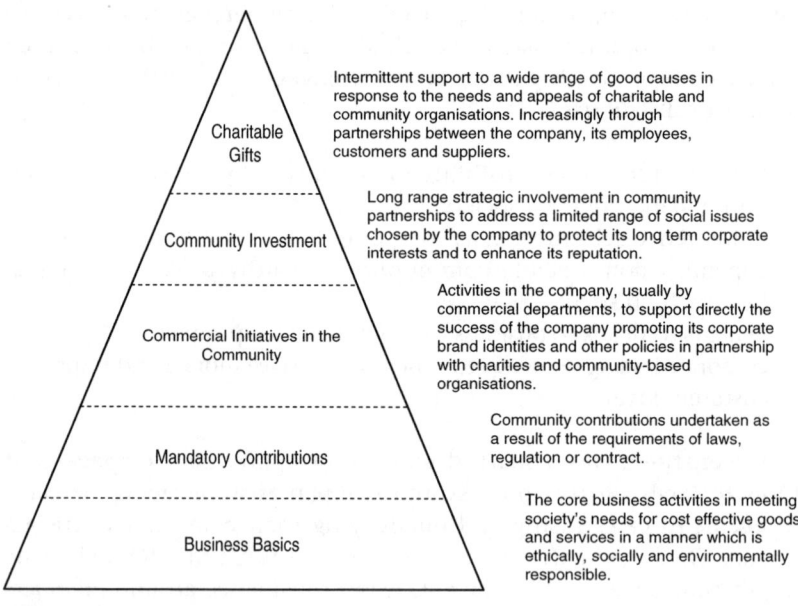

Figure 3.1   The LBG Model

Table 3.3 Diageo's community investment in £ Sterling by LBG category

	2001	2002	2003	2004	2005
Philanthropy	5,475,000	2,131,000	2,366,000	1,072,000	1,915,000
Social Investment	8,176,000	12,110,000	11,249,000	11,764,000	14,667,000
Commercially-led Initiatives	1,615,000	2,730,000	5,386,000	4,686,000	6,042,000
Total	15,266,000	16,971,000	19,001,000	17,522,000	22,624,000

Source: Diageo Corporate Citizenship Report 2003, p. 17 and Corporate Citizenship Report 2005, p.14.

- Community investment strategy – carefully focussed by the company to secure some long-term returns to the business.
- Commercial initiative – gives direct advantage to the company.
- Business basics – activities solely for commercial benefit. These are not evaluated as part of the application of the LBG model.[11]

Companies can pay the Corporate Citizenship Company (see profile below), who manage the LBG, to evaluate their community programmes (Corporate Citizenship Company, 2004; LBG, 2004b). In 2004 the annual fee for membership was £1,950 plus VAT. Some companies choose to apply the model themselves. Such companies may ask the Corporate Citizenship Company to audit their findings. The model is constantly reviewed and further evolutions occur as new challenges are imposed by changes in business practices. In 2006 much thought is being devoted to the issue of how to ring-fence the impacts of CC as it becomes increasingly mainstreamed within daily business practice. The trend towards responsible advertising, which has both commercial and citizenship objectives, is a case in point. Thus, the LBG is moving towards its self-styled 'Fourth Generation' whereby the LBG committee intend to embed their model as the international standard for measuring Corporate Community Involvement (LBG, 2005). Certainly significant progress has been made in this regard: in 2001 the LBG was launched in Australia as the Australian Benchmarking Group, in 2002 the model was adopted under the title of The Corporate Giving Standard in the USA and in 2004 as the Group Français de Référence, working with the Cap Juby in France (LBG, 2005).

It should be noted that evaluation is a controversial arena for debate. Firms are increasingly coming under pressure to audit and benchmark many of their activities including corporate citizenship. As a result issues of compliance are extremely important to the modern firm. A burgeoning consultancy industry is developing supporting the evaluation process as greater openness and transparency is demanded of corporations. The emergence of the LBG can be understood as an industry-led response to the demands of this broader context. A senior source within one corporation reflected that demands and interventions from (unspecified) 'busybodies' acts as a distraction and a source of some frustration to corporate managers.

The Corporate Responsibility Index (CRI) – 'the 1st authoritative voluntary benchmark of responsible business practice' (BITC, 2003)

The CRI has been devised by Business in the Community (BITC). BITC has been involved in analysing and benchmarking non-financial aspects of companies' performance since 1995, when they introduced the Business in the Environment Index (Kent, 2003). Subsequently it was realised that a corporate responsibility benchmark was needed so that companies and business/city analysts could comprehend the impact and relative worth of CSR practices. The CRI is a 'voluntary self-assessment survey that provides a benchmark of how companies manage, measure and report their impact on society' (*Sunday Times* Business Section 3/04/05). The CRI is produced in partnership with *The Sunday Times* who publish the results in March each year in a special supplement. The performance of the 100 top companies is presented in table form and a series of accompanying articles discussing various aspects of CSR are also printed.

CRI methodology

The CRI benchmarks the CSR performance of companies by evaluating three aspects of CSR: 1) the existence of strategies, 2) the extent to which these strategies are integrated into overall business operations, 3) broader management practices that impact upon the community, environment, marketplace and workplace (BITC, 2003; Kent, 2003).

In 2005 participating companies completed a 68-page online survey answering questions in six categories. Points are awarded based on the answers provided. The maximum score available is 100. The six categories are: Corporate Strategy, Integration of Corporate Responsibility into company operations, Management Practice, Performance and Impact, Level of Assurance provided for the submission by which the responses can be verified and Series of Supplementary Questions the responses to which may support the previous answers.

Approximately 15% of companies are visited as part of a BITC-led verification process (*Sunday Times*, 2005). Furthermore each submission is signed off by the executive with responsibility for CSR. The Index process itself is assured by Arthur D. Little.

The first Index, which was announced in March 2003, listed companies alphabetically within five groups. Companies' individual scores were not disclosed without permission. On that occasion top quintile companies each scored 82% or better, bottom quintile companies scored below 52%, whilst the average score was 67% (Baue, 2003). Over 500 FTSE100, FTSE250 and Dow Jones companies were offered the opportunity to complete questionnaires for the 2003 survey. Of these 139 did so, an increase of 12% on the previous year (BBC News, 2003). In contrast to the first year, the 2003 and 2004 surveys listed companies in rank order. Certainly there had been concerns that the notion of a 'bottom' quintile had been misleading at face value as the majority of UK companies have not been prepared to submit themselves for scrutiny via the CRI (Kent, 2003). Thus, even low ranking companies may be amongst the most responsible in the UK.

The management category is further evaluated by the deployment of A, B, C profiles to indicate how well companies are managing the measurement and reporting processes within different aspects of their corporate responsibility programmes. Thus, five rating profiles are provided for each company in the following areas: Corporate Strategy and Integration combined, and Management Practice in each of the following realms: Community, Environment, Marketplace and Workplace.

The A/B/C profiles are interpreted according to the following level descriptors:

A – Companies are measuring and reporting progress.
B – Companies are moving beyond a basic commitment.
C – Companies are beginning to measure progress.

The performance of Diageo, Anglo American and Vodafone in the first CRI is shown in Table 3.4 (NB. GSK are not listed, thus it is to be assumed that they did not provide data to the BITC). The companies' ranking in the 2003 and 2004 surveys is provided in the right hand column.

The 2003 survey was topped by the National Grid followed by BP, Unilever, Veolia Water and Aviva (BBC News, 2003). The 2004 survey was headed by Westpac Banking Corporation, National Grid Transco, BT Group, The Co-Operative Bank and BAA (BITC, 2004). The 2006

Table 3.4   CRI performance, 2002–2006

	2002 Quintile	2002 Management Profile	2003 Ranking	2004 Ranking	2006 Ranking
Anglo American	2	AAABA	57	32=	31=
Diageo	3	AAABB	34	32=	48=
Vodafone	3	AABAC	83	50=	N/A

Sources:
http://www.bitc.org.uk/document.rm?id=3382,
http://www.bitc.org.uk/document.rm?id=1577,
http://www.bitc.org.uk/document.rm?id=774, www.bitc.org.uk/document.rm?id=163

survey was headed by The Co-Operative Bank, BAA, Barclays, BT Group and National Grid (BITC, 2006).

Comments on the CRI

Analysis of the detail within the CRI results has revealed some interesting trends (Kent, 2003). For example, in 2002 companies scored an average of 80% for their CSR strategy but only 61% for integration within overall business operations. In other words, the exposition of theory has proven less challenging than CSR practice. Furthermore, companies have reported that managing CSR activity within their supply chain is particularly difficult. Finding effective ways of measuring the impacts of CSR activities upon communities was also highlighted as a problem area. Interestingly the publication of the Index has fuelled debates about the issue of government regulation within the CSR realm. Industry sources believe that their voluntary involvement in the CRI process is evidence that regulation is unnecessary. Indeed, some express a view that legislation leads to a 'compliance mentality' in which companies only aim to achieve the legal minimum. NGOs and other lobbyists believe that regulation would help set a minimum standard and that in reality firms would compete to exceed the minimums set via voluntary systems (Kent, 2003). Some companies have articulated concerns about the length of the CRI questionnaire and thus the resources required to complete it. This issue is accompanied by the growth in indices and reporting schemes that are becoming available within the broad realms of ethical business conduct, environmental management and corporate social responsibility. The CRI is perceived as an important mechanism for measuring CSR and is 'setting the early pace' amongst the various indices and measurement systems that are emerging. It is likely that consolidation will occur in time as the utility of various systems becomes clearer.

The Global Reporting Initiative (GRI)

The GRI was convened by the Coalition for Environmentally Responsible Economies (CERES) and the United Nations Environment Programme (UNEP) in 1997 (GRI, 2005a; UNEP DTIE, 2005). The GRI has become an established institution headquartered in Amsterdam with a Board of Directors. The GRI operates in official collaboration with UNEP and the UN Secretary General's Global Compact. The GRI's core mission is to develop guidelines that provide a framework for organisations to report on the economic, environmental and social dimensions of their business activities. The GRI represents a concerted effort to fill a void in CSR reporting, specifically that there has been no framework that is widely understood and applied by all organisations. Without agreement on the core data required for such reporting there has been a tendency for 'reports...to contain photos of happy smiling children and not much else' (Baker, 2005). A significant strength of the GRI is that it is a wide ranging collaborative effort which brings together businesses and a range of other stakeholders.

The aims of the GRI Guidelines[12] are as follows:

- To provide reporting principles that assist organisations in providing sustainability reports.
- Help organisations present a balanced view of their broader economic, environmental and social performance.
- Promote comparability between reports produced by organisations operating in diverse locations and economic sectors.
- Support benchmarking and assessment processes.
- Facilitate stakeholder engagements.

It should be recognised that the guidelines do not set performance standards nor do they represent a code of conduct.

Since its inception GRI has been committed to a process of continuous improvement driven by the insights and experiences of stakeholders familiar with the Guidelines and other GRI reporting framework components. In 2006 the Guidelines are being reviewed based on extensive stakeholder input gained from nearly 500 people worldwide through the Structured Feedback Process. The result will be the third generation of GRI Guidelines (built on prior versions in 2000 and 2002) due for release in mid-2006 (GRI, 2005b). The GRI website is extremely

Table 3.5 The global spread of the GRI

Region	Number of Reporters
Africa	31
Asia	154
Europe	316
Latin America	22
Northern America	92
Oceania	45

Source: http://www.globalreporting.org/guidelines/ReportersStats.xls#'Reporters per Region'!Default__statsReportersPerRegion

Country	Number of Reporters
Japan	124
United Kingdom	72
USA	69
Spain	42
Australia	36
France	31
Netherlands	30
Germany	28
South Africa	26

Source: http://www.globalreporting.org/guidelines/ReportersStats.xls#'Reporters per Country'!Default__statsReportersperCountry

detailed and extensive. It also provides links to individual corporation's Annual Sustainability/Social/Responsibility Reports via a searchable database: http://www.globalreporting.org/guidelines/reports/search.asp. Firms who utilise the GRI Guidelines refer to this in their reports. Some provide very detailed accounts of the ways in which they have utilised the Guidelines.[13]

Evaluating the GRI

The GRI must be understood as a work in progress. There is much still to be done in terms of streamlining the technicalities of measurement and more broadly in terms of defining the precise purpose of the whole process and orientating the mechanisms accordingly. Early drafts of the Guidelines have included as many as 100 indicators. These have been streamlined to just over 50 core indicators and a number of supplementary ones (Baker, 2005). However, as company time has to be expended collecting data for each indicator questions have to be asked about the fitness for purpose of many of the indicators. As one critic has asked 'what information can I get from knowing the percent of purchasing spent per supplier and main invoicing country?' (Baker, 2005). The social and environmental indicators are particularly fuzzy in terms of measurement of performance. Indeed, more than 20 of the indicators just ask whether policies or procedures exist. There is no accountability in terms of measuring the outcomes of these policies in practice. For example, a company can have a policy that declares that no child labour is to be utilised. Yet, there is no requirement for companies to assess or report on whether they or their suppliers actually do use child labour. If the GRI is to be taken seriously in the medium term it must be seen to measure performance as well as management process. There is also a lack of information concerning the impact of the company's products and services upon society – as Mallen Baker observes (2005), 'society must make space for the possibility of a socially responsible tobacco company, but I would expect such a one to report fully on the current impact of the product – something not required by the core indicators of the GRI'.

It is early days for the GRI. It has rapidly attained global institution status. However, its very character as a multi-stakeholder body inevitably induces tensions and the need for compromise. On the one hand it is possible to say that the GRI is not business-led enough as firms are being expected to collect some data that is not really of use to them. On the other hand the emphasis upon measuring policies without also focussing upon the outcomes of policies leaves non-business actors feeling dissatisfied. However, if the GRI is seen to be a creature of compromise and lacking in meaningful data then the 'power and role of social reporting will…be weakened immeasurably', Baker (2005).

Reporting has been on the increase amongst UK firms, with 132 FTSE250 companies producing social reports in 2003 compared to 54 in 2001. More companies reference CSR activities within their annual reports and their corporate communications. Web-based reporting has also risen, with many firms providing accounts of their CSR programmes, including details of individual projects and partnerships. In the USA reporting is on the increase with 45% of Fortune Global 250 Companies producing a separate social, environmental or sustainability report in 2002 – an increase of 10% since 1999. Independent verification has also increased from 19% to 29% over the same time period (Conley and Williams, 2004).

Table 3.6 Involvement in LBG, CRI and GRI of our case study companies

	LBG	CRI	GRI
Anglo American	Member	Participate	Use Guidelines
Diageo	Member	Participate	Use Guidelines
GSK	Member	Do not participate	Use Guidelines
Vodafone	Member	Participated until 2006	Use Guidelines

Notes

1. Cited in Fernandez-Young et al. (2004, p.2).
2. *Source*: www.kenan-flagler.unc.edu?KI/kiWashington.csrpolicues/consensus.cfm
3. *Sources*: csr.gov.uk (2005, a, b, c, d, e).
4. csr.gov.uk (2005a), *Corporate Social Responsibility: a Government Update*. Available at: http://www.csr.gov.uk/pdf/dti_csr_final.pdf. Accessed 04/08/2005.
5. Moon (2004, p.11).
6. See Moon (2004, p.12).
7. Amnesty International UK et al. (2006, p.5).
8. Amnesty International UK, et al. (2006), *Flagship or failure? The UK's implementation of the OECD guidelines and approach to corporate accountability*. Availableat: http://www.christian-aid.org.uk/indepth/601flag/ Final%20OECD%20Report.pdf. Accessed 18/07/2006.
9. Jenkins (2005, p.530).
10. Finlay (2004), and Johannesburg Securities Exchange (2003, 2005).
11. *Source*: www.employeevolunteering.org.uk/resources/details.asp?id=184& the meid=104
12. These are available online at http://www.globalreporting.org/guidelines/2002.asp
13. See for example GSK's website: http://www.gsk.com/financial/reps03/EHS03/GSKehs-1.htm

References

AccountAbility.org.uk (2005), *AccountAbility – About Us*. Available at: www.accountability.org.uk/aboutus/default.asp. Accessed 20/07/2005.

Action Aid (2006a), *Action Aid International*. Available at: www.actionaid.org.uk/index.asp?page_id=1391. Accessed 09/05/2006.

Action Aid (2006b), *Action Aid Reports*. Available at: www.actionaid.org.uk/100223/corporates.html. Accessed 09/05/2006.

Action Aid (2006c), *How are we doing?* Available at: http://www.actionaid.org.uk/_content/documents/ActionAid_Review_2003.pdf. Accessed 09/05/2006.

Action Aid (2006d), *How we Work*. Available at: www.actionaid.org.uk/index.asp?page_id=100031. Accessed 09/05/2006.

Action Aid (2006e), *Our History*. Available at: www.actionaid.org.uk/100041/our_history.html. Accessed 09/05/2006.

Alexander, M. (2006), *Black Economic Empowerment*. Available at: http://www.southafrica.info/pls/procs/iac.page?p_t1=692&p_t2=3185&p_t3=3522&p_t4=0&p_dynamic=YP&p_content_id=890427&p_site_id=38. Accessed 02/10/2006.

Amnesty International UK, Christian Aid and Friends of the Earth (2006), *Flagship or failure? The UK's implementation of the OECD guidelines and approach to corporate accountability*. Available at: http://www.christian-aid.org.uk/indepth/601flag/Final%20OECD%20Report.pdf. Accessed 18/07/2006.

Arango, M. (2005), *Philanthropy in Mexico*. Available at: http://www.fas.harvard.edu/~drclas/publications/revista/Volunteering/mexicophil.html. Accessed 04/10/2006.

Baker, M. (2005), *Global Reporting Initiative – GRI*. Available at: www.mallenbaker.net/csr/CSRfiles/GRI.html. Accessed 23/05/2005.

Baue, W. (2002), *Report Argues that Europe Outperforms the U.S. in Corporate Social Responsibility*. Available at: http://www.socialfunds.com/news/article.cgi/778.html. Accessed 08/08/2006.

Baue, W. (2003), *New UK Index Rates Corporate Social Responsibility Performance*. Available at: www.socialfunds.com/news/print.cgi?sfArticleId=1062. Accessed 17/05/2005.

BBC News (2003), *Poll shows most ethical companies*. Available at: http://newsvote.bbc.co.uk/ mpapps/pagetools/print/news.bbc.co.uk/1/hi/business/3509470.stm. Accessed 17/05/2005.

BITC (2003), *'Corporate Responsibility Index Executive Summary'*, Business in the Community.

BITC (2004), *Corporate Responsibility Index 2004*. Available at: http://www.bitc.org.uk/document.rm?id=1577. Accessed 18/08/2006.

BITC (2005a), *Frequently asked questions*. Available at: http://www.bitc.org.uk/about_bitc/faqs.html. Accessed 18/05/2005.

BITC (2005b), *History of Business in the Community*. Available at: http://www.bitc.org.uk/ about_bitc/history.html. Accessed 18/05/2005.

BITC (2005c), *Programme directory*. Available at: http://www.bitc.org.uk/programmes/programme_directory/index.html. Accessed 18/05/2005.

BITC (2005d), *Who we are*. Available at: http://www.bitc.org.uk/about_bitc/index.html. Accessed 18/10/2005.

BITC (2006), *Corporate Responsibility Index 2006*. Available at: http://www.bitc.org.uk/document.rm?id=3382. Accessed 18/08/2006.

Christian Aid (2004a), *Behind the mask. The real face of corporate social responsibility*. Available at: http://www.christianaid.org.uk/indepth/0401csr/index.htm. Accessed 21/07/2005.

Christian Aid (2004b), *Report Reveals the true face of corporate social responsibility*. Available at: www.christianaid.org.uk/news/media/pressrel/040121p.htm. Accessed 18/07/2005.

Christian Aid (2005a), *About Christian Aid*. Available at: http://www. christianaid.org.uk/aboutca/strategic_framework/index.htm. Accessed 21/07/2005.

Christian Aid (2005b), *Recent Reports from Christian Aid*. Available at: http://www.christianaid.org.uk/indepth/index.htm. Accessed 21/07/2005.

Christian Aid, Friends of the Earth and Action on Smoking (2004), *BAT in its own words – Behind the mask of corporate social responsibility*. Available at: http://www.christianaid.org.uk/indepth/504bat/bat_report.pdf. Accessed 11/11/2005.

Conley, J. and Williams, C. (2004), *Engage, Embed and Embellish: Theory versus Practice in the Corporate Social Responsibility Movement*. Available at: http://papers.ssrn.com/sol3/papers.cfm?abstract_id=691521. Accessed 31/07/2006.

CORE (2006a), *FAQs*. Available at: www.corporate-responsibility.org/C2B/faq/indes.asp?CatID=1. Accessed 09/05/2006.

CORE (2006b), *What is CORE?* Available at: www.corporate-responsibility.org. Accessed 09/05/2006.

Corporate Citizenship Company (2004), *Case study – Pilot Initiative in Poland*. Available at: www.corporate-citizenship.co.uk/social/casestudy.asp. Accessed 02/08/2004.

Corporate Citizenship Company (2005a), *About Us*. Available at: www.corporate-citizenship.co.uk/aboutus/default.asp. Accessed 20/05/2005.

Corporate Citizenship Company (2005b), *Assignments*. Available at: www.corporate-citizenship.co.uk/aboutus/assignments.asp. Accessed 20/05/2005.

Corporate Watch (2005a), *About Corporate Watch*. Available at: www.corporatewatch.org.uk/?lid=58. Accessed 11/11/2005.

Corporate Watch (2005b), *About Corporate Watch: Statement of Aims*. Available at: www.corporatewatch.org.uk/?lid=52. Accessed 11/11/2005.

csr.gov.uk (2005a), *Corporate Social Responsibility: a Government Update*. Available at: http://www.csr.gov.uk/pdf/dti_csr_final.pdf. Accessed 04/08/2005.

csr.gov.uk (2005b), *Corporate Social Responsibility: International Strategic Framework*. Available at: http://www.csr.gov.uk/pdf/dti_csr_finaldoc.pdf. Accessed 04/08/2005.

csr.gov.uk (2005c), *Policy & Legislation – International*. Available at: www.csr.gov.uk/international.shtml. Accessed 04/08/2005.

csr.gov.uk (2005d), *Policy and Legislation (International)*. Available at: www.csr.gov.uk/international.shtml. Accessed 04/08/2005.

csr.gov.uk (2005e), *UK national initiatives – by theme*. Available at: www.csr.gov.uk/ukbytheme.shtml. Accessed 05/08/2005.

DFID (2003), *DFID and corporate social responsibility*. Available at: http://www.csr.gov.uk/pdf/e2dfidandcsr.pdf. Accessed 04/08/2005.

DFID (2004), *Factsheet, February 2004, Extractive Industries Transparency Initiative*. Available at: http://www.csr.gov.uk/pdf/e2eitifactsheet.pdf. Accessed 04/08/2005.

DFID (2006), *Eliminating World Poverty: Making governance work for the poor*, DFID.

Economist (2000a), *If not for NAFTA, when?* Available at: http://www.economist.com/research/backgrounders/PrinterFriendly.cfm?story_id=403131. Accessed 03/10/2006.

Economist (2000b), *Revolution ends, change begins*. Available at: http://www.economist.com/surveys/displayStory.cfm?story_id=403102. Accessed 02/10/2006.

Economist (2003a), *Country Briefings: Mexico – History in Brief*. Available at: http://www.economist.com/countries/Mexico/PrinterFriendly.cfm?Story_ID=2282341. Accessed 03/10/2006.

Economist (2003b), *Country Briefings: Poland Economic Structure*. Available at: http://www.economist.com/countries/Poland/PrinterFriendly.cfm?Story_ID=2296177. Accessed 02/10/2006.

Economist (2004), *Country Briefings: Mexico – Economic Structure*. Available at: www.economist.com/countries/Mexico/PrinterFriendly.cfm?Story_ID=2570664. Accessed 03/10/2006.

Economist (2005), *Backgrounders: Mexico's Economy*. Available at: http://www.economist.com/research/backgrounders/displayBackgrounder.cfm?bg=629589. Accessed 03/10/2006.
Economist (2006a), *Backgrounders: Poland*. Available at: http://www.economist.com/research/backgrounders/displayBackgrounder.cfm?bg=912671. Accessed 02/10/2006.
Economist (2006b), *Chasing Rainbows*. Available at: http://www.economist.com/surveys/displayStory.cfm?story_id=5678229. Accessed 02/10/2006.
Economist (2006c), *Cheer Up*. Available at: http://www.economist.com/surveys/displayStory.cfm?story_id=6875707. Accessed 02/10/2006.
Economist (2006d), *Economic Data*. Available at: http://www.economist.com/countries/Poland/profile.cfm?folder=Profile-Economic%20Data. Accessed 02/10/2006.
Ethical Corporation (2005), *The Business and Human Rights Management Report*. Available at: www.ethicalcorp.com/content.asp?ContentID=2608. Accessed 20/07/2005.
ETI (2005), *Experimental Projects*. Available at: http://www.ethicaltrade.org/Z/actvts/exproj/index.shtml. Accessed 09/11/2005.
Fernandez-Young, A., Moon, J. and Young, R. (2004), 'The UK Corporate Social Responsibility consultancy industry: a phenomenological approach', ICCSR, Nottingham University Business School.
Finlay, A. (2004), *Investing in social responsibility*. Available at: http://www.southafrica.info/pls/procs/iac.page?p_t1=692&p_t2=1827&p_t3=2677&p_t4=0&p_dynamic=YP&p_content_id=342050&p_site_id=38. Accessed 12/08/2005.
FTSE4Good.com (2005), *FTSE4Good Homepage*. Available at: www.ftse.com/ftse4good/index.jsp. Accessed 21/07/2005.
GAO (2005), *Globalization: Numerous Federal Activities Complement U.S. Business's Global Corporate Social Responsibility Efforts*. Available at: http://www.gao.gov/new.items/do5744.pdf. Accessed 29/07/2005.
GRI (2005a), *GRI-goverance*. Available at: www.globalreporting.org/images/GRIstructure.gif. Accessed 23/05/2005.
GRI (2005b), *Introducing the G3*. Available at: http://www.globalreporting.org/G3/. Accessed 26/05/2005.
Gwynne, R. and Kay, C. (1999), *Latin America Transformed. Globalization and Modernity*, London: Arnold.
Hilton, S. and Gibbon, G. (2002), *Good Business: Your world needs you*, London: Texere.
IBLF (2006), *IBLF Supporters*. Available at: http://www.iblf.org/supporters.jsp. Accessed 18/08/2006.
Jenkins, R. (2005), 'Globalisation, Corporate Social Responsibility and Poverty', *International Affairs*, Vol.81 (3), pp.525–540.
Johannesburg Securities Exchange (2003), *SRI Index – Background and Selection Criteria*. Available at: http://www.jse.co.za/sri/docs/Background%20and%20Criteria.final.06%2010%2003.pdf. Accessed 12/08/2005.
Johannesburg Securities Exchange (2005), *The SRI*. Available at: www.jse.co.za/sri/. Accessed 12/08/2005.
Jones, I. and Pollitt, M. (eds.) (2002), *Understanding how issues in business ethics develop*, Palgrave.

Kent, T. (2003), *The Launch of the UK Corporate Responsibility Index*. Available at: www.ethicalcorp.com/content_print.asp?ContentID=450. Accessed 17/05/2005.

LBG (2004a), *The Corporate Responsibility Group*. Available at: www.lbg-online.net/about/crg.asp. Accessed 02/08/2004.

LBG (2004b), *FAQs*. Available at: www.lbg-online.net/model/faq.asp. Accessed 02/08/2004.

LBG (2004c), *History*. Available at: www.lbg-online.net/about/history.asp. Accessed 18/05/2005.

LBG (2005), *Measure for Measure: Celebrating the LBG's First 10 years*, London Benchmarking Group.

maketradefair.com (2002), *Rigged Rules and Double Standards – trade, globalisation and the fight against Poverty*. Available at: http://www.maketradefair.com/assets/english/report_english.pdf. Accessed 17/07/2006.

Moon, J. (2004), *Government as a Driver of Corporate Social Responsibility*. Available at: http://www.nottingham.ac.uk/business/ICCSR/pdf/ResearchPdfs/20-2004.pdf. Accessed 10/11/2005.

Murgasova, Z. (2005), *Post-Transition Investment Behaviour in Poland: A Sectoral Panel Analysis, IMF Working Paper 05/184*. Available at: http://www.imf.org/external/pubs/ft/wp/2005/wp05184.pdf. Accessed 02/10/2006.

Oxfam, Save the Children and VSO (2002), *Beyond Philanthropy*. Available at: www.savethechildren.org.uk/temp/scuk/cache/cmsattack/622_beyondphil.pdf. Accessed 28/06/2005.

Oxfam International (2006), *Offside! Labour rights and sportswear production in Asia*. Available at: http://oxfam.intelli-direct.com/e/d.dll?m=234&url=http://www.oxfam.org.uk/what_we_do/issues/trade/downloads/offside_sportswear.pdf. Accessed 17/07/2006.

Oxfam.co.uk (2006), *History of Oxfam – In the Beginning*. Available at: www.oxfam.org.uk/about_us/history/index.htm. Accessed 17/07/2006.

Oxfam.org.uk (2006), *History of Oxfam-Oxfam Today*. Available at: www.oxfam.org.uk/about_us/history/history9.htm. Accessed 17/07/2006.

Oxford Economic Forecasting (2004), *Twenty-year Evaluation of the Tomorrow's People Trust*, Draft final report August 2004.

politics.co.uk (2005), *Blair: Enterprise key to African development*. Available at: http://www.politics.co.uk/printerfriendly.aspx?itemid=16095324. Accessed 26/04/2006.

Powell, C. (2003), *Remarks at the 2003 Corporate Excellence Awards*. Available at: http://www.state.gov/secretary/former/powell/remarks/2003/25209.htm. Accessed 08/08/2006.

SouthAfrica.Info (2006a), *Foreign Direct Investment Soars*. Available at: http://www.southafrica.info/pls/procs/iac.page?p_t1=692&p_t2=1828&p_t3=0&p_t4=0&p_dynamic=YP&p_content_id=176880&p_site_id=38. Accessed 02/10/2006.

SouthAfrica.Info (2006b), *South Africa: economy overview*. Available at: http://www.southafrica.info/pls/procs/iac.page?p_t1=692&p_t2=1827&p_t3=0&p_t4=0&p_dynamic=YP&p_content_id=309265&p_site_id=38. Accessed 02/10/2006.

Sunday Times (2005), 'Companies that Count: The Top 100 Companies That Count', *The Sunday Times*, 3 April, London.

UNEP DTIE (2005), *Global Reporting Initiative*. Available at: www.uneptie.org/outreach/reporting/gri.htm. Accessed 23/05/2005.

Wikipedia.org (2006a), *Mexico.* Available at: http://en.wikipedia.org/wiki/Mexico. Accessed 02/10/2006.
Wikipedia.org (2006b), *Poland.* Available at: http://en.wikipedia.org/wiki/Poland. Accessed 02/10/2006.
Wikipedia.org (2006c), *South Africa.* Available at: http://en.wikipedia.org/wiki/South_africa. Accessed 02/10/2006.
World Bank (2005), *What Does Business Think about CSR in Central and Eastern Europe?* Available at: www.csrwire.com/PressReleasePrint.php?id=4698. Accessed 03/10/2006.

4
Social Capital and Multinationals

Context

We live in world of rising concern about the contribution of multinationals to society. Naomi Klein's (2000) *No Logo* and Noreena Hertz's (2001) *The Silent Takeover* have raised the spectre of global corporations who show little concern for their effect on vulnerable host communities and who are more powerful than many of the governments that welcome them across their borders. As such multinationals are often perceived to be in the process of destroying local cultures and replacing them with homogenised western values. Multinational production methods are accused of exploiting desperate workers and having low labour and environmental standards. The process of globalisation which multinationals represent is credited with undermining the power of national governments to control their economic destiny, leaving them vulnerable to the subsequent exit of footloose capital and undermining their tax base, by promoting tax competition among governments to attract them in the first place. Even more moderate writers such as Stopford, Strange and Henley (1991) recognise that a world with increasingly significant large global firms poses a fundamental challenge for developing country governments: change national economic policies (good or bad) or lose multinational investments.

Whatever the economic reality of the wilder criticisms of multinationals and their impact one thing is clear: the global public perception of multinationals is poor. A 2002 World Economic Forum survey on trust in institutions in 42 countries found global businesses near the bottom of a list, just above large national companies.[1] A larger 2004 survey put global companies as the least trusted institutions among a smaller list of institutions.[2] As Zinkin (2004) points out multinationals seem to be the subject of such declining trust for three reasons: globalisation's negative image; recent US corporate governance scandals which have shed light on the internal workings of a number of globally acquisitive companies, such as Enron and Worldcom; and increased appetite on the part of consumers to punish companies for poor ethics.

That there should be rising concern about the behaviour of such corporations is unsurprising. Sociologist Ronald Inglehart pointed out as early as 1977 that there was a connection with rising income and increased concern about 'the way' business was done relative to the 'economic success' of business. This move from materialism to post-materialism has been a feature of almost all OECD countries.[3] Multinationals were always going to be vulnerable to this trend in society due to their size and geographic spread and the relative ease of getting information on their activities. Increasing western affluence and awareness of the economic plight of others was always going to increase calls on multinationals to do more. They could not expect to simply maximise short-term profits in their host communities for the benefit of their shareholders in rich countries.

The negative perception of corporations' role in globalisation has further been heightened by very success of business in gaining a world trading system that works increasingly to its advantage. As a greater percentage of manufacturing consumption in advanced countries is sourced in Asia this has allowed multinationals to exploit Asia's lower labour and environmental standards. Attempts to broaden the scope of free trade and further remove restrictions on the movement of capital within the World Trade Organization (WTO) arrangements have been accused of disproportionately favouring rich country interests. The long awaited Multilateral Agreement on Investment has not yet been agreed. Meanwhile OECD governments have recognised the need to begin some regulation of companies' activities in host companies by issuing the OECD Guidelines for Multinational Enterprises (2000). African under-development has recently become a big issue with multinationals that exploit natural resources on that continent becoming a focus of NGO activity.

In the last two chapters we have discussed corporate citizenship (CC) programmes and their associated terms. We now seek to extend our understanding by focussing on the developmental impact of CC policies. In doing this we have in mind two questions. First, what is it that CC policies are trying to do? This implies that we need a theory of how CC might be working to the benefit of society. Second, how can we measure the impact of CC policies? Here we need to measure inputs and outputs. It is to the concept of social capital that we turn in order to get a handle on both of these issues. We begin by discussing the descriptive features of social capital and go on to a discussion of how social capital can be measured empirically and how it applies to the multinational firm.

Social capital

Assessing the effect of multinationals' corporate citizenship programmes on society requires us to define what it is that they might be impacting on. What we suggest is that the concept of social capital provides us with a good way of thinking about this.

Robert Putnam defines social capital as those 'features of social organization such as trust, norms and networks that can improve efficiency by facilitating coordinated action'.[4] Social capital is thus capital in that it reflects a capacity that can be increased or reduced over time, it is also social in that it reflects wider benefits than the economic and is not reserved for private use.

For Putnam, who initially examined social capital in Italy (1993), membership of a choir is and reflects social capital. Social capital is constituted on the one hand by the social norms that affirm that joining a choir is a good way to spend one's leisure time and on the other hand by the existence of trust in people from different backgrounds, whose only thing in common is that they can sing. In the US he uses bowling leagues and the scout movement as examples of positive social networks (Putnam, 2000). The groups that Putnam identifies as good for social capital are sometimes referred to as P-groups. These can be contrasted with O-groups, such as trade unions and the mafia (and indeed the extended family), which exist for rent seeking at the expense of social welfare.[5] P-groups are said to be strong in producing *bridging* social capital between different groups in society. O-groups are said to be strong in producing *bonding* social capital between similar individuals in society. Both types of capital can be necessary for a happy society. Strong bonding social capital within families is better for children's development. However it is bridging social capital that is harder to produce and which seems to vary more significantly between societies.

Thus social capital as a concept focusses attention away from produced capital, such as machinery, human capital (the value of education) and natural capital (natural resource endowments) on to another dimension of the capacity of society for economic development. Like the CSR concept social capital has also focussed attention on the importance of voluntary initiatives. The voluntary origin of much social capital is fundamental to its rise to prominence and differentiation from earlier forms of capital. Such social capital, like CSR, is to be contrasted with the rather formal regulations historically used to govern society and business.[6]

Putnam takes the credit for popularising the term 'social capital' in much the same way that Francis Fukuyama (1995) takes the credit for popularising the associated term 'Trust'.[7] Putnam's focus was to explain differential performance of Italian regions, where choir membership is strongly positively correlated with income per head, and the decline in social capital in the US since the 1950s.

While Putnam's work was squarely on societies, there is an earlier tradition that examines the social capital of individuals.[8] Coleman and Hoffer (1987) examined the effects of schooling on individual social capital suggesting that those who went to Catholic schools did less well educationally than those who travelled to public schools. Clearly Putnam's social capital represents an aggregation of this type of individual social capital.

The Putnam definition also incorporates a well-researched area of economics, that of trust. Francis Fukuyama had already highlighted this aspect of social capital by linking the relative performance of different economies across the world to the level of trust existing within their societies. High trust societies were those where property rights were respected and consistently enforced, low trust ones were those where property was at risk from corrupt or ineffective police forces and courts.

Dasgupta defines a social norm as 'a behavioural strategy that is subscribed to by all.'[9] This implies that norms play an important role in defining socially acceptable behaviour. A norm of always honouring your side of a business deal is clearly better than one that says it is ok to defraud strangers at the first transaction. Norms of good behaviour engender trust and may be promoted by social networks.

Both social norms and social networks reflect a richness of concept that can be further developed. The usage of the analytical category 'social' suggests that these terms possess elements that are non-conventional and difficult to pin down and measure. This suggests it may difficult to model formally or to measure accurately. Indeed, Portes (1998) argues that social capital is a shorthand for sociability. The fact that the components of what makes up social capital may be desirable for their own sake also poses a conceptual problem for some in that capital is an input to production not an outcome of it. This however poses problems for the use of social capital in causally explaining economic development not for the usefulness of actual measures of it.

Although the term social capital was developed for use in advanced economies, the World Bank has made extensive use of the term empirically and conceptually in their quest for 'A World free of Poverty'.[10]

'Social capital refers to the institutions, relationships and norms that shape the quality and quantity of a society's social interactions...Social capital is not just the sum of the institutions which underpin a society it is the glue that holds them together.'[11]

This definition is wider than that of Putnam in that it includes formal institutions, such as government development agencies as part of social capital. It is useful in highlighting that social capital is important for the quality of social relations and that it is a quantifiable concept.

Michael Woolcock (2000) suggests that social capital is useful because it provides a common language to discuss the complex problems of development across a range of disciplines: economists, political scientists, sociologists, geographers and management scientists have all made extensive use of the concept. For Woolcock getting social relationships right is the key to the facilitation of successful development.

Grootaert and Bastelear (2002a) distinguish the scope, form and channel of social capital. The scope of social capital can be micro (person to person), meso (across hierarchical groups or between groups) or macro (affecting macro institutions such as development agencies). The form of social capital can be structural (e.g. facilitating meeting others as in a club) or cognitive (e.g. changing one's attitude to strangers). The channel can be via information (e.g. exchanging business cards at a sports club) or collective action (e.g. the formation of a group to campaign for a new public road).

Social capital, like physical capital, is not necessarily good. Just as machines can be used to produce guns or pornography; social clubs can produce terrorists or racists and social norms can be oppressive and trust limited to those 'who look like me'.[12] Echoing the World Bank definition above, Padlam (2000) observes social capital can be a 'glue' or a 'lubricant'. The glue that holds people to traditional but oppressive ways of social relating is clearly bad, while social lubricants that help people 'to rub along' with those different to them is clearly a good thing. It may even be the case that at the individual level one person's increase in social capital reduces everyone else's, either by restricting social access of the less socially well off or by reducing the willingness of the less well off to cooperate with each other.[13]

Defining what makes for good social capital – in the form of healthy social relations – is something that several authors have focussed on. Granovetter (1973) distinguished social relations characterised by strong and weak ties. Strong ties exist between family members, weak ties between members of choirs. Weak ties tend to facilitate more merit-based and less segregated social relations. These are the sorts of relationships that are good for economic development more generally. Thus in traditional communities associations which encourage inter-tribal mixing would facilitate the development of good social capital.

This idea of encouraging social relations with those outside ones family and tribe is carried over to the network analysis. Well-networked individuals and organisations only have to travel via a smaller number of contacts (or links) to reach large numbers of relevant contacts. Individuals who bridge different groups are those with information advantages over those who do not. Where certain groups or individuals are poorly connected to other groups they suffer from what Burt (2001) calls 'structural holes' in their networks. Burt suggests the value of individuals who can bridge structural holes in network maps. In this vein, organisations that facilitate social relations among already closely socially related individuals are much less valuable than those that eliminate structural holes.

The idea of the differential quality of social links in society is developed further by Lin (2001). If Burt's analysis is about the quality of horizontal links, Lin's is about the quality of vertical links. Lin highlights social relations in China where it matters how high up your links go in the hierarchy: knowing a General is better than knowing a Corporal. This reflects the fundamental problem of the poor, they may know each other but they do not know rich relatives, friends or co-workers who can help them. A self help group made up solely of other poor people is going to be much less helpful than one which includes input from the well educated or well connected. Both Burt and Lin suggest that simply counting the quantity of links an individual has will not accurately reflect the value of those links. Lin suggests that it is the position of contacts and the nature of the relation to them that needs to be measured.

For Lin social capital is a useful term because it embodies the importance of having the right structures in society to facilitate the building of healthy social relations, the existence of opportunity for gaining social access to others and the idea that social relations can be used to facilitate individual or collective action useful to society.

We are not arguing that social capital is the only form of capital that contributes to development in the host countries of multinationals. This is not the case, it is perhaps not even the most significant. However what is the case is that communities with higher levels of social capital are likely to be the ones where returns to physical and human capital investments flourish. Serageldin and Grootaert (1999) usefully point out that although human or social capital/natural capital/produced assets are all required for successful economic development, such development is likely to be most sustainable when it works to keep stocks of each sufficiently high and non-decreasing.

How social capital works to raise economic development

Before looking at causal mechanisms by which higher social capital raises economic wellbeing it is important to note that social capital may be a very good thing in itself. Lin (2001) points out that having social capital yields direct private benefits. Well-networked individuals are happier and live longer. This is unsurprising as casual observation would suggest that the more 'sociable' an individual the 'happier' they are.

Thus company investment in social capital may have a direct payoff to the individuals involved in the process. This may imply happier, better disposed employees and external stakeholders. Clearly this sort of labour market and public relations effect is an important part of what companies think they are doing in promoting corporate citizenship programmes, as our case studies in later chapters illustrate.

The indirect effects of social capital require more explanation. Both the trust and norms aspects of the Putnam definition are well explored via the literature on repeated games. It is a standard result of game theory that if a game is repeated an indefinite number of times cooperation will emerge such that the players will depart from short term profit maximisation and 'cooperate' to achieve higher aggregate returns over the course of repeated plays of the game.

In the language of social capital trust will be created over time by repeated interaction. The value of creating this trust is that the sooner the players start cooperating the greater the benefits from cooperation will be. The trust created may encourage additional business or collaboration. It is also the case that multiple equilibrium paths may exist, such that higher levels of initial cooperation produce permanently higher returns.[14]

Game theory can also be applied to norms of behaviour. One of the problems of any human interaction is opportunism. Such opportunism may be difficult to identify (especially if there are many players) or difficult to punish (if penalties for cheating are small). Norms of behaviour can reinforce incentives to cooperate by making it unseemly not to play the game cooperatively. Social norms almost always carry social sanctions for non-compliance in the form of ostracism, criticism or denial of access to social networks. In certain situations these can be associated with direct financial costs, in other cases the social stigma alone may be very high. Norms of behaviour may also act to reduce monitoring costs. Such norms and their associated sanctions make playing the game cooperatively yield the highest payoff in the long run. Sethi and Somanathan (1996) show that norms can both be robust with respect to some opportunism but also very difficult to re-establish once some threshold level of self-interested behaviour has been exceeded. This explains the persistence of good norms over centuries (e.g. in Northern Europe) but also the difficulty of recovering norms that may have been lost through some extreme set of events (e.g. such as the communist revolutions in Russia and Eastern Europe).

Economists have made a lot of progress in explaining how cooperation emerges and where trust comes from. Once established trust has additional beneficial consequences. Sato and Helper (1996) distinguish competence and goodwill trust. Competence trust is the belief in the ability of business partners as distinct from their trustworthiness; where the belief in trustworthiness is the foundation of goodwill trust. Both must be present for maximum economic benefit. Such trust encourages further investment and a process of continuous mutual learning (as observed with the Japanese buyer-supplier system).[15]

Social networks act as vehicles for spreading trust and norms of behaviour. Thus membership of a club or project may be an excellent way to get to know people, initially at very low cost. This allows trust and norms of trusting behaviour to develop between the individuals involved. Fukuyama (1999) suggests that networks are more successful when they are large, internally cohesive, have small radius of distrust (i.e. the number of those regarded by network members as untrustworthy) and a large radius trust (i.e. the number of those regarded by network members as trustworthy). This is because organisations with a clear purpose with a positive attitude towards others and few enemies are likely to be those most valued by society.[16] Putnam's bowling leagues and scout clubs are clearly in this category, whereas a small terrorist cell is the exact opposite.

Isham (2002) asks whether investment in social capital, such as setting up a management committee for a neighbourhood water project in Africa, can improve local development. He suggests that social capital works to aid development by allowing the sharing of information, reducing the transaction costs between individuals and groups, facilitating collective action and allowing individual risks to be mitigated. This suggests that investments in social capital can have the characteristics of physical investments and should be compared to them when physical investment capital is low.

Collier (2002) suggests that certain forms of social interaction can be good for solving certain externalities. Teaching is good for solving the knowledge externality by allowing copying. Networks are good at solving the knowledge externality by pooling information. Similarly networks can solve opportunism by building trust. Clubs can solve free riding behaviour by norms of cooperation. The problem for developing countries is that pooling by associations may be regressive for income. Formal markets may work better, independent media and courts and a competitive credit market may be better ways of solving the knowledge externality.

If companies see social capital as an outcome of, rather than an input to, their corporate citizenship policies it might be appropriate to ask how social capital is created. The evidence is that social capital is strongly correlated with education. Taking a four-year university degree in a typical OECD country increases the probability of an individual volunteering for a social project by 10%.[17]

Glaesar, Laibson and Sacerdote (2002) shed light on the incentives to create social capital mechanism by considering investments in social capital as private investment by individuals to which they expect to earn a return. Their model assumes that the return to a social capital investment is a function of the individual's social capital and aggregate social capital. They find that social capital investment is likely to rise when individuals are more concerned about the future, less mobile with respect to their job, as the opportunity cost of time declines, the rate of social capital depreciation increases and as the amount of aggregate social capital goes up. Social capital investment declines with relocation and age. In short social capital investment is going to be highest for stable individuals with a commitment to their local neighbourhood and aged in their 40s and 50s.

Characterising the social capital of corporate citizenship (CC) projects

In order to analyse our individual case study CC projects we make use of the form of Table 4.1. This summarises two different CC projects.

Table 4.1 Summarising social capital aspects of CC projects

		Project 1	Project 2
Scope-			
Micro:	Person to person	**	**
Meso:	Vertical relationships	***	*
Macro:	Institutional	**	*
Form-			
Structural:	Networks	**	**
	Bridging structural holes	**	*
	New membership	*	*
	Ties & glue/lubricant	*	**
Cognitive:	Competence/goodwill	**	***
Channel-			
Information:	Improve education	**	
Collective action:	Correct government/ social failure	***	
Misc:	Employment stability	**	
	Cohesion	**	**
	Radius of trust/distrust	**	*
	Norms of behaviour	**	**

Key: no stars – minimal impact, * – some impact, ** – notable impact, *** – potent impact.

The features of the social capital are listed following the discussion above. Each aspect is scored as no stars, one, two or three stars, according to how significant each of the features appears to be.

Summarising our discussion on the elements of social capital we can link each of the elements of the table as follows. Social capital can be characterised as having scope, form and channel (Grootaert and Bastelear, 2002b). Scope refers to which sorts of actors are involved. This can be micro (person to person), macro (society level) or meso (vertical, e.g. between a senior company official and local inhabitant). Form refers to the method by which social capital is created. This can be cognitive (by changing attitudes and perceptions) or structural (via creating a forum for interaction, such as a committee). Cognitive forms of social capital can involve competence trust whereby social actors become more willing to trust the ability of counterparties to deliver or goodwill trust where social actors are more willing to risk social or commercial dealings in the expectation (rather than the evidence) of a positive outcome (Sato and Helper, 1996). Structural forms of social capital either involve creating new social networks or forums for co-operation, adding members to existing networks or improving links between social actors. Improved links between social actors are particularly important when weak ties are created (Granovetter, 1973). Social capital in this sense can either be glue that provides social cohesion or the lubricant that helps members of society to rub-along together (Padlam, 2000). Forms of social capital which bridge structural holes in society may be particularly important (Burt, 2001), because these build social relations between otherwise poorly connected groups (such as local villagers and national politicians). Vertical relationships between the well connected and the poorly connected also add potency to social capital (Lin, 2001). Channel refers to the way in which the acquired social capital translates into positive social outcomes. Channels of social capital include the improved education that the forms of social capital facilitate and the collective action that they make possible (Collier, 2002). Collective action can correct government and social failures. Additional channels are via improved employment stability (Glaesar, Laibson and Sacerdote, 2002), social cohesion, an improved radius of trust (Fukuyama, 1999) and improved norms of behaviour.

We make use of the summary in Table 4.1 in chapters 7–10.

How can we measure social capital

So far we have concentrated on describing social capital, now we want to go on to suggest how it might be measured. One of the great claims for the concept of social capital is that it offers the prospect of measuring some explanatory factors of economic development. This offers the opportunity to statistically model the effect of these factors.

There have been many measures of social capital that have been applied in the literature, reflecting the multidimensional nature of the concept and the purpose for which it is being measured.

Putnam (2000) uses 14 measures to produce a composite measure of social capital in the US. These measures include the number of club memberships, the amount of volunteering and the participation in Presidential elections, attendance at political meetings and participation in election campaigns.[18] Putnam's measures can be criticised because they do not reflect the depth or economic significance of the social interaction involved.

One issue that arises in the literature is how to construct a social capital index from a large number of potential survey questions. The preferred method of doing this is Principal Component Analysis (PCA). This constructs an index as a weighted sum of each of the components. The construction works by calculating weights on each of the component questions that maximise the total sum of the squared correlations between the composite variable and each component. Thus higher weights are given to components that are more highly correlated with each other whilst outlier components get low weights.[19] PCA analysis of social capital is often based on detailed surveys of local attitudes and can cover a wide range of trust, norm and network-related attitudes. For instance Onyx and Bullen (2000) analyse 68 questions in five communities in Australia.[20] These sorts of studies have been used to link broad measures of social capital with measures of other types of capital (natural, produced and human).[21] The nature of the method also allows questions that get a low weight initially to be disregarded as unrelated to composite social capital.[22]

Formal social network analysis is now a well-developed field.[23] It is possible to draw detailed maps linking individuals to one another and establishing how attenuated certain individuals might be and what subgroups exist. This however does not address the issue of how economically significant these ties might be. How strong social ties actually are, is related to the concept of a composite measure of social capital. Using a variant of PCA Marsden and Campbell (1984) attempt to measure the strength of social relations. They find that the closeness or the emotional intensity of a relationship is most strongly correlated with a composite measure of tie strength. They also find that time spent with the other person and the depth of relationship are distinct aspects of the strength of the social tie. This leads to the suggestion that simple measures of the frequency and duration of contact may not be good predictors of tie strength. This suggests that the Putnam measures of social capital do not get at the whole story of what makes social capital good for the economy. However actual time spent with the other person is positively correlated with the constructed measure of tie strength. Marsden (1990) goes on to question whether individuals questioned in surveys provide accurate information on the strength of their ties and whether there is accurate sampling of the whole of the networks under study.

There have been a number of studies that have directly measured individual economic performance with measures of social capital, many of them in a developing country context.

Using World Values Survey (WVS) data Knack and Keefer (1997) examined the relationship between economic growth rates in 29 countries over the period 1980–1992 and measures of social capital. The World Values Survey is a regular survey of individuals that asks them a number of questions directly related to the trust and norms components of social capital. The percentage of people responding yes to

'In general, do you trust other people?' was used a key measure of trust. It was found that a 10% rise in this variable was correlated with a 0.8% p.a. rise in the growth rate over the period. Trust measures were strongly correlated with International Country Risk Guide index numbers. Knack and Keefer also used some of the attitude to authority questions such as 'Do you think it is always wrong to cheat on your taxes?' as measures of civic norms.

Other studies have made use of surveys of club membership at the village level to assess the impact of social capital. Membership of groups is related to household expenditure. Narayan and Pritchett (1999) looked at group membership in a sample of villages in Tanzania finding that group membership was positively correlated with income. Maluccio, Haddad and May (2000) found that in their sample of households in Kwa-Zulu Natal, South Africa group memberships had increased substantially between 1993 and 1998 with higher stated levels of trust in 1993 correlated with higher membership in 1998.[24] They suggest that while those with more memberships have higher income, increases in membership are not associated with higher income. The most significant memberships were religious societies, savings clubs and burial societies (death expenses insurance clubs). As savings clubs and burial clubs cost money it is not clear that any direction of causality from club membership to increased household expenditure can be inferred. The index of social capital equally weights the density, performance and participation in the groups.

Club memberships do not operationalise how social capital might be raising income. In order to gain insight into this process Piazza-Georgi (2002) surveys attitudes to wealth. She asks subjects to choose between two statements. On wealth, the statements were:

1. I admire the man or woman who has managed to become rich.
2. Most rich people have become rich dishonestly.

On community, the statements were:

1. You need the help of your community to succeed.
2. You must struggle alone if you want to succeed, you cannot count on others.

Answering 1 to each of these questions implied more positive attitudes to wealth and higher social capital. Similarly, Krishna (2003) also used a survey with the following question with a direct economic relevance to the question of how sociable members of different villages in rural Pakistan were:

Suppose a friend of yours in this village faced the following alternatives: which one would he or she prefer?

1. Own and farm ten units of land by themselves.
2. Own and farm 25 units of land with one other person in the village.

Interestingly in this case high social capital was not found to be enough, on its own, to raise village incomes. It was important that this was combined with the presence of a new village leader who knew about state agency help and was informed about external market opportunities. Social capital and local government had to work together. This finding is supported in the context of the US Community Reinvestment Act that mandates banks to lend a certain percentage of their portfolio to the poor via NGOs.[25] There is more community lending to poor communities with more of both NGOs and social capital. This indicates that in local development, social capital, appropriate local institutional support and external financing go together.

Buerkle and Guseva (2002) have examined the importance of personal networks in determining income in the Czech Republic and Poland. They found those who subsequently worked in the same town as the university they attended earned significantly more. Those who had attended night classes to gain their degree earned significantly less than those who had studied full-time.[26] They took this as evidence that the informal networks established at university were more valuable if formed during a full-time course and were less valuable if the individual subsequently left the university town.

Many of the above studies have been heavily criticised. There are two sets of criticisms. First, the quality of the data is poor. Second, the econometrics is suspect due to the nature of social capital.

Van Deth (2003) makes a number of serious criticisms of data quality. First, the World Values Survey does not incorporate a modern concept of social capital: there are no questions about network membership in the older surveys. Second, interview data often asks about perceived membership and does not measure actual memberships. Third, measures of aggregate trust cannot be inferred from individual trust and vice versa. Hall (1999) points out that the UK appears to be a high trust environment on the basis of number of memberships and voluntary organisations but scores poorly on the WVS trust question. This suggests that the WVS question is too broad and open to misinterpretation to be meaningful. Fourth, the same questions asked across a number of countries are not contextualised to account for the different nature of social capital in different countries. Finally, it is also not clear what the right way to construct a composite variable is, since it depends on the number and nature of the questions asked even under PCA. Related to this is the assumption that there are no missing variables in the analysis either in the construction of measures of social capital or in measures of their effects.

Durlauf (2002) focusses on the econometric problems arising from econometric analysis that seeks to link social capital to economic performance.[27] He suggests that studies which link trust variables to economic growth rates are often too simple and suffer from large numbers of missing variables. This gives rise to the possibility that social capital may simply be an inaccurate proxy for the real underlying drivers of differential economic performance. There also remains the problem of distinguishing trust and trustworthiness. What people say about how much they trust each other is clearly not as important as how trustworthy in business transactions they actually are. Durlauf makes that the point that social experiments carried out in conditions where many factors are held constant may be more fruitful than regression analysis of survey data. He suggests that one of the key insights of experimental psychology is how fragile social relations can be in the face of external stress and the challenge is to explain the resilience of social capital and its associated institutions.[28]

Such experiments have been used in the analysis of trust.[29] Glaeser et al. (2000) use experimental games to test the nature of trust and trustworthiness. They use 189 Harvard undergraduates in two game experiments:

The Trust Game: A two-player game where the first player is given $15. That player can then choose how much to send to the second player. The amount sent is doubled and the second player can choose to return a portion of the amount to the first player. In this case the amount of money sent by the first player is a measure of how trusting they are, the amount returned is a measure of how trustworthy the second player is.

The Envelope Drop: Players are asked how much would they pay for a $10 bill in an envelope addressed to them dropped in a public place. They higher the sum of money that they would pay the more trusting the player is.

The results of the Trust Game suggest that repeated play facilitates trust, race and nationality differences between the players reduce trustworthiness and non-cognitive social skills improve overall returns. The results of the Envelope Drop Game suggest that people who trust strangers more are willing to pay more for the envelope. Crucially this experiment finds that the answer to the standard Trust question in the WVS is strongly correlated with the trustworthiness of the individual.

Holm and Danielson (2005) conduct the Trust Game on similar students in Norway and Tanzania. They find the degree of trust in others is the same in both but the amount of money returned is lower in Tanzania than in Norway. These results suggest that lower levels of income create more expectation of a lack of reciprocity in business relationships. This could be related to the idea that multinationals are fair game for exploitation in business relationships in some developing countries on the part of local communities and governments.

In closing we note that both companies and the World Bank have developed tools to assess the impact of their social projects on social capital. In a subsequent chapter we discuss Anglo American's Socio-Economic Assessment Toolbox (SEAT) that they use to assess the wider community impact of each of their manufacturing and production facilities.[30] The World Bank have also developed an Assessment Tool to look specifically at the social capital impact of their project lending.[31] These tools do attempt to draw on many of the insights that the empirical literature on social capital has highlighted.

Firms and social capital

While there has been a significant amount written about social capital and individuals, social capital and countries, and social capital and communities, very little of this literature is related directly to companies. In this section we highlight some of the points of connection in the literature.

La Porta et al. (1997) look at the relationship between the WVS measure of trust and the share of the largest 20 companies in GDP across 40 countries. There is a strong correlation. This suggests that countries with higher levels of social capital can support larger firms. The argument is that strong family ties are bad for the sort of weak tie based trust that the operation of large stock market-based companies require. Thus the bridging social capital that is required to support large firms is important for advanced capitalist development.

If high social capital encourages the formation of successful large companies, Tolbert (2005) argues for a different direction of causation. He suggests that small local firms encourage the formation of social capital. He looks at the correlation between social capital in US states with the share of local (rather than chain) retailers. He finds a positive correlation between measures of local orientation and lower crime and poverty. He argues that these types of businesses serve as meeting places for the formation of social capital within communities. This is a rather similar argument to arguments for the community-building role of local (and often financially non-viable) post offices in the UK.

That companies rely on high amounts of internal capital is something explored by Cohen and Prusak (2001). They highlight that the internal organisation of large successful firms such as UPS and Alcoa involves high degrees of networking within the firm. An example of this would be the daily meetings of UPS drivers to informally reallocate jobs to minimise travel distance. They also discuss the new Alcoa headquarters that includes lots of open space and informal meeting areas complete with equipment for impromptu use of whiteboards etc. Such cooperative working environments require high levels of individual and group trust to work.

This sort of effect has been observed in empirical studies. Tsai and Ghosal (1998) examined social capital within 15 business units of a multinational. This company was interesting because the business units were allowed a significant amount of freedom as to whom they cooperated with, both within the firm and outside it. They found that existence of shared vision, greater social interaction and higher levels of trust and trustworthiness facilitated superior rates of resource exchange between business units and greater value creation through product innovation.

Our focus in this book is however on the relationship between companies and the external society in which they are embedded. The distinction between the different ways in which firms can contribute to social capital is discussed in Westlund and Nilsson (2005). They define four types of social capital: social capital internal to the enterprise and three types of external social capital – production-related (e.g. links to suppliers), environment-related (e.g. links to government) and market-related (e.g. customer relations built through marketing). Of the three types of external social capital, CC programmes would be included under 'environment-related', though this category includes other elements such as informal links with local politicians. For a sample of Swedish businesses in one industrial estate Westlund and Nilsson find a positive relationship between indicators of firm growth and amount of local sponsorship.

The external social relations of the firm is something that has been an increasing focus over recent times. Zadek (2001) appeals for the creation of a 'civil corporation' that takes its external obligations seriously:

> 'A corporation that is said to be civil is understood as one that takes full advantage of opportunities for learning and action in building social and environmental objectives into its core business by, effectively developing its internal values and competencies.'[32]

The term Corporate Social Investment (CSI) further focusses on the external nature of a company's community involvement.

Thus 'CSI encompasses projects that are external to the business or outward looking projects undertaken for the purpose of uplifting communities in general and those which have a strong developmental approach. It also includes projects with a focus on social, developmental or community aspects where the investment is not primarily driven as a marketing initiative.'[33]

This view links back to a long literature on the link between corporate financial performance (CFP) and corporate social and environmental responsibility. Milton Friedman (1970) famously wrote '[t]he social responsibility of business is to make profits.' This view remains a powerful one. It suggests that firms fundamentally advance social welfare through focussing on profit maximisation. It also suggests that it is up to governments to maximise social welfare directly. It is consistent with modern concerns about the transparency of company decision-making. An open process of decision-making about social projects might involve an unhealthy invasion of government into the operation of private firms and of private firms into government.[34]

However many studies have investigated the link between CFP and CSR. Margolis and Walsh (2003) compare 127 studies over the period 1972 and 2002. They find evidence of a positive relationship between CSR reputation and profits or share prices, though the relationship between CSR disclosure and profits is much more mixed. They also find a positive relationship between corporate giving and profits, though the direction of causality is unclear. However the great question of whether corporate social actions make any difference to society is unanswered.

Orlitzky et al. (2003) criticise Margolis and Walsh for simply counting the number of positive and negative studies. They apply a meta-analysis that weights studies by the number of observations that they contain. They find that the relationship between share prices and CSR is stronger than the relationship between profits and CSR. However they also conclude that corporate social performance is positively related to CFP from the analysis of 30 years of studies. However measurement error, sampling error and missing variables may explain 15–100% of the variation in corporate financial performance making the relationship far from stable. They also argue that the relationship is clearly bidirectional as current corporate social investment must be limited by past corporate profitability. Separate analysis of corporate environmental responsibility and corporate social responsibility suggests that the impact of environmental responsibility on profits is weaker than the relationship between CFP and CSR generally. This is possibly due to the tendency for some of these studies to rely on how much environmental disclosure there is, rather than measures of environmental reputation.

Companies have become much more interested in assessing the impact of their community involvement in recent years. A good example of systematic thinking in this area is the London Benchmarking Group Model, developed by Logan and Tuffrey (1999; 2000). This model categorises not only the nature of the community involvement: charitable gifts, community investment and commercial initiatives in the community. It measures the outputs of such projects in terms of leveraging additional support (e.g. from government), community benefits and business benefits. It categorises inputs as: cash, employee time, in-kind contributions and programme management costs. Community benefits can be analysed in terms of local groups supported, volunteering opportunities created, number of people being helped and training opportunities offered. The business benefits to the firm can include: making employees feel more positive towards the firm and improvements in the public's perception of the business or brand. While all of these inputs and outputs lend themselves to some form of measurement, overall assessments of projects remain difficult and expensive. To measure these properly would require measures of wider community impact, such as whether a literacy project increased literacy rates, and direct financial impact on the firm's business, such as amount of new business created. As we note later in our case study of Diageo, only the largest projects are often assessed in such a careful and comprehensive way.

We close this section with a discussion of two studies that highlight the operation of the business benefits of social capital.

Fafchamps and Minten (2002) examine the impact of social capital among agricultural goods traders in Madagascar. They survey a sample of over 800 traders in 1997. They find that business value added and sales are positively correlated with measures of personal social capital. The social capital variables that they correlated with performance included the number of fellow traders known, the number of individuals who can help with the business, the number of suppliers known personally and the number of customers known personally. Interestingly they found the number of relatives in the trade was negatively correlated with performance. The authors suggested that there were three channels through which social capital worked: relations with other traders reduced transaction costs; relations with individuals who can help provide informal insurance; and family relationships could lead to a reduction in business efficiency. These findings support the view that weak ties between individuals in business are good for performance.

At the other end of the scale of company size, Hilb and Rotstein (2005) look at the impact of the computer chipmaker, Intel's corporate citizenship in Costa Rica. Intel in Costa Rica is an excellent case study because of the sheer size of Intel's impact on the Costa Rican economy (around 10% of GDP). Intel's investment in a chip plant in Costa Rica required 2,000 skilled workers. In order to increase the capability of the Costa Rican economy in providing sufficient human capital Intel worked closely with the government and the education sector to improve capacity. It invested in partnerships with universities. There was also a significant amount of local opposition to the construction of the chip plant. This was overcome with a significant investment in the local community and a large visiting programme for local people to the chip factory. Teacher training initiatives at the school level were very popular. Its 'Teach to the Future Course' for school teachers had the beneficial side effect of increasing Intel-based computer sales to teachers on the courses by 60%. The ongoing success of Intel in Costa Rica suggests that such outreach initiatives can contribute significantly to facilitating wider economic development, as well as the narrow business success of the initiating firm.

Multinationals and social capital

Multinationals are a special class of firms. As Buckley and Casson (1985) point out what makes a successful national firm become a multinational is that it is better at systematising and adapting its business processes such that it is possible to export them to affiliates in other countries. Thus multinationals, at the same time, mould the environments in which they operate and are sufficiently open to being adapted by them. Kostova and Roth (2003) discuss the particular difficulty of creating social capital within the multinational. This involves the action of individuals who can span the boundary between headquarters and the business units and harness the social relations so created to improve the value of the business. Friendly relations are not enough, clearly the ability to harness the most appropriate internal resources across borders is the key to successful headquarter – subsidiary interaction. This theoretical suggestion is backed up by the empirical work of Tsai and Ghosal (1998) discussed above.

Multinationals relationship to wider economic and social development has a long and chequered history. Litvin (2003) sees the current global hostility to multinationals as a function of the early pioneers of the multinational: the British East India Company and British South Africa Company. These companies were licensed by the British state to make profits within exclusive territories and to essentially administer the areas in which they operated. They thus combined the power of the state, foreignness and resource exploitation in the minds of many of the inhabitants of the host countries in which they operated. Their licences were only revoked when it became clear that such private monopolists could not be expected to operate as well as a benign state.[35]

This finding that multinationals have a bad legacy to overcome finds support in some of the literature on the survival of firms. For instance Zaheer and Mosakowski (1997) find that the survival rates of foreign firms in the interbank currency trading market are lower than for domestic firms. Interestingly the size of the discrepancy diminishes over time suggesting the importance of factors such as experience of the local market and, perhaps, a decline in perception of being foreign. Taking a different angle Mezias (2002) finds that foreign owned subsidiaries are facing greater rates of labour lawsuits in the US than US-based companies. Again suggesting something about the lack of knowledge of the environment exhibited by the foreign subsidiaries or the greater willingness of employees to sue them.

More recently multinationals have been the target of a backlash due to globalisation. Eighty-five percent of international trade involves multinationals and their significance in world trade continues to increase. The liberalisation of the world trading rules that followed the successive post World War Two GATT negotiations has been massively to the benefit of multinationals. There have also been well publicised corporate business ethics failures since the 1970s. Thus the foreign business dealings of large US defence contractors lay behind the 1977 Foreign Corrupt Practices Act, which unleashed the Corporate Compliance movement in the US, and the failures of BCCI and Maxwell

Communications spurred the Corporate Governance movement in the UK since 1990. Increasing awareness of global differences in income and environmental standards and the impact of globalisation on them has spurred the 'Global Value Chain critique' in which NGOs have attacked the behaviour of multinationals at their weakest global point in their value chain (which could be sweatshops in Asia or oil production facilities in Africa).[36]

Multinationals corporate citizenship activities in developing countries can be very significant. The sheer scale of the multinationals and their comparative organisation in often badly served (by national government) regions of underdeveloped countries makes them significant players in local development. Frynas (2005) estimates that in 2001 multinational oil, gas and mining companies spent $500 million worldwide on corporate social investment. They were motivated by the desire to gain competitive advantage (licences are often informally or formally conditional on local social spending), the need to create a safe working environment for employees, managing external expectations (including those of western NGOs) and the desire to keep their employees happy more generally and attract better job applicants.

Litvin (2003) gives a fascinating account of the sheer difficulty of doing business in some developing countries. Shell's compound in Warri – their local headquarters in the oil rich areas of the Niger Delta – is a fortress with employees needing to leave it under guard due to the frequent risk of kidnap. Shell's 6000 km of pipelines leave it vulnerable to criminal damage and associated environmental damage caused by oil spills. Part of the local resentment has been that only 3% of the government's oil revenues from this poor region have been spent there until recently. Its relations with the Nigerian government are close because Shell is the managing partner of the largest oil joint venture in Nigeria in which the government has a majority stake and Shell has a 30% share. BP had its stake in the venture nationalised in 1979. Community projects in Nigeria cost Shell $4 million p.a. in the late 1980s and $60 million p.a. by 2000. Shell employs 170 community development staff in the region. As one might imagine Shell faces challenges in rolling out a community programme. Social investments are politically controversial. Two hundred people were killed in 1999 protesting against the relocation of a government office. In this context Shell has been criticised in a 2001 report because only one-third of its social projects were operational at any one time and some of them appear to be socially wasteful (such as building three new town halls in one town to satisfy different tribal demands).

Frynas (2005) also discusses the experience of Shell in Nigeria in this context. He suggests that multinationals find it difficult to adapt to the country context in which they find themselves. In particular, they do not sufficiently involve beneficiaries; there is a lack of human resources in the management of projects; firm managers are overly technical in their approach and lack development training; and projects are not integrated into an overall development plan for an area or region. Frynas suggests that in another region of Nigeria, Statoil have been more successful in promoting a wider development plan through a close association with a development NGO, Pro Natura. However this may be because of the region being easier to operate in than the one covered by Shell's operations.

The example of Shell in Nigeria is clearly an extreme one, but it does raise the issue of whether companies possess capabilities for playing a significant role in development beyond their core business. As Frynas points out 70–80% of oil revenues go to the government in Nigeria and criticism of Shell deflects attention from the misuse of much of this income over decades. However the positive example of Intel in Costa Rica clearly provides a counterweight to this.

It is important to explore the likely limitations of multinationals in community development. The first is the significance of the scale of community investment. In South Africa, where many multinationals proudly discuss their community involvement, the total value of such social investment is only 1.5% of the education and health budget of the central government.[37] For multinationals to be significant there clearly needs to be substantial leverage of their actual community expenditure. Indeed it is the case that the tax contributions of multinationals are many times their CSI in most developing countries. Clearly if it were the case that CSI expenditure reduced tax revenue by buying fiscal goodwill, the overall effect of CSI expenditure could be significantly negative. Newell (2005) explores this in the South African context arguing that much CSI involves good public relations, placating local communities and buying tax avoidance. He argues that Community Driven Development where the poor build their own development capacity is likely to be more effective than CSR. This is because this sort of pressure will ensure that communities are not bought off too cheaply and more importantly that effective state regulation is enacted or enforced rather than left to voluntarism and self-regulation.

The relationship between firms and social capital is reflected in the relationship between multinationals and firms. However there are some additional dimensions. Banai and Reisel (1999) highlight the issue of whether local employees trust foreign managers in London banks. The answer seems to be 'yes' independently of whether they are appointed on pure merit or because of a tradition of parent company officials holding key roles. This suggests that multinationals are firms which must not only build trust within the same country but also between people of different nationalities.

Countries and social capital

In this section we highlight some of the particular issues that have arisen in the analysis of social capital in the three developing countries that we focus on this study: Poland, Mexico and South Africa. Our purpose is not to comprehensively describe the nature of social capital in the three countries but to provide a sketch of what other authors have sought to highlight in their analysis.

Poland

Is a former eastern bloc country that has recently joined the European Union. The country has had something of a free market tradition in the past and the communist era lasted from 1945 to 1989 when it became one of the first eastern bloc countries to emerge from Soviet control. Relatively little has been written applying social capital explicitly to Poland. However, the existing literature does reflect upon the ways in which social capital has been affected during the three key periods of modern Polish economic development.

Chloupkova et al. (2002) compare the creation and destruction of social capital by looking at the agricultural cooperative movement in Poland and Denmark. The authors find that the movement develops similarly in both countries, relying on and giving rise to high levels of social capital in the 19th century. However comparison of the current level of social capital shows much lower levels in Poland. This suggests that the communist period, by socialising most economic relations, worked to destroy social capital.

This legacy of destruction of social capital becomes important in the recent period. Poland has suffered a significant decline in its traditional manufacturing industries since the end of communism. An examination by Stachowicz and Walukiewicz (2003) of the setting up of pro-innovative networks in the region of Silesa shows the importance of such networks. The networks were supported by the arrival of a tyre maker Goodyear, which set up a plant in the area. A lack of large Polish companies to lead such innovative clusters is a problem in this area. This paper notes that since 1990, 300 private universities have been set up in Poland without any support from the central government and the number of students enrolled at university has quadrupled.

The nature of social capital within Poland's growing private small and medium sized company sector is explored in two studies. Wallace, Shumulyar and Bedzir (1999) examine the informal social networks that exist among small-scale post-communist traders and how these help minimise trading risks. Pollard and Jemicz (2004) highlight the importance of social capital in facilitating the successful internationalisation of small and medium sized businesses in Poland. They show that high levels of social capital facilitate the overcoming of the barriers to entry that exist for these firms.

Mexico

Mexico is a large developing country that shares an economically significant border with the US.[38] It is a federal country with a weak central government and democratic institutions. One party consistently won elections for 70 years until 2000. That party (the PRI or Institutional Revolutionary Party) practised *Personalismo*: a political culture characterised by strong personal ties of loyalty. Of the 32 states, five of the six bordering the US have the highest growth rates. From 1985 income per head has been diverging between the states. US multinationals are significant in the Mexican economy but so too is migration (legal and illegal to the US). The 1985 North American Free Trade Agreement provides the context for the liberalisation of trade between Mexico and the US and the facilitation of US multinational investment on the Mexican side of the border. There was a significant rebellion in the southerly Chiapas region in 1990 driven by poverty and lack of interest by the central government. Robey (1999) notes that the cultural differences between the average northern Mexican and the US citizens of El Paso are much less than that between northern Mexico and the southerly provinces.

Lall (2002) finds that firms that make use of informal networks (as measured by frequency of business lunches and reunions) have better economic performance. Decuir-Viruez (2003) finds that 45% of the variation in regional growth rates over the period 1994–2000 can be explained by variations in social capital, however economic freedom is much more significant than social capital by itself. His measure of social capital is an index that includes percentage voting for the opposition and the institutional density of P versus O groups.

Like many developing countries Mexico is plagued by high crime rates. Paras (2003) uses a survey to link personal experience of crime in Mexico City with trust in individuals, institutions and membership of formal organisations, behavioural change, good personal health and preference for democracy. Trust and participation in society declines with experience of crime. This suggests that reducing actual crime and fear of crime is very important for creating a society with high social capital.

Casson and Guista (2004) evaluate two microfinance projects in Mexico and find that the involvement of trust brokers and the policy of subsidising trust building projects is very important for the success of these projects. Healy (2002) notes the success of a project to create local museums in building social capital in Yucatan. He found that such projects encouraged volunteerism as being on the local committee of such a museum could be the first step to a political career. The museums were then marketed in the US as part of a holiday tour package, creating substantial economic benefits for small local communities.

Jonathan Fox (1996; 1997) has evaluated a number of World Bank programmes in Mexico. He strongly criticises the lack of social capital building by the Bank in Mexico, citing its own lack of engagement with local communities, which is illustrated by the production of most of its documents in English. However he does discuss three projects: covering community forestry, aquaculture and sustainable development, which illustrate a more engaged approach to local communities (Fox, 1997). In a related finding Fox finds that the success of social capital building efforts depends on the involvement of state and local actors combined with external actors in civil society (Fox, 1996). While social capital can be produced from the grassroots up external allies turn out to be crucial to the survival of local civic initiatives. Fox and Gershman (2000) also find that social capital projects in Mexico fail due to project managers being ignored or being hostile to existing forms of pro-poor social capital. In a successful community forestry case the World Bank project staff involved with the project have been consistently supportive of their Mexican project manager in debates with the national treasury and environment ministry.

South Africa

South Africa is a key test-bed of many theories of social capital and there have been a significant number of papers which make use of it in empirical work. South Africa was a British Colony, which following independence moved towards an apartheid state. This process accelerated sharply after the Second World War when a series of laws were passed limiting the democratic access of the non-white communities and restricting their freedom of movement. In one of the terrible legacies of this system black workers were separated from their families with ongoing consequences for the social fabric of society. Blacks were also concentrated in poorer agricultural areas in so-called homelands. It was in this context that 'townships' – illegal settlements close to large cities developed. South Africa became a multi-racial democracy in 1994 under majority-black rule. Since then government policy has sought to bring about gradual social change without fundamentally weakening the economic system that supported the apartheid system for so long. However an important part of this change is a significant move towards Black Economic Empowerment (BEE), which has set targets of 26% black ownership of business capital over a ten-year period.[39]

Maluccio, Haddad and May (2000) and Mbigi (2000), align social capital with the analogous African concept of 'ubuntu', the level of which they feel has diminished in the face of the rapid and rather unique changes in the last century in South Africa. Ubuntu is enshrined in the Zulu maxim *ubuntu ngumuntu ngabantu*, i.e. 'a person is a person through other persons'.[40] This traditional African aphorism articulates a basic respect and compassion for others. It can be interpreted as both a factual description and a rule of conduct or social ethic. Maluccio et al. suggest that a decline in social capital in South Africa followed the end of Apartheid. This decline is the result of the decrease in time available to the key players who help to maintain social networks (as they have moved into government), an increase in demographic mobility post-apartheid, and an increase in government efficiency, which has negated the requirement of social capital as a compensatory mechanism.

During the 1980s multinationals that remained in South Africa were the target of long-running campaigns to get them to disinvest. Since 1994 companies have been under some pressure to make amends for their perceived complicity in the apartheid system, under which they benefited from cheap black labour built on segregation and poor social conditions and a tax system that supported disproportionately small transfers of economic wealth to the poorest communities. There has also been a legacy of environmental degradation in the regions of industrial activity built on non-existent or inadequately enforced environmental regulations.

Lund-Thomson (2005) highlights some of the attempts by multinationals to build community relations in this context. Some companies have signed Good Neighbourhood Agreements. The problem is that the spatial distribution of poor communities around industrial plants means that civil society is weakest in those places where it could do most good. He notes that there is a fragmentation of government agencies concerned with social and environmental problems and many NGOs have been weakened by the brain drain into the ANC government following their ascent to power in 1994. Emmett (2000) also argues strongly that many areas of South African society have low initial levels of social capital. As such it is not enough to seek community participation in the development of social projects, it is necessary to assess and increase their capacity to participate first.

Fig (2005) is critical of some voluntary initiatives by business in the CSR area. Many have not woken up to the huge challenge of AIDS among their workforce. As we will discuss later in our case study of Anglo American, infection rates are as high as 30% among some large company's workers. The process of industry certification and the creation of a Johannesburg Stock Exchange Social Responsibility Investment Index do not appear to go far enough and misses out large areas of 'responsibility' such as in the payment of fair wages. Fig points out that BEE may even have been counterproductive for CSI as many black entrepreneurs do not feel that CSI is their responsibility. However it is the case that overseas listed companies are under greater pressure to raise standards, even though the standards in question tend to reflect first world concerns for the environment rather than the plight of the poor.

Most studies of social capital in South Africa do not highlight the role of companies in social capital creation and destruction. Reinke (1998) examines the shortcomings of social lending in South Africa. He finds the transaction costs of informal lending clubs supported by the Small Enterprise Foundation (SEF) are very high. The financial return on the small loans undertaken covers only 7% of their costs. This leads him to question whether the large amount of development assistance that supports the SEF could be better spent. A much more successful example of social capital building is the Stutterheim Local Economic Development Initiative.[41] This did bring together a number of competent, experienced, enthusiastic social entrepreneurs and community leaders to link formerly antagonistic social groups to promote economic development. From 1990 to 1995 the Stutterheim Development Forum was successful in bringing groups together and led to the building of schools and community halls. Since then the rise of the ANC government and the taking over of some its functions has reduced its rationale.

Carter and Maluccio (2003) find that a household panel survey of the link between child nutritional status and social capital found that higher levels of personal and community social capital was associated with healthier children. This is because higher social capital provided insurance against losses when subsistence levels of expenditure were threatened.

Mubangizi (2003) finds that group efforts to raise economic development in the Maluti district are more successful when there is commitment from the state, the business sector and civil society. The business sector can help with organisational management, skills and attitudes to running a successful enterprise and promoting AIDS/HIV awareness. She recommends that local government should establish a development desk to help coordinate between different project groups and within project groups.

The importance of the link between business and AIDS is highlighted in a paper by Campbell and Mzandume (2001). They document a peer education project that involved a group of prostitutes living in a mining shanty town. This town consisted of 200 sex workers and hangers on living next to a mine. The demand from the miners was a function of the fact that many lived away from home. The shanty town was under the control of low level gangsters who ran the protection and prostitution businesses in the town. The paper makes depressing reading as to the limited nature of the self-help available to these women. The best they could hope for was a reduced risk of AIDS if they could persuade more of their clients to use condoms. Escape from the community, or the institution of proper democratic control of it was unthinkable. The fact that it was beside a rich mine illustrates the scale of the social capital building effort that it is required right at the doorstep of large, often global companies.

The nature of the environmental problem in South Africa is illustrated in a paper by Peek (2002) on a waste management plant owned by Mondi in South Durban. This story illustrates the legacy of environmental racism and government and industrial indifference. Mondi is a subsidiary of Anglo American, one of our case study firms. Mondi were using a particular site in a poor residential area to dump ash in a landfill site. Mondi had no permit for this site. Local campaigning forced Mondi to commission a report in 1998 that suggested the waste was not hazardous. However this report was not commissioned with the approval of the local community. Following a locally commissioned study Mondi admitted that the waste was hazardous. Eventually the local community secured an assurance, following a visit from the government environment minister that the site would be closed by 31 July 1999. The case highlighted the relative cost to the community of gaining such a decision against the resistance of a multinational. It also illustrates the lack of an effective environmental protection agency in South Africa to launch investigations and monitor compliance and the difficulty poor communities have in getting the right scientific, technical and legal advice.

Conclusions

Multinationals are rightly concerned about the communities in which they operate. As such they should be concerned for their impact on the social capital of those communities. This is because it is through the community that many problems that cannot be handled by individuals acting alone, governments or the operation of the market can be solved (Bowles and Gintis, 2002). Investments in social capital are thus investments in the ability of the community to govern itself.[42] Of all the classes of companies in existence multinationals are best placed to undertake, innovate and evaluate such investments. Multinational firms are also capable of creating bridging social capital that links local, national and international communities. This is what makes them important case studies.

As we have argued social capital is fundamentally about the trust, norms and networks within society. Companies can contribute to it by building these components both within the firm and in wider society. Our focus in the rest of this book will be on the external component of social capital. We will seek to highlight how corporate citizenship programmes may contribute to societal well being by impacting on trust, norms and networks. We will use the insights of the social capital literature to develop measures of social capital that are appropriate to the multinational and capable of being meaningfully compared across companies and countries. Clearly such measures need to be observable and capable of handling the differences in context which different companies in different countries find themselves in. Social capital offers us the prospect of some useful ways forward for measuring the inputs to and the outputs from CC programmes. We will do this in two ways: by detailed case studies that make use of the insights from the theoretical social capital literature; and via empirical analysis that draws on the measurements used in empirical social capital studies. We develop our empirical measures more fully in chapters 5 and 6 and take up the detailed case studies in chapters 7 to 10.

As Blowfield (2005) argues CSR's biggest contribution has been to stimulate new thinking about the relationship between business and society. This chapter's use of social capital as a device by which to analyse the contribution of business to building up local communities reflects a similar strength of the social capital concept. It helps us to look at an old problem in new ways and stimulates new theories of what causes social capital, how it may be dealt with and new measurements which help us to analyse it.

Notes

1. The *Voice of the People Survey* questioned 34,000 people about which institutions could be most trusted to act in society's interests (See World Economic Forum, 2002). It included a list of 17 national and international institutions.
2. *The Fifth Annual Corporate Social Responsibility Monitor 2004* conducted by Globescan Inc (2005). This survey of 23,067 individuals globally reveals that the global companies are the least trusted institutions in terms of whether they operate in the best interests of society. The list includes NGOs, UN, National Government, Trade Unions, Domestic Companies and the Media.
3. For an updated version of the thesis, see Inglehart (1997).
4. Putnam (1993, p.167).
5. O-groups are named after Mancur Olson (1982) who famously derived a theory of interest group behaviour to describe groups such as trade unions.
6. See Blowfield and Frynas (2005) for this view of CSR.
7. Schuller (2000) attributes the rise in the profile of the term to its incorporation in a State of the Union Address. Putnam's identifies television (in Putnam, 1996) as the chief culprit in reducing measured social capital in the US, its linking to the politics of the Third Way in the US and the UK and sheer fluidity of the term. Fukuyama (1995) develops the Trust concept for a popular audience.
8. See James Coleman (1988) for a seminal treatment of this.
9. Dasgupta (2000, p.341).
10. See www.worldbank.org.
11. Quoted in Schuller (2000, p.28).
12. Ogilvie (2003) has an account of how male dominated craft associations acted to exclude and reduce the pay of women who did similar work in early modern Germany. She refers to this as 'the dark side of social capital'.
13. See Waldstrom (2003) for this critique of social capital.
14. See Kreps et al. (1982) for a seminal theoretical treatment of this phenomena and Jones and Pollitt, (1996) for a discussion in a business context.
15. Sato and Helper (1996) observe higher levels of trust in Japan than in the US and Europe within the buyer-supplier system.
16. Fukuyama (1999) summarises this in an equation:
Social Capital = $\Sigma[(1/r_n).r_p.c.n]_{1,T}$ where n = size of membership of organisation T, c = degree of internal cohesion, r_p = radius of trust, r_n = radius of distrust.

17 Denny (2003) finding using International Adult Literacy Survey Data. Denny uses this to suggest that there are significant external benefits to education whereby others benefit from the individual's education. This study also finds that the better paid do more volunteering. Helliwell and Putnam (1999) find that rises in population average education reduce individual volunteering (at a given educational level). This may be because of the increased availability of alternative well-qualified volunteers. However this effect is not enough to offset the positive impact of equivalent increases in one's own education on volunteering.
18 Putnam finds sharp declines in most of his 14 measures across the US for the 1955 period onwards. These results may not generalise to other OECD countries, Hall (1999) found no general decline in club membership between 1951 and 1991 in the UK.
19 See Hjollund and Svendsen (2000).
20 They find that the rich are not necessarily more connected than the poor. However employed people do find connectedness at work and this suggests that their links may be more valuable, even if no more dense.
21 Stimson, Western, Baum and Van Gelecun (2003) do this in the context of five Australian communities.
22 Sabatini (2005) examines 51 questions divided into five classes in order to see which of the individual questions and entire classes of questions are correlated with the composite measure of social capital.
23 See for example Wasserman and Faust (1994) for a comprehensive introduction to the field of social network analysis.
24 Haddad and Maluccio (2003) connect the two periods to look at the impact of changing membership on outcomes.
25 See Holyoke (2004).
26 This effect was stronger in Poland than in the Czech Republic. The effects in Poland were to increase income by $57.35 per month in the first case and $47.38 per month in the second.
27 Durlauf (2002) uses Narayan and Pritchett (1999) and Knack and Keefer (1997) as two of his case study papers. The Narayan and Pritchett paper is singled out as confusing the trust and trustworthiness issue. The Knack and Keefer paper is accused of using equations that are too simple to explain macro-economic growth. Knack and Keefer (1997) is compared, unfavourably, to a paper by Easterly and Levine (1997). This paper makes the rather interesting point that at face value certain climate related and colonial factors can explain differential growth rates in former colonies. However these factors become insignificant when measures of the current state of institutions of democracy and property rights are added. They use this to make the point that although deep-seated cultural characteristics are no doubt important in explaining economic performance, the mechanism by which they have their effect (and indeed the way that they can be mitigated) is via the institutions that either reflect them or over-rule them.
28 The famous robbers cave experiment (Sherif et al., 1961) demonstrated how quickly social relations can break down in a controlled experiment.
29 See Carpenter (2002) who discusses the Trust Game, the Ultimatum Game, the Dictator Game and the Voluntary Contribution Game. All of which can

be used in the field to test the trust and trustworthiness of individuals under study.
30 See Anglo American (2005) for full details.
31 See Grootaert and Bastelear (2002b) for a full description of this and two examples of its implementation.
32 Zadek (2001, p.9).
33 Altron Group (2004, p.3) quoted in Fig (2005).
34 Margolis and Walsh (2003).
35 Litvin implicates the British East India company in the Indian Mutiny of 1857 and in the legacy of the British South Africa company in the ongoing situation of the white farmers in Zimbabwe.
36 See Jenkins (2005, pp.526–528) for a brief history of the rise of global CSR.
37 Vanessa Hockey (2004), cited in Fig (2005).
38 See Decuir-Viruez (2003) and Robey (1999) for general discussions of the cultural and economic position of Mexico in a social capital context.
39 As a sign of the extent to which the ANC government has moved back from its original radical vision, this target was reduced from an initial proposal of 51%.
40 Shutte (1993, p.46).
41 See Nel and McQuaid (2002).
42 Bowles and Gintis (2002) suggest that social capital should actually be called 'community governance'. This would seem to provide an echo of something close to every corporation's heart: corporate governance.

References

Altron Group (2004), *Policy document and implementation guidelines*, Johannesburg: Altron Group.
Anglo American (2005), *SEAT Socio-Economic Assessment Toolbox*, London: Anglo-American.
Banai, M. and Reisel, W.D. (1999), 'Would you trust your foreign manager? An empirical investigation', *International Journal of Human Resource Management*, Vol.10 (3), pp.477–487.
Blowfield, M. (2005), 'Corporate Social Responsibility: reinventing the meaning of development?', *International Affairs*, Vol.81 (3), pp.515–524.
Blowfield, M. and Frynas, J.G. (2005), 'Setting new agendas: critical perspectives on Corporate Social Responsibility in the developing world', *International Affairs*, Vol.81 (3), pp. 499–513.
Bowles, S. and Gintis, H. (2002), 'Social Capital and Community Governance', *Economic Journal*, Vol.112 (November), pp.F419–F436.
Buckley, P. and Casson, M. (1985), *The economic theory of the multinational enterprise: selected papers*, London: Macmillan.
Buerkle, K. and Guseva, A. (2002), 'What Do You Know, Who Do You Know? School as a Site for the Production of Social Capital and its Effects on Income Attainment in Poland and the Czech Republic', *American Journal of Economics and Sociology*, Vol.61 (3), pp.657–680.
Burt, R.S. (2001), 'Structural Holes versus Network Closure as Social Capital', In N. Lin, K. Cook and R.S. Burt (eds), *Social Capital Theory and Research*, New York: Adeline De Gruyter, pp.31–56.

Campbell, C. and Mzandume, Z. (2001), 'Grassroots Participation, Peer Education, and HIV Prevention by Sex Workers in South Africa', *American Journal of Public Health*, Vol.91 (12), pp.1978–1986.
Carpenter, J.P. (2002), 'Measuring social capital: adding field experimental methods to the analytical toolbox', In J. Isham, T. Kelly and S. Ramaswamy (eds), *Social capital and economic development: well being in developing countries*, Aldershot: Edward Elgar, pp.119–137.
Carter, M.R. and Maluccio, J.A. (2003), 'Social Capital and Coping with Economic Shocks: An Analysis of Stunting of South African Children', *World Development*, Vol.31 (7), pp.1147–1163.
Casson, M. and Guista, M.D. (2004), 'The Costly Business of Trust', *Development Policy Review*, Vol.22 (3), pp.321–342.
Chloupkova, J., Svendsen, G.L.H. and Svendsen, G.T. (2002), 'Building and destroying social capital: The case of cooperative movements in Denmark and Poland', *Agricultural and Human Values*, Vol.20, No.3, pp.241–252.
Cohen, D. and Prusak, L. (2001), *In Good Company – How Social Capital Makes Organizations Work*, Cambridge, Mass: Harvard Business School Press.
Coleman, J. (1988), 'Social Capital in the Creation of Human Capital', *American Journal of Sociology*, Vol.94, Supplement, pp.S95–S120.
Coleman, J.S. and Hoffer, T.B. (1987), *Public and Private Schools: The Impact of Communities*, New York: Basic Books.
Collier, P. (2002), 'Social capital and poverty: a microeconomic perspective', in C. Grootaert and T. Van Bastelear, *The role of social capital in development: an empirical assessment*, Cambridge: Cambridge University Press, pp.19–41.
Dasgupta, P. (2000), 'Economic progress and the idea of social capital', In Dasgupta, P. and Serageldin, I. (eds), *Social Capital: A multifaceted perspective*, Washington, D.C.: World Bank, pp.325–424.
Decuir-Viruez, L. (2003), *Institutional Factors in the Economic Growth of Mexico*, Paper to the 43rd ERSA Congress, Finland.
Denny, K. (2003), *The Effects of Human Capital on Social Capital: A Cross-Country Analysis*, Institute for Fiscal Studies Working Paper, WP03/16.
Durlauf, S.N. (2002), 'On the Empirics of Social Capital', *Economic Journal*, Vol. 112 (November), pp.F459–F479.
Easterly, W. and Levine, R. (1997), 'Africa's growth tragedy: policies and ethnic divisions', *Quarterly Journal of Economics*, Vol.16 (5), pp.563–576.
Emmett, T. (2000), 'Beyond community participation? Alternative routes to civil engagement and development in South Africa', *Development Southern Africa*, Vol.17 (4), pp.501–518.
Fafchamps, M. and Minten, B. (2002), 'Social capital and the firm: evidence from agricultural traders in Madagascar', in C. Grootaert and T. Van Bastelear, *The role of social capital in development: an empirical assessment*, Cambridge: Cambridge University Press, pp.125–154.
Fig, D. (2005), 'Manufacturing Amnesia: Corporate Social Responsibility in South Africa', *International Affairs*, Vol.81 (3), pp.599–617.
Fox, J. (1996), 'How Does Civil Society Thicken? The Political Construction of Social Capital in Rural Mexico', *World Development*, Vol.24 (6), pp.1089–1103.
Fox, J. (1997), 'The World Bank and Social Capital: Contesting the Concept in Practice', *Journal of International Development*, Vol.9 (7), pp.963–971.

Fox, J. and Gershman, J. (2000), 'The World Bank and social capital: Lessons from ten rural development projects in the Philippines and Mexico', *Policy Sciences*, Vol.33, pp.399–419.

Friedman, M. (1970), 'The social responsibility of business is to make profits', *The New York Times Magazine*, September 13.

Frynas, J.G. (2005), 'The false developmental promise of Corporate Social Responsibility: Evidence from multinational oil companies', *International Affairs*, Vol.81 (3), pp.581–598.

Fukuyama, F. (1995), *Trust*, New York: The Free Press.

Fukuyama, F. (1999), *Social Capital and Civil Society*, Institute of Public Policy, George Mason University, October 1.

Glaesar, E.L., Laibson, D. and Sacerdote, B. (2002), 'An economic approach to social capital', *Economic Journal*, Vol.112 (November), pp.F437–F458.

Glaesar, E.L., Laibson, D.I., Scheinkman, J.A. and Soutter, C.L. (2000), Measuring Trust, *Quarterly Journal of Economics*, August 2000, pp.811–846.

Globescan Inc. (2005), *Corporate Social Responsibility Monitor 2004 Executive Summary*, Ontario: Globescan Inc. Available at http://strategic.ic.gc.ca

Granovetter, M.S. (1973), 'The Strength of Weak Ties', *American Journal of Sociology*, Vol. 78, pp.1360–1380.

Grootaert, C. and Van Bastelear (2002a), 'Introduction and Overview', In C. Grootaert and T. Van Bastelear (eds), *The role of social capital in development: an empirical assessment*, Cambridge: Cambridge University Press, pp.1–18.

Grootaert, C. and Van Bastelear, T. (eds) (2002b), *Understanding and Measuring Social Capital: A Multi-Disciplinary Tool for Practitioners*, Washington, D.C.: World Bank.

Haddad, L. and Maluccio, J.A. (2003), 'Trust, Membership in Groups, and Household Welfare: Evidence from KwaZulu-Natal, South Africa', *Economic Development and Cultural Change*, Vol.51 (3), pp.573–601.

Hall, P.A. (1999), 'Social Capital in Britain', *British Journal of Politics*, Vol.29, pp.417–461.

Healy, K. (2002), 'Building Networks of Social Capital for Grassroots Development among Indigenous Communities in Bolivia and Mexico', in J. Isham, T. Kelly and S. Ramaswamy (eds), *Social capital and economic development: well being in developing countries*, Aldershot: Edward Elgar.

Helliwell, J. and Putnam, R. (1999), *Education and Social Capital*, NBER Working Paper, No.7121.

Hertz, N. (2001), *The Silent Takeover: Global Capitalism and the Death of Democracy*, London: Heinemann.

Hilb, M. and Rotstein, F. (2005), *The Role of Multinational Firms in Strengthening the Societal Fabric of Capability Development: The Case of Intel in Costa Rica*, mimeo.

Hjollund, L. and Svendsen, G.T. (2000), *Social Capital: A Standard Method of Measurement*, mimeo.

Hockey, V. (ed.) (2004), *Corporate social investment handbook 6th edn*, Cape Town: Trialogue.

Holm, H.J. and Danielson, A. (2005), 'Tropic trust versus Nordic trust: Experimental Evidence from Tanzania and Sweden', *Economic Journal*, Vol.115 (April), pp.505–582.

Holyoke, T.T. (2004), 'Community Mobilization and Credit: The Impact of Nonprofits and Social Capital on Community Reinvestment Act Lending', *Social Science Quarterly*, Vol.85 (1), pp.187–205.

Inglehart, R. (1997), *Modernization and Postmodernization, Cultural, Economic and Political Change in 43 Societies*, Princeton: Princeton University Press.

Isham, J. (2002), 'Can investments in social capital improve local development and environmental outcomes? A cost-benefit framework to assess policy options', In J. Isham, T. Kelly and S. Ramaswamy (eds), *Social capital and economic development: well being in developing countries*, Aldershot: Edward Elgar, pp.159–175.

Jenkins, R. (2005), 'Globalisation, Corporate Social Responsibility and poverty', *International Affairs*, Vol.81 (3), pp.525–540.

Jones, I.W. and Pollitt, M.G. (1996), 'Economics, Ethics and Integrity in Business', *Journal of General Management*, Vol.21 (3), pp.30–47.

Klein, N. (2000), *No Logo: no space, no choice, no jobs*, London: Flamingo.

Kostova, T. and Roth, K. (2003), 'Social Capital in Multinational Corporations and a micro-macro model of its formation', *Academy of Management Review*, Vol.28 (2), pp.297–317.

Knack, S. and Keefer, P. (1997), 'Does Social Capital Have an Economic Payoff? A Cross Country Investigation', *Quarterly Journal of Economics*, Vol.112, pp.1251–1288.

Kreps, D., Milgrom P., Roberts J., and Wilson R. (1982), 'Rational Cooperation in the Finitely Repeated Prisoners' Dilemma,' *Journal of Economic Theory*, Vol.27, pp.245–252.

Krishna, A. (2003), *Understanding, measuring and utilizing social capital: clarifying concepts and presenting a field application from India*, CAPRi Working Paper No.28.

Lall, S. (2002), 'Learning by Dining. Informal Networks and Productivity in Mexican Industry', *The World Bank, Working Paper* No. 2789.

La Porta, R.F., Lopez-de-Silanes, F., Shleifer, A. and Vishny, R. (1997), 'Trust in Large Organizations', *American Economic Review*, Vol.87, pp.333–338.

Lin, N. (2001), Building a Network Theory of Social Capital, in N. Lin, K. Cook and R.S. Burt (eds), *Social Capital Theory and Research*, New York: Adeline De Gruyter, pp.3–29.

Litvin, D. (2003), *Empires of profit: commerce, conquest and corporate responsibility*, London: Texere.

Logan, D. and Tuffrey, M. (1999), *Companies in communities: valuing the contribution*, West Malling: Charities Aid Foundation.

Logan, D. and Tuffrey, M. (2000), *Companies in communities: assessing the impact using the London Benchmarking Group model to assess how the community and the company benefit from community involvement*, West Malling: Charities Aid Foundation.

Lund-Thomson, P. (2005), 'Corporate Accountability in South Africa: the role of community mobilizing in environmental governance', *International Affairs*, Vol.81 (3), pp.619–633.

Maluccio, J., Haddad, L. and May, J. (2000), Social Capital and Household Welfare in South Africa, 1993–1998, *Journal of Development Studies*, Vol.36, pp.54–81.

Margolis, J.D. and Walsh, J.P. (2003), 'Misery loves companies: rethinking social initiatives by business', *Administrative Science Quarterly*, Vol.48 (2), pp.268–305.
Marsden, P.V. (1990), 'Network Data and Measurement', *Annual Review of Sociology*, Vol.16, pp.435–463.
Marsden, P.V. and Campbell, K.E. (1984), 'Measuring Tie Strength', *Social Forces*, Vol.63 (2), pp.482–501.
Mbigi, L. (2000), 'Managing Social Capital', *Training and Development*, Vol.54 (1), pp.36–40.
Mezias, J.M. (2002), 'Identifying Liabilities of Foreignness and Strategies to Minimize their Effects: The Case of Labor Lawsuit Judgments in the United States', *Strategic Management Journal*, Vol.23, pp.229–244.
Mubangizi, B.C. (2003), 'Drawing on social capital for community economic development: Insights from a South African rural community', *Community Development Journal*, Vol.38 (2), pp.140–150.
Narayan, D. and Pritchett, L. (1999), 'Cents and sociability: household income and social capital in rural Tanzania', *Economic Development and Social Change*, Vol.47 (4), pp.871–897.
Nell, E.L. and McQuaid, R.W. (2002), 'The Evolution of Local Economic Development in South Africa: The Case of Stutterheim and Social Capital', *Economic Development Quarterly*, Vol.16 (1), pp.60–74.
Newell, P. (2005), 'Citizenship, accountability and community: The limits of the CSR agenda', *International Affairs*, Vol.81 (3), pp.541–557.
OECD (2000), *The OECD Guidelines for Multinational Enterprises*, Paris: OECD. Available at: www.oecd.org/department/0,2688,en_2649_34889_1_1_1_1_1,00.html
Ogilvie, S. (2003), *A bitter living: women, markets, and social capital in early modern Germany*, Oxford: Oxford University Press.
Olson, M. (1982), *The rise and decline of nations: economic growth, stagflation and social rigidities*, New Haven: Yale University Press.
Onyx, J. and Bullen, P. (2000), 'Measuring Social Capital in Five Communities', *Journal of Applied Behavioural Science*, Vol.36 (1), pp.23–42.
Orlitzky, M., Schmidt, F.L. and Rynes, S.L. (2003), 'Corporate social and financial performance: A meta-analysis', *Organization Studies*, Vol.24, pp.403–441.
Padlam, M. (2000), 'Social Capital: One or Many? Definition and Measurement', *Journal of Economic Surveys*, Vol.14 (5), pp.629–653.
Paras, P. (2003), *Unweaving the Social Fabric: The Impact of Crime on Social Capital*, Center for US Mexico Studies, Working Paper 2003–04.
Peek, S. (2002), 'Doublespeak in Durban: Mondi, waste management, and the struggles of the South Durban Community Environmental Alliance', in D. McDonald (ed.), *Environmental justice in South Africa*, Athens: Ohio University Press, pp.202–219.
Piazza-Georgi, B. (2002), 'Human and social capital in Soweto in 1999: report on a field study', *Development Southern Africa*, Vol.19 (5), pp.615–639.
Pollard, D. and Jemicz, M. (2004), 'Social capital theory and the internationalisation of Polish SMEs', *Transformations in Business and Economics*, Vol.3, No.2 (6), pp.138–150.
Portes, A. (1998), 'Social Capital: its origins and application in modern sociology', *Annual Review of Sociology*, pp.1–14.

Putnam, R.D. (1993), *Making Democracy Work: Civic Traditions in Modern Italy*, Princeton, NJ: Princeton University Press.
Putnam, R.D. (1996), 'The Strange Disappearance of Civic America', *American Prospect*, Vol.7, Issue 24, available at www.prospect.org/archives/24/24putn.html.
Putnam, R.D. (2000), *Bowling Alone. The Collapse and Revival of the American Community*, New York: Simon and Schuster.
Reinke, J. (1998), 'Does Solidarity Pay? The Case of Small Enterprise Foundation, South Africa', *Development and Change*, Vol.29, pp.553–576.
Robey, J.S. (1999), 'Civil Society and NAFTA: Initial Results', *Annals of the American Academy of Political and Social Science*, Vol.565, pp.113–125.
Sabatini, F. (2005), *Social capital as social networks: A new framework for measurement*, Working Paper No.83, University of Rome La Sapienza, Department of Public Economics.
Sato, M. and Helper, S. (1996), *Does Trust Improve Business Performance?*, Prepared for the 8th International Conference of the Society for the Advancement of Socio-Economics, Geneva, Switzerland.
Schuller, T. (2000), 'Social and Human Capital: The Search for Appropriate Technomethodology', *Policy Studies*, Vol.21 (1), pp.25–35.
Serageldin, I. and Grootaert, C. (1999), 'Defining social capital: an integrating view', in Dasgupta, P. and Serageldin, I. (eds), *Social Capital: A multifaceted perspective*, Washington, D.C.: World Bank, pp.40–58.
Sethi, R. and Somanathan, E. (1996), 'The Evolution of Social Norms in Common Property Resource Use', *American Economic Review*, Vol.86 (4), pp.766–788.
Sherif, M., Harvey, O., White, B., Hood, W. and Sherif, C. (1961), *Intergroup Conflict and Cooperation: The Robbers Cave Experiment*, Norman: Institute of Group Relations, University of Oklahoma, reprinted by Wesleyan University Press, 1988.
Shutte, A. (1993), *Philosophy for Africa*, Rondenbosch, South Africa: UCT Press.
Stachowicz, J. and Walukiewicz, S. (2003), *Setting up proinnovative networks in Silesia*, Contribution to the 43rd Congress of the European Regional Sciences Association, Finland.
Stimson, R., Western, J., Baum, S. and Van Gelecun, Y. (2003), Measuring Community Strength and Social Capital, Paper given at The European Regional Science Association, 2003 Congress.
Stopford, J.M., Strange, S. and Henley, J.S. (1991), *Rival states, rival firms: competition for world market shares*, Cambridge: Cambridge University Press.
Tolbert, C.M. (2005), 'Minding Our Own Business: Local Retail Establishments and the Future of Southern Civic Community', *Social Forces*, Vol.83 (4), pp.1309–1328.
Tsai, W. and Ghosal, S. (1998), 'Social Capital and Value Creation: The Role of Intrafirm Networks', *Academy of Management Journal*, Vol.41 (4), pp.464–476.
Van Deth, J.W. (2003), 'Measuring social capital: orthodoxies and continuing controversies', *International Journal of Social Research Methodology*, Vol.6 (1), pp.79–92.
Waldstrom, C. (2003), *Social Capital in Organizations – Beyond Structure and Metaphor*, Aarhus School of Business, Department of Management and International Business, Working Paper No.2003-7.

Wallace, C., Shumulyar, O. and Bedzir, V. (1999), 'Investing in Social Capital: The Case of Small-Scale, Cross-Border Traders in Post-Communist Central Europe', *International Journal of Urban and Regional Research*, Vol.23 (4), pp.751–770.

Wasserman, S. and Faust, K. (1994), *Social Network Analysis: Methods and Applications*, Cambridge: Cambridge University Press.

Westlund, H. and Nilsson, E. (2005), 'Measuring Enterprises' Investments in Social Capital: A Pilot Study', *Regional Studies*, Vol.39 (8), pp.1079–1094.

Woolcock, M. (2000), 'Social Capital in Theory and Practice – Where do we Stand?', In J. Isham, T. Kelly and S. Ramaswamy (eds), *Social capital and economic development: well being in developing countries*, Aldershot: Edward Elgar, pp.18–39.

World Economic Forum (2002), *Results of the Survey on Trust*, Davos: World Economic Forum. Available at: www.weforum.org/site/homepublic.nsf/Content/Annual+Meeting+2003%5 CResults+of+the+Survey+on+Trust#pdf

Zadek, S. (2001), *The Civil Corporation*, London: Earthscan.

Zaheer, S. and Mosakowski, E. (1997), 'The Dynamics of the Liability of Foreignness: A Global Study of Survival in Financial Services', *Strategic Management Journal*, Vol.18 (6), pp.439–464.

Zinkin, J. (2004), 'Maximising the 'Licence to Operate', CSR from an Asian Perspective', *Journal of Corporate Citizenship*, Vol.14, pp.67–80.

5
Multinationals and Community Engagement in South Africa and Mexico

Introduction

The next two chapters seek to use the social capital concept, discussed in the previous chapter, to measure the community engagement activities of multinationals undertaken as part of their corporate citizenship programmes. A major advantage of the social capital literature is that it facilitates measurement of the inputs and outputs of corporate citizenship programmes in a way that allows comparisons of levels and distribution of corporate community engagement activities to be made. The measures of community engagement are reported for each firm in two samples of multinationals and subjected to some statistical analysis. A major benefit of our analysis in contrast to previous studies of corporate giving is that we can focus on community engagement in individual countries (for which corporate giving data is not usually available).

In this chapter we look at two samples of multinationals: UK multinationals in South Africa and US multinationals in Mexico. These samples were selected because of the high degree of involvement of UK and US multinationals in these countries and the relative ease of collecting data on them. In each case we construct two main variables for each firm in the sample: an engagement score which measures the amount of community projects that the firm has and a norm score which measures the quality of the firm's reporting of its community activities. Both of these measures draw heavily on the trust, norms and networks elements of social capital and directly on some of the empirical social capital literature's measurement indices. We provide some reporting of the component elements of these scores in terms of industry of origin, type of project and level of engagement. We then attempt to correlate the company engagement scores with possible explanatory factors such as industry of origin, size of company, age of subsidiary and local stock market listing.

This analysis is intended to give a broad overview of the differences between companies in terms of their corporate citizenship policies from a social capital perspective. It highlights some important differences and similarities between multinationals from different countries, a theme that we shall explore more fully in the next chapter which uses a similar methodology to look at multinationals from a number of EU countries operating in Poland and goes on to put engagement in one country in a global context.

Together these two chapters provide the context for more detailed studies of individual company corporate citizenship programmes and projects that we undertake later in the book. They draw heavily on the research carried out for Jones, Nyland and Pollitt (2001; 2002; 2004a; and 2004b).

Measurement issues

As we have seen in the previous chapter there have been only limited attempts to measure the social capital impact of multinationals. One issue is that multinationals operate at a number of different levels – local, national and international – in contrast to the normal focus of developmental social capital analysis on the village *or* the country. They also operate in several countries and are complex communities in their own right.

Impediments to MNC analysis

The geographical spread and scope of MNCs cause three important complications that must be negotiated in social capital measurement. First, there is the fact that whilst the metrics of previous studies focussed at the micro and macro levels might complement one another, they *do not necessarily integrate* successfully into one standard for measurement: such that there are no major studies that have attempted to do this. The pressure to integrate macro and micro level analysis is highlighted by Woolcock

> 'the collective panoply of micro and macro measures of "social capital" – and their correspondingly eclectic theoretical moorings – has led many critics to accuse social capital of having become all things to all people, and hence nothing to anyone.' (2000, p.7)

Nevertheless he is equally quick to point out that focussing excessively on micro definitions (as Portes, 1998 and Putnam, 2000 do) 'tends to overlook the broader institutional environment in which communities are inherently embedded.' (2000, p.7). Care must be taken.

Second, there is the issue of *cogency* – it is entirely possible that a MNC, either structurally or through the acts of a few individuals at different levels, can simultaneously generate and destroy social capital: inappropriate pressure on governments at one level can systemically nullify progress made in successful work at the local level. Thus a pharmaceutical company that funds community healthcare schemes but lobbies against extension of national healthcare system may not be improving overall health outcomes.

Third, there is the problem of *circularity and causality*: social capital is often self-generating, leading to problems of measurement, again highlighting why we need to look at the whole MNC at once. The concern which stems from this (but which is difficult to measure) is the spirit behind the social capital created, in particular that it is not seen as parochial, or might stifle or subsume more grassroots level initiatives.

The ultimate aim is to classify the best practice of MNCs around the world, not just in their home nation. This is important because the most influential studies of social capital tend to be focussed on developed countries (e.g. Putnam, 1993; 2000) or the activities of firms in their country of origin (e.g. Cohen and Prusak, 2001). The reason why these studies have done this is partly practical: there are a greater number of social and cultural variables and therefore implementation risks for MNCs, which neither Cohen and Prusak (nor Putnam, 2000) have had to encounter in their focus on the highly homogenised culture, society and economy of the US (or UK).

The central issue in this chapter is how UK-listed MNCs build social capital in South Africa and how US-listed MNCs build social capital in Mexico. UK firms have a long and often troubled history in South Africa with significant involvement in both the building and destroying of social capital. In Mexico there is also a long history of US firm involvement that has accelerated since the NAFTA agreement of 1994.

Defining suitable measures

Rose (1997) suggests that finding suitable measures of social capital is founded somewhere between analysing previous surveys and creating social capital 'best practice' models (suggesting sensitivity to the particular context). We have looked at some of these studies in the previous chapter in the context of exploring what we mean by social capital. Here we look at the actual measures employed in empirical studies with a view to designing measures appropriate to the corporate citizenship programmes of MNCs.

Since the MNC has an impact on the micro, meso and macro levels, it is important to look at the work that has been undertaken in each of these areas. There have been various different studies that have measured social capital at different levels. In 1996 Richard Rose remarked that it is essential for the credibility of social capital to be able to measure it: 'the measurement challenge is to turn anecdotes about social networks into quantified data.'[1]

Some of the most pertinent analyses have been those by: Rose (1996), Knack and Keefer (1997), Narayan and Pritchett (1997), Maluccio, Haddad and May (2000), Grootaert (1999) and Putnam (1993; 2000). We review each in turn.

1. Rose (1996)

Rose focusses largely on the micro and meso level of social capital. He criticises using the 'number of formal institutions in a society' as a measure of social capital, because he feels that people rely far more on informal types of social capital in their day-to-day lives.[2] He featured

Table 5.1   Rose's (1996) social capital measures

Variable	Measure		Measurement criterion
Social Capital	Type of social capital		On whose help do you rely in the first instance when having problems?
	Usefulness of social capital for	...coping in transition economies	What percentage able to get by in a year without spending savings or borrowing?
		...social protection	Would a friend loan as much as a week's wages if your household was very short of money?
Trust	Quantity of trust		Percentage of workers who trusted/distrusted union officials
	Quality of trust		Who households would trust with their savings

Table 5.2 Knack and Keefer's (1997) measures

Variable	Measure
Trust	Percentage of respondents who replied that 'most people can be trusted'
Strength of norms of civic cooperation	Claiming benefits when you are not entitled to
Measured on a scale of 1 (always justifiable) to 10 (never justifiable). The scales were reversed and the values summed over the five items. The average score (out of 50) was 39.4. India ranked 'highest' with a score of 42.7. 34.5 was the lowest score.	Avoiding a fare on public transport
	Cheating on taxes if you have the chance
	Keeping money that you have found
	Failing to report damage you have done accidentally to parked vehicle

three measures of social capital and two for trust used in Russia (see Table 5.1). None are directly applicable to the investigation in hand because they require specific questions, although they do provide useful pointers to the direction that should be taken.

2. Knack and Keefer (1997)

Knack and Keefer measure trust and norms of association across different cultures. Their work is based on some of the results of the World Values Survey, a worldwide investigation of socio-cultural and political change carried out in more than 65 societies on all six inhabited continents, containing almost 80% of the world's population (see Table 5.2). This study has given rise to more than 300 publications, in 16 languages. Whilst useful indicators of the type of activity to look for, these metrics are not particularly applicable to the investigation of MNC activity, since they focus more on public values.

3. Narayan and Pritchett (1997)

Narayan and Pritchett looked at village level 'social capital' in rural Tanzania. Their work was largely based on the 'Social Capital and Poverty Survey,' carried out in randomly selected clusters of villages in April–May 1995 as part of a larger participatory poverty assessment exercise. Individuals were asked to list the groups to which they belonged (from an enumerated list of six: church, Muslim group, political party, women's group, burial society, farmers' group). From this, the individuals were asked to suggest which group was the most important to

Table 5.3 Narayan and Pritchett's social capital measures (1997)

Variable	Measure	Criterion
Overall group membership	Membership	'How many groups are you a member of?'
	Degree of importance	'If you could only join one group, what would it be?'
Characteristics of up to three groups for each individual	Kin heterogeneity of membership	Who are members? 1 – Close relatives 2 – Same clan 3 – Different tribes 4 – Anyone in the village
	Income heterogeneity of membership	Are all members from 1 – Same livelihood 2 – Mostly same livelihood 3 – Mixed livelihoods Do the leaders have 1 – Different livelihood 2 – Same livelihood
	Group functioning	How do you rate group functioning? (Scale 1–5: 1 = very poor; 5 = excellent) If there is a fee, what happens if not paid? 1 – Asked to leave the group 2 – Delay in payment accepted 3 – Nothing happens
	Group decision-making	N/A
	Voluntary membership	N/A

them. A secondary set of questions defined the group in term of five characteristics (see Table 5.3).

The quality of their index has arguably been surpassed by Maluccio, Haddad and May (2000) and Grootaert (1999), although their group listings are indicative of possible community-level organisations with which a MNC might be linked.

4. Maluccio, Haddad and May (2000) (MHM)

MHM used two different but related surveys to prepare a comparative analysis of change in social capital in KwaZulu-Natal. The original

Table 5.4 MHM's (2000) social capital measures

Variable	Measure	Question
Density	The number of group memberships per household	Self explanatory
Performance	The average reported performance of the most important groups in the household	'Overall, how well do/did you think the group works?' (Asked for both 1993 and 1998. Scale 1–5: 1 = very poor; 5 = excellent))
Participation	Average reported frequency of meeting attendance for the most important groups in the household	'How many of the group's meetings do/did you usually attend?'

datasets came from the 1993 'Project for Statistics on Living Standards and Development' and the 1998 'KwaZulu-Natal Income Dynamics Survey' ('KIDS').

They attempted to measure group membership in KwaZulu by looking at the following three variables: density, performance, and participation. This is a useful span of dimensions, by which any group affiliation at any level can be measured (see Table 5.4).

5. Grootaert (1999)

Grootaert investigated the effects of 'local associational' social capital on household welfare in three Indonesian provinces: Jambi, Jawa Tengah and Nusa Tenggara Timur. Within each province two districts were selected to participate in the study, within each district two sub-districts were selected. Within each sub-district, four villages were selected based on location criteria, (upland/lowland and near/far to growth centre), and within each of the 48 villages, 25 households were selected randomly to participate in the household survey. Units were selected purposively so as to represent a range of social, economic and institutional backgrounds.[3] The measures are explained in Table 5.5.

Again, whilst it has limited its focus to the micro and meso level, Grootaert's work is a useful indicator of possible measures of social capital. When combined with MHM, it provides a useful means of assessing the significance of membership within a group.

Table 5.5 Grootaert's (1999) social capital measures

Variable	Measure
Density of membership	The number of group memberships per household
Heterogeneity index 1. Using the three most important associations for a household. 2. Score from 0–8, 0 = members all from different backgrounds; 8 = all from same background. 3. Average of the three taken and indexed.	Neighbourhood Kin group Occupation Economic status Religion Gender Age Level of education
Meeting attendance	Average per month
Decision-making Index 1. Using 3 most important associations for a household. 2. Level of participation played in the group from 0 = 'not very active' to 2 = 'very active'. 3. Average taken, indexed.	Self-assessed level of involvement
Membership dues	Quantity paid (as indicator of seriousness)
Community orientation	Whether the association is community founded or from externally imposed groups

6. Putnam (1993; 2000)

Putnam has conducted two major surveys (1993; 2000), with strikingly different measures of social capital. Putnam's first major survey was on civic engagement in Italy. His second is on civic engagement in the US. The second should not necessarily be seen as a development of the former: whilst Putnam's models and thinking have definitely evolved during this time, the specific details of his work are ultimately reliant on the nature of the dataset with which he is working.

The data for the first survey was based on the collation of several surveys in local regions in the North and South of Italy (see Table 5.6.1)

For the second study Putnam created a Social Capital Index (SCI) based on research conducted across US States looking at levels of engagement. It encompasses individual and aggregated state-level responses, and can be seen as a useful means of transcending the micro-/meso-/macro dichotomies.

Table 5.6.1 Putnam's (1993) social capital measures

Variable	Measure	Criterion
Index of civic community	Political behaviour of citizens	Newspaper readership Availability of sports and cultural associations
	Measure of breadth and depth of civic community	Turnout in referenda and the incidence of preference voting
Index of institutional performance	Composite measure on the comparative performance of regional governments	12 separate elements from timeliness of budgets to legislative innovation
Citizen satisfaction	People asked whether they were 'very' or 'rather' satisfied with regional govt	Large sample survey between 1977 and 1988

Table 5.6.2 Putnam's (2000) SCI variables

Variable		Measure
Community organisational life	1	Served on committee of local organisation in last year
	2	Served as officer of some club or organisation in last year
	3	Civic and social organisations per 1,000 population
	4	Mean number of club meetings attended in last year
	5	Mean number of group memberships
Engagement in public affairs	6	Turnout in presidential elections
	7	Attended public meeting on town or school affairs in last year
Community voluntarism	8	Number of non-profit organisations per 1,000 population
	9	Mean number of time did volunteer work in last year
	10	Mean number of times did volunteer work in last year
Informal sociability	11	Agree that 'I Spend a lot of time visiting friends'
	12	Mean number of times entertained at home in last year
Social trust	13	Agree that 'most people can be trusted'
	14	Agree that 'most people are honest'

Summary

None of the surveys listed above is perfect by design: each is constrained by the nature of the dataset available. None has made any over-inflated claims about the comprehensiveness of the data contained within. Some have delivered a great deal, both in terms of the specific suggestions of the ways in which various aspects of social capital can be measured at various levels, as well as implicit suggestions of possible new measures which could be developed for the measurement of social capital. What emerges is that it is possible to find data that measures the numbers of commitments, the type of commitments and the values behind them. Some of the most insightful measures have arisen as a result of the constraints of the original study, and other opportunities may present themselves in the unique circumstances presented here. Nevertheless applying these measures to the MNC requires very careful selection of key criteria, not only in terms of what is required but also as a reflection of what is available. With the need to survey as many eligible companies as possible, we made use of the internet, which inherently limits the richness of the available data. However we rectify this later with our company case study chapters.

Suitable measures for the MNC

The measurement of social capital has tended to limit itself to the investigation of what we term as norms, and the measurement of networks has been overlooked or remains unsophisticated. What is proposed here is a new combination of measures: network maps and a norm index.

A simple linear measure of social capital does disservice to the richness and multidimensionality of network structures. Freeman (2000) points to the usefulness of charts as a means of visualising social networks. As such, it is useful to provide some means of charting the engagements of a single MNC.

Network mapping

Network maps aim to measure the engagements of firms with different varieties of organisation, at a number of levels, and on a variety of issues. The range of issues was chosen on the basis of issues most typically addressed by MNCs (listed in Table 5.7), and the organisations with which they are most likely to interact at international, national or local levels – the three different spheres at which the multinational corporation somewhat uniquely exists (listed in Table 5.8).[4] A residual other category was also added. For US firms in Mexico, the crime issue was dropped as this was specific to South Africa. We make explicit reference to the type of organisation with which the MNC interacts at each level for the US firms in Mexico.

Table 5.7 Project issue/focus definitions

Issue	Definition
Education	Develop *intellectual capability* at any age.
Youth	Foster social skills in the young.
Health	Augment health directly or through health education.
Environment	Improve environmental conditions.
Development	Develop the economy as a whole.
Employment	Create jobs within the local region, and not nationally.
Ethics	Establish a code of conduct for participants.
Crime	Aim to reduce crime.
Arts	Patronise the arts.

Table 5.8 Regional level institutions: definitions

Level	Entity	Definition and/or example
International	International organisation	Serves as a colloquium for international governments, such as the UN.
	NGO	A non-governmental international organisation, e.g. the Red Cross.
	Academic	Academia, and research.
	Firms	Any multinational firms.
National	Government	National government.
	NGO	A non-governmental national organisation, e.g. a national interest group or a union.
	Institution	A national institution, such as the South African Football Association.
	Firms	Firms based predominantly in host country.
Local	Local gov.	Local-level government bodies such as councils.
	Local institution	For example, libraries, hospitals and schools.
	Local firms	Firms that operate within a fairly limited geographical scope, i.e. not at the national level.
	Individual	When there is an attempt to address people on an individual-by-individual basis, rather than a group-by-group basis, for example, scholarships and sponsorship.

An ordinal score was then given to measure extent of a particular engagement. The scoring system is described in Table 5.9. At the international and national levels, the company under scrutiny has six possible scores from 0 to 5. The basic scores are 1 for endorsement of a network or convention, 3 for active non-committee membership, and 4 for active committee membership. A further point can be added depending upon whether or not resources are donated to the relationship, which is an extension of Grootaert's (1999) use of membership dues to signal strength of connection. Thus by this logic non-committee membership with the donation of funds is held to be approximately equivalent to committee membership without the provision of funds. At the local level points scoring is simplified and limited in order to reflect the smaller scale of a project. If a company's single engagement takes in a variety of types of organisations, for example a multilateral venture between government organisations and other MNCs, then points are awarded twice to reflect the multidimensionality of engagement. For the South African sample where ownership of the sponsoring subsidiary is shared we proportionally reduce the score for relevant projects to facilitate comparison. An example of an individual project and how it was scored is given in Box 5.1.

The resultant map provides a reliable sense of the extent to which a firm is typically involved in various different issues with different organisations at different geographical levels. It may be likened to a mediaeval map – lacking topographical precision but an offering sufficiently accurate sketch to afford one a sense of location and space.

Norm indexing

If a network map measures the spatial rudiments of engagement, then norms help to give a crude indication of their longevity. Naturally, the

Table 5.9 Scoring system for engagements in a project

Regional Level	Score			
	1	3	4	+1
International	Endorses	Active non-committee member	Active committee member	Donation of resources
National	Endorses	Active non-committee member	Active committee member	Donation of resources
Local	Endorses	Loans	Donates	

Box 5.1 Schlumberger – the SEED Connectivity Grant Program

Schlumberger is a global technology services company with corporate offices in New York, Paris and The Hague. Schlumberger has more than 80,000 employees, representing 140 nationalities, working in nearly 100 countries. The company consists of two business segments: Schlumberger Oilfield Services, which includes Schlumberger Network Solutions, and SchlumbergerSema.

Schlumberger's community engagements come under the broad bracket of its 'SEED' (Schlumberger Excellence in Educational Development) non-profit community development programme. Whilst the programme itself is international and appears to form a cogent strategy on the part of Schlumberger to address social issues, it is run very much at a grassroots level, which explains why the company's network engagement scores are exclusively in the local domain.

The key projects all revolve around a similar theme – the provision of computers and Internet access to those who cannot afford it themselves for education and training purposes. There are five such projects listed in Mexico, according to the Schlumberger site. Three are in Reynosa (a town of 750,000 nine miles south of the Mexico-US Border), and two of these are hosted at different Centers for Industrial and Services Technological Studies (upper-secondary level schools) in the city.

A similar programme is also run in Ciudad del Carmen, where a primary school is used at weekends to allow students access to computers. This programme also encourages students at the local business school to participate as volunteer teachers, and also fosters links with government organisations such as the National Ministry of Education (*la Secretaría de Educación Pública* or SEP) and the Campeche region's Ministry of Education (*la Secretaría de Educaciónen Campeche* or SACUD). The final programme in Mexico is run in Villahermosa in Tabasco, and is an initiative to offer the school's computer facility to three nearby schools.

The SEED programme is highly interesting, and most definitely conducive to the building of social capital for a number of reasons. Firstly, it naturally provides a concrete scheme which allows Schlumberger to detail an explicit commitment to the community. The long-term nature of these projects (all of which are scheduled to

> **Box 5.1 – *continued***
>
> run for more than two years) indicates commitment. Schlumberger stipulates that the recipients of its funding also create a public statement of intent and update reports every six months which it will publish on its website. The framework and structure apparent within these reports helps to foster strong reciprocal behaviours.
>
> The programmes also show a very strong leaning towards networking – all of the different projects have themselves spawned collaborative networks which are themselves social-capital building. The potentiality of access to the Internet as a means of fostering human or intellectual capital is therefore supplemented by positive social networking. Following Tables 5.8 and 5.9, the five projects in the programme are recorded as occurring at the *Local* level interacting with *Local Institutions*, are listed as an *Education* project and score 4 each because they include donation of resources.

relatively recent emergence of much of the corporate social responsibility discourse has meant that there is a paucity of evidence of continuity in the actions of firms from any time preceding 1999, so it is difficult to assess the trajectory of many of the firms – in this survey those repenting at haste appear equal to those with a steady, time-honoured commitment to social and environmental engagements.

The bases for the measures of norms that we use can be found in the key works on social capital. Typically, the measures were chosen on the basis of the available data, which was often collated from secondary sources. Typically these have attempted to compile an index of public trust and civic norms using various questions. For instance Knack and Keefer's (1997) question about whether it is justifiable to cheat on taxes if you have the chance suggests a similar set of questions that could be asked of companies. Does your company think it is justifiable to increase profits by not having explicit values, not publicly committing to CSR and not giving to the local community? Public statements of commitment to norms of social responsible corporate behaviour are thus used to measure this aspect of multinationals contribution to social capital.

Questions that address the MNC should be – as with the other surveys – a reflection both of the sensible expectations and pragmatic consideration of what is available to survey. Using the Minnesota prin-

Table 5.10 Minnesota principles

Number	Proposition
1	Stimulating economic growth is the particular contribution of business to the larger society.
2	Business activities must be characterised by fairness.
3	Business activities must be characterised by honesty.
4	Business activities must be characterised by respect for human dignity.
5	Business activities must be characterised by respect for the environment.

ciples (see Table 5.10) as a foundation for the expectations of good ethical behaviour, and the limits of the dataset of how to assess this, we might derive the subsequent measures of positive norms.

The first important measure is whether the firm has explicit social values or not – one point for yes, none for no. This same scoring system is used to acknowledge the existence of a foundation and a clear guide to funding. We also look at the method of CSR reporting. There is the very simple ordinal scale of commitment (scores 0), moving from no data, to HTML-encoded (and more ephemeral) data (scores 1), to the downloadable and more immutable Adobe™ Portable Document Format (PDF) electronic versions of their annual report. The PDF encoded social information is classified further into whether it is included in a chapter within their annual report (scores 2), or in a separate, self-contained report (scores 3). A separate report is preferable since it typically reflects a greater commitment to social engagement. Another measure looks at the ease with which this data can be accessed, on a scale from zero (in the absence of data) to difficult to find (i.e. can often only be found using a third-party search engine, which scores 1) relatively easy to find (scores 2) and is within one click of the company's homepage (scores 3). For UK firms in South Africa we were able to add a final referent measure of whether or not the firm is listed in the FTSE4Good ethical investment index,[5] which offers an indication of a minimum standard of ethical performance. For ease of comparison we sum the norm scores (excluding the FTSE4Good measure).[6] For US firms in Mexico we added a final measure of whether external responsibility information is provided in Spanish. Reporting social capital building in the language of the host community itself builds social capital within that community.

In closing our discussion of what data we collect it is worth noting that we concentrate on measuring the input side of social capital rather then the output side (to the extent that engagements and norms are not ends in themselves). One could imagine looking explicitly at the economic and social change output of social capital building activity (such as number of people affected by a particular project). To look at this would require another and more extensive research effort than the one undertaken for this book.

Survey dataset

The dataset was compiled as follows.

For the UK firms in South Africa, all UK-listed companies in the Waterlow Directory of Multinationals (1998) with an operation in South Africa (with a minimum of 250 employees, local or not) were noted. This generated a list of 37 companies. All pertinent external network engagements and behaviours which these companies described on their own websites in the week beginning 16th July 2001 were then recorded.

For the US firms in Mexico, all US-headquartered companies in the Waterlow Directory of Multinationals (1998) which listed an operation in Mexico were identified, and then scrutinised to find credible evidence of a significant presence in Mexico (taken to be an operation with more than 250 employees).[7] This generated a list of 73 firms. Following this, the survey went on to record all pertinent external responsibility which the company described on its own website in the period from 8th July to 22nd July 2002.

There are obvious pitfalls with using this data. First, Internet data seems ephemeral. However, this risk can be turned into an analytical advantage since there are measurable variations in data immutability on the Internet, as explained below. Second, how does one ensure that the MNC is not *fabricating* information, or is *withholding* it? Given the need for transparency, and the scrutiny which the glare of the Internet is able to put on the assertions of MNCs, one would anticipate that lying is rare. Since a firm *may* exaggerate the significance of an engagement, information was recorded based on the *bare minimum quantifiable* commitment. Only evidence backing up an assertion would merit a score, regardless of hints of other commitments or of a deeply imbued significance.

In terms of non-disclosure, there are three obvious constraints: *expediency*, limiting the supply of information due to a lack of demand; *modesty*, where MNCs wish to avoid charges of bragging or neocolonialism; and *associational risk*, that is reluctance on the part of either the company or the second party to disclose an engagement based on the past, present, or future negative association. One must assume that with the modern imperative for corporate external responsibility, large MNCs consider the benefits of listing engagements to be greater than each of these costs, although there do appear to be counter-examples.[8]

In addition to data on network engagements and norms described above we also collected additional information, subject to availability, which might help explain the network engagement score.

For the South Africa sample we had data on worldwide revenue, profit and employees and total charitable donations. This was drawn from company accounts. In addition we made use of industry data (based on FTSE sector information) and the presence of a Johannesburg Stock Market listing.[9] We also collected information on South African subsidiaries: revenue, number of employees and the presence of a joint venture.[10] This subsidiary data was only available for some of the sample. The age of firms in the year 2000 is recorded. All data was for the calendar year 2000 or a reporting period including a substantial part of 2000. Financial data is measured in millions of UK pounds.

For the Mexican sample we had data on worldwide revenue, profit and employees from company accounts. In addition we made use of industry data (based on 4-digit NACE categories). We also collected on Mexican subsidiaries: revenue, number of employees and the presence of a joint venture.[11] This subsidiary data was only available for some of the sample. The age of firms in the year 2001 is recorded. All data was for the calendar year 2001 or a reporting period including a substantial part of 2001. Financial data is measured in millions of US dollars.

Survey findings for UK firms in South Africa

The results are broken into two major groups: aggregates of network maps (Table 5.11); and indicators of transparency and mechanisms that may help to build social capital (Table 5.12). There is significant variation both across and within industries in the reportage of actions undertaken to increase social capital in South Africa.

There seems to be greater overall engagement amongst 'extractive' (mining and oil) sector corporations. This should not be surprising. These firms are obliged to create social capital because they have already artificially assembled communities at the site of the resource they wish to harvest. This leaves them with two major options. First,

Table 5.11 Network maps: UK firms in South Africa

Extractive sector	Issue									Level[12]			
	Educn	Youth	Health	Environ	Develop/ Employ	Crime	Arts	Ethics	Other	Total	TN	N	L	Total
Anglo American	9	5	5	8	12	10				49	8	34	7	49
Billiton	18	9	4	14	11	10	2.4		5	73.4	8	25	40.4	73.4
BP			4	13	4			3		24	1	11	12	24
Lonmin	8		1	4						14		4	10	14
Rio Tinto	10	8	14	12	11.5		2		1	64.5	16	2	46.5	64.5
Shell	9			5	4				7	18		14	4	18
Total	54	22	28	56	42.5	20	4.4	3	13	242.9	33	90	119.9	242.9
Mean	9	3.7	4.7	9.3	7.1	3.3	0.7	0.5	2.2	40.5	5.5	15	20	40.5

Industrial sector	Issue										Level			
	Educn	Youth	Health	Environ	Develop/ Employ	Crime	Arts	Ethics	Other	Total	TN	N	L	Total
BOC	20	4	4		1.5		2		4.5	36		2.5	33.5	36
Cookson										0				0
GKN	8			2						10	2		8	10
ICI									1	1	1			1
Invensys										0				0
Johnson Matthey										0				0
Total	28	4	4	2	1.5	0	2	0	5.5	47.0	3.0	2.5	41.5	47.0
Mean	4.7	0.7	0.7	0.3	0.3	0	0.3	0	0.9	7.8	0.5	0.4	6.9	7.8

Table 5.11 Network maps: UK firms in South Africa – continued

Consumer sector	Issue									Level			
	Educn	Youth	Health	Environ	Develop/ Employ	Crime	Arts	Ethics	Other	Total	TN	N	L	Total
SAB									2	2		2		2
BAT										0				0
Cadbury Schweppes			4	4	4	9			9	30		10	20	30
Diageo	9	9	4	8	26			2	12	70	2	20	48	70
Imperial Tobacco										0				0
Reckitt Benckiser										0	2		2	0
Unilever	10								3	13	3	5	5	13
Total	19	9	8	12	30	9	0	2	26	115	7	37	75	115
Mean	2.7	1.3	1.1	1.7	4.3	1.3	0	0.3	3.7	16.4	0.7	5.3	10.4	16.4

Medical sector	Issue									Level			
	Educn	Youth	Health	Environ	Develop/ Employ	Crime	Arts	Ethics	Other	Total	TN	N	L	Total
AstraZeneca			12							12	8	4		12
GSK			28							28	20		8	28
Smith&Nephew			0							0				0
Total	0	0	40	0	0	0	0	0	0	40	28	4	8	40
Mean	0	0	13.3	0	0	0	0	0	0	13.3	9.3	1.3	2.7	13.3

147

Table 5.11 Network maps: UK firms in South Africa – *continued*

Information Leisure sector	Issue										Level			
	Educn	Youth	Health	Environ	Develop/ Employ	Crime	Arts	Ethics	Other	Total	TN	N	L	Total
Bass									2	2	2			2
EMI										0				0
Great Universal Stores										0				0
Pearson										0				0
Reuters	4	4								8			8	8
UBM										0				0
WPP	4	8		4						16		8	8	16
Total	8	12	0	4	0	0	0	0	2	26	2	8	16	26
Mean	1.1	1.7	0	0.6	0	0	0	0	0.3	3.7	0.3	1.1	2.3	3.7

Infrastructure Finance sector	Issue										Level			
	Educn	Youth	Health	Environ	Develop/ Employ	Crime	Arts	Ethics	Other	Total	TN	N	L	Total
Dimension Data										0				0
HSBC								1		1	1			1
Marconi										0				0
P&O	4									4			4	4
Spirent										0				0
Standard Chartered										0				0
Tibbett & Britten										0				0
Vodafone[13]	2.835	1.26	2.26	1.26		1.26	1.575			10.45	1	3.15	6.3	10.45
Total	6.835	1.26	2.26	1.26	0	1.26	1.575	1	0	15.45	2	3.15	10.3	15.45

Table 5.12 Norms by industry grouping: UK firms in South Africa

Company	Explicit values	CSR info availability	Ease of finding CSR info	Foundation	Funding guide	FTSE 4Good?	Total
Anglo American	1	2	3	1	0	0	7
Billiton	1	3	3	1	1	0	9
BP	1	3	3	1	0	1	9
Lonmin	0	0	0	0	0	0	0
Rio Tinto	1	3	3	1	0	0	8
Shell	1	3	3	1	1	1	10
Mean Extractive	0.8	2.3	2.5	0.8	0.3	0.3	7.2
BOC	1	1	1	0	0	0	3
Cookson	0	1	2	0	0	0	3
GKN	1	1	2	0	0	0	4
ICI	1	2	1	1	0	1	6
Invensys	0	2	2	0	0	0	4
Johnson Matthey	1	1	0	0	0	0	2
Mean Industrial	0.7	1.3	1.3	0.2	0.0	0.2	3.7
BAT	0	1	1	0	0	0	2
Cadbury Schweppes	1	3	3	1	0	1	9
Diageo	1	3	3	1	1	1	10
Imperial Tobacco	0	0	0	0	0	0	0
Reckitt Benckiser	1	1	0	0	0	0	2
SAB	1	0	0	0	0	1	2
Unilever	1	3	3	1	1	1	10
Mean Commercial	0.7	1.6	1.4	0.4	0.3	0.6	5.0

Table 5.12 Norms by industry grouping: UK firms in South Africa – *continued*

Company	Explicit values	CSR info availability	Ease of finding CSR info	Foundation	Funding guide	FTSE 4Good?	Total
AstraZeneca	1	1	2	1	0	1	6
GSK	1	3	3	1	1	1	10
Smith & Nephew	1	3	3	1	0	1	9
Mean Medical	**1.0**	**2.3**	**2.7**	**1.0**	**0.3**	**1.0**	**8.3**
Bass	1	1	3	0	0	1	6
EMI	1	3	3	1	1	1	10
Great Universal Stores	1	1	2	1	0	0	5
Pearson	1	1	2	1	0	1	6
Reuters	1	3	2	1	1	1	9
UBM	0	0	0	0	0	1	1
WPP	1	0	0	0	0	1	2
Mean Information/Leisure	**0.9**	**1.3**	**1.7**	**0.6**	**0.3**	**0.9**	**5.6**
Dimension Data	0	0	0	0	0	1	1
HSBC	1	3	3	0	0	1	8
Marconi	0	1	1	0	0	0	2
P&O	0	2	2	0	0	1	5
Spirent	0	0	0	0	0	0	0
Standard Chartered	1	1	2	0	0	1	5
Tibbett & Britten	0	0	0	0	0	0	0
Vodafone	1	3	3	1	0	1	9
Mean Infrastructure/Finance	**0.4**	**1.3**	**1.4**	**0.1**	**0.0**	**0.6**	**3.8**

Table 5.13 Issue popularity by sector: UK sample

	Rank		
	1	2	3
Extractive	Environment	Education	Development
Industrial	Education	Other	Youth; Health
Consumer	Development	Other	Education
Medical	Health		
Information & Leisure	Youth	Education	Environment
Infrastructure & Finance	Education	Health	Crime

they can attempt to create communities and relocate families through the construction of schools, libraries and housing. Second – more cure than prevention – is to fight against sexually transmitted diseases contracted where workers live away from their families in hostels and encounter prostitution.

There are interesting patterns in the overall spread of issues addressed by the different sectors (see Table 5.13). Environment is the

Table 5.14 Sectoral engagement by level percentage: UK sample

	Level		
	Transnational	National	Local
Extractive	13.6%	37.1%	49.4%
Industrial	6.4%	5.3%	88.3%
Consumer	4.3%	32.2%	63.5%
Medical	70.0%	10.0%	20.0%
Information & Leisure	7.7%	30.8%	61.5%
Infrastructure & Finance	12.9%	20.4%	66.7%

Table 5.15 Sectoral engagement by level: UK sample

	Rank by most engaged		
	1	2	3
Transnational	Medical	Extractive	Infrastructure & Finance
National	Extractive	Consumer	Information & Leisure
Local	Industrial	Infrastructure & Finance	Consumer

main area of focus in the extractive and industrial sectors, development/employment in the consumer sector, health in the medical sector. In terms of the level of activity the industrial and consumer sectors tend to have commitments skewed towards the local level, the medical sector focusses on the international level – perhaps as a result of its focus on health (see Table 5.14). There is an overlap between issues and geographical level – medical issues are felt to be best addressed internationally, whilst educational ventures are more specifically targeted (see Tables 5.14 and 5.15).

Within the different sectors some firms provide rich engagement information, in particular the extractive industry, for whom all firms provide easy access to some type of special social report. There is also a far higher average likelihood of a firm having a charitable foundation in the mining and medical sectors. This may to a great extent be the result of the difficulty that these firms have not only in communicating information, but the scepticism of the audience. The probable location of shareholders may also be a factor. Table 5.16 appears to indicate that amongst Industrial and Extractive firms, those with a Johannesburg Stock exchange listing report any social engagements in South Africa more thoroughly than those who do not, although other factors may also be at play.

There is a general convention to include a list of company values, and in almost all of the sectors the majority of firms do this. However,

Table 5.16 Engagement scores and Johannesburg Stock Exchange listing: Industrial and extractive sector firms

Firm	Engagement score	JSE listing? Yes/No
Cookson	0	N
Invensys	0	N
Johnson Matthey	0	N
ICI	1	N
GKN	10	N
Lonmin	14	Y
Shell	18	N
BP	24	N
BOC	36	Y (Afrox Healthcare)
Anglo American	49	Y
Rio Tinto	66.5	Y (Palabora Mining Company)
Billiton	73.4	Y

the Infrastructure/Finance sector has a far lower incidence of this occurring, although it is the extractive and industrial sector firms that have most commonly fallen foul of the FTSE4Good ethical index selection criteria. We investigate this statistically later on.

The limitation of the results here is their somewhat static nature – there are several dynamics which might help to explain the reasons why certain firms act in the way they do which cannot be highlighted by any means other than historical analysis. The extractive sector companies may be more highly engaged out of a sense of guilt and a desire to redress perceived social failings during the apartheid era. Regardless, the different statistics above are the collected data of how firms present themselves on the Internet.

Survey findings for US firms in Mexico

This survey offers an interesting set of results. What becomes immediately apparent is that whilst many firms (34) report engagements in Mexico, more do not. This is not to say that these firms are not engaged in communities; many are quite explicit in their support for projects in the US, but do not list anything in Mexico. This often accounts for the disparities that emerge between the norm scores of the firm and their engagement in Mexico (see Tables 5.17 and 5.18).

An absence or paucity of information concerning engagement is attributable to one of two causes. The first is that firms are simply not engaged in Mexico. The second, and more controversial, is that they do have engagements but do not choose to list them for one of several possible reasons. If either of these were a factor, it might be possible to suggest that the moral marketplace, where firms ethics is judged (Hess et al., 2002), has a geographical bias. That is to say, the firms involved choose not to list their engagements in Mexico and to emphasise their engagements in the US as that is where the bulk of shareholders are.

There are striking parallels with the results from South Africa in that it is firms involved in labour-intensive industrial work and healthcare-related work which perform most strongly. There are numerous potential reasons for this, and not necessarily the same in each sector or for each firm. There are arguably three key factors which encourage the disclosure of engagement: the greater size of the workforce; the need to relocate whole families and provide the means to do so (which appears to be of less significance in the case of Mexico than in South Africa); and finally the desire to defend corporate reputations which are frequently under attack in these sectors, perhaps a result of the

Table 5.17 Network maps: US firms in Mexico

Pharmaceuticals & healthcare	Edcn	Yth	Hlth	Env	Dvpt	Ethic	Arts	Oth	Total	TN	N	L
Abbott Labs												
AHP/Wyeth												
Baxter International	2	12	8					4	26		10	16
Becton Dickinson & Company			9						9		5	4
Bristol Myers Squibb			3	2	10				15	5	7	3
Eli Lilly							3		3		3	
Merck			14						14	1	13	
Pfizer												
Pharmacia Corp												
Total	2	12	34	2	10		3	4	67	6	38	23
Mean	0.2	1.3	3.8	0.2	1.1		0.3	0.4	7.4	0.7	4.2	2.6
St Dev	0.7	4	5.3	0.7	3.3		1	1.3	9.3	1.7	4.9	5.3
Max	2	12	14	2	10		3	4	26	5	13	16
Min												

Edcn = education; Yth = youth; Hlth = health; Env = environment; Dvpt = development/employment; Ethic = ethics; Oth = others

Table 5.17 Network maps: US firms in Mexico – *continued*

	Issue									Level		
Other chemicals	**Edcn**	**Yth**	**Hlth**	**Env**	**Dvpt**	**Ethic**	**Arts**	**Oth**	**Total**	**TN**	**N**	**L**
Avon Products			5						**5**		5	
Colgate Palmolive												
Dow												
Du Pont				1					**1**			1
Eastman		4		4				4	**12**			12
FMC												
Goodyear												
Johnson & Johnson	4	10	11	6	4	4		2	**41**	17	8	16
PPG												
Praxair												
Procter & Gamble	24	12		6	1			2	**45**		41	4
Total	**28**	**26**	**16**	**17**	**5**	**4**		**8**	**104**	**17**	**54**	**33**
Mean	2.5	2.4	1.5	1.5	0.5	0.4		0.7	**9.5**	1.5	4.9	3
St Dev	7.2	4.5	3.5	2.5	1.2	1.2		1.3	**17**	5.1	12.3	5.6
Max	24	12	11	6	4	4		4	**45**	17	41	16
Min												

Table 5.17 Network maps: US firms in Mexico – continued

Food & retail	Edcn	Yth	Hlth	Env	Dvpt	Ethic	Arts	Oth	Total	TN	N	L
Campbells												
Coca Cola	20								20			20
Conagra												
Gap												
Kellogg		4							4			4
McDonalds		5		1					6		5	1
Pepsico												
Philip Morris		1						4	5		5	
Walmart			5					4	9		9	
Total	**20**	**10**	**5**	**1**				**8**	**44**		**19**	**25**
Mean	2.2	1.1	0.6	0.1				0.9	4.9		2.1	2.8
St Dev	6.7	2	1.7	0.3				1.8	6.5		3.4	6.6
Max	20	5	5	1				4	20		9	20
Min												

Table 5.17 Network maps: US firms in Mexico – *continued*

Industrial machinery and equipment	Issue									Level			
	Edcn	Yth	Hlth	Env	Dvpt	Ethic	Arts	Oth	Total	TN	N	L
Caterpillar				1	4				5	4	1	
Cummins				8					8			8
Deere & Co												
Dell												
Emerson Electric												
Hewlett Packard												
IBM	4	4		1		1	4		14	2	8	4
Ingersoll-Rand												
ITT				12					12	12		
Raytheon												
RR Donnelly												
Total	4	4		22	4	1	4		39	18	9	12
Mean	0.4	0.4		2	0.4	0.1	0.4		3.5	1.6	0.8	1.1
St Dev	1.2	1.2		4.1	1.2	0.3	1.2		5.4	3.7	2.4	2.6
Max	4	4		12	4	1	4		14	12	8	8
Min												

157

Table 5.17 Network maps: US firms in Mexico – *continued*

Electrical and electronic equipment & services	Issue									Level		
	Edcn	Yth	Hlth	Env	Dvpt	Ethic	Arts	Oth	Total	TN	N	L
3Com												
Cooper Industries				5					5		5	
Corning												
Eaton	4								4			4
EDS							3		3			3
GE	4	8	4	9					25		9	16
Lucent												
Motorola												
Texas Instruments												
United Technologies	1							2	10	9		1
Verizon	3	8		7	4				15			15
Total	12	16	4	21	4		3	2	62	9	14	39
Mean	1.1	1.5	0.4	1.9	0.4		0.3	0.2	5.6	0.8	1.3	3.5
St Dev	1.7	3.2	1.2	3.4	1.2		0.9	0.6	8.1	2.7	3	6.1
Max	4	8	4	9	4		3	2	25	9	9	16
Min												

Table 5.17 Network maps: US firms in Mexico – *continued*

Manufacturing	Issue									Level		
	Edcn	Yth	Hlth	Env	Dvpt	Ethic	Arts	Oth	Total	TN	N	L
3M		5							5		5	5
Alcoa	12	11	20	25	3		4	20	95	8	5	82
Crown Cork & Seal												
Eastman Kodak	5								5			5
Fluor												
Ford	15		5	32	7		1		60	26	29	5
Fortune Brands												
General Motors	9			4				3	16		5	11
Georgia Pacific												
Gillette												
Nike					5			4	9		5	4
Parker – Hannifin												
Phelps Dodge		2							2		2	
Total	41	18	25	61	15		5	27	192	34	51	107
Mean	3.2	1.4	1.9	4.7	1.2		0.4	2.1	14.8	2.6	3.9	8.2
St Dev	5.4	3.2	5.6	10.7	2.3		1.1	5.5	29.1	7.4	7.9	22
Max	15	11	20	32	7		4	20	95	26	29	82
Min												

Table 5.17 Network maps: US firms in Mexico – *continued*

Highly diversified & miscellaneous	Issue									Level			
	Edcn	Yth	Hlth	Env	Dvpt	Ethic	Arts	Oth	Total	TN	N	L
American Airways				2					2	1	1	
Disney												
Fedex												
Marriott												
Schlumberger	20							4	24			24
Tyco												
UniSys												
United Airways					4				4			4
Weyerhaeuser												
Total	20			2	4			4	30	1	1	28
Mean	2.2			0.2	0.4			0.4	3.3	0.1	0.1	3.1
St Dev	6.7			0.7	1.3			1.3	7.9	0.3	0.3	7.9
Max	20			2	4			4	24	1	1	24
Min												

Table 5.18 Norms by industry grouping: US firms in Mexico

Pharmaceutical & healthcare	Explicit values	CSR info availability	Ease of access	Foundation	Funding guide	Spanish?	Total
Abbott	1	3	1	1	2	0	8
Baxter International	1	3	1	1	3	1	10
Becton Dickinson	1	2	1	1	3	1	9
Bristol Myers Squibb	1	3	1	1	2	1	9
Eli Lilly	1	1	1	1	2	0	4
Merck	1	1	1	1	3	1	8
Pfizer	1	1	1	1	2	0	6
Pharmacia	1	1	1	1	3	0	7
AHP/Wyeth	1	1	1	1	1	0	5
Total	9	16	9	9	21	4	48
Mean	1	1.8	1	1	2.3	0.4	5.3

Retail & food	Explicit values	CSR info availability	Ease of access	Foundation	Funding guide	Spanish?	Total
Campbells	1	3	1	1	2	1	9
Coca Cola	1	1	1	1	2	0	6
Conagra	1	3	1	1	3	0	9
Gap	1	3	1	1	3	0	9
Kellogg	1	1	1	1	2	0	6
McDonalds	1	1	1	0	2	1	6
Pepsico	1	1	1	1	2	0	6
Philip Morris	1	3	1	1	3	0	9
Walmart	1	1	1	1	2	0	6
Total	9	17	9	8	21	2	66
Mean	1	1.9	1	0.9	2.3	0.2	7.3

162 *Multinationals in their Communities*

Table 5.18 Norms by industry grouping: US firms in Mexico – *continued*

Other chemicals	Explicit values	CSR info availability	Ease of access	Foundation	Funding guide	Spanish?	Total
Avon	1	3	1	1	2	1	9
Colgate Palmolive	1	3	1	1	2	0	8
Dow	1	1	1	1	3	1	8
Du Pont	1	1	1	1	2	0	6
Eastman	1	3	0	0	3	0	7
FMC	1	1	0	0	3	0	5
Goodyear	1	1	1	1	2	0	6
J&J	1	1	1	1	2	1	7
PPG	1	3	1	1	2	1	9
Praxair	1	0	1	1	0	0	3
Procter & Gamble	1	1	1	1	3	1	8
Total	11	18	9	9	24	5	76
Mean	1	1.6	0.8	0.8	2.2	0.5	6.9

Industrial machinery and equipment	Explicit values	CSR info availability	Ease of access	Foundation	Funding guide	Spanish?	Total
Caterpillar	1	3	1	1	3	0	9
Cummins	1	3	1	1	2	0	8
Deere & Co	1	3	1	1	2	0	8
Dell	1	1	1	1	3	0	7
Emerson	1	3	1	1	3	0	9
Hewlett Packard	1	1	0	0	3	0	5
IBM	1	3	1	1	3	0	9
Ingersoll-Rand	1	1	1	1	2	0	6
ITT	1	1	1	1	3	0	7
Raytheon	1	1	1	0	3	0	6
RR Donnelley	1	3	1	1	3	0	9
Total	11	23	10	9	30	0	83
Mean	1	2.1	0.9	0.8	2.7	0	7.5

Table 5.18 Norms by industry grouping: US firms in Mexico – *continued*

Manufacturing	Explicit values	CSR info availability	Ease of access	Foundation	Funding guide	Spanish?	Total
3M	1	1	1	1	2	1	7
Alcoa	1	3	1	1	3	0	9
Crown Cork & Seal	1	1	0	0	1	0	3
Eastman Kodak	1	1	1	1	2	0	6
Fluor	1	1	1	1	2	0	6
Ford	1	3	1	1	3	1	10
Fortune Brands	1	0	0	0	0	0	1
General Motors	1	1	1	1	3	1	8
Georgia Pacific	1	3	1	1	3	0	9
Gilette	1	3	1	1	3	0	9
Nike	1	3	1	1	3	1	10
Parker Hannifin	1	1	1	1	2	1	7
Phelps Dodge	1	3	1	1	3	0	9
Total	13	24	11	11	30	5	94
Mean	1	1.8	0.8	0.8	2.3	0.4	7.2

Electrical and electronic equipment & services	Explicit values	CSR info availability	Ease of access	Foundation	Funding guide	Spanish?	Total
3Com	1	1	2	0	2	0	6
Cooper Industries	1	3	1	1	2	0	8
Corning	1	1	1	1	2	0	6
Eaton	1	1	1	1	2	0	6
EDS	1	1	1	0	2	0	5
GE	1	1	1	1	3	1	8
Lucent	1	1	0	0	3	0	5
Motorola	1	3	1	1	3	0	9
Texas Instruments	1	3	1	1	3	0	9
United Technologies	1	1	0	0	2	1	5
Verizon	1	2	1	1	3	1	9
Total	11	18	10	7	27	3	76
Mean	1	1.6	0.9	0.6	2.5	0.3	6.9

Table 5.18 Norms by industry grouping: US firms in Mexico – *continued*

Highly diversified and miscellaneous	Explicit values	CSR info availability	Ease of access	Foundation	Funding guide	Spanish?	Total
American Airways	0	0	1	1	0	0	2
Disney	1	1	1	0	3	0	6
Fedex	1	1	1	1	2	0	6
Marriot	1	1	1	1	2	0	6
Schlumberger	1	3	1	1	3	0	9
United Airways	1	1	1	1	3	0	7
UniSys	1	1	0	0	1	0	3
Weyerhaeuser	1	3	1	1	3	0	9
Total	7	11	7	6	17	0	48
Mean	0.9	1.4	0.9	0.8	2.1	0	6.0

Table 5.19 Issue popularity by sector: US sample

	Rank		
	1	2	3
Pharmaceuticals & healthcare	Health	Youth	Development
Other chemicals	Education	Youth	Environment
Food & retail	Education	Youth	Other
Industrial machinery & equipment	Environment	Education; Youth; Development; Arts	
Electrical and electronic equipment & services	Environment	Youth	Education
Manufacturing	Environment	Education	Other
Highly diversified & Miscellaneous	Education	Development; Other	

Table 5.20 Sectoral engagements by level percentage: US sample

	Level		
	Transnational	National	Local
Pharmaceuticals & healthcare	9.0%	56.7%	34.3%
Other chemicals	16.3%	51.9%	31.7%
Food & retail		43.2%	56.8%
Industrial machinery & equipment	46.2%	23.1%	30.8%
Electrical and electronic equipment & services	14.5%	22.6%	62.9%
Manufacturing	17.7%	26.6%	55.7%
Highly diversified & miscellaneous	3.3%	3.3%	93.3%

Table 5.21 Sectoral engagements by level: US sample

	Rank		
	1	2	3
Transnational	Industrial machinery & equipment	Manufacturing	Other chemicals
National	Pharmaceuticals & healthcare	Other chemicals	Food & retail
Local	Highly diversified & miscellaneous	Electrical and electronic equipment & services	Food & retail

conditioning influence of the scrutiny firms are under. The interests of the different sectors in issues is similar to South Africa (see Table 5.19). However the level of engagement shows different involvement in international projects than in South Africa (see Table 5.20) with Industrial Machinery and Equipment, rather than Pharmaceuticals and Healthcare leading the way in international engagement (Table 5.21).

There are interesting patterns of engagements as regards the nature of a project and the parties with whom there is engagement, as shown in the aggregated table of all engagements on the part of firms (Table 5.22).

The bulk of collaboration at the International level is undertaken between MNCs and NGOs, predominantly addressing environmental

Table 5.22 Summary engagements for US sample

		Issue								
		Edcn	Yth	Hlth	Env	Dvpt	Ethic	Arts	Other	Total
Transnational	Int org	5		1	2					8
	NGO	5		10	22	12	4		4	57
	Acad				8					8
	Firms				7	4	1			12
	Total	10		11	39	16	5		4	85
		Edcn	Yth	Hlth	Env	Dvpt	Ethic	Arts	Other	Total
National	Gov	24	6	5	24	3			2	64
	NGO	5	18	23	15	6			6	73
	Institution	2	22		5			4	6	39
	Firms	5				5				10
	Total	36	46	28	44	14		4	14	186
		Edcn	Yth	Hlth	Env	Dvpt	Ethic	Arts	Other	Total
Local	Local gov	4	3	6	8				4	25
	Local Institution	68	25	32	29	4		8	16	182
	Local Firms	5			2	4			4	15
	Individual	4	12	7	4	4		3	11	45
	Total	81	40	45	43	12		11	35	287

and developmental issues (see Table 5.22). At the National level, education and youth, health and the environment are the key areas of focus. The chosen collaborator appears to vary according to the nature of the project and probably therefore the extent of leverage that a particular organisation can have. Naturally, education and environmental issues are often addressed in cooperation with government (although NGOs are prominent in environmental issues); youth movements favour collaboration with a combination of national NGOs and national-level institutions; and health initiatives work largely with NGOs. At the Local level, local institutions are very definitely the grassroots partners of choice, and education the dominant issue, with youth, health and the environment following, although inevitably there is a far greater number of projects which simply defy definition at this level (painting a fire-station, for example, in the case of Alcoa).

Econometric analysis of network engagement scores[14]

UK multinationals in South Africa

We conducted a number of regressions in order to explain the network engagement score. In our reported regression analyses we use NETSA to denote the network engagement score in South Africa. INPT is the intercept. For South Africa industry dummies EXTRACT, INDUSTR, CONSUMER, MEDICAL, INFO and INFRA refer to the Extractive,

Table 5.23 Explaining South African network engagement scores

	1	2	3	4
Dependent variable	NETSA	NETSA	NETSA	NETSA
No. of observations	37	37	37	37
R^2	0.451	0.376	0.469	0.396
Adjusted R^2	0.342	0.339	0.421	0.341
F-statistic	4.1155***	10.2459***	9.7108***	7.2094***
	(6,30)	(2,34)	(3,33)	(3,33)
INPT	48.814***	9.234***	8.248**	7.322*
	(5.468)	(2.872)	(2.714)	(1.980)
INDUSTR	−39.825***			
	(−3.664)			
CONSUMER	−29.938***			
	(−2.943)			
MEDICAL	−33.305**			
	(−2.644)			
INFO	−43.9682***			
	(−4.162)			
INFRA	−45.418***			
	(−4.445)			
EXTRACT		38.347***	2.620***	28.588**
		(4.363)	(2.949)	(2.227)
REVENUE	0.00021	0.00018	−0.00057**	0.000067
	(−1.455)	(−1.247)	(−2.700)	(−0.376)
CHARIT			0.938**	
			(2.402)	
JSE				10.862
				(1.042)

* = significant at 10%, ** = significant at 5%, *** = significant at 1%.
t-statistics in parentheses.

Industrial, Consumer, Medical, Information, Infrastructure (and other) sectors respectively (equals 1 if firm is in the industry, 0 otherwise). REVENUE is worldwide revenue. CHARIT is charitable donations. JSE equals 1 if the firm is also listed on the Johannesburg Stock Exchange (0 otherwise). NORM is the norm score.

The most interesting regressions are summarised in Table 5.23. We report R-squared, R-bar squared (which adjusts for number of independent variables) and an F-statistic for the overall regression. Equation 1 is a base regression looking at the impact of industry relative to extractive industries. This indicates that firms in all other sectors do less engagement than firms in the Extractive sector. This result is made clearer in Equation 2 where dropping all the industry dummy variables in Equation 1 and replacing them with a single dummy on the Extractive firms. Equation 3 shows that given the industry effect (EXTRACT) and a positive donations effect (CHARIT) the pure size effect is significantly negative (REVENUE). JSE listing has the right sign in Equations 4. Further equations adding the norm score do not find it significant. Equation 3 has the highest R-bar squared of the regressions that do not include the potentially endogenous norm variable. Unreported regressions including South Africa revenue and employees indicated that the worldwide size variables were, if anything, more significant than the size of the local subsidiary. We could find no effect of the presence of a joint venture. Though it should be pointed out that we had limited data on subsidiaries (15–19 firms) and hence the degrees of freedom for these regressions were low.

These results suggest that Extractive Industries are significantly more engaged (Network map score increases by up 38). They also suggest that larger UK MNCs that make more corporate donations do more social capital building in South Africa. JSE listing has a moderate positive effect.

US multinationals in Mexico

In our reported regression analyses of US firms in Mexico we use NETMEX to denote network engagements of each firm. INPT is the intercept. CHEMICAL, FOOD, INDUST, ELECTRIC, MANUFACT, MISC refer to industry dummies for the Other Chemicals, Food and Retail, Industrial machinery and equipment, Electrical and electronic equipment and services, Manufacturing, Highly Diversified and Miscellaneous sectors (equals 1 if firm is in the industry, 0 otherwise). This leaves Pharmaceuticals and Healthcare as the base sector against which other sectors are measured. REVENUE is worldwide revenue. MEXREV100 is

Table 5.24 Explaining Mexican network engagement scores

	1	2	3	4
Dependent variable	NETMEX	NETMEX	NETMEX	NETMEX
No. of observations	73	42	33	33
R^2	0.176	0.415	0.336	0.427
Adjusted R^2	0.087	0.274	0.114	0.166
F-statistic	1.983*	2.931**	1.516	1.636
	(7,65)	(8,33)	(8,24)	(10,22)
INPT	5.029	4.115	19.690***	13.408
	(1.022)	(1.158)	(2.781)	(1.374)
CHEMICAL	2.350	−0.007	−1.998	−2.542
	(0.359)	(−0.001)	(−0.394)	(−0.516)
FOOD	−6.348	−7.898	−10.499*	−11.189**
	(−0.909)	(−1.287)	(−1.925)	(−2.083)
INDUST	−4.493	−5.582	−8.471	−7.855
	(−0.687)	(−1.029)	(−1.649)	(−1.568)
ELECTRIC	−3.220	−4.440	−11.297*	−12.705**
	(−0.491)	(−0.830)	(−1.924)	(−2.208)
MANUFACT	5.052	−2.327	−9.698*	−5.753
	(0.795)	(−0.433)	(−1.811)	(−1.016)
MISC	−4.031	−8.089	−7.586	5.370
	(−0.588)	(−1.195)	(−0.828)	(0.476)
REVENUE	0.00013***	0.00019***	0.00013***	0.00011**
	(2.902)	(4.279)	(2.773)	(2.294)
MEXREV100		−0.070		
		(−0.322)		
AGESUBSID			−0.249**	−0.303**
			(−2.081)	(−2.474)
JV				−4.924
				(−1.182)
NORM				1.352
				(1.468)

* = significant at 10%, ** = significant at 5%, *** = significant at 1%.
t-statistics in parentheses.

the share of Mexican revenue in worldwide revenue. AGESUBSID is the age of the oldest subsidiary in Mexico. JV equals 1 if the firm has a more than 5% partner in a subsidiary. NORM is the norm score.

The most interesting regressions are summarised in Table 5.24, which is in a similar form to Table 5.23 above. Equation 1 is the base regression looking at the impact of industry relative to Pharmaceuticals and Healthcare. This regression suggests no role for industry and a significant revenue effect. However the R-bar squared is low indicating that less than 9% of the variation in scores is explained by the equation. Equation 2 shows that Mexican revenue (MEXREV100) significantly improves the fit of the regression but the parameter is insignificant and negative (though the sample size is reduced to 42). Equations 3 and 4 suggest a significant negative role for age of subsidiary (AGESUBSID). Joint ventures (JV) are negative but not significant. Norm scores have no significant effect in Equation 4.

The US results therefore suggest that industry effects, which were strongly present via the extractive sector in South Africa do not exist. The overall explanatory power of the regression analysis is low. They also suggest that if anything US firms engage disproportionately if they are newer entrants into Mexico (when Mexico is a smaller part of their worldwide operations). A subsidiary that has been in Mexico 20 years will have a Network map score of 3 less than one which has been in existence for ten years. Joint venturing makes engagement less likely (perhaps because this itself acquires societal goodwill). The absence of significant norm effect indicates that for US firms good reporting is not associated with actual engagement on the ground, similar to South Africa.

Conclusions

This chapter illustrates how social capital concepts can be used to analyse corporate citizenship projects. We have been able to score projects in order to compare companies in different industries and different countries in terms of the amount of community engagement they are undertaking and their reporting norms. We have been able to distinguish between the different types of projects focussed on and the level of engagement at which they operate. There are some clear patterns such as health sector firms favouring healthcare projects and international initiatives. Our regression analysis has scratched the surface of what could be done with network map score and norm score data of this type. Further regression analysis of the type of project and the level of engagement could be made.

The results indicate that there are considerable differences between individual firms and that particularly in the case of US firms in Mexico these are difficult to explain statistically. Size plays some role but not in the way one might expect. Many US firms do very little in the way of community engagement but this may be driven by strategic concerns at the commencement of new operations in Mexico.

The results from South Africa are easier to explain. Extractive industries are significant in taking the lead on social capital building. Size does play a role and social capital building and worldwide donations are related to what is done in South Africa. Our results are consistent with the view that these firms are significantly different in their attitude to community engagement.

Taken together the results suggest a surprisingly weak role for industry effects in terms of total engagement and a small size effect. They also suggest that some countries in which multinationals operate receive more attention than others. One might suggest that US and UK multinationals are different in their focus on corporate citizenship projects, or that South Africa and Mexico have different drivers of community engagements. Certainly in combination the samples yield very different results. The role of country of origin and host country effects is difficult to entangle with the two samples we have. We investigate this further in the next chapter by looking at a sample of different country of origin multinationals in a single host country.

Notes

1 Remarks at a World Bank Workshop on Social Capital, 16–17 April 1996, as quoted in Morris (1998, p.4).
2 This is perhaps a result of the fact that Rose has devoted significant time to looking at the collapse of formal institutions in the Ukraine (Rose, 1995a, b, c).
3 Grootaert (1999, pp.13–14).
4 International engagements were included only if they pertained to South Africa or Mexico as relevant. We note the limitations of our focus on self-declared engagements. If a multinational were to ban a union this would actively destroy a potentially beneficial social network. Measures of this type are (unsurprisingly) not readily available.
5 http://www.ftse4good.com
6 This raises the issue of the extent to which different measures with differing scales can be summed and what the overall numbers mean. However we feel that such summation does convey some basis for overall comparison.
7 These statistics are rarely listed on either the US homepage or the Mexican page, although this occurred in some instances. Where there was no evidence, the companies in question were telephoned either at their US, Latin American or Mexican offices to inquire as to whether or not they had more than 250 employees. In the few instances where this failed to produce an answer, sensible estimations of employee numbers were surmised, based on – for example – the existence of factories.

8 We found two, by Anglo American and HSBC, where projects were not listed on the firms own sites but were mentioned elsewhere. These projects were not included in the scores.
9 Sources: www.ftse.com and www.jse.co.za
10 We collected this information from company accounts, Thomson Financial databases and a telephone survey.
11 We collected this information from company accounts, Thomson Financial databases and a telephone survey.
12 TN = International, N = Nation L = Local.
13 Vodafone's score is restricted by its holding only 31.5% of Vodacom in South Africa.
14 Our regression analyses are deliberately straightforward to aid interpretation. We did experiment with log formulations of variables, but this did not substantially alter the results. We could have undertaken censored regressions but have wished to keep the presentation generally accessible.

References

Cohen, D. and Prusak L. (2001), *In Good Company: How Social Capital Makes Organizations Work*, Boston, MA: Harvard Business School Press.

Freeman, L.C. (2000), 'Visualising Social Networks', *The Journal of Social Structure* Vol.1 (1). Available online at http://www.cmu.edu/joss/content/articles/volume1/Freeman.html.

Grootaert, C. (1999), Social Capital, Household Welfare and Poverty in Indonesia, World Bank Social Development Department: Revised Draft.

Hess, D., Rogovsky, N. and Dunfee, T.W. (2002), 'The Next wave or Corporate Community Involvement: Corporate Social Initiatives', *California Management Review*, Vol.44 (2), pp.110–125.

Jones, I.W., Nyland, C.M. and Pollitt, M.G. (2001), *How do multinationals build social capital? Evidence from South Africa*, December, CBR Working Paper, No.220.

Jones, I.W., Nyland, C.M. and Pollitt, M.G. (2002), *How do multinationals build social capital? Evidence from Mexico*, December, CBR Working Paper, No.249.

Jones, I.W., Nyland, C.M. and Pollitt, M.G. (2004a), 'Multinationals in Developing Communities: How UK Multinationals Build Social Capital in South Africa', *New Academy Review*, Vol.3, No.2, pp.70–91.

Jones, I.W., Nyland, C.M. and Pollitt, M.G. (2004b), *Multinationals in Developing Communities: How EU Multinationals Build Social Capital in Poland*, March, CBR Working Paper, No.285.

Knack, S. and Keefer, P. (1997), 'Does Social Capital Have an Economic Payoff? A Cross-Country Investigation', *Quarterly Journal of Economics*, CXII, pp.1251–1258.

Maluccio, J., Haddad, L. and May J. (2000), 'Social Capital and Household Welfare in South Africa, 1993–1998', *The Journal of Development Studies*, XXXVI(6), pp.54–81.

Morris, M. (1998), *Social Capital and Poverty in India*, IDS working Paper 61.

Narayan, D. and Pritchett, L. (1997), *Cents and Sociability: Household Income and Social Capital in Rural Tanzania*, Social Development Policy Research Working Paper No 1796: Washington: World Bank.

Portes, A. (1998), 'Social Capital: Its Origins and Applications in Modern Sociology', *Annual Review of Sociology*, XXIV, pp.1–24.

Putnam, R.D. (2000), *Bowling Alone: The Collapse and Revival of American Community*, New York: Simon and Schuster.

Putnam, R.D. (1993), *Making Democracy Work: Civic Traditions in Modern Italy*, Princeton: Princeton University Press.

Rose, R. (1995a), 'Adaptation, Resilience, and Destitution: Alternative Responses to Transition in Ukraine', *Problems of Post-Communism*, XLII, 6, pp.52–61.

Rose, R. (1995b), *New Russia Barometer IV – Survey Results*, Studies in Public Policy 250, Centre for the Study of Public Policy, University of Strathclyde.

Rose, R. (1995c), 'Russia as an Hour Glass Society: A Constitution without Citizens', *East European Constitutional Review*, IV, 3, pp.34–42.

Rose, R., (1996), *Social Capital: definition, measure, implications*. Remarks at a World Bank Workshop on Social Capital, 16–17 April.

Rose, R. (1997), *Measure of social capital in African Surveys*, World Bank Social Capital Initiative.

Woolcock, M. (2000), *Social Capital in Theory and Practice: Where Do We Stand?*. Paper prepared for the 21st Annual Conference on Economic Issues, Department of Economics, Middlebury College, VT, April 7–9, 2000.

6
Multinationals and Community Engagement in Poland

Introduction

The previous chapter introduced comparable measures of community engagements by multinationals. That chapter looked at two different country of origin multinationals operating in two different host countries. This chapter extends this work by looking at a single host country (Poland) but multinationals from a range of different countries (six developed EU countries). This allows us to make direct comparisons between the behaviour of multinationals from different countries controlling for the operating environment.

As we discuss below Poland is interesting choice as a host country. It is not a particularly 'needy' or high profile developing country. One could argue that South Africa is a special case for the UK multinationals operating there, with unique and high social demands being place on MNCs for historical reasons. One might also argue that Mexico is also a special case for US multinationals due to its geographic proximity, its importance in US foreign policy and its significance as a recipient of outsourcing of US manufacturing. Differences between UK-German-French (and other EU) multinationals in Poland might be expected not to reveal differences in foreign policy or be affected by the sheer scale of need but genuine differences in the level of development and sophistication of corporate citizenship programmes themselves.

In addition to repeating the analysis of the previous chapter on a new and more international dataset this chapter extends the previous analysis in two major ways. First, we look at the wider development context of corporate engagement policies. In particular we highlight the number and type of projects involved and how this compares to governmental development efforts in Poland. This allows us to offer some insights into the significance of corporate social development policies against those of governmental development agencies. Second, we look at the company engagement activity in Poland in the context of their global engagement activity. This allows us to extend our analysis to a preliminary consideration of the disposition of global engagements and whether what companies are doing in one country is representative of what they are doing globally.

Social capital and Poland

As part of the former 'eastern bloc' Poland provides an interesting area for study, because its social capital development differs so strongly from the western countries that are often the focus of analysis. Our analysis was conducted during 2003, hence most of our data refers to this period. Economically, GDP per capita was $9,500 in 2002.[1]

The social capital situation in Poland arguably mirrors that of the former East Germany, as surveyed by Offe and Fuchs (2003). That analysis can be summed up thus: social capital was manifest in two parallel tiers of social capital: 'formal associations and...semi-oppositional private underground networks'. Formal associations tended to be work-related, and 'frequently mandated by imperative political and economic considerations.'[2] The collapse of the East German government and state-sponsored industry removed the foundations for this type of association. Likewise, the unofficial opposition networks lost their centre of focus.

As far as the top-down social capital is concerned sociologist Jerzy Krzyszkowski confirms a similar state of affairs in Poland:

> 'A crisis of the centralized protective state based on three institutions: the labor market, the social insurance system, and the public system of social assistance has led to a massive growth in the number of citizens socially excluded and marginalized.'[3]

The bottom-up social capital of the communist era in Poland was a means of bypassing the strictures of the official system. Local individuals maintained a very loose but wide-reaching community, which did two things. First, it facilitated the flows of economic, political and social life around ossified governmental strictures. Second, it consistently eroded government structures through workplace-based underground organisations, such as Lech Walesa's 'Solidarity', to the point of collapse. It is perhaps the strength of these bottom-up organisations that lead Francis Fukuyama to predict that Poland would be better placed among the post-communist European nations to develop its economy and nurture democracy.[4]

But the collapse of the communist state has had a negative impact on the parallel tiers of social capital: without the workplace to provide systems of association and engagement, and without the formal institutional apparatus to ward off social exclusion, social capital declined. Whilst wealth and jobs are no predictor of a healthy social capital, unemployment and poverty will always undermine it.

In what areas does Poland apparently need the greatest amount of assistance? The Development Gateway, which provides information on development projects around the world, suggests that education, social services, agriculture and government administration, water and sanitation, industry, energy, health and environment projects take up more than 75% of the 881 inter-governmental assistance projects in Poland.[5] Development projects build social capital in various ways. Universally, any creation of contacts and networks in order to facilitate a project is social capital by default. In addition to this, there may also be 'secondary' social capital created depending upon the nature of the project. For example where a development project builds a social centre, social capital emerges in two ways: the creation of links and organisations from various parts of the community in order to complete the centre; and the creation and maintenance of links to subsequent users.

Alongside this, the breakdown of projects by source is as follows:

Table 6.1 Number of projects funded, by nation

Nation	Projects funded
UK	598
Sweden	232
France	134
Canada	75
Germany	48
Italy	41
UNFPA (United Nations Population Fund)[6]	21
Austria	20
United States	19
Japan	14

Source: www.developmentgateway.org – 23rd August 2003.

As regards the issues in which governments and governmental organisations invest, they are broken down by the Development Gateway as follows:

Table 6.2 Breakdown of investment by issue: development gateway categories

Issue	Projects listed	% of total projects
Education	135	15.3
Social services	89	10.1
Agriculture	82	9.3
Government administration	70	7.9
Water and sanitation	56	6.4
Industry	52	5.9
Energy	43	4.9
Health	41	4.7
Environment	36	4.1
Banking and financial services	36	4.1
Emergency assistance	32	3.6
Multi-sector	29	3.3
Transport	29	3.3
Communications	24	2.7
Debt relief	19	2.2
Employment	17	1.9
Civil society and democracy	13	1.5
Forestry	13	1.5
Trade policy and regulations	12	1.4
Unspecified	11	1.2
Urban development	10	1.1
Housing	7	0.8
Mineral resources and mining	6	0.7
General programme assistance	5	0.6
Rural development	5	0.6
Construction	4	0.5
Food aid	2	0.2
Population and reproductive health	2	0.2
Tourism	1	0.1
Total	881	100

Source: www.developmentgateway.org – 23rd August 2003.

Tables 6.1 and 6.2 suggest a quantity and distribution by project type against which the activities of multinationals in Poland might be compared. We note here the significance of UK government projects in the total of all foreign government development projects and also that the

Box 6.1 Danone Child Malnutrition initiative

In 2003 Danone employed 92,209 people across the world,[7] and 1,079 in Poland.[8] It engaged in a project that attempts to address the problem of child malnutrition. The initiative explicitly looks at the social means by which the problem can be addressed.

The ongoing initiative has two major parts. The first of these was a conference in Warsaw in April 2003, which Danone co-hosted, and which was attended by 116 participants (of whom two were from Danone) from 75 local and national institutions and organisations (other than Danone).

Danone's April 2003 conference assisted in the construction of common dialogue and terminology, the lack of which was felt to be hampering the multilateral approach to the problem of malnutrition. The two-day conference included workshops, debates and presentations from representatives from various different organisations and institutions.

The second stage has been the resultant working group, which encompasses 23 national and local institutions (other than Danone). The project is very much focussed on the issue of delivery: how can it be properly ensured that assistance will be accepted, and how can it be certain that those who are in need of assistance are the ones that receive it? The need is quite clear. According to studies undertaken by the initiative, the areas of high unemployment in Poland are amongst those where aid is most keenly needed.

In assisting both in the setting up of the initiative and playing such as active role, Danone can be said to be building social capital at three levels. Firstly, there is the social capital between itself and the other participants in the initiative: it has created networks and helped to establish clear norms of the behaviour that can be expected of it. In its report to the committee, it even goes as far as to explicitly state that the initiative was 'not a one-off act but an element of the company's philosophy.'

Further social capital is built by the facilitation of dialogue amongst the other members, both of the conference and also of the working group. Danone provides material resources to facilitate the meetings, which help to underpin the building of mutual understandings and contact networks.

Box 6.1 – *continued*

The third, and most indirect type of social capital is a two-dimensional type. On the one hand, the 'linking' network that emerges between the initiative and malnourished children is of clear benefit. On the other hand, it fosters social capital and trust by helping to shore up one of the three 'pillars' whose erosion has undermined social capital and the general spirit of trust in Poland, that is the social insurance system which might have been relied upon to provide food in the past.

The provision of food within schools to schoolchildren also facilitates the building of social capital. A recent study undertaken by Buerkle and Guseva, which looked at the importance of schools as a resource for building social capital, concluded that:

> '[w]hen scholars argue that education has an effect on occupational success, they overestimate the role that human knowledge and skills play in distributing social rewards and overlook the social component of education. Thus, by emphasizing the role that social capital plays in translating schooling experience into societal awards, we suggest a way for economic sociology to make an important contribution to the study of education and inequality. Acknowledging the effects of school-based networks is important, not simply because networks impact individual mobility. Employees' networks, which are often initiated through schooling contacts, also facilitate the way in which firms do business.'[9]

Taken together, therefore, the initiative undertaken by Danone should be seen as an example of best practice in building social capital in numerous dimensions. It is also engaged in other initiatives within Poland, and its malnutrition project is not the sole locum of engagement in CSR terms. This project was scored as a *Health* project occurring at the *National* level involving both *Government* and *Institutions*. It involved donation of resources. Hence it scored a maximum 5 under both Government and Institutions.

top five issues being addressed by government projects are Education, Social Services, Agriculture, Government Administration and Water and Sanitation.

Network mapping and norm indexing

The approach to scoring the social capital impact of the companies was very similar to that of the previous chapter. However there are some adjustments for the particular circumstances of Poland and in order to facilitate some of the later analysis. An example of the scoring for a Poland project is given in Box 6.1.

Network mapping

The range of issues were chosen on the basis of 11 issues most typically addressed by MNCs and the organisations with which they are most likely to interact. The list is very similar to that in Table 5.7 but includes Disaster (mainly flood-related), Community at Large, Shelter and Sport, which were not worthy of being picked out in the previous studies. The list is supplemented partly because we also go on to look at projects of the sample companies in the rest of the world. Those issue types are described in Table 6.3. Community engagements were scored as in Table 5.9 of the previous chapter. However in order to facilitate comparison with government programmes and globally the

Table 6.3 Groupings of EU MNC focus

Issue (with abbreviation)	Definition
Education (Ed)	Develop intellectual capability at any age.
Youth (Yth)	Foster social skills in the young.
Health (Hlt)	Augment health directly or through health education.
Disaster (Dis)	Attempt to provide relief for disasters (typically natural: does not include AIDS).
Environment (Env)	Projects that aim to improve environmental conditions.
Development (Dev)	Develop the economy as a whole.
Community at large (CAL)	Involvement in local initiatives such as the fire brigade.
Shelter (Shel)	Involvement in the provision of permanent or temporary housing.
Ethics (Eth)	Establish a code of conduct for participants.
Arts (Art)	Patronise the arts and culture.
Sport (Spt)	Promote the playing of sport.
Other (Oth)	Any other type of engagement.

absolute number of projects, their main issue type and level of engagement were also recorded.

Norm indexing

Reporting norms are recorded in a similar way to that described in Chapter 5. We replace the UK specific membership of the FTSE4Good Index and the US specific presence of CSR information in Spanish question with two questions. First, whether the firm provides CSR information in Polish. And second, whether the firm subscribes to the Global Reporting Initiative (GRI) criteria, which involves additional checking and ratification and the obligation to provide particular varieties of data. This is a UN Environment Programme initiative to standardise sustainability reporting and provides a useful common standard against which firms from different countries can be measured. We discussed this earlier in Chapter 3.

The full scoring system for the Norm index is given in Table 6.4.

As in Chapter 5 data was gathered from the information provided on the firms' own websites from European multinationals (as defined in Waterlow's Directory of Multinationals, 1998) who employ more than 250 individuals in Poland. This generated a list of 49 multinationals from six EU countries. Relevant measures of external network engagements and norms were recorded from their websites during August 2003. Together this group of multinationals employed almost 114,000

Table 6.4 Constituent criteria of the norm index

1. Method of social reporting				
Score	0	1	2	3
Basis for Score	Nothing	HTML-based report	PDF in *annual* report	PDF *separate* report
2. Ease of access				
Score	0	1	2	3
Basis for Score	No information	Information difficult to find	Information relatively easy to find	Information directly linked to homepage

	Yes	No
3. Does the firm have explicit social values?	1	0
4. Does the company have a foundation?	1	0
5. Is there a clear guide on funding application?	1	0
6. Is external responsibility information provided in Polish?	1	0
7. Does the firm subscribe to the Global Reporting Initiative?	1	0

182 *Multinationals in their Communities*

people – 0.8% of Poland's 13.9 million workforce.[10] Poland's manufacturing sector – where the bulk of the firms in the dataset operate – employs 2.73 million people, meaning that as much as 4% of the manufacturing sector is represented by the dataset.

In addition to data on network engagements and norms described above we also collected additional information, subject to availability, which might help explain the network engagement score. We also collect data on the absolute number of engagements worldwide for each firm.

We have data on country of origin, worldwide revenue, profit and employees. This was drawn from company accounts. In addition we made use of industry data (based on European NACE industry classification). We also collected information on Polish subsidiaries: revenue, number of employees, age of subsidiary and the presence of a joint venture.[11] This subsidiary data was only available for some of the sample and is relevant to 2002. All data was for the calendar year 2002 or year including a substantial part of 2002. Financial data is measured in millions of Euros.

Results on network mapping and norm indexing in Poland

The resultant survey revealed several interesting characteristics. What became apparent very quickly is that many firms do not list any community engagement at all in Poland: 18 firms list some engagement in or pertaining to Poland, whilst 31 do not. These results are clearly seen in Table 6.5 where we report Network Map and Norm Index score by firm and also report industry code (NACE). NACE codes are reported in Table 6.6. As with our previous samples there is a strong industry effect. High scores are recorded in some sectors, e.g. DA (food products; beverages and tobacco) and DF (coke, refined petroleum products). Zero network map scores are recorded in others, e.g. DK (machinery and equipment not covered elsewhere) and F (construction).

We also collected the number of social or corporate citizenship engagements anywhere around the world. We analyse this later in the chapter. These engagements were not scored according to the 'depth' of the engagement.

The significance and type of MNC engagements

Amongst our MNC initiatives in Poland, the breakdown, maintaining our earlier classifications, is shown in Table 6.7.

Table 6.5   Scores broken down by industry (NACE) and country of origin

Firm	NACE code	Country of origin	Network map score	Norm index score
Provimi	A/B	France	0	0
Danone	DA	France	28	8
Heineken	DA	Netherlands	10	8
Associated British Foods	DA	UK	0	7
BAT	DA	UK	14	9
Cadbury Schweppes	DA	UK	12	10
Imperial Tobacco	DA	UK	0	5
Unilever	DA/DG	UK	5	10
Svenska Cellulosa Aktiebolaget	DE	Sweden	0	8
BP	DF	UK	68	11
Shell	DF	UK	4	11
Sanofi-Synthelabo	DG	France	5	7
Bayer	DG	Germany	42	10
Henkel KGAA	DG	Germany	15	8
Akzo Nobel	DG	Netherlands	0	5
GSK	DG	UK	0	9
ICI	DG	UK	0	10
Lafarge	DI	France	9	7
Heidelberger Zement	DI	Germany	0	0
Pilkington	DI	UK	0	8
RMC Group	DI	UK	8	7
Peugeot	DK	France	0	5
Linde Group	DK	Germany	0	5
VW	DK	Germany	0	8
Fiat	DK	Italy	0	5
Sandvik AB	DK	Sweden	0	0
Volvo	DK	Sweden	0	6
Schneider Electric SA	DL	France	0	8
Siemens	DL	Germany	28	11
Koninklijke Philips Electronics NV	DL	Netherlands	0	8
Electrolux	DL	Sweden	0	5
Ericsson	DL	Sweden	0	6
Valeo	DL/DM	France	0	4
GKN	DN	UK	0	6
Eiffage	F	France	0	0
Bilfinger Berger	F	Germany	0	0
Hochtief	F	Germany	0	0
Strabag	F	Germany	0	0
Skanska AB	F	Sweden	0	6
Carrefour	G	France	9	9
Casino Guichard-Perrachon	G	France	0	9
L'Oreal	G	France	5	5
Beiersdorf	G	Germany	0	4
Royal Ahold	G	Netherlands	10	7
Kingfisher	G	UK	27	7
Accor	H	France	0	5
Sodexho	H	France	0	4
Bouygues	I	France	0	8
Vodafone	I	UK	5	9

Table 6.6 Definitions of the relevant NACE codes

Relevant NACE code	Meaning
A	Agriculture, hunting and forestry
B	Fishing
D	Manufacturing
DA	Food products; beverages and tobacco
DE	Pulp, paper and paper product; publishing and printing
DF	Coke, refined petroleum products and nuclear fuel
DG	Chemicals, chemical products and man-made fibres
DI	Other non-metallic mineral products
DJ	Basic metals and fabricated metal products
DK	Machinery and equipment not covered elsewhere
DL	Electrical and optical equipment
DN	Manufacturing items not covered elsewhere
F	Construction
G	Wholesale and retail trade; repair of motor vehicles, household
H	Hotels and restaurants
I	Transport, storage and communication

Whilst it is difficult to elicit exact comparisons in terms of the numbers, scales and classification of projects undertaken, certain trends do appear. The top five areas of concentration for government agencies (listed in Table 6.2) – taking up almost 55% of their work – are education, social services, agriculture, government administration, and water and sanitation. However for MNCs, the top five areas of focus – which take up almost 80% of the projects, are the youth, education, environment, health, and development. This may be due to a delegation of labour or that there are certain engagements to which MNCs feel more responsive or responsible, or simply a structural consequence of MNCs desire to build social capital more quickly than government agencies in certain areas.

There are various examples of this: environmental initiatives account for 4.1% of projects for government-based initiatives, but 14% of MNC initiatives. This may, for example, be more concerned with issues of

Table 6.7 MNC initiatives in Poland – breakdown by issue

Issue	Projects listed	Percentage of total projects
Youth	14	25
Education	9	16
Environment	8	14
Health	7	12
Development	7	12
Disaster	5	9
Arts	4	7
Ethics	2	4
Sports	1	2
CAL	0	0
Shelter	0	0
Other	0	0
Total	**57**	**100**

perceived responsibility. 'Emergency Assistance' accounts for only 3.6% of government-based initiatives, but 9% of MNC engagements in Poland were concerned with this – in particular in the deluge of floods that hit Poland recently. In this particular instance, the type of engagement listed by the bulk of the MNCs was the simple provision of manpower, coordination facilities and basic resources, in assistance of emergency services and volunteer groups: with a presence 'on the scene,' they were better placed to respond. Likewise, the greater relative and absolute focus on educational initiatives on the part of government-based organisations suggests that it might be felt that this is a domain in which MNCs should dabble less, dependent on the prevailing conditions of the host country.

Although it is difficult to make absolute comparisons of the scale of governmental and MNC involvement, we note that MNC projects in our sample are 57 against 881 governmental projects. This suggests the potential and the limitation of the total impact of MNCs. Clearly government projects are an order of magnitude greater than those of MNCs. However the number of MNC projects is non-negligible. If these projects were to be the more innovative and more current their effective share could be several times greater than these raw numbers might suggest.

Patterns of engagement

In this subsection we map the focus, level and depth of the engagements of MNCs in Poland and offer some comparison between this and

Table 6.8 Number of engagements by focus and level

Level	Edu	Yth	Hlt	Dis	Env	Dev	CAL	Shl	Eth	Art	Spt	Oth	Tot
International	2				1								3
National	3	4	3	6	11	5			1				33
Local	5	11	6		3	2				1	4	1	33

Table 6.9 Pattern of engagement by focus and level weighted by depth of engagement

Level	Edu	Yth	Hlt	Dis	Env	Dev	CAL	Shl	Eth	Art	Spt	Oth	Tot
International	10				3								13
National	18	16	15	28	57	21			5				160
Local	22	41	24		11	9				4	16	4	131

Table 6.10 Average depth of engagement (Table 6.9/Table 6.8)

Level	Edu	Yth	Hlt	Dis	Env	Dev	CAL	Shl	Eth	Art	Spt	Oth	Tot
International	5.0				3.0								4.3
National	6.0	4.0	5.0	4.7	5.2	4.2			5.0				4.8
Local	4.4	3.7	4.0		3.7	4.5				4.0	4.0	4.0	4.0

the patterns of engagement seen in our South African and Mexican samples.

First, one can look at the number of engagements undertaken by firms, incorporating the variety of different engagements represented by a single project. Thus the 57 projects in Table 6.7 translate into the 69 engagements in Table 6.8.

If depth of engagement (network map score) is factored in, we have the pattern of Table 6.9.

This means that their average depth of engagement in projects is as in Table 6.10.

This initially appears puzzling, but can be understood by virtue of the fact that there are often multiple engagements in projects at a given level. For example, at the national level government, NGOs and firms might be involved in a common initiative for health or the environment. What this tells us is that there are sometimes rich patterns of engagement in particular issues. It is unsurprising that this is lacking somewhat at the international level, since all engagement is channelled through one organisation that then acts, rather than through a coalition-based workgroup of some sort.

Table 6.11 Number of engagements, categorised by partner organisation and geographical level

Regional level	Partners	Score
International	International Organisation	1
	NGO	2
	MNCs	0
National	National Government	6
	National NGO	11
	National Institution	11
	National Firm	5
Local	Local Government	1
	Local Institution	19
	Local Firm	1
	Individual	12

Note: See Table 5.8 for definitions.

Focus varies, therefore, according to the particular level of institution with which the firm is acting. At the international level, the firms tend to focus on educational issues. At the national level, there is a more dominant focus on environmental issues, and at the local level there is a greater focus on youth initiatives. This is likely to be – in part – a function of where the greatest leverage is considered to be. For example, youth initiatives necessarily function more effectively at the grassroots level because of the need for personalised attention and focus. Environmental issues tend to rely more on national-level coordination to have an effectiveness that merits mention in a report. Health is an issue which could arguably be said to lend itself to both, in part because it relies both on national policy, on the one hand to administer the formal system, and because preventative initiatives tend to rely on more individualised approaches.

Bringing the level of focus in even more closely, it is possible to look at the preferred partnership through which firms undertake initiatives in Poland (in Table 6.11). The clear indication is that, whilst at the national level, government, NGOs and other institutions are all engaged relatively equally, the local level government is typically bypassed in favour of more direct engagement. It appears, therefore, that there is a preference to avoid direct dealings with both other firms and also with formal government.

Comparing the results for Poland with those for South Africa and Mexico, we see that disaster projects are important for the Wholesale and retail trade (Table 6.12). We note the relative lack of importance in Poland of international initiatives, which are a negligible part of the total (see Table 6.13). International initiatives were significant in South Africa and Mexico, and very significant in some sectors such as Pharmaceuticals and Healthcare. By contrast national initiatives are generally the most important in Poland as opposed to local initiatives in Mexico. This must reflect the focus of international institutions on poorer countries and the relative competence of national Polish-based organisations as partners in corporate projects. Interestingly Polish national and local government play a relatively minor part in the engagement strategies of multinationals. For US firms in Mexico one-third of national engagement involved national government. It is only half that for EU multinationals in Poland. In terms of the leading sectors at the different levels DG (analogous to Pharmaceuticals and Healthcare in Mexico and Medical in South Africa) is not the leading sector (as we might expect) at any level (Table 6.14). This is perhaps because the sector includes chemicals as well as pharmaceutical firms and because the engagement score is equally split between local and national projects, reducing its ranking in one or other of the levels.

Patterns of norms

The various constituent parts of the norm index of the companies are interesting. Only eight firms in the survey provide information in

Table 6.12 Issue popularity by sector: Poland

	Rank		
	1	2	3
A			
B			
DA	Health	Youth	Environment
DE			
DF	Youth	Development	Environment
DG	Environment	Youth	Arts
DI	Environment	Development	
DL	Education	Arts	Development
DN			
F			
G	Disaster	Education	Health
H			
I	Education		

Table 6.13 Sectoral engagements by level percentage: Poland

	Level		
	Transnational	National	Local
A			
B			
DA		69.0%	31.0%
DE			
DF	6.9%	47.2%	45.8%
DG		55.0%	45.0%
DI	17.6%	17.6%	64.7%
DL		39.3%	60.7%
DN			
F			
G	9.8%	49.0%	41.2%
H			
I		100%	

Table 6.14 Sectoral engagement by level: Poland

	Rank		
	1	2	3
Transnational	DI: Other non-metallic mineral products	G: Wholesale & retail trade; repair of motor vehicles, household	DF: Coke, refined petroleum products & nuclear fuel
National	I: Transport, storage and communication	DA: Food products; beverages and tobacco	DG: Chemicals, chemical products and man-made fibres
Local	DI: Other non-metallic mineral products	DF: Coke, refined petroleum products & nuclear fuel	DG: Chemicals, chemical products and man-made fibres

Polish and, of these, six firms are UK-based. Adherence to the Global Reporting Initiative is still relatively low, with just 18 of the 49 firms in the study adhering to its practices, and similarly there are only 16 firms with foundations. However, the average level of information provision is high, with 27 firms providing downloadable booklets detailing their worldwide social engagements, (although these do not necessarily pertain to Poland) and only seven firms do not provide any information at all regarding their social engagements.

National and international performance

There is an interesting variation in the performance of multinationals, depending upon the country in which they are headquartered, which is summarised in Table 6.15. As regards network map scores, the stronger average performance is among UK, German and Dutch firms, although the size of the standard deviation is a clear indicator of the discrepancy within the national groupings. As regards norms, UK, and Dutch firms again score highly, and there is a greater degree of consistency among the UK and Dutch firms. Overall, there was a weak positive correlation between network map scores and norm indices, with a coefficient of 0.45.

It appears that the clearest indicator of a firm's engagement in Poland is its degree of engagement worldwide. At the national level there is a strong positive correlation with a coefficient of 0.97 between the number of projects declared in Poland and those declared anywhere else in the world (including the home country).

There are clear differences in the absolute number of projects taken on by the average representative national firm in this dataset. The total numbers of project listed by firms are reported in Table 6.16.

Nonetheless, there are different relative degrees of focus, depending upon the country. Table 6.17 below indicates the relative preference for projects in the home nation or outside it.

Table 6.15 Average scores for network maps and norm indices, organised by country

Country	No. of firms in dataset	Network map average	Network map st devn	Norm index average	Norm index st devn
France	14	4	7.7	5.6	3.0
Germany	10	8.5	15.1	4.6	4.5
Italy	1	0	0	5.0	0
Netherlands	4	5	5.8	7.0	1.4
Sweden	6	0	0	5.2	2.7
UK	14	10.2	18.3	8.5	1.9

Table 6.16 Average number of projects undertaken

Nation (number of firms)	Average projects undertaken around the world
France (14)	18.8
Germany (10)	31.7
Italy (1)	0
Netherlands (4)	10.3
Sweden (6)	7.7
UK (14)	38.5

Table 6.17 Relative preference for projects

| Nation | Projects undertaken (%) | | |
| | At home | Abroad | |
		Poland	Elsewhere
France	27	3	70
Germany	22	5	73
Italy	0	0	0
Netherlands	12	7	80
Sweden	11	0	89
UK	12	6	82

French firms tend to focus more on projects in France, with some 27% of projects undertaken in the home country. The majority of these projects are focussed on youth initiatives. For German firms within Germany, the focus tends to be on the arts and sport. Outside Germany, education and youth receive the lion's share of attention, followed by health and the environment. The Dutch firms listed most engagements in the Americas and Asia, with a fairly even spread of low scores around the major issues. The companies from Sweden tend to involve themselves in projects on international-level initiatives with a dominant focus (some 63% of projects) on disaster relief, particularly in Africa, Latin America and European Countries outside the EU. UK firms' projects focus primarily on Africa and the EU, and are typically concerned with the environment as an issue at the global level, although they also score very strongly in education, youth and health. The breakdowns of the different MNC nationality by region are listed in Table 6.18.

Table 6.18 Numbers, locations and foci of projects, arranged by MNC nationality

		Ed	Yth	Hlt	Dis	Env	Dev	CAL	Shl	Eth	Art	Spt	Oth	TTot	Av
France	Poland	1	1	3	1	2								8	0.7
	Home	4	49	5	6		1	3			3			71	5.9
	Abroad	22	79	25	12	12	10		10	11	4		5	190	15.8
	Total	27	129	33	19	14	11		13	11	7		5	269	22.4
Germany	Poland	2	2	1	1	2	2			1	4			15	1.3
	Home	9	3	2							23	31		68	5.7
	Abroad	39	76	42	12	28	8	3		7	20	6		241	20.1
	Total	50	81	45	13	30	10	3		8	47	37		324	27
Italy	Poland													0	0
	Home													0	0
	Abroad													0	0
	Total													0	0
Netherlands	Poland				1	1	1							3	0.3
	Home	3					1				1			5	0.4
	Abroad	6	1	7	4	3	4	2	1	1	3	1		33	2.8
	Total	9	1	7	5	4	6	2	1	1	4	1		41	3.4
Sweden	Poland													0	0
	Home	1	1	1							1	1		5	0.4
	Abroad	2	1	2	32	1	1			4			3	46	3.8
	Total	3	2	3	32	1	1			4	1	1	3	51	4.3
UK	Poland	6	11	3	2	3	4			1		1		31	2.6
	Home	16	18	1		10	2	10	2	1	5	1		66	5.5
	Abroad	71	81	86	21	137	40	19	1	16	10	3	4	489	40.8
	Total	93	110	90	23	150	46	29	3	18	15	5	4	586	48.8

Econometric analysis of network engagement scores in Poland and the number of worldwide engagements

EU multinationals in Poland

We conducted a number of regressions in order to explain the network map score in Poland. In our reported regression analyses we used NETPOL to denote network engagement score in Poland. INPT is the intercept. FRANCE, GERMANY, ITALY, NLANDS, SWEDEN represent country dummies (1 if firm has headquarters in country, 0 otherwise). The base country is the UK. We made use of the following industry dummies: AB, DA, DE, DF, DG, DI, DN, F, G, H, and I refer to the NACE industries in Table 6.6 (equals 1 if in industry, 0 otherwise). The

Table 6.19 Explaining Poland network engagement scores

	1	2	3	4
Dependent variable	NETPOL	NETPOL	NETPOL	NETPOL
No. of observations	49	49	34	32
R^2	0.234	0.341	0.168	0.083
Adjusted R^2	0.125	0.097	0.019	−0.185
F–statistic	2.1389*	1.3960	1.1268	0.30990
	(6,42)	(13,35)	(5,28)	(7,24)
INPT	4.372	−0.594	7.720	7.955
	(1.156)	(−0.097)	(1.305)	(1.587)
FRANCE	−2.577		−6.007	−1.209
	(−0.548)		(−0.903)	(−0.227)
GERMANY	1.184		−1.212	4.707
	(0.233)		(−0.173)	(0.819)
ITALY	−11.173			
	(−0.899)			
NETHERLANDS	−2.849		−7.267	1.129
	(−0.416)		(−0.758)	(0.139)
SWEDEN	−5.964		−10.384	−7.737
	(−0.988)		(−1.058)	(−0.633)
REVENUE	0.00012***	0.000015		0.00000015
	(2.920)	(0.167)		(0.003)
AB		0.570		
		(0.042)		
DA		10.564		
		(1.461)		
DE		0.446		
		(0.033)		
DF		33.215*		
		(1.714)		
DG		10.199		
		(1.420)		
DI		4.716		
		(0.565)		
DL		5.513		
		(0.750)		
DN		−0.537		
		(−0.043)		
F		0.459		
		(0.058)		

Table 6.19 Explaining Poland network engagement scores – *continued*

	1	2	3	4
G		8.607 (1.217)		
H		0.442 (0.043)		
I		2.455 (0.246)		
REVPOL			0.009 (1.640)	
AGESUBSID				–0.246 (–0.393)
JV				–0.910 (–0.197)

* = significant at 10%, ** = significant at 5%, *** = significant at 1%.
t-statistics in parentheses.

base industry is DK (other machinery and equipment). REVENUE is worldwide revenue. REVPOL is subsidiary revenue in Poland. AGESUBSID is age of subsidiary. JV indicates the presence of a joint venture (equals 1, 0 otherwise).

The most interesting regressions are summarised in Table 6.19. We use the same results reporting format as in chapter 5. The results indicate that, as for Mexico, the regressions struggle to explain much of the variation in the score. Equation 1 shows that the country effects are insignificant (though the parameter values are mostly negative indicating that UK firms do more engagement). Worldwide revenue is significant and positive. Equation 2 suggests that industry effects are better than country effects at explaining the data in terms of R-squared (though not R-bar squared). DF is significant indicating that the energy firms (BP and Shell) do significantly more than the automobile manufacturers in the base DK. Equation 3 indicates no role for subsidiary revenue in explaining engagement, while age of subsidiary and the presence of a joint venture are also not significant.

Overall the results suggest that it is difficult to explain the pattern of community engagement in Poland. However it is interesting to note that country of origin effects are not significant, in contrast to the results suggested by observation in Table 6.12. This suggests that the differences we observe between countries are driven by the size and industry characteristics. Thus UK firms apparently do more because of their larger global size and their existence in industries (such as resources) that do more, not because they are from the UK per se.

Worldwide number of projects

We have data on the number of projects undertaken worldwide by our sample of EU multinationals. This provides for some indicative analysis of worldwide engagements. The sample is not representative in the sense that it is made up of firms with operations in Poland. However it does provide an interesting extension of the analysis by allowing us to examine whether it is easier to explain the global rather than the local behaviour of MNCs in corporate citizenship.

In our reported regression analyses we use PRWORLD to denote the global number of projects for each firm. INPT is the intercept. The country and industry dummy variables are as for the previous sample. REVENUE is worldwide revenue. PROFIT is worldwide profit. NORM is the norm score.

The most interesting regression results for this sample are in Table 6.20. The equations are more significant than those reported in Table 6.19, though it is important to stress that we measure depth of engagements in Table 6.19 and only the number in Table 6.20. Equations 1 and 2 focus on country and size effects. Once again the UK has higher engagement scores but insignificantly so. Revenue and Profit do partially explain the number of projects, with profits providing a better fit of the data. Equations 3 and 4 show that industry effects are stronger than country effects, improving the fit and providing some significant industries. Chemicals firms (DG) are now significantly better than the auto firms (DK), as are electrical and optical equipment firms (DL). Equation 4 shows a significant role for the norm score.

These results suggest that industry and norms of reporting, as well as absolute size explain a significant part of the number of projects globally (R-squared is around 50% in Equation 4). They also suggest no role for country effects (though this may be captured to some extent by national differences in reporting requirements).

Conclusions

This chapter has further extended the work on applying social capital concepts statistically to companies. The total number of projects in Poland is small compared to government projects but is still material.

Table 6.20 Explaining worldwide network map scores

	1	2	3	4
Dependent variable	PRWORLD	PRWORLD	PRWORLD	PRWORLD
No. of observations	49	49	49	49
R^2	0.217	0.244	0.454	0.504
Adjusted R^2	0.106	0.136	0.251	0.299
F-statistic	1.9438* (6,42)	2.2554* (6,42)	2.2387** (13,35)	2.4653** (14,34)
INPT	26.540** (2.238)	29.540*** (2.723)	−11.693 (−0.677)	−26.202 (−1.420)
FRANCE	−13.107 (−0.888)	−15.238 (−1.070)		
GERMANY	−1.860 (−0.117)	−1.561 (−0.100)		
ITALY	−44.369 (−1.138)	−9.402 (−0.235)		
NETHERLANDS	−25.405 (−1.182)	−19.085 (−0.889)		
SWEDEN	−22.214 (−1.174)	−20.999 (−1.129)		
REVENUE	0.00031** (2.442)		0.00036 (1.401)	0.000095 (0.330)
PROFIT		0.0042*** (2.763)		
AB			11.137 (0.290)	26.055 (0.685)
DA			30.070 (1.472)	8.278 (0.360)
DE			18.213 (0.473)	−5.839 (−0.150)
DF			25.364 (0.463)	42.162 (0.785)
DG			73.666*** (3.631)	50.704** (2.182)
DI			24.165 (1.025)	12.632 (0.534)
DL			43.582** (2.100)	28.233 (1.300)
DN			7.843 (0.223)	−2.018 (−0.059)

Table 6.20 Explaining worldwide network map scores – *continued*

	1	2	3	4
F			9.101 (0.409)	19.793 (0.888)
G			13.524 (0.677)	1.383 (0.068)
H			25.116 (0.863)	19.128 (0.675)
I			15.601 (0.555)	–2.463 (–0.085)
NORM				5.141* (1.846)

* = significant at 10%, ** = significant at 5%, *** = significant at 1%.
t-statistics in parentheses.

The results in this chapter further suggest that local community engagement by MNCs is difficult to explain in some countries. Many companies do little or no community engagement as measured by corporate citizenship projects. There is significant variation between companies and this cannot be easily reconciled with available metrics on the characteristics of global and local operations. The focus of the projects in Poland – on the environment and education – is somewhat different to South Africa where health and development projects were significant. In terms of level of engagement international initiatives were much less significant in Poland than in South Africa and Mexico.

There appear to be significant differences between countries of origin in terms of reporting and engagement. However on statistical testing this is found to reflect the industry of operation of the firms from those countries rather than a pure country effect. This result is borne out at the global level in our analysis of the number of projects worldwide.

As with the South Africa and Mexico samples the characteristics of the local subsidiary play only a limited role in explaining community engagement in the host country. The impression remains that many multinationals have not given much thought to the rationale behind the global distribution of corporate citizenship projects and how these might be justified to local stakeholders.

Notes

1. CIA online World Factbook, 2002 estimate, http://www.reference-guides.com/cia_world_factbook/Poland/ Economy/ GDP__per_capita/
2. Offe and Fuchs, 2003, p.220.
3. Krzyszkowski, 2003, p.546.
4. Fukuyama, 1995, p.361.
5. Data from the Development Gateway website, 17th August 2003: http://www.developmentgateway.org/. It is important to note that many of the projects listed here appear to have finished thus it is not clear that our measures of largely ongoing MNC projects are comparable to these figures.
6. The UNFPA is a United-based organization, which 'works to ensure universal access to reproductive health'.
7. Danone website. Most recently checked 29th November 2003, http://www.danonegroup.com/group/index_group.html>
8. Data provided by Danone's HR Office in Poland in late August 2003.
9. Buerkle and Guseva, 2002, p.675.
10. Polish Workforce statistics are from ILO reports. There are at least a further 27 MNCs, employing on average 93 individuals, that were not included in the study because they had insufficient employees.
11. We collected this information from company accounts, Thomson Financial databases and telephone survey.

References

Buerkle, K. and Guseva, A. (2002), 'What do you know, who do you know? School as a Site for the Production of Social Capital and its Effects on Income Attainment in Poland and the Czech Republic', *American Journal of Economics and Sociology*, Vol.61 (3): pp.657–680.

Fukuyama. F. (1995), *Trust: The Social Virtues and the Creation of Prosperity*, New York: Free Press.

Krzyszkowski, J. (2003), *Preparing Social Professionals for Building Social Capital to Combat Social Exclusion at Local Level*, in C. Labonte-Roset, E. Marynowicz-Hetka, J. Szmagalski (eds) *Social Work Education and Practice in Today's Europe: Challenges and the Diversity of Responses*, Katowice: Śląsk.

Offe, C. and Fuchs, S. (2003), *A Decline of Social Capital? The German Case*, in R.D. Putnam (ed.) *Democracies in Flux*, Harvard: Harvard University Press.

7
Diageo and its Corporate Citizenship Programme

A brief corporate biography

Diageo is the world's leading premium alcoholic beverage company. Its portfolio of high profile brands includes Smirnoff, Guinness, Johnnie Walker, Bells, Baileys, J&B, Captain Morgan, Cuerva and Tanqueray. Whilst these renowned brands are themselves long-established, Diageo is a relatively new creation. In 1997 the food and drinks business Grand Metropolitan, which included Burger King, Pillsbury, Baileys and Smirnoff amongst its assets, merged with the brewer Guinness. The new corporation was named Diageo, derived from the Latin for 'day' (dia) and the Greek for 'earth' (geo) (NYSE Magazine, 2004).

The company's strategic focus has subsequently been shaped through the sale of all its non-beverage components; Pillsbury was sold in 2001 and Burger King in 2003 (Diageo, 2004h). In December 2001 Diageo and Pernod Ricard jointly acquired the Seagram spirits and wine business from Vivendi (NYSE Magazine, 2004). Thus, Diageo can now claim to be the world's pre-eminent premium brand alcoholic beverage company 'with an outstanding collection of brands across spirits, wine and beer categories' (Diageo, 2003a, p.2). The company focusses upon developing its core spirits business and corporate strategy is driven by the goal of developing Diageo's eight 'global priority' brands which include, Smirnoff premium Vodka, Johnnie Walker whisky and Guinness stout (NYSE Magazine, 2004). Seven of these products are either number one or two in their sales categories. The company is listed on both the London and New York stock exchanges and trades globally in over 180 markets. It is clear from the tables below that the North American and European markets are currently the most important for Diageo in terms of turnover and sales. Diageo is

Table 7.1   Regional data for Diageo 2004

Region	Turnover £ millions	% of total turnover	Employees	% of total employees	Equivalent units* sold (million)	% of total sales	% of total community spend**
Europe	3,922	44.1	11,373	48	42.1	35	58.8
North America	2,701	30.4	3,742	16	45.2	37	27.2
Asia Pacific	996	11.2	2,415	10	11.1	9	8.5
Latin America	460	5.2	1,496	5	8.8	7	4.4
Africa, Middle East	812	9.1	4,694	20	14.9	12	1.1
Totals	8,900		23,720		122.1		

* An equivalent unit is that volume which contains the same number of servings as a nine-litre case of spirits.
** Data relates to premium drinks business only.
Source: Diageo Corporate Citizenship Report 2004, pp.2, 3 & 14.

a relatively unusual firm due to the lack of obvious connection between the overall corporate brand and the product brands. Establishing an internal brand across the various business divisions spread across the globe has been a significant challenge since 1997.

Corporate citizenship – strategy and management

As an alcoholic beverages company Diageo has to confront a number of issues in terms of its relationship with broader society. Whilst the firm produces goods that bring pleasure to many millions of people alcohol abuse in various forms and religious objections to alcohol consumption present challenges for the firm to consider. Indeed, concern over alcohol abuse and irresponsible drinking result in the firm facing the constant threat of regulation in many of its markets. By adopting a firm position on Corporate Citizenship Diageo is able to negotiate these various challenges. Thus, Corporate Citizenship (CC) is an integral component of the way that Diageo does its business. CC and involvement with communities are seen as being central to the company's ongoing objective of creating long-term shareholder value as this determines the impact on its stakeholders. Through its community activities the company aims to 'build and enhance corporate reputation, help build a sustainable business environment, build team spirit and build trust and the licence to operate with shareholders' (Business in the Community, 2002). Diageo is a leading advocate for community involvement and has led the way by being one of the first corporations to appoint a professional director for CSR. Diageo's CEO is the executive owner of CC, whilst strategy and policy are dealt with through a CC committee. The strategic direction of CC is clearly driven from the top of the firm. The CEO chairs the CC committee meetings, which occur three times a year. The committee is composed of members drawn from the Executive level of the company, which makes Diageo different from many other firms. During 2004 this committee merged with the Brand Committee, whose main remit is to protect and develop the Diageo brand. The CC committee develops corporate policies on matters such as Human Rights, genetically modified organisms (GMOs) and so forth. Principles for dealing with these sorts of issues are established, codes of conduct drawn up and the Compliance committee then ensure their full application. Recent internal restructuring has meant that the Director of CC now reports to the Communications Director.

Diageo's community programme is embedded within its business activities at all levels and is aligned to corporate objectives and values. Diageo in effect inherited a wide range of community-based corporate community projects and schemes from its constituent businesses. Guinness, for example, had a long history of community involvement around their sites in Dublin, whilst Grandmet had been inextricably linked with the urban regeneration focussed charity Tomorrow's People. Formulating a unified and coherent CC strategy aligned to the goals of the new corporation was one of the major challenges in the late 1990s. Considerable efforts were subsequently made by key players to devise an appropriate strategy and embed it within daily business practice. The impacts of the firm's history remain evident in the geographical spread of community spending (see Table 7.1) with a disproportionate amount being directed towards Europe, whilst international markets receive much lower proportions of community investment. During 2004 the firm revised its approach to community involvement. A three-day conference was held during which strategies for external affairs, communication and corporate citizenship were debated. Concerns have been articulated suggesting that Corporate Citizenship, 'seems mainly "top-down" with limited evidence of strong commitment at middle management level and below' (ProbusBNW, 2004, p.8).

In 2005 Tomorrow's People were adjudged winners of the BUPA-sponsored Healthy Communities Award in the BITC Big Tick Awards. The firm was ranked 32 out of the 132 participating companies in the BITC's 2004 Corporate Responsibility Index – the leading company in the beverages sector. The firm's actual rating was 90%, up from 68 in 2002. Diageo is included within both the FTSE4Good Index and the Dow Jones Sustainability Index. During 2005 Diageo was included in a list of the 100 most sustainable firms in the world (see www.global100.org). The firm has recently launched its own award for African Business Reporting. The intention is to challenge negative perceptions of Africa and to encourage the presentation of more balanced views of the business opportunities in the African continent.

Community spending

An annual contribution representing 1% of pre-tax profits to community programmes has been agreed. The firm has undertaken a benchmarking exercise and believe that a 1% spend represents corporate best practice. In 2003 the actual value of this commitment totalled £19 million. Diageo states that this figure does not match the entirety of its commitment as the firm always 'underclaims'. A senior figure within the company stated that the total community spend in 2003 was in fact £28 million. It is possible that this higher figure

Table 7.2 Community investment performance (£) according to the Annual Giving List

	Cash donation £m	Staff/ management costs £m	Gifts in kind £m	Total donation £m	% of pre-tax profits	Rank
2005	20.13	1.22	1.27	22.62	1.2	18
2004	15.13	1.19	1.21	17.52	0.9	35
2003	15.13	1.78	2.70	19.61	1	24
2002	16.7	2.1	1	19.8	1	27

Sources:
http://image.guardian.co.uk/sys-files/Society/documents/2004/11/08/giving.pdf
http://image.guardian.co.uk/sys-files/Guardian/documents/2004/04/28/2003amendedtable.pdf
http://society.guardian.co.uk/givinglist/tables/0,10999,848892,00.html
http://image.guardian.co.uk/sys-files/Society/documents/2005/11/28/GivingList_paper_281105.pdf

Table 7.3 Community investment in £thousand Sterling by LBG category

	2001	2002	2003	2004	2005
Philanthropy	5,475	2,131	2,366	1,072	1,915
Social Investment	8,176	12,110	11,249	11,764	14,667
Commercially-led Initiatives	1,615	2,730	5,386	4,686	6,042
Total	15,266	16,971	19,001	17,522	22,624

Sources: Diageo Corporate Citizenship Reports, 2003, p.17 and 2005, p.14.

incorporates 'socially responsible advertising', which is not normally included within benchmarked expenditure totals (Diageo, 2003b). According to the *Giving List*, published in the Guardian newspaper, Diageo was ranked 18th amongst FTSE100 companies in terms of the value of its donations as a share of profits in 2005. A proportion of the annual community investment spend (£7.2 million in 2005) is accounted for by contributions to the Thalidomide Trust (Diageo, 2004i). The latter body supports the victims of the drug Thalidomide, which was distributed by a subsidiary of United Distillers in the late 1950s. The ongoing moral commitment to fund this out of court settlement rests with Diageo.

Diageo is one of an increasing number of major companies who utilise the LBG model to evaluate their community involvement activities (Corporate Citizenship Company, 2004; LBG, 2004). Indeed, Diageo was a the founder member of the LBG and the Head of CC is still actively involved within the highest strategic levels of the LBG.

Diageo uses the LBG model to assess aspects of their CC programme (Diageo, 2003b). The costing mechanisms provided by the LBG are helpful in calculating the total spend. As Table 7.3 indicates, there has been a recent shift away from philanthropic spending and an increase in commercially-led initiatives in recent years. Individual projects are evaluated using the input-output matrix, some examples of which are included within the annual Corporate Citizenship report (Diageo, 2003b, p.17). Following the strategic review of CC undertaken when Diageo was created a decision was taken to commit more resources to fewer projects, to focus upon key themes and develop sustainable partnerships with other bodies (Business in the Community, 2002). Recently, a further review of CC activities has taken place and the key focus areas have been re-defined. In 2004 CC activities were built around the three following domains: *Alcohol Education*, *Local Citizens* (later separated into *Local Citizens* and *Skills for Life*) and *Water of Life*.

In 2004 the Diageo website listed 13 projects that have been supported through the *Alcohol Education* focus area. Diageo recognises that its position as the world's leading alcoholic drinks company places a significant burden upon the firm to take a lead in promoting responsible alcohol consumption (Diageo, 2003a; Diageo, 2003b). As a result Diageo is involved in a wide range of responsible drinking-related projects across the world. Table 7.4 below illustrates how spending classified as *Alcohol Education* consumes an increasing proportion of CC spending. The *Water of Life* programme is Diageo's leading environmental and humanitarian initiative. Forty-six projects were listed on the website in 2004. *Water of Life* is the English translation of the Gaelic 'uisge beatha', which is the origin of the modern word 'whisky'. Projects are funded via *Water of Life* under three classifications: conservation and biodiversity, public health and sustainability (Diageo, 2004j). As water is central to Diageo's production and manufacturing processes it is entirely logical that many projects demonstrate a commitment to water and sanitation provision. Constructive engagement with local communities is central to Diageo's philosophy as a corporation. The *Local Citizens* focus area acts as a way for the corporation as a whole to support Diageo's businesses in their interactions with their communities. The Diageo website listed 37 projects that have been supported via *Local Citizens*. A wide range of sub-themes are also dealt with via Diageo's overall portfolio of projects including *Disaster Relief, Leadership, Our People* and *Poverty Relief*. The impact of historical commitments upon CC spending patterns remains considerable.

Initiating projects

There are three main routes by which projects can become initiated. The majority of projects are funded through formal applications to the Foundation via the 'application toolkits' provided for each Focus Area. During the financial year 2002/2003 the Foundation received 37 fully developed project proposals from their businesses and over 700 exter-

Table 7.4 Community investment in £ Sterling by focus area, 2001–2005

Focus area	2001	2002	2003	2004	2005
Alcohol Education	4,500,000	3,700,000	6,151,000	6,354,000	7,431,000
Water of Life	160,000	200,000	160,000	375,000	1,101,000
Skills for Life				1,749,000	2,051,000
Local Citizens	10,606,000	13,071,000	12,690,000	9,044,000	12,041,000

Source: Diageo Corporate Citizenship Reports, 2003, p.17 and 2005, p.14

nal applications (Diageo Foundation, 2003). The Foundation also receives many other informal requests. Some projects become driven by the interest or passion of key Diageo employees who act as Champions. These individuals tend to have an important role to play in making the 'business case' for a project to be pursued. The CEO of Grandmet initiated the establishment of the Tomorrow's People Trust, whilst the recently established Earthwatch project is in no small part the product of lobbying by middle ranking Diageo employees. Finally, some projects are externally driven via direct approaches from leading establishment figures. A famous example within the Diageo portfolio is the Skills Centre that was developed in Colesberg, South Africa at the insistence of Nelson Mandela, who has devoted much time to persuading corporate figures of their central role in the transformation of post-apartheid South Africa (Diageo, 2004g).

The Diageo Foundation

The Diageo Foundation was established in 1997 to support the company's businesses in their community engagement endeavours. The Board appoints trustees, drawn from across Diageo's business divisions. The Director of Corporate Citizenship chairs the Foundation's meetings, whilst a member of the five-person strong CC team manages the day-to-day operations of the Foundation. The Foundation works closely with a number of specialist not-for-profit organisations that act as project partners. Foundation funds and expertise tend to be used to kick-start projects with the intention that projects will be maintained through support from local business divisions, project partners or through the attainment of self-sustainability. Thus, the impacts of the Foundation can be characterised as catalytic. The Foundation seeks to 'push out' responsibility for CC to local markets, who can then take ownership for the firm's conduct within local communities. The Foundation's budget varies from year to year. During the financial year 2003/4 the Foundation contributed £2.9 million of the total corporate CC spend of £17.5 million. The Foundation makes charitable donations, matches employee fundraising and provides funding for longer-term social investment. Considerable efforts are made to leverage further resources through matched funding and the transfer of skills and material items from Diageo's businesses. Corporate reputation consultants ProbusBNW note, 'there seem to be some potential for tensions between the independent charitable status of the Foundation and the Company's own more business focussed strategy for community investment' (ProbusBNW, p.8). Furthermore, ProbusBNW questions the precise purpose of the Foundation – 'is the Foundation a **driver** of strategic initiatives or a **supporter** of existing good causes?' (ProbusBNW, 2004, p.10).

Reporting and evaluation

Diageo has produced annual Corporate Citizenship Reports since 2003. The 2005 Report focusses mainly upon the impacts of the firm upon Society (with detailed sub-sections covering *responsible drinking, understanding consumers, community investment,* and *realising the potential of our people*). In addition, there are sections on Environment, Economy and Governance. The report is assured by the Corporate Citizenship Company and is prepared in accordance with the 2002 GRI Guidelines. Furthermore, a number of regional and country corporate citizenship reports have been published. In 2005 such reports have been published for Africa and the Seychelles. Diageo utilises the services of a range of other external bodies to evaluate their larger individual programmes and projects. The long-running *Tomorrow's People* charity (see Case Study 1) has recently been evaluated by Oxford Economic Forecasting (2004) whilst the New Economics Foundation (2003) have evaluated *Working it Out*. Partners also play a key role in performing evaluations. Earthwatch, for example, have set in place a series of systems for evaluating the Diageo-Earthwatch programme.

Case Study 1: Tomorrow's People[1]

Location: UK, some international spin-offs
Duration: 1984–present

How the programme started

The inner city riots of the early 1980s motivated Grandmet's CEO and other key players to take action against unemployment and poor social conditions. This motivation stemmed from awareness that the broader socio-economic environment was negatively affecting the business environment, to coin a phrase, 'healthy back streets equal healthy high streets'. There was also a realisation that corporate restructuring, necessitated by the business climate, would worsen social conditions. Planning for the original Trust started in 1981.

Programme outline

Tomorrow's People is a charity which helps the unemployed into work through training, advice and support. The charity was initially known as the *Grandmet Trust*, which ran government funded training programmes leading to vocational qualifications and the development of relationships between employers and clients. The charity operates as an intermediary between government, business and individuals. The unemployed are given the opportunity to gain the skills and qualifications sought by the local labour market. Once trained the clients are introduced to local businesses. By the early 1990s the Trust had a national network of 80 operational centres making it one of the UK's largest training providers.

In 1996 the Trust was renamed Tomorrow's People and the organisation's strategic objectives shifted from a training base to a broader focus on advice and mentoring, particularly for the long-term unemployed, especially those facing significant barriers to employment. Advisers now take their expertise and experience out into the community to places where the unemployed can easily access them, such as libraries, JobCentres, training providers, community groups, and shopping centres. A network of supportive employers has also been built to ensure that opportunities for progression will exist for Tomorrow's Peoples clients.

Approximately 30 programmes are currently in operation, which aim to help client groups such as single parents, the disabled and ex-offenders. Examples of programmes include, *New Steps* (targeted at 16–18 years olds who are assisted in working on community-based projects), *Working it Out* (which targets Year 11 pupils who have dropped out of mainstream education) and *Getting London Working* (a project which challenges the negative impacts of unemployment).

Tomorrow's People has 170 full-time equivalent staff and had an income of £6.1 million in 2002/3. Tomorrow's People operates as an organisation that 'conducts its activities in a philanthropic, but also highly professional and business-like manner, enabling access to other sources of funds and corporate support' (Oxford Economic Forecasting, 2004, p.3).

Working with partners

Diageo has been intimately involved with the Tomorrow's People charity (www.tomorrows-people.co.uk) since its inception. Diageo continues to be involved via donations and various forms of staff support. In March 2005 the trust became legally independent from Diageo as the firm aims to ensure the total independence and sustainability of the charity. Diageo is committed to support Tomorrow's People for a further five years.

Inputs from Diageo

Diageo has contributed financial resources worth £20 million (at today's prices) over 20 years with a further £5 million coming via other forms of financial input such as taking on unwanted property leases. Diageo's contributions represent approximately 8% of Tomorrow's People total income. Diageo personnel have been involved from the outset at many levels. Diageo's Director of Corporate Citizenship is a Trustee, chairs the advisory committee to the board and provides support to management. In total he devotes about 10% of his time to Tomorrow's People. Diageo's staff also provides information on human resource management, risk management and other specialist areas. Diageo's premises are made available for meetings, conferences and events. Work placements are offered within Diageo's business divisions and staff provide advice and mentoring support to Tomorrow's People's clients.

Outcomes for the corporation, its partners and the community

- Tomorrow's People has provided 382,000 people with assistance, of whom 165,000 have gained employment, whilst 50,000 have undertaken education/training or voluntary work. Other clients have received general advice and mentoring.
- Until the mid-1990s approximately 24,000 people per annum received assistance. The switch in strategic focus, which required more intensive work with clients, led to a drop to 7,400. At this point in time the emphasis was more upon those facing major barriers to employment such as ex-offenders, ex-addicts, the unskilled, the uneducated and the socially excluded. Successful outcomes for this more challenging clientele run at about 33% (compared to a long term average of 43%).
- Tomorrow's People's income has been in the region of £285 million (at today's prices) over 20 years. The majority has come from contracts, *Jobcentre Plus*, local and regional government, *Single Regional Funding* and the *European Social Fund*. Donations have been received from the private sector and individuals. In 2002/3 14% of total income came from the latter sources. Diageo has historically been the single highest contributor.
- It is estimated that the total benefits to society of Tomorrow's People's work has been in the region of £430 million. During this time a small charity has evolved to become a 'national force'. It has inspired innovative projects in the UK and beyond and helped create a blueprint for effective engagement between private sector and communities.

- Diageo has gained an excellent reputation as a corporate citizen, opportunities have been provided for employee involvement and partnerships have developed with local and national government actors. Diageo has benefited from strengthened links with government.
- Employees within Diageo have gained new skills and broadened their experience. Successful projects have been used as examples of best practice and applied around the world. For example, the Tomorrow's People *Bar Skills* programme has been rolled out in Brazil and other developing nations.
- Other programmes aimed at the homeless and unemployed have been established, including the *Foyer Federation, Fullemploy* and *INCLUDE* and many community programmes. Government programmes, (such as the *Welfare to Work* strategy) have also been influenced by Tomorrow's People.
- Tomorrow's People has become increasingly involved in governmental activities including: contributing submissions to House of Commons' Select Committee Inquiries on employment issues; being consulted by departments such as the UK Treasury's Cross-Cutting Review of the Role of the Voluntary Sector; providing briefing papers for members of parliament and ministers in the UK and European parliaments; and working with think-tanks such as Demos.

Evidence of sustainability

Tomorrow's People has been a tremendously influential programme stimulating a number of spin-offs within the UK and overseas. Network development has been a crucial component of the programme's evolution with contacts extending into the highest level of government. Diageo's financial and human resources have been pivotal in driving Tomorrow's People throughout its history. Diageo's ability to effect a viable exit-strategy will be the greatest test of the project's overall institutional sustainability.

How the programme is evaluated

Oxford Economic Forecasting has produced a thorough evaluation of Tomorrow's People during 2004. Individual programmes have also been evaluated, e.g. *Working it Out* was evaluated by the New Economics Foundation. The programme is also assessed regularly according to the criteria set by the LBG model.

Case Study 2: Youth Business Initiative (YBI)[2]

Location: Global
Duration: Diageo involved since 2000

How the programme started

Diageo became involved at the launch stage following requests from leading figures behind YBI to support the launch Conference, which took place in October 2000.

Programme outline

The Youth Business International (YBI) is taking a lead in working with business to support and promote youth entrepreneurship around the world. It is an international network of programmes helping disadvantaged young people (usually 18–30 year olds although in some countries the range broadens to incorporate 16–35 year olds) to become entrepreneurs by providing start-up funds and mentoring. YBI is a unit of The Prince of Wales *International Business Leaders Forum* (IBLF). Paul Walsh, Diageo's Chief Executive, sits on the board of IBLF. YBI works alongside local partners such as business, governments and NGOs to help young people into work and to build their self-esteem, prosperity and future prospects. In 2000 the United Nations (UN) adopted a series of Millennium Development Goals one of which focussed on *'decent and productive work for youth'*. A Youth Employment Network was established focussing upon employment creation, equality, entrepreneurship and employability. The YBI was selected to work within the entrepreneurship group. Diageo has been involved with YBI in a number of community projects around the world through its *Keep Walking Fund*.

YBI projects operate through the provision of seed capital that enable the young person to start their own business. These loans have to be repaid and a nominal administration charge is made. Loans average between US$250–$5000 depending on the relative cost of living in each country. Business mentoring is a core component of the programme whereby a volunteer business person acts as a friend, guide and coach to the young entrepreneur over the first three years of their new venture.

The projects are components of autonomous national programmes that adopt and adapt the YBI model to local needs and conditions. Youth business programmes join the YBI network once the central YBI unit accredits them. The Johnnie Walker *Keep Walking Fund* has operated a joint programme with YBI in India and Mexico. Diageo presently has an 'ongoing, ad-hoc, informal commitment to support YBI'.

Working with partners

Diageo sits on YBI's advisory council, which includes representatives from the Prince's Trust, PriceWaterhouseCoopers, Rotary International and Lovells. Individual YBI projects link in with locally specific partners.

Inputs from Diageo

It is estimated that resources totalling £500k have been donated (to October 2004). This sum comprises: annual subscription to the IBLF; in-market partnerships with YBI in India and Mexico; a commitment to run future programmes in Latin America and China; and part sponsorship of, and presence at, YBI's global conference in Buenos Aires, Oct 2004.

A number of key Diageo personnel are committed to supporting YBI activities. These include: the Head of Diageo Corporate Citizenship who is a member of YBI's International Steering Committee and along with the Head of External Affairs, Latin America is on YBI's Latin American Advisory Group; two Finance Directors have assisted in developing the Youth Development Bond (a tool to package and merchandise the youth entrepreneurship model); a firm Consultant has helped develop YBI's brand essence; a Marketing Director has been seconded to YBI for six months to develop a global marketing plan for the Youth Development Bonds and create a new brand identity for YBI; and Diageo's General Manager in India is a trustee of YBI's local venture.

Outcomes for the corporation, its partners and the community

- YBI is run by a small team and has therefore benefited from its link with Diageo in a number of areas. YBI has benefited from developing a partnership with a global organisation experienced in fostering local partnerships. Funding is provided at global and local levels, such as sponsorship of the YBI conference and local support for programmes and projects.
- Diageo has provided marketing and financial expertise, which has assisted with brand positioning, brand building strategies and innovation (e.g. input into creation and development of Youth Development Bond, a financial instrument for seed-funding of young entrepreneurs).
- Diageo personnel have been appointed as members of advisory committees. In India and Mexico, employees have become mentors

and this support is expected to increase in Latin America. Access to Diageo's corporate contacts and partners has been provided.
- A Project Advisory Committee has been initiated in Latin America in order to build a network of corporations to develop CSR and to support YBI projects as part of the Inter American Development Bank project.
- The individual local YBI projects allow Diageo's business knowledge and experience to be transferred, thus helping young people seeking to build SMEs. Marginalised young people have been able to develop their potential by accessing formal business networks. The support of mentors significantly increases the sustainability of start-ups.
- Each new entrepreneur tends to stimulate the creation of two new jobs, this increases employment, reduces youth alienation and associated social problems and helps to generate wealth. Youth entrepreneurs are given a route out of the informal sector.
- Spin-offs include Youth Development Bonds (YDBs), which have been devised to package and merchandise the youth entrepreneurship model. These are being piloted in Argentina, Canada and China. Diageo is providing assistance in putting together a brand plan for this international roll-out. The UN, World Bank and ILO have established the Youth Employment Network (YEN) to promote youth entrepreneurship globally and are supporting YDBs as a means towards achieving the Millennium Development Goal to provide *'decent and productive work for youth'*.
- The YBI partnership offers Diageo's local markets an opportunity to work with governments, business and civil societies in the promotion of youth entrepreneurship.
- Diageo's employees have benefited from opportunities to act as business mentors to young entrepreneurs or panel members on a volunteer basis. Diageo's presence at the YBI conference provides exposure to representatives from UN, ILO, World Bank, Governments and the International Youth Foundation. Thus, Diageo has been able to strengthen and deepen its networks of association, particularly with globally influential institutions. For example, the World Bank is providing US$5 million to promote the YBI model in Latin America; Diageo, Unilever and BP have been approached to advise on this.
- India and China are keen to develop the concept as a solution to youth poverty – both governments hosted high profile summits in 2004. Diageo has strong business interests in these countries. HM Treasury have also shown an interest.

- There have also been some benefits to Diageo's Johnnie Walker whisky brand in its leverage of the Johnnie Walker *Keep Walking*/YBI partnership. The corporate learning outcomes from the association between Johnnie Walker and YBI are clear and have led to a focus on corporate rather than brand association.

Evidence of sustainability

YBI has demonstrated many characteristics of effective sustainability. The sheer density of high level actors within the YBI network is indicative of enduring institutional strength. Importantly, YBI does not appear to be overly dependent on any single organisation for financial or institutional support. The extent to which the programme is being spun off around the world is also an important indicator of the sustainability of the YBI model.

How the programme is evaluated

The partnership between Diageo and YBI is relatively recent and it is therefore too early to fully evaluate the effectiveness of the relationship. However, a thorough internal review of the programme was conducted within Diageo during 2004. Local projects tend to be evaluated at the discretion of local partners.

Case Study 3: Diageo-Earthwatch Champions Programme[3]

Location: Global spread within Diageo markets
Duration: Since 2002

How the programme started

The programme gained its initial impetus from two Diageo employees, one of whom had participated in an Earthwatch project as a Millennium Volunteer. These individuals were heavily involved in the internal persuasion process – 'making the business case'. One of these individuals is still involved in the promotion, development and administration of the programme within Diageo. An approach was made to the Diageo Foundation and the programme evolved from there. Earthwatch's excellent reputation and Diageo's past involvement with them via *Water of Life* projects facilitated the process. Diageo gained an awareness of other corporations' partnerships with Earthwatch through its membership of the Corporate Environmental Research Group (CERG).

Programme outline

Employees from across the entire corporation (see Table 7.5 below) are invited to apply for a place on a two-week conservation research project run by the Earthwatch Institute. The 15 employees selected (from 243 applications in 2003) are known as 'environmental champions'. They subsequently attend one of six projects chosen by the CC team at Diageo with the support of Earthwatch (see list below). In the first year of the programme the field projects involved the themes of water and forests. Now agriculture, biodiversity and climate change are emerging as key themes. These projects bring together Diageo employees from different parts of the world, who work on the project with a mix of international volunteers and individuals sponsored by other corporations. On their return from the field the employees undergo a personal development review with their line manager and subsequently identify and implement a local environmentally-based project (known as a Local Action Plan, LAP) using the knowledge and skills they have gained in the field. An e-forum through which the Champions can share ideas, frustrations and experiences is intended to facilitate the delivery of the LAPs. The centrality of environmental sustainability and employee development to the programme's ethos reinforces its relevance to current CC strategy.

Table 7.5   Geographical distribution of environmental champions 2003–2004

Region	Number of winners	Percentage of winners	Number of employees	Percentage of employees
Europe	13	43.33	11625	47.33
North America	6	20	3914	15.94
Asia Pacific	3	10	2681	10.92
Africa	7	14	5025	20.46
Latin America	1	3	1316	5.36

Table 7.6   Selection of Earthwatch field projects attended by Diageo's champions

1) Brazil's Pantanal: Conserving an Ecosystem
2) Costa Rica's Tropical Forest
3) Lakes of the Rift Valley
4) Mountain Waters of Bohemia
5) Rainforests of Northern Australia
6) South Africa's Hidden Species

Working with partners

The Earthwatch Institute (Europe) is the principal partner, (www.earthwatch.org). Earthwatch takes the lead in most aspects of the day-to-day running of the programme. For example, Earthwatch draws up shortlists of potential field projects, shortlists potential winners from the employee applications and supports Champions in the development of their LAPs. An efficient, mutually beneficial working relationship exists between Diageo and Earthwatch. Diageo takes an active role in the partnership and seeks to input ideas and resources throughout the process. Various Diageo business sections are involved in the process including risk management experts, the environmental working group and the CC team. Diageo has made a transition from being donors to being active partners in project delivery. Each project (both in the field and in the locality) involves co-operation from local partners. The precise nature of the relationship between Diageo and its local partners varies from project to project.

Inputs from Diageo

Diageo input approximately £100K per year to the programme, which covers Earthwatch's fees for the projects. The individual business divisions meet the cost of travel and one week's extra paid leave. The employee contributes a week of their paid leave entitlement and contributes their own time to the development of the LAPs. Line managers may occasionally include the delivery of the LAP within a Champion's job description. The costs of the local projects are usually covered through the Diageo Foundation, mainly via *Water of Life*. In Years 3 and 4 the Foundation is seeking to reduce the level of centralised inputs by 50%. Local businesses will then be expected to meet the costs of the LAPs in full. This approach is consistent with Diageo's broader policy of encouraging project self-sustainability. After 2006 efforts will be made to embed the programme within the businesses, thus moving away completely from financial inputs from the Foundation. Work is ongoing to ensure buy-in from the local business heads. It is estimated that Diageo's CC team input approximately two 'man-months' to planning and administering each annual cycle.

Outcomes for the corporation, its partners and communities

- The execution of the programme has proved to be an excellent internal communications exercise for Diageo as effective information flows are required across all divisions and subsidiaries of the corporation across the globe. This is an important element of the

evolution of Diageo as a coherent global company and can be seen as part of the drive to establish an internal Diageo brand.
- A Champion based in Australia commented that it initially seemed implausible that a person in a distant outpost of the corporation could possibly win – *'I have now shown that it is possible to get there – even for employees all the way Down Under'*. Thus, the programme does help to promote a sense of unity within the global corporate structure.
- There have been important dividends in terms of the Champions' personal and professional development, for example, learning about team dynamics and new ways of approaching problem solving. The enthusiasm of the Champions can have beneficial impacts upon colleagues and tends to stimulate volunteering via the LAP.
- In addition, the first Earthwatch programme enabled employees to contribute 1500 hours of work to conservation, in countries such as Australia, Kenya, Costa Rica and opportunities to work with local partners including communities have been stimulated via the LAPs.

Evidence of sustainability

During its initial years the Earthwatch programme has been dependent upon funding from Diageo. For the programme to prove sustainable in the longer term it will be important for local businesses to commit to maintaining their support through the input of financial resources. The sustainability of individual Local Action Plans varies from place to place. Where there is strong local commitment new practices and initiatives will become embedded within daily operations. However, in other locations management buy-in may not be as strong and the LAP process will make little impact.

How the programme is evaluated

Earthwatch evaluate each field project and report back to Diageo. Line managers utilise the programme as a focus within Champions' personal development reviews. Earthwatch review each annual cycle of field projects and report back to Diageo. Progress with the local projects is closely monitored.

Local Action Plans

Outline

On return from their field project Champions are expected to initiate and deliver a Local Action Plan (LAP) based in or around their place of work. Both the Diageo Foundation and Earthwatch support this process. The latter appoints a community advisor to assist the Champion in identifying and planning their project. Funding for these projects has been obtainable from the Diageo Foundation's *Water of Life* programme with approximately £3.5k being set aside for each project. Champions are usually expected to work on the project in their own time, although some line managers have built this work into people's job descriptions where there is a business case for doing so.

The types of project initiated by Champions have varied considerably in their scale and scope, reflecting the embryonic nature of the programme, the diversity of local needs and perhaps the varying ability of individual Champions to command access to resources. Thus, some projects have been relatively small in scale, such as the introduction of litterbins to a factory site, whereas others have impacted directly upon business practices, such as changing product-packaging processes, whilst others have focussed exclusively upon microelements of the local ecosystem, such as encouraging the nesting of specific bird species. An interesting element of the programme has been the way that it has kick-started many 'nice to do' environmental projects, which otherwise would have remained on the drawing board. Several LAPs include paper and plastic recycling, for example, which required on-site Champions to get them off the ground.

A selection of Local Action Plan projects, 2003 and 2004

1) Pollution in the local (Cheshire, UK) landscape, improving a neglected wildlife area and recycling at the Diageo packing plant.
2) Conservation of Sand Martin species and habitat management (Scotland).
3) Greening site at Diageo Maryland including recycling.
4) Standardising environmentally friendly packaging at Diageo plants and providing recycling bins for mineral water bottles used by staff (Italy).
5) Reducing litter around Benin City and Guinness Nigeria sites. Introducing paper recycling.
6) Conservation related to effects of chemical and water pollution upon a local river (Philippines).
7) Project H_2O – improved water efficiency at Huntingford factory site in Australia.

Outcomes for the corporation, its partners and the community

- The Earthwatch Environmental Champions programme is particularly interesting as the LAP element offers an opportunity to further the benefits gained through the field project.
- Various stakeholders are in a position to gain through the LAPs. The Champions themselves are able to disseminate their new found knowledge and enthusiasm, the local community may benefit, the Champion's colleagues can be drawn in to new ventures, the business can benefit from the increased motivation levels amongst staff and the local environment will benefit.
- Best practice examples of LAPs are now under development, which will assist future Champions in identifying and delivering workable projects.

Case study 4: Projeto Bartender, Brazil[4]

Location: Pilot in Sao Paulo, then rolled out to other cities
Duration: Started June 2000

How the programme started

The programme began in 2000, when the company felt the necessity to make a social contribution. Diageo established a citizenship committee with 12 employees who considered the necessity to take action related to the business but which would help the society. They devised the Bartender Project, which is a course offering professional skills to young people on low incomes.

Programme outline

The programme trains young (usually 18–21) unemployed people in bartending skills via a 4–8 month course. The national commercial training service (Servicio Nacional de Aprendizaje Comercial – SENAC) advertises the programme and takes charge of the selection procedures. The following criteria are applied: applicants cannot have a family income superior to three times the minimum salary, which is around US$260 per month, they must be between 18 and 21 years old and unemployed. SENAC analyse the candidates' profiles and call them for an interview, in order to ensure that the programme and its conditions meet their expectations. This process reduces the number of people giving up in the middle of the course.

The programme includes work experience. Two months of the course are spent on citizenship and the promotion of responsible alcohol consumption. Field trips to bars, restaurants, drink plants and museums take place. Conferences are provided with talks from restaurant owners, bartenders and industry experts, including Diageo staff. Course includes training in: IT, health and hygiene, presentation skills, customer service, consumer rights, labour legislation and serving skills. Understanding the role of the Bartender in promoting responsible drinking is essential to the course. The students are taught about the social problems that alcohol abuse can cause. The pilot projects were conducted in urban areas with key On-Trade accounts.

Working with partners

The training provider SENAC, are the primary partners in the scheme. Local organisation 'English Culture' contributes basic English lessons. An external consultant supervises the execution of the programme in every city. In Curitiba, Diageo has just established a very good partnership with bar and restaurant owners, who are sponsoring some of the students. Diageo keeps them posted on the evolution of the programme, the partners are invited to contribute to activities, such as lectures on alcohol responsibility, parents meetings and so forth. They usually provide an opportunity for the students to complete their training programme in their bars and restaurants. Hotel chains such as Accor have been key employers. Barbecue Restaurants were formal partners in the programme but the partnership was discontinued because they require waiters rather than bartenders. Operational matters are organised through the training agency, but Diageo aims to maintain a very close relationship with the other partners because they are Diageo's clients in the market. An exit strategy has been built into the scheme via the development of strategic partnerships with On-Trade clients. The intention is to rollout the project via independent partners. There is an intention to produce a spin-off project aimed at older, low-income unemployed servers. Tomorrow's People are being solicited to provide support for the venture.

Inputs from Diageo

The Diageo Foundation has contributed £60,000 annually for three years with an extra £20,000 coming from other sources. Since 2001/2 funding has been increasingly sourced via On-Trade clients in order to achieve some level of project self-sustainability. Diageo pays for the course entirely, unless there are other sponsors as in Curitiba. Diageo gives employees the opportunity to volunteer either lecturing to the students on their specific area of work or being shadowed during the execution of their duties. The On-Trade partners play an important role by helping students to find a job when they graduate. One-third of Guinness UDV Brazil employees have provided voluntary assistance. Each employee contributes approximately one hour per month to the project. External Affairs and Human Resources offer management support. Volunteers from Finance, Marketing and Human Resources initiated the business plan, set the objectives and checked the resource allocation and budgeting arrangements. No financial support is offered to the students but Diageo tries to negotiate with the training agency in terms of ensuring the provision of extra items like transport and snacks, according to the needs of people in each different city. People from Recife (North East of Brazil) tend to have more difficulties and they require more support. Diageo endeavours to adapt and respect people's regional culture and background.

Outcomes for the corporation, its partners and the community

- All 54 students involved in the pilot gained work with the On-Trade. More than 150 students have graduated in the Sao Paulo area. Of the first 50 graduates in Sao Paulo ten graduates were employed as trainees at partner firm Barbecue Restaurants, 12 went to Accor and On-Trade clients took on 18. The project is now in its fourth year in Sao Paulo and three years have been completed in Rio de Janeiro. Seventy percent of Rio students have gained linked employment. Fifty-nine students have graduated from Recife (home of Smirnoff and Bell's bottling plants) programme (40% female). The programme has been extended to Curitiba and Salvador.
- The scheme has demonstrated Diageo's commitment to corporate citizenship by targeting alcohol education and providing assistance to disadvantaged young people. Diageo has concrete cases where this course changed not only the student's life but also their family's quality of life as a whole.
- Other hospitality-related industry members are considering becoming involved. On-Trade owners consider the trainees to be highly qualified and very well trained. The project motivates Diageo's employees and helps to build closer relationships with outside clients. It provides opportunities for positive PR exposure for the drinks industry. Overall, it is *'an educational project that's also a strategic initiative'*.

- Recognition has been gained from Federal government as the Secretary of Health attended a certificate awarding ceremony. Diageo has gained government recognition as providers of an outstanding preparation course for first-time job seekers.
- The programme has spread to other markets (including Bangkok and Venezuela) as an example of best practice and Diageo has recently received a request from Australia for more details on how to implement the programme.

Evidence of sustainability

Projeto Bartender has been ongoing for several years. The gradual transition to funding via the On-Trade is indicative of the sustainability of both the delivery model and the underlying concept driving the development of the project. The spread of the project within Brazil and other markets is further evidence of the enduring nature of the project and its principles.

How the programme is evaluated

The programme is reviewed by the training providers and by Diageo in Brazil.

Project-by-project assessment of social capital impacts

In this section we summarise the social capital aspects of each project. We conclude by using the format of Table 4.1 to create a table, which allows a comparison of the social capital elements of each project (see Table 7.7).

Tomorrow's People

The Tomorrow's People project is a first class example of the beneficial social capital impacts that an MNC can generate through its engagements with broader society. Potent social capital impacts are evident in several areas. Such extensive and profound impacts result from the lengthy duration of involvement on the part of Diageo and the range of resource inputs invested into the programme. The programme is particularly notable for the fact that it has consistently succeeded in improving people's employability when other programmes, especially government sponsored ones, have struggled to make a lasting impact. Thus, government failures have been corrected and employment stability promoted. The project has succeeded in bridging structural holes by drawing together organisations and individuals with the skills and aptitudes to challenge the problem of long-standing unemployment. Network development has been particularly strong at both interpersonal and interorganisational levels. Very important vertical relationships have been developed linking local bodies with national ones. In this regard there have been very important dividends for Diageo in terms of developing links with the UK government. Whilst the final resources donated by Diageo have clearly been instrumental to the enduring success of Tomorrow's People it is the human inputs that have enabled the project to stand out. Commitment from the highest levels of the firm has been crucial in facilitating social capital development in so many realms and ultimately rendering the project a model of best practice. However, such profound levels of involvement do pose problems for the firm in terms of making it difficult to scale down its engagement.

YBI

YBI is another programme that scores very well in social capital development terms. Due to the programme's institutional density it is difficult to identity the precise impacts generated by the involvement of Diageo. However, the fact that Diageo is involved at the highest level of the programme and has invested considerable resources is indicative of the extent of their impacts. High level network development involving influential institutional actors is perhaps one of the most potent processes occurring during the evolution of YBI. Important person-to-person interventions are evident both at the highest institutional level of YBI and in the delivery of individual projects at country level. Collective action is very important in challenging government's market failures and thus in the promotion of employment stability. Ultimately YBI scores well in terms of its impacts upon all forms of social capital development. This is to be expected due to the project's intrinsic structure which relies upon strong institutional development at the global and national levels facilitating the delivery of effective local programmes. There are important social capital outcomes for Diageo as their role in the YBI enables the firm to be involved in influential networks incorporating national governments in the firm's venture markets. YBI projects are an important way for the firm to build trust with consumers and government in such markets.

Earthwatch

The social capital outcomes from the Earthwatch programme are relatively limited. This is due to the nature of the programme whereby the particular skills of the Earthwatch Champions are relatively unimportant in terms of their contribution to the field project and there is little scope for significant network development or skill/knowledge transfer. Indeed, whilst the work completed through the Earthwatch programme is extremely worthy some observers have noted that the programme's full potential is not developed due to the way that the programme is commonly practised. Diageo's variant of the Earthwatch programme does, however, generate some social capital developmental through its follow-up LAPs. At a local level these can stimulate beneficial outcomes including the promotion of positive norms of behaviour in relation to attitudes to the environment and the promotion of goodwill within the firm. Indeed, many of the beneficial outcomes are internalised within the firm itself in terms of building networks amongst the Champions and in promoting cohesion and structural ties across the firm.

Table 7.7 Diageo case studies – summary assessment of social capital impacts

		Tomorrow's People	YBI	Earthwatch	Projeto Bartender
Scope-					
Micro:	Person to person	***	***	**	**
Meso:	Vertical relationships	***	**	*	**
Macro:	Institutional	***	***	*	**
Form-					
Structural:	Networks	***	***	**	**
	Bridging structural holes	***	**	*	**
	New membership	**	**	*	*
	Ties & glue/lubricant	**	**	**	*
Cognitive:	Competence/goodwill	***	***	***	**
Channel-					
Information:	Improve education	***	**		**
Collective action:	Correct government/ social failure	***	***		**
Misc:	Employment stability	***	***		***
	Cohesion:	***	**	**	**
	Radius of trust/distrust	**	**	*	*
	Norms of behaviour	***	**	**	***

Key: no stars = minimal impact, * = some impact, ** = notable impact, *** = potent impact.

Projeto Bartender

The Bartender project produces a good range of positive impacts upon social capital. The primary objective of this programme is to tackle joblessness amongst young people, thus making a contribution to the promotion of employment stability. The programme also generates very important dividends in terms of the norms that it promotes. For example, trainee bartenders learn how to spot counterfeit liquor, are encouraged to work in the formal sector and are trained to promote responsible drinking practices amongst their clients. There are notable impacts in terms of network development as various public and private sector bodies are involved in the delivery of the bartender project. These come into play through the direct contribution of Diageo's Brazilian-based staff to the delivery of the project including face to face contact with trainees. The input of corporate human resource managers is particularly important in placing the trainees in jobs. At present many of these impacts may best be judged as 'notable'. However, if the project continues to be successfully scaled up, operating within more localities in Brazil and even being rolled out into other international markets then the project is likely to have achieved potent impacts across a wide range of criteria.

Notes

1 Sources: Diageo, 2004a; Diageo, 2004b; Diageo, 2004e; New Economics Foundation, 2003; Oxford Economic Forecasting, 2004; Tomorrow's People, 2004.
2 Sources: Diageo, 2003c; Diageo, 2003d; Diageo, 2004c; IBLF, 2004; Prince's Trust, 2004; Youth Business, 2003.
3 Sources: Diageo, 2004d; Diageo, 2004k; Diageo, 2004l; Earthwatch, 2003; Earthwatch, 2004a; Earthwatch, 2004b; Earthwatch, 2004c; Earthwatch and Diageo, 2004; Wallace, 2003. Secondary sources have been supplemented by primary data supplied in interviews and electronic communications with Earthwatch Champions and Earthwatch's Corporate Liaison Manager.
4 Sources: Anon, 2004; Daniele, 2003; Diageo, 2001; Diageo, 2004f; Diageo Brazil, 2004; Guinness UDV, 2000; Senac Brazil, 2004. Secondary sources have been supplemented by primary data supplied via electronic communications with a Diageo representative in Brazil.

References

Anon (2004), *English Culture- Bartender Project*. Available at: www.culturainglesasp.com.br/prospects/perfil/proj_soc/bartenders.jsp. Accessed 17/08/2004.

Business in the Community (2002), *Community Involvement 2002, Corporate Community Investment 2002*. Available at: www.bitc.org.uk/ resources/case_studies/diageo.html. Accessed 10/09/2004.

Corporate Citizenship Company (2004), *Case study – Pilot Initiative in Poland*. Available at: www.corporate-citizenship.co.uk/social/casestudy.asp. Accessed 02/08/2004.

Daniele, P. (2003), *Program Education for the Work of the Senac enables young to the market*. Available at: http://216.239.39.104/translate_c?hl=en&sl=pt&u= http://www.setor3.com.br/senac2/cala. Accessed 17/08/2004.

Diageo (2001), *Tomorrows' People in Brazil: The Bartender Project*. Available at: http://www.diageo.com/download%5C3000—R160.pdf. Accessed 02/08/2004.

Diageo (2003a), *Annual Review*, Diageo plc, London.

Diageo (2003b), *Corporate Citizenship Report*, Diageo plc, London.

Diageo (2003c), *Diageo announces Youth Development Bond at Asian Summit on Youth Entrepreneurship, India*. Available at: http://www.diageo.com/pageengine.asp?site_id=0&section_id=0&page_id=1042&status_id=3000. Accessed 03/08/2004.

Diageo (2003d), *Diageo India support creates new enterprises, jobs and productive partnerships*. Available at: http://www.diageo.com/pageengine.asp?menu_id=0&site_id=4&section_id=21&page_id=736. Accessed 08/08/2004.

Diageo (2004a), *Case study: Tomorrow's People helps thousands find work*. Available at: www.diageo.com/pageengine.asp?menu_id=0&site_id=4&section_id=21&page. Accessed 04/08/2004.

Diageo (2004b), *Diageo – Supporting Tomorrow's People Trust*. Available at: http://www.diageo.com/pageengine.asp?site_id=4&section_id=21&page_id=783. Accessed 08/07/2004.

Diageo (2004c), *'Diageo Corporate Citizenship Case Study: A Partnership with Youth Business International'*, Internal management report.

Diageo (2004d), *The Diageo Earthwatch Champions programme*. Available at: http://www.diageo.com/pageengine.asp?site_id=4&section_id=21&page_id=899. Accessed 04/08/2004.

Diageo (2004e), *Diageo helps Fullemploy build a more inclusive society*. Available at: http://www.diageo.com/pageengine.asp?site_id=4&section_id=21&page_id=799. Accessed 07/07/2004.

Diageo (2004f), *Factfile: Diageo India support creates new enterprises, jobs and productive partnerships*. Available at: http://www.diageo.com/pageengine.asp?menu_id =0&site_id=4&section_id=21&page_id=700. Accessed 27/07/2004.

Diageo (2004g), *Guinness South Africa – Skills for Life Centre*. Available at: http://www.diageo.com/pageengine.asp?site_id=4&section_id=21&page_id=759. Accessed 15/08/2004.

Diageo (2004h), *Our history*. Available at: http://www.diageo.com/pageengine.asp?status_id= 3000&page_id=22&site_id=3&section_id=24. Accessed 13/09/2004.

Diageo (2004i), *Thalidomide long-term issue*. Available at: http://www.diageo.com/pageengine.asp?site_id=4&section_id=21&page_id=811. Accessed 13/09/2004.

Diageo (2004j), *"Water of Life" funding application toolkit*. Available at: http://www.diageo.com/pageengine.asp?menu_id=0&site_id=4&section_id=21&page_id=1008. Accessed 20/08/2004.

Diageo (2004k), *What is the Earthwatch Programme?* Available at: http://diageo24.intranet.diageo/CorpCommWebApp/CorpCommCMSPortal.portal?_nf. Accessed 04/08/2004.

Diageo (2004l), *'What's new? Diageo Earthwatch Champions Programme'*, May 2004 Special Edition internal newsletter.

Diageo Brazil (2004), *'The Bartender Project, Hospitality Training for Low-Income Young Adults'*, Internal powerpoint presentation.

Diageo Foundation (2003), *'Trustees' report and financial statements'*, Diageo.

Earthwatch (2003), *Champions Programme Report 2002 and 2003*, internal evaluation document.

Earthwatch (2004a), *About the Corporate Environmental Responsibility Group*. Available at: www.earthwatch.org/europe/corporate/aboutcerg.html. Accessed 10/08/2004.

Earthwatch (2004b), *'Become an Earthwatch Champion'*, promotional material.

Earthwatch (2004c), *Mountain Waters of Bohemia*. Available at: www.earthwatch.org/expeditions/krecek.html. Accessed 10/08/2004.

Earthwatch and Diageo (2004), *'Diageo Earthwatch Programme Management'*, internal management document.

Guinness UDV (2000), *Bartender, O Manual do profissional de bar*, published by Guinness UDV, Latin America.

IBLF (2004), *Education and leadership development – the corporate response*. Available at: http://www.iblf.org/csr/csrwebassist.nsf/content/a1a2e3b4.html. Accessed 31/07/2004.

LBG (2004), *The Corporate Responsibility Group*. Available at: www.lbg-online.net/about/crg.asp. Accessed 02/08/2004.

New Economics Foundation (2003), *Working it Out*, project evaluation.

NYSE Magazine (2004), *Under CEO Paul Walsh, Diageo has sold off its food holdings to focus on premium drinks*. Available at: www.nyse.com/events/1047970081651.html. Accessed 02/09/2004.

Oxford Economic Forecasting (2004), *'Twenty-year Evaluation of the Tomorrow's People Trust'*, Draft final report August 2004.

Prince's Trust (2004), *Pump up the volume*. Available at: www.princes-trust.org.uk/Main%2520Site%2520v2/downloads/the%2520business%2520spring%252004.pdf+princes+trust+ybi&hl=en. Accessed 31/07/2004.

ProbusBNW (2004), *ProbusBNW CCI Index 2004/5: Report for Diageo*. Available at: http://www.diageo.com/report/downloads/cci_index_report.pdf. Accessed 23/05/2006.

Senac Brazil (2004), *Institutional Profile*. Available at: http://www.sp.senac.br/jsp/default.jsp?newsID=a1158.htm&testeira=544&sub=3. Accessed 29/09/2004.

Tomorrow's People (2004), *'Working Wonders. Celebrating Tomorrow's People's 20 years of helping the UK defeat long-term unemployment'*, Tomorrow's People, Hastings.

Wallace, J. (2003), *Mountain Waters of Bohemia*, internal evaluation document.

Youth Business (2003), *Diageo*. Available at: http://www.youth-business.org/YBI/Homepage/1,2289,Support-304-3041-0-0-2-0,00.html. Accessed 31/07/2004.

8
Anglo American and its Corporate Citizenship Programme

A brief corporate biography

Anglo American, which is comprised of various subsidiaries, joint ventures and associates, is one of the world's largest corporations within the mining and natural resource sectors (AMVESCAP, 2005; Anglo American, 2004b). The corporation has significant interests in a range of products including gold, platinum, diamonds, coal, base and ferrous metals, industrial minerals and forest products. The corporation was founded in 1917 by Sir Ernest Oppenheimer in order to exploit South Africa's gold reserves (Anglo American, 2005f). Business interests within the Southern African region grew in subsequent years: Anglo became the largest shareholder in De Beers; the company instigated development of the Zambian copperbelt and became involved in the exploitation of platinum group ores in South Africa. Further business and geographical diversification followed in subsequent decades as the company built businesses or made acquisitions within the coal, steel and paper industries. The company also developed interests in chemicals, construction, newspapers and financial services. From the mid-late 1990s, accelerating after 1999, considerable corporate restructuring was undertaken including the sale of non resource-based businesses and the 'unravelling many of the cross holdings which had previously characterised many leading South African corporations'. Thus, various subsidiaries were bought out and operational functions within De Beers were streamlined.

In May 1999 Anglo American Corporation of South Africa was combined with Minorco and the new company was listed in London (primary listing), Johannesburg and Switzerland. Subsequently the company has disposed of $10 billion of non-core assets (such as indus-

> *Examples of Anglo American plc's subsidiaries, joint ventures and associates (as of May 2006):*
>
> - **Anglo Coal** is wholly owned by Anglo American plc and has mining operations in South Africa, Colombia, Venezuela and Australia.
> - Anglo American plc owns a 41.8% stake in its independently managed subsidiary **AngloGold**, which is one of the world's leading gold producers.
> - The group owns a significant stake (74.8%) in **Anglo Platinum** which has the highest market capitalisation of any platinum mining company.
> - A 45% shareholding in **De Beers Investments**, world leaders in diamond exploration, mining and marketing.
> - Anglo American owns (100%) **Anglo Base Metals**, which has copper, zinc, nickel and mineral sands operations in South America, Africa and, Ireland.
> - **Anglo Industrial Minerals** (100%) has two subsidiaries – **Tarmac** (100%), construction materials in Europe and **Copebras** (73%), a Brazilian producer of phosphate fertilizers and related materials.
> - **Mondi Packaging** (100%) is a leading player in the business papers and corrugated packaging sectors in both Europe and South Africa.
>
> Sources: AMVESCAP, 2005; Anglo American, 2004b.

trial and financial services) and acquired $15 billion of new businesses as of May 2006. The latter include: Tarmac plc in the UK, Shell's coal interests in Australia and Venezuela, Chilean-based low cost copper producer Disputada and Russian forest enterprise business Skytyvkar, which has strengthened Mondi's European paper and packaging interests. The company operates in more than 50 countries worldwide (AMVESCAP, 2005). In October 2005 the firm announced that it intended to further rationalise its assets and to focus increasingly upon its core mining business. The company has announced plans to reduce its shareholding in AngloGold Ashanti, whilst paper, steel, aluminium and sugar subsidiaries all face disposal as the firm looks to transform itself from a diversified South African giant into a global mining company (Economist, 2006).

Table 8.1   Regional data for Anglo American plc 2004

	South Africa	Rest of Africa	Europe	Americas	Australia/ Asia
Operating profit (by origin) $US millions	1318	452	818	1721	229
% contrib. to operating profit	29	10	18	38	5
Employees ('000)	127	22	42	12	6
% of total employees	61	11	20	6	3
CSI as % of total	76	4	11	8	1

Sources: Financial data from Anglo American plc Annual Report 2004, pp.55 and 58. CSI data from Anglo American plc Report to Society 2004, p.33.

N.B. Figures include group subsidiaries, joint ventures and associates.

Corporate citizenship – strategy and management

'The aim of this group is, and will remain, to make profits for our shareholders, but to do so in such a way as to make a real and lasting contribution to the communities in which we operate', Anglo American founder Sir Ernest Oppenheimer, 1954.

Anglo American's 'Good Citizenship' business principles define the firm's approach to business conduct (Anglo American, 2005h). These principles cover issues of business integrity, obligations to stakeholders, human and labour rights, safety, health and environmental issues. These principles apply to all the firm's operations and the company seeks to apply comparable standards to significant suppliers and to associates and joint ventures. The staging of the World Summit on Sustainable Development in Johannesburg in 2002 acted as a stimulus to Anglo American to re-conceptualise the nature of the relationship with the environment and society. From this point forward 'Sustainable Development' has been deployed to capture the ways in which the firm interfaces with physical and human environments. The Chairman's Foreword to the 2004 Report to Society (Anglo American, 2004a) specifies the ways in which the firm conceptualises its relationship with broader society; whilst 'there must be boundaries to corporate responsibility...we cannot disengage from the societies in which we work'. The benefits of this approach include making Anglo American 'more acceptable as an investor, as an employee, as a neighbour and a business partner...reduc(ing) risk and increasing the sustainability of our business'. Corporate citizenship is treated as one specific component of sustainable development. Corporate Citizenship is not delivered through a dedicated CSR department, instead a more devolved management structure has been deployed cutting across Safety, Health and Environment (SHE), Human Resources and External Affairs (Anglo American, 2005h). Each year individual operations report to their divisional CEO outlining progress in complying with the firm's SHE and Good Citizenship principles (Interview with Head of External Affairs). These reports are aggregated at a divisional level and written as detailed Letters of Assurance to the Board. These are discussed by the Board and the Chief Executive then responds individually to the letters outlining areas for improvement. It is interesting to note that Anglo American refers to Corporate Social Investment (CSI) – a term used widely by South African-based corporations to refer to their corporate citizenship spending. Whilst the firm notes that 'we are increasingly integrating sustainable development concepts into our core business practices' (Anglo American, 2005h), some critics, in this instance Friends of the Earth International, present a different perspective, 'Anglo has a poor social and environmental track record' (Friends of the Earth, 2004; see also Corporate Watch, 2005).

Reporting

Anglo American produces an annual 'Report to Society' (Anglo American, 2005a) which, for each of the last four years, have focussed upon 'sustainable development'. In 2002 the report was entitled 'Towards Sustainable Development', in 2003 'Working for Sustainable Development', in 2004 'Creating Enduring Value' and in 2005 'A climate of change'. The 2004 Report is structured around the five capitals model of sustainable development via the following chapter headings, 'Sustainable Development, Governance and Ethics, Economic Value, Human Capital, Social Capital, Natural Capital, Man Made Environment'. Human Capital refers to safety, occupational health, training, whilst Social Capital refers to community development, corporate social investment, HIV/AIDS, human rights and ethics. The Corporate Responsibility section of the 2004 Annual Review opens as follows, 'During 2004 Anglo American pursued an active programme to align the business more closely with the objective of sustainable development' (Anglo American, 2004b, p.18). The 2004 Report includes greater transparency on government relations and more disclosure on 'man-made' capital (Anglo American, 2005i). The content and style of the report fits the criteria laid down by the Global Reporting Initiative (GRI) and the Draft Boundary Protocol. KPMG provides an assurance statement within the report to confirm that to the best of its knowledge the analysis of various sustainable development indicators presented within the report is fair and accurate (Anglo American, 2005i).

CSI spending – geographical and sectoral patterns

According to firm's 2004 Report to Society Anglo American and its subsidiaries contributed $47.4 million, equivalent to 1.1% of pre-tax profits to charitable causes and social investments (Anglo American, 2005g; Anglo American, 2005h). This figure excludes activities with a social dimension that are related to the 'core business', such as work on local business development, workplace HIV programmes and so forth (Anglo American, 2005g). Anglo American emphasises that it does not seek to exploit the methodologies employed by the LBG in order to maximise its claims (Interview with Head of External Affairs). Projects or activities that have an explicit business rationale are excluded from social investment data. Table 8.2 below records the distribution of donations according to LBG categories as noted within the Giving List, 2002–5. In terms of geographic distribution (see Table 8.1) the majority of social investment, 76%, is directed towards a single country – South Africa. In fact the quantity of CSI directed towards South Africa is disproportionate to that country's operations contribution to profits. This reflects several things – firstly, the acute developmental needs that exist in that nation, which is one of the most unequal in the world. Secondly, Anglo has its origins in South Africa and key figures within Anglo are active within the nation's political, social and economic institutions. Thirdly, the company faces moral and legislative imperatives to contribute directly to the nation's process of socio-economic transformation. Such imperatives emanate from the requirements of Black Economic Empowerment (BEE) legislation, the Mining Charter, the public sector's slow response to the HIV/AIDS crisis and direct requests for contributions to community projects.[1] Furthermore, the firm has been placed under explicit pressure by President Mbeki to contribute significantly to socio-economic change following the decision to list the firm on the London Stock Exchange (Mbeki, 2004).

Just over a third of total CSI is directed towards 'community' projects, a quarter towards education and youth, 10% towards housing and 7% to health and HIV/AIDS projects. The focus upon these sectors reflects the nature of the impacts generated by Anglo's main operations. Communities tend to be heavily affected by major mining operations, thus, there is logic in providing targeted support. Provision

Table 8.2 Community investment performance (£m) according to the Annual Giving List

	Cash	Staff/ management	Gifts in kind	total	% of pre-tax profits	Rank
2005	23.26	2.49	0.6	26.35	1.2	19
2004	21.73	1.61	0.81	24.15	1.6	16
2003	18.00	0.10	0.06	18.16	0.91	29
2002	13.93	0.13	–	14.06	0.60	46

Sources:
http://image.guardian.co.uk/sys-files/Society/documents/2005/11/28/GivingList_paper_281105.pdf
http://image.guardian.co.uk/sys-files/Guardian/documents/2004/04/28/2003amendedtable.pdf
http://society.guardian.co.uk/givinglist/tables/0,10999,848892,00.html
http://society.guardian.co.uk/givinglist/tables/0,10999,580050,00.html

Table 8.3 Overall corporate social investment by sector 2004

Community	Education/ youth	Housing	Health & HIV/AIDS	Arts, culture & heritage	Environment	Other
37%	25%	10%	7%	6%	2%	15%

Source: Anglo American plc Report to Society 2004, p.34 (estimated).

of accommodation in mining areas has long been a contentious issue. Anglo is involved in upgrading worker accommodation and also in resettlement schemes. Occupational health concerns related to mine working have also come to the fore in recent years, thus firms such as Anglo have been required to produce an appropriate response. The HIV/AIDS crisis, particularly in southern Africa poses considerable moral and business challenges for firms such as Anglo American, 23% of whose workforce are HIV+. The firm has been proactive in responding to these challenges by initiating educational and prevention programmes since the mid-1980s and offering Voluntary Counselling and Testing, supported by the provision of free anti-retroviral drugs since 2002. As of the end of 2005 the company had 3,500 employees on anti-retroviral treatment and a further 8,500 in the earlier stages of infection on health monitoring and support programmes. This has been particularly important in light of the South African government's controversial and lethargic policy response. Bearing in mind the company's heavy focus upon sustainable development it is interesting to note that environmental projects only consume 2% of CSI, perhaps reflecting the extent to which environmental spending has become integrated into the company's daily business operations.

In 2005 Anglo American was the recipient of BITC's International Award, which on this occasion focussed upon business' contribution to development in Africa (Anglo American, 2005b). The firm's entry featured work on HIV/AIDS, community engagement via SEAT, local business development initiatives, community social investment and involvement in various good governance initiatives, such as the EITI and the Business Trust in South Africa. During 2004/5 Anglo American gained recognition as the top mining company in both the Basic Resources Sector of the World Index of the Dow Jones Sustainability Index and its equivalent in Europe, the STOXX Index (Anglo American, 2004a). Furthermore, Anglo American plc and three of its subsidiaries were included in the Johannesburg Stock Exchange SRI Index.

Anglo Chairman's Fund

The Anglo Chairman's Fund is the principal mechanism for distributing funds for social investment within Anglo American in South Africa, although individual subsidiaries, such as AngloGold Ashanti operate their own funds (Anglo American, 2003b; Anglo American, 2005e; McIntosh Xaba and Associates, 2005). The Chairman's fund operates solely (with the occasional exception) within South Africa. Prior to July 1998, when a phase of significant corporate restructuring was completed, the Fund had been known as the Anglo American and De Beers Chairman's Fund. The Fund has a broad remit and operates according to the following philosophy, 'to make effective and sustainable use of limited resources to create an environment enabling people to assume greater control of their lives. The Fund supports a wide variety of causes and diverse programmes recognising the varied socio-economic and educational needs facing South African communities' (McIntosh Xaba and Associates, 2005). The Fund supports any cause that can be considered as 'socially constructive' (McIntosh Xaba and Associates, 2005). Whilst the causes and programmes are diverse, funds are 'carefully targeted' and 'informed giving' occurs in order to enhance social benefit. Thus, resources are carefully directed towards South Africa's specific developmental needs. For example, South Africa suffers from a shortage of school leavers sufficiently equipped with skills and knowledge in

Table 8.4 Sectoral giving through the Anglo Chairman's Fund 2003

Sector	Number of grants	Value (in SA Rand)	%
HIV/AIDS	48	16154000	22
Area committees	1	193707	<1
Arts and Culture	28	2907154	4
Education	210	37287046	51
Entrepreneur Development	18	1888000	3
Environment	15	1212000	2
Health	28	1927158	3
Policy /Advocacy	11	2270400	3
Welfare/ Development	83	9672506	12
Total	442	73,511,971	

N.B.: US$1 = approx 6.41 Rand

Source:
http://www.angloamerican.co.uk/social/downloads/Chairmans%20Fund%20Review%202003.pdf, p.4

Table 8.5 Chairman's Fund – number and value of projects 1999–2003

Year	Number of projects	Value millions Rand
1999	670	30.6
2000	630	37.7
2001	610	59.2
2002	550	63.4
2003	450	73.5

Source: www.angloamerican.co.uk/social/chairfund.asp.

maths and science. In partnership with the Department of Education the Fund has devised a Maths and Science Awards programme that rewards schools in disadvantaged communities that demonstrate exemplary performance and participation in maths and science. HIV/AIDS programmes are also supported very heavily. The Chairman's Fund has developed a partnership, profiled later in this chapter, with the youth-oriented NGO loveLife in order to enhance the provision of HIV/AIDS services in government clinics.

There are 11 Key Focus Areas: Arts and Culture, Community Development, Education, Environment, Health, HIV/AIDS, Housing, Job Creation, Poverty Alleviation, Rural Development and Welfare. The

Fund is managed by Tshikululu Social Investments (TSI), a not-for-profit corporate social investment consultancy which reviews each request, puts forward recommendations for consideration to Fund Committees and Trustees and ensures that proper accounting and reporting is adhered to by projects once assistance has been approved. TSI manages a number of other South African corporations' social investment funds, including AngloGold Ashanti's Fund.

Anglo American's SEAT methodology

During 2004 the Anglo American Socio-Economic Assessment Toolbox (SEAT) was launched (Anglo American, 2003c; Anglo American, 2003d; Anglo American, 2004b; TheTimes100.co.uk, 2005) in order to assist the firm meeting the following Good Citizenship business principle, 'We seek to make a contribution to the economic, social and educational well-being of the communities associated with an operation' (Anglo American, 2005h, p.3). The objective of this potentially groundbreaking initiative is to facilitate improved understandings of the impacts of Anglo's operations upon local communities, the needs, priorities and concerns of communities and the range of stakeholders and the dynamics between them. Such local relationships have at times been fraught generating problems for the firm and its local operations (Anglo American, 2002b; Anglo American, 2004c). The methodology was developed with the support of consultancy firm Environmental Resources Management (ERM) (ERM, 2004). The methodology does not replace a full Social Impact Assessment (which are mandatory for new operations and expansions) but is a voluntary attempt to improve the management of the socio-economic impacts of mature operations. Three pilot projects were undertaken in South Africa, Australia and Brazil to facilitate the development of the toolbox. SEAT consists of 22 tools for guiding best practice in areas such as local business development, assessing human capital, establishing partnerships, improving the quality of community investment and in planning for the social dimensions of mine closure. The SEAT process is delivered in 4 stages: 1) Profiling the operation and its associated communities, 2) Identifying socio-economic impacts and sharing the results with stakeholders, 3) Developing management responses to key issues raised, 4) Reporting the results. SEAT is implemented by Anglo American staff supported where required by local experts such as academics or local consultants. The SEAT process aims to enable local social and economic impacts to be managed more effectively at the site level. Operational managers are able to better understand their existing 'footprints' and engage in culturally appropriate ways with local stakeholder communities. SEAT assessments enable community needs and expectations to be understood and sources of friction and distrust identified. In addition, partnerships can be developed that enable local Anglo operations to support sustainable livelihoods. The focus within the SEAT methodology upon the development of partnerships is indicative of Anglo American emerging philosophy in this regard as they endeavour to adapt the demands of the new wave of corporate citizenship. As Chairman Sir Mark Moody-Stuart observes (Foreword in the 2004 Report to Society), 'In some areas our managers are having to learn new skills to enable them to work with others. We are finding that partnerships offer solutions which are beyond our capacity to deliver alone'.

A similar – but 'lighter weight' toolbox has been developed for use in areas of exploration – the Safety, Health, Environment and Community (SHEC) List. The SEAT process has acted as a mechanism for building capacity in terms of dealing with community and social issues within the firm. Approximately 200 Anglo employees have received training related to the implementation of SEAT. Workshops have been held in Southern Africa, Latin America, Central Europe and China. More than 50 SEAT assessments have been completed covering two-thirds of Anglo's significant operations in some 15 countries.

The adoption of the SEAT methodology is revolutionising Anglo American's relationship with its operations' neighbouring communities and is sharpening the focus of the firm's approach to sustainability in general and corporate citizenship in particular. Whilst a targeted philanthropic element to the firm's interactions with communities is occurring via SEAT's outputs, sources within the firm emphasise that the dominant objectives of SEAT are to improve the management of the firm's business operations.

Summaries of a cross-section of SEAT Reports

Hippo Valley Estates (HVE) Ltd, Zimbabwe, SEAT Report 2004

HVE is major sugar cane growing estate located in the south-eastern area of Zimbabwe.

Positive impacts identified by the SEAT process included: employment creation, investment in employee welfare, capacity building amongst local suppliers and contractors, tax contributions and social investment. The latter include road maintenance, provision of potable water and contributions to health and education facilities.

Issues of concern included: poor condition of employee housing, insufficient dialogue with local chiefs and a need for greater partnering with local organisations.

Way forward: As a result of SEAT efforts are being made to develop an issue-based Community Engagement Plan. SEAT has enabled HVE management to identify a series of Key Performance Indicators (KPIs) which will enable HVE to improve its social performance. These include: number of complaints or compliments received, HIV/AIDS infection rates amongst employees and their dependants, stakeholder attendance at community meetings and quantity of new or improved employee housing.

Source: Anglo American (2004d).

New Denmark Colliery, Mpumalanga, South Africa, SEAT Report 2004

New Denmark Colliery (NDC) is located 150 km from Johannesburg in the Lekwa Municipality. The colliery extracts bituminous steam coal. NDC has faced several difficult challenges in recent years following the closure of two shafts between 1999–2001.

Positive impacts identified by the SEAT process included: Between 2002 and 2004 production has risen substantially whilst injuries and coal contamination levels have declined. NDC has sought to engage local contractors and made a variety of social contributions within the community such as the provision of buses for school transport and provision of blankets for the local TB hospital.

Issues of concern included: NDC should honour the government's 'people's contract' more explicitly, more effort should be put into supporting the local micro-economy especially via procurement policies, retrenchment should be reduced, employee housing is a concern, relationships with local schools have declined and NDC's transformation claims should be subject to more transparency.

Way forward: KPIs have been developed such as: attendance levels at community liaison forums, HIV/AIDS rates within the workforce and communities, provision of infrastructure and numbers of businesses supported by NDC. NDC community projects will increasingly focus upon areas neglected within local government plans.

Source: Anglo American (2004d).

Mondi Business Paper (MBP) SCP Ruzomberok, Slovak Republic, SEAT Report 2005

MBP SCP is the largest integrated pulp and paper mill in the Slovak Republic. The mill has been recently modernised via the IMPULS project which has substantially improved technical and environmental performance.

Positive impacts identified by the SEAT process included: direct and indirect employment, human capital and skills development in the areas of health and safety, quality, environment, management and occupational training and investment in a wide range of community initiatives.

Issues of concern included: the impacts of retrenchment and the new technical demands caused by technological change at the plant. Concerns were expressed about salaries especially in comparison with Austrian colleagues. Internal stakeholders noted the threat of a brain-drain caused by the development of the local car industry and the impacts of young people's increased expectations.

Way forward: Management will continue to evaluate the mill's performance using the Community Engagement Plan using KPIs identified via SEAT. Specifically, the firm will strive to improve the following elements: internal communication of Corporate Social Investment strategy, alignment of education investment to the company's needs and support for women employees.

Source: Anglo American (2005k).

Case study 1: Anglo Zimele Empowerment Initiative Ltd[2]

Location: South Africa mainly but also some activity in Zambia and Kazakstan

Duration: Zimele established in May 2000 building on a pre-existing model initiated in 1989

How the programme started

In 1989 Anglo American formed the Small and Medium Enterprise Initiative in a joint venture with De Beers specifically to create business opportunities for companies with a black ownership component. In 1998 the partner organisations separated and set up their own ventures. In 2000 the programme was re-launched as 'Zimele', meaning 'to be independent and to stand on one's own feet'. Four years later the company was re-branded as Anglo Zimele in order to reinforce the association with the Anglo American brand.

Programme outline

Zimele is described as Anglo American plc's vehicle for small business development and BEE. Zimele seeks to integrate small and medium sized enterprises (SMEs) into the mainstream economy of South Africa. More broadly Anglo aims to integrate its own economic development initiatives with the development frameworks created by local, provincial and national government.

Zimele operates in two complementary areas:

1) Procurement. Business development managers in Anglo's subsidiaries and divisions identify opportunities to procure goods and services from BEE companies. For a company to be considered as a black enterprise there should be a minimum of 40% black equity with black partners taking an active part in management. Training and mentoring are offered to support firms who must be able to meet key business criteria of quality, price and service delivery. Zimele invests much time in identifying BEE suppliers who can participate within Anglo American's supply chains. In 2004 R5.76 billion (US$895,433,845) worth of procurement was awarded to BEE companies.

2) Business Development. Zimele aims to facilitate the development of new black-owned businesses, sometimes by people employed within Anglo companies. Such business can provide products and services to Anglo through its outsourcing programme. Zimele has invested in a wide range of businesses operating in different sectors, such as IT, engineering, manufacturing and retail. All the businesses have at some point in their history provided services for Anglo American. Zimele supports the development of these businesses through funding and the sharing of business skills and knowledge. Zimele takes a minority equity share (c. 20%) within the nascent firms and is represented on the board of directors, which allows it to share its business skills and assist in the execution and implementation of action plans. Zimele assists in the development of strategic and financial skills as well as market development and expansion. Zimele provides assistance with business plans, the development of strategy and the setting of targets. Zimele is highly proactive in identifying new customers, mainly through introductions. In the longer term entrepreneurs are encouraged to broaden their customer base and thus reduce their reliance upon Anglo's operations. A survey revealed that 13% of Zimele's former beneficiaries were no longer reliant on Anglo at all, whilst 46% remained reliant on Anglo for 50% or more of their business and 42% had a highly diversified customer base.

Furthermore, Anglo Zimele acts as the fund manager for the ***Anglo Khula Mining Fund***, which is a R40 million (US$6,270,045) joint initiative between Anglo American and Khula Enterprise Finance, which is a Department of Trade and Industry initiative.

Zimele has a core operational staff of six, who are responsible for all Zimele activities, including procurement and the management of Zimele's portfolio of companies. External support is provided on a needs-led basis by Anglo managers or external business consultants. The annual cost for administering Zimele is approximately R3.5 million (US$544,456.81). Zimele generates revenue from returns on investment, annual dividends, interest on loans and small management charges for basic administrative work. Zimele prioritises the identification of exit strategies and gradually seeks to facilitate increasing independence on the part of the SME – 'independence through enterprise'. Three years is the usual target duration for involvement by Zimele. Zimele will operate for the foreseeable future. Zimele preceded the regulatory requirements created by the South African Government to promote BEE. Since 2003, corporations have been legally bound by the Mining Charter to meet various BEE criteria and Zimele is now contributing to Anglo American's ability to meet these obligations whilst sustaining a supply of suitable contractors.[3]

The Anglo Zimele model has received various forms of international recognition. The International Finance Council has recognised the value of the model as a mechanism for developing linkages between large and small businesses, while the World Association for small and medium enterprises has also drawn lessons from the Zimele approach. Anglo were selected as speakers at the September 2002 UNCTAD Conference on effective business linkages in Rio de Janeiro and the model has been presented at a number of World Bank and UNDP events.

In broad terms the establishment of Zimele can be seen as a response to the need to develop the black-owned business sector in South Africa. The Government's Mining Charter has reinforced the legislative requirement for corporations to support BEE. Furthermore although most of the contracts won by Zimele businesses have been for already outsourced activities the programme is compatible with the firm's strategy of outsourcing non-core activities in order to engender cost efficiencies.

Working with partners

Zimele has worked with various local government departments, the national government's Department of Trade and Industry, several of Anglo American's local divisions/subsidiaries and support has been received from business consultants.

Inputs from Anglo American

The business development aspect of Zimele's activities operates with an investment fund of R15 million. A team of business development officers focusses upon the administration and delivery of the programme. Anglo American's Corporate Communications Department provides wider exposure for Zimele and its start-ups through press coverage. Anglo American's own legal and taxation departments provide advice and support to individual firms.

Outcomes for the corporation, its partners and the community

- As of July 2005 Zimele was investing in 27 companies, turning over R351m (US$54,601,073) and employing in excess of 2,000 people. Since its inception Anglo Zimele has been directly responsible for the development of over 100 small businesses. Of these, data is available on some 64 SMEs which collectively generate an annual turnover of R542 million (US$84,309,044) and directly employ approximately 4,000 people. Although some other start-ups have not been sustained individuals have received an income for at least a short duration of time and benefited from the transfer of entrepreneurial skills and knowledge.
- Survival rates for SMEs initiated via Anglo Zimele are twice that of other SME start ups in South Africa.
- Zimele facilitates the transfer of knowledge and skills to South Africa's previously disadvantaged communities thus helping to challenge poverty and inequalities. According to the World Business Council for Sustainable Development (WBCSD) Zimele makes direct contributions to two of the Millennium Development Goals (MDG) – income and hunger – and indirect contributions to a further four – education, gender equality, youth employment and technology transfer.
- Zimele has been recognised an example of excellence by the South African President Thabo Mbeki who requested a showcase of the programme and its activities. Mbeki is reputed to have been keen to learn why a private sector model of Small, Medium and Micro Enterprises (SMME) generation has been substantially more successful than government-led initiatives.
- Anglo American is able to sub-contract an increasing proportion of non-core activities thus increasing the firm's economic efficiency. Anglo American achieved a 23% growth in procurement from black SMEs during 2002. Further growth of 20% was attained during 2003.
- The programme plays a part in helping Anglo American to meet its statutory responsibilities regarding the government's BEE Scorecard.
- Anglo American has received international recognition for the quality of their business linkage programmes.

Case study of a Zimele supported business – Bambanani Health and Safety Products

Background
Bambanani was set up in 1999 by Solly Majola. The firm sells top of the range ear, eye and respiratory protective equipment. Majola had previously worked as a production manager for a division of the mining services firm Sturrock and Robson. During the late 1990s Majola attended a health and safety presentation which inspired him to consider the opportunities offered by setting up a business distributing health and safety products. Shortly afterwards the opportunity to develop this idea arose. Zimele were approached for a loan to help get the business off the ground. The application was successful with Zimele taking a 33% share in the company. In cash terms this loan covered Majola's salary during the first year of operation whilst the business was set up.

The roles of Zimele, Anglo American and Sturrock and Robson
Sturrock and Robson have provided much of the business infrastructure such as office and warehouse space. Zimele has introduced Majola to individuals within firms who would be likely to procure goods from Bambanani. Many of the firms concerned are from the Anglo American stable. Zimele has also assisted Majola by helping him obtain a vendor number, which allows him to gain access to the mines. Zimele has actively promoted Bambanani to potential clients. Approximately 85% of Bambanani's sales are to Anglo American and its affiliates. Zimele staff have been helpful in responding to questions and ideas posed by Majola. Majola has received no formal training through the Zimele scheme, he has 'learned by doing' with staff at Zimele and Sturrock and Robson providing verbal advice. Bambanani was featured in a TV documentary that showcased some of the more successful corporate social investment stories from across South Africa.

Bambanani's development and future prospects
During 2005 Majola was able to take on a member of staff to support him and he moved into an independent office. Zimele have now divested from Bambanani. It is estimated that the firm will turnover R5 million (£440,000) during 2005. Majola notes that the competition is very strong for young businesses such as his as established firms have many years of experience and a great density of contacts to draw upon.

Source: Interview with Solly Majola, 31st August 2005.

Evidence of sustainability

Zimele exhibits strong evidence of sustainable characteristics in several key areas. The SMME survival rate is indicative of the robustness of the Zimele model, lessons from which are being drawn by other bodies in South Africa and beyond. Anglo American is rolling the model out in other parts of the world. The ability of the central Anglo Zimele organisation to be self-financing is an important indicator of sustainability.

How the programme is evaluated

Zimele continually reviews the progress of the businesses. An Independent Management Review was conducted in mid-2005 and an internal report published in September 2005.

Case Study 2: Application of SEAT – Mondi Forests: Richmond Business Unit (RBU)[4]

Location: KwaZulu Natal, South Africa
Duration: Since 1997 (SEAT became part of the process in 2002/3)

How the programme started

Following an upsurge in problems with the local community Mondi initiated a long term relationship with the Farmer Support Group (FSG), an NGO with considerable experience in social development issues. FSG has played a major role in developing various aspects of Mondi's social management systems and practice. Parallel processes in operation at that time included the national imperative to challenge the socio-economic disparities inherited from apartheid, a growing awareness of the need for major firms to lead the way on corporate citizenship and the need to meet the standards set by Forestry Stewardship Council (FSC) certification.

Programme outline

RBU has several forestry plantations in KwaZulu Natal, which collectively incorporate 18 low-income, black communities. During the late 1990s, in common with other operators in the forestry sector, RBU changed its business model such that the majority of plantation management and harvesting activities were contracted out thus substantially altering the dynamic between the company and local communities. Mondi's workforce was reduced substantially in size – indeed only eight full-time staff remained whilst 1,150 were employed through sub-contracting. In addition, various social facilities provided directly by Mondi were transferred to government or terminated, such as schools, clinics and accommodation. As some contractors were brought in from outside the area relationships with local stakeholders declined. RBU experienced a number of problems due to the resultant deterioration in the local economy and people's negative reactions to the sub-contracting policy. For example, community livestock were grazed on Mondi's land without permission causing damage to saplings. Confiscation of livestock led to a further breakdown in relations. Local people were smoking out bees in order to harvest honey, causing fires in the process. In some cases tensions flared to the point that Mondi's personnel were threatened and property was subjected to arson attacks.

Mechanisms for responding to these problems were identified through the application of the SEAT methodology. In fact this evaluation was one of three pilot studies undertaken to facilitate the development of a generic SEAT methodology within Anglo America. A 22-page report was produced during 2002. A widespread consultation exercise was undertaken with 20 stakeholder groups, including corporate management, contractors, NGOs, government departments, residents from the Ntembeni community and school head teachers. The report identified a range of key issues facing the company and its stakeholders and identified opportunities for improvement.

The SEAT process has enabled the RBU to identify a range of social risks that have impacts upon both local communities and the business itself. Many of these problems arise from the sub-contracting process and are indicative of the challenges of managing sub-contractors' broader performance. Such risks include: a decline in safety, health, environment and social performance, an increase in safety and health risks due to deteriorating infrastructure, problems of uncontrolled grazing and squatting, poor water quality and pollution from landfills. By identifying these risks, their root causes and the stakeholders affected Mondi is in a position to initiate corrective actions. The company has appointed a full-time Social Development Coordinator who liaises with 16 locally based Social Development Managers (SDMs) who are trained in participatory approaches to community engagement and in small business support. This network facilitates a flow of information between Mondi and local communities. For example, the SDMs work with communities identifying developmental ideas and formulating solutions. Community Liaison Forums, which involve a range of stakeholders, have been initiated and a fund for social investments (such as grants and loans to support social needs and entrepreneurial activities) has been set up. Permits for grazing and firewood gathering are now also issued.

Mondi has supported training amongst local communities in the following areas: cattle management, soil conservation, HIV/AIDS awareness, bee keeping, market gardening, marketing skills development for craft workers and entrepreneurial skills development. Such actions are usually facilitated through the SDMs and include upgrading the local infrastructure such as the supply of potable water within local communities and improving waste management systems. In order to strengthen the broader social infrastructure Mondi Forestry provide various forms of support for a local NGO – the Farmer Support Group (FSG), an NGO specialising in social development based at the University of Natal in Durban, including funding the cost of the head of the unit. Mondi recruited a community development officer from FSG. Mondi have been closely involved with FSG throughout the SEAT process.

In addition, efforts have been made to broaden the range of obligations faced by sub-contractors to include more community-related matters. The practice of sub-contracting, whilst driven by competitiveness pressures, is responsible for many of the social problems in the area and thus the risks confronting Mondi. Mondi has been obliged to review various aspects of the sub-contracting process. For example, initial contracts tended to be short (less than three years) leaving companies with little time (or incentive) to develop meaningful relationships with local communities nor, arguably, were payment levels received from Mondi, sufficient to facilitate these processes. Equally Mondi's tendering process failed to devote sufficient attention to contractor obligations to engage with social performance management.

Evidence of the impacts of Mondi's improved social performance following the application of SEAT includes, a reduction in fires, theft and vandalism and increasing community support for Mondi activities. A key to the success of Mondi's social engagement is the two-way nature of their relationship with communities. An ethos of partnership with communities has been created such that communities now contribute to looking after the broader physical and natural environment.

Mondi also sponsors other social investments within KwaZulu Natal, which operate at a divisional level. These include *The Black Gold Products Charcoal project*. Waste timber from Mondi's plantations is converted into charcoal, which can be sold under the Forestry Stewardship Council banner significantly increasing the price that can be achieved in European markets. Mondi worked with DFID to finance the project (Mondi put in R1 million (US$155,411) and DFID R2 million), which supports local black entrepreneurs. The pilot project created 125 jobs and as of 2005 the numbers employed in such projects had risen to 400–500.

Working with partners

Mondi's CSR strategy is consistent with Anglo American's overall approach of seeking to deliver community goals through partnerships with other organisations with appropriate skills and resources. The NGO Farmer Support Group has been a major player in Mondi's community work in KwaZulu Natal. Local government departments have also been important partners as SEAT has identified needs that local authorities should meet as service providers. Mondi has sought to work with local authorities who often lack capacity and financial resources. Multi-partner approaches offer a way forward. National government departments have been approached for resources and advice. The UK's DFID have provided finance for the 'Black Gold Forest Products' project.

Inputs from Mondi

Mondi provides financial support for FSG and Mondi staff contributes to training activities within communities. US$20,000 provided for social and community programmes.

Outcomes for the corporation, its partners and the community

- Mondi social investments have generated indirect employment for 20 people which is more than double the directly employed management cadre of the Richmond Business Unit.
- Localised problems (fire, vandalism, theft) previously experienced by Mondi Forests in the area have been substantially reduced.
- The local economy has been bolstered and key social infrastructure maintained.
- Mondi is demonstrating competence as corporate citizens and are meeting obligations to contribute to socio-economic transformation in South Africa. Mondi's management have become more aware of the firm's broader social impacts and now have a more nuanced understanding of their stakeholders' socio-economic priorities.
- Constructive relationships with local communities are being rebuilt to the benefit of all stakeholders.
- Mondi's reputation as a good corporate citizen has been restored.
- The negative externalities encountered by RBU arising from poor integration of local needs into RBU's activities have been reduced.
- Mondi is able to direct their CSI resources to areas of greatest need.

- SEAT has also produced important dividends for the firm as employees have been able to raise concerns about their working environment and management have been able to take appropriate action. For example, ensuring that employees' children have access to schooling.
- Mondi is now credited with taking its responsibilities seriously and is receiving recognition as a leading local exponent of CSR.

Evidence of sustainability

Mondi's experiences in KwaZulu Natal have been important in facilitating improved engagement with stakeholders. Lessons have been learned and disseminated more broadly within the company. This process has reduced some of the risks facing the firm when operating within certain socio-economic environments.

How the programme is evaluated

Certain findings from the SEAT process can be used as indicators to monitor and measure performance. These include, number of arson incidents, HIV rates and total spend on community investment. These key performance indicators can be measured on an annual basis in order to monitor the benefits gained via the implementation of SEAT recommendations.

Case Study 3: HIV/AIDS Community Partnership – loveLife

Location: South Africa
Duration: Three years from 2003

How the programme started

Having recognised the severity of the HIV/AIDS crisis within their operations Anglo American sought support from an NGO with an innovative approach to the problem. loveLife's focus upon targeting young people made them an attractive proposition as a partner.[5]

Programme outline

More than 5 million South Africans (>15% of the workforce) are estimated to have HIV/AIDS; this figure could double by 2010 causing South Africa's GDP to decline by 17%. The challenges faced by corporations in this context are significant. AngloGold, for example, estimates that HIV/AIDS presently costs the firm $5–6 an ounce. Approximately, 30,000 of Anglo American's workers in South Africa are

HIV+ representing more than a quarter of the workforce in some business units. However, the South African government have been criticised for their slow response to the problem and President Mbeki has gone on record questioning the very scientific basis for HIV. Furthermore, there has been controversy, including court actions, in relation to the pricing of anti-retroviral drugs and the production of generics in South Africa. It was against this controversial and complex backdrop that Anglo American became one of the first companies to recognise the potential threat of HIV/AIDS, both to their business and to society more broadly and initiated a series of steps in an attempt to tackle the problem. During 2001 it was recognised that prevention programmes alone could not contain the risks and thus consideration was given to the provision of a company-wide treatment programme. In a pilot project 97% of Anglo employees gaining access to HIV/AIDS medication were able to return to full-time work. In November 2002 Anglo American launched an anti-retroviral programme (ART) for its employees and appointed a full-time health economist to monitor the impacts of the programme. A decision was taken that ways should be sought to increase access to treatment for workers' dependants, contractors and wider communities. It was recognised that Anglo American could not deliver such a wide ranging objective on their own and external specialist support was solicited and a particular focus was to seek to build capacity in the public health system. A partnership with a ground-breaking NGO, loveLife, was brokered for this purpose.

In 2003, whilst speaking at the 2003 Nelson Mandela Awards for Health and Human Rights, Anglo American's senior vice-president Brian Brink announced that the Chairman's Fund would provide three years of funding to loveLife, South Africa's national HIV prevention programme for youth. loveLife aims to improve the accessibility of comprehensive HIV prevention services, voluntary counselling and testing for HIV as well as enhanced care, support and treatment for sufferers. loveLife's work is particularly focussed upon youth as 50% of HIV infections – especially amongst young women – occur before the age of 20. loveLife aims to provide quality HIV/AIDS services in a 'non-stigmatised setting' as HIV/AIDS sufferers often fear the social stigma attached to visiting AIDS treatment facilities. Further financial support for this broader programme has been garnered from a variety of sources including the Kaiser and Mandela Foundations. According to Dr. Drew Altman, President of the Kaiser Family Foundation, 'Anglo American is to be congratulated for its leadership in advancing efforts for a truly comprehensive approach to managing South Africa's HIV/AIDS epidemic' (loveLife, 2005b).

The scheme is operating as a pilot programme helping to identify the nature of the delivery infrastructure required to support the rollout of Anti-Retroviral Treatment (ART) throughout the national public health system. Anglo American has helped their partners devise a system for improving the standard of care provided in clinics. Thus, efforts are being made to ensure that clinics meet ten key performance indicators, which include appropriate provision of opening hours, existence of appropriate reporting and medication supply systems. In addition, it has been important to create a welcoming environment within the clinic and ensure that staff receive sensitivity training. Whilst, systems are being put in place to enable people to access 'wellness' and immune status monitoring programmes. An important precedent is being set as the treatment is not only available for Anglo's workers but also to the wider community. Anglo's operations provide staffing input to work with loveLife and other partners in order to build capacity in public sector care clinics.

One Anglo American subsidiary offers a loveLife supported *lifestyle programme* for young people in its apprenticeship training. At each site a project team operates. Typically this team will be composed of a 'champion' from the local business unit, Anglo American's area manager, a private doctor, a representative from the government health department, loveLife's CEO and a representative from Anglo American's Chairman's Fund. The initial community and operational partners have included: Saldanha Bay, Vredendal and Lutzville in the Western Cape where Namakwa Sands (Anglo Base Metals) are located and Melmouth and Richards Bay in KwaZulu Natal home to Mondi (Anglo Paper and Packaging).

Working with partners

loveLife, The Nelson Mandela Foundation, the Henry J. Kaiser Family Foundation and the Global Fund to fight AIDS, TB and Malaria and the South African Department of Health.

Inputs from Anglo American

Anglo American initially committed $4.5 million from the Chairman's Fund, further monies have been committed by the Mandela Foundation (R10 million or US$1,567,000), the Kaiser Foundation ($10 million a year) and the Global Fund ($12 million).[6] The company is also contributing expertise from its business units. In each unit a manager has been appointed to champion the programme. Anglo American has made its medical infrastructure available and is also providing site-specific training for nurses involved in rolling out ART via the public health system.

Outcomes for the corporation, its partners and the community

- Anglo American's funding commitment is enabling loveLife to set up adolescent friendly clinics in the six provinces where Anglo American has business units. Specifically, 900 public clinics are being rehabilitated in areas where Anglo American has operations. In this way loveLife can establish their outreach programme into more remote geographical areas.
- Business skills and practices are being shared with project partners. In the case of loveLife the funds provided by Anglo American are enabling the improvement of management systems and the building of capacity within clinics.
- During 2005 two loveLife outreach coordinators were employed directly by Anglo.
- The overriding objective from Anglo's perspective is to enhance the health sector response at the community level. Thus, lessons regarding appropriate mechanisms for delivering public health programmes are being learned and disseminated.
- The health of Anglo American's workers, their families and broader communities is being improved.
- Absence from work is being substantially reduced and the treatment is bringing gains in staff morale and productivity.
- Workers' concerns about long term access to medication are being allayed.
- Corporate life, disability and medical insurance premiums will be minimised.
- The firm is being associated with a successful community programme.
- Reducing HIV/AIDS amongst the young will ensure the firm has a workforce to draw upon in the future.

Evidence of sustainability

HIV/AIDS programmes are notoriously difficult to assess due to the complex political, social and cultural contexts within which they operate. The partnership with loveLife certainly yielded a number of beneficial outcomes and important lessons are being learned by all stakeholders. Improvements in the management of HIV/AIDS are critical in terms of increasing the sustainability of Anglo American's business units. In relation to Anglo American's own workplace programmes, its health economics study is indicating that in its best performing operations – especially some of its collieries – participation in voluntary counselling and testing is now around 90% and the benefits of its treatment programmes, in terms of reduced absenteeism and reduced loss of skilled workers to the disease, now balance the costs of providing treatment.

How the programme is evaluated

loveLife's work has been evaluated as part of an academic review of HIV prevention in South Africa (see Pettifor et al., 2005). loveLife continually reviews the effectiveness of its strategies as the programme is evidence-based and thus must continually review its performance in the light of data (loveLife, 2001).

Project-by-project assessment of social capital impacts

In this section we summarise the social capital aspects of each project. We conclude by using the format of Table 4.1 to create a table, which allows a comparison of the social capital elements of each project (see Table 8.6).

Anglo Zimele

Perhaps the most striking aspect of the Zimele programme is the wide array of social capital impacts being facilitated. The principal constituencies benefiting through these impacts are the individual entrepreneurs and Anglo American itself, although it should be acknowledged that there are broader benefits being stimulated within society as a whole and the top levels of the South African government. The scope of Zimele's impacts is evident in several ways. Zimele has opened up unheralded opportunities for individual black entrepreneurs who are able to access person to person support from staff members at Anglo American and Zimele itself. The most significant effect of Zimele is the way that doors are opened for the entrepreneurs such that they are able to access senior managers within Anglo American's subsidiaries and divisions. Such access is critical to the potential success of their businesses as these individuals are the gatekeepers to the contracts that are the lifeblood of the embryonic businesses. The direct facilitation of such connections can be seen as a classic example of Lin's vertical relationships of scope. At an institutional level the programme has enabled constructive links to be developed between Anglo American and the highest levels of South Africa's government. In this context it should be noted that relationships between the government, especially President Thabo Mbeki, and Anglo American's senior management have recently been fraught.[7] However the President's interest in Zimele may be perceived as a form of rapprochement, helping to build institutional trust and develop a sense of goodwill. Equally, the Presidential showcase of Zimele projects has the potential to assist government advisors in devising means to support the nation's SME sector; an area where the government has struggled to make an impact. By bringing major corporations into the policy-making loop and thus providing an opportunity for the 'DNA of business' to be disseminated there is a possibility that a significant structural hole within policy-making networks can be rectified.

There are other clear social capital gains being made by Anglo American via Zimele. The firm's divisions and subsidiaries are able to access a new network of suppliers of goods and services. The fact that these small firms are backed by Zimele acts as a form of recommendation implying that the standards of services/products will be of a good quality. Thus, the link with Zimele helps to build networks of trust. From Anglo American's perspective the existence of a growing network of new suppliers is important as it validates their commercial decision to focus upon subcontracting and enables them to meet the BEE targets set by the government. As well as building links with national government, Anglo American plc has been able to use Zimele as a vehicle to access global institutional networks via the development of connections with the United Nations and the International Finance Corporation.

Clearly the promotion of BEE via legislative means is central to the ANC's overall policy platform and Anglo American's high profile support for this policy via Zimele can be seen as important in normalising BEE within South Africa's broader business environment. Furthermore, Zimele's promotion of good business practice, including debt servicing, fulfilment of contractual obligations and so forth is important in constructing the type of business culture that is essential for generating an entrepreneurial culture within South African society.

Richmond Business Unit, KwaZulu Natal

The application of the SEAT methodology at the Richmond Business Unit has explicitly benefited the following constituencies: local communities, Mondi, local government and the NGO FSG. The most potent social capital impacts are evidenced in Mondi's relationships with communities. Previously these relationships had declined severely, however the implementation of SEAT has enabled distrust to be overcome and trust built. In this way a significant contribution has been made to social cohesion within these local regions and the notion that business can be a constructive contributor to wider society has been established and reinforced. Such impacts are particularly important in geographically isolated regions where resistance to external agencies, especially MNCs, can be considerable. Such problems had been exacerbated in the aftermath of Mondi's decision to expand its subcontracting policy.

Perhaps the most significant impacts of the changing relationship between the firm and the community have occurred within Mondi itself. The firm's own culture has changed through the application of the SEAT process and there is a greater understanding of the firm's impacts upon local society and the ways that relationships may be managed more effectively. These improvements have resulted from Mondi's desire to develop partnerships, broaden their networks and develop direct relationships with key locally based institutions. The NGO FSG has played a crucial role in introducing Mondi to new ways of thinking about local communities.

There have been important developments at the institutional level as Mondi have engaged with local government departments in mutually beneficial relationships. Provision of effective local services is a challenge for the local government in the region of KwaZulu Natal where RBU operates. Local governments tend to face critical shortages in terms of the financial and human resources required to deliver local services and assist local economic development. However, the form of social capital being developed through SEAT can be seen as helping to bridge the evident structural deficits within local and regional networks. Mondi is able to interface with local government officials and collaborate on mutually advantageous projects bringing in other expert partners, such as FSG, where required.

loveLife partnership

The constituencies receiving the most social capital benefit through the loveLife partnership are: loveLife, local communities, Anglo American plc and the national government's Department of Health. The most potent impacts in terms of scope occur at the macro-level through the facilitation of inter-organisational connections which are having profound structural impacts in terms of network development. The changes here are fundamental due to the paucity of previous provision. Anglo American has taken the lead in generating a network to tackle the HIV/AIDS crisis. Thus, loveLife, the public sector health service and Anglo American are operating in a novel form of partnership. The importance of this work cannot be underestimated as there were previously severe structural deficits in HIV/AIDS services in these localities. Anglo's lead has enabled important ties to be initiated and relationships between partners constructed. In this sense there is a clear lubrication effect. There are clear benefits for Anglo in terms of stabilising their workforce, promoting social cohesion and improving relationships with local communities. An outcome of this process should be increased levels of goodwill being directed towards the corporation. A crucial aspect of this programme is that it has acted to correct what may be perceived as government failure in terms of tackling the HIV/AIDS crisis. Social cohesion is clearly being improved as a result of the programme. The targeting of support for whole communities rather than just employees is critical in this regard.

Table 8.6 Anglo American case studies – summary assessment of social capital impacts

		Zimele	RBU	loveLife
Scope-				
Micro:	Person to person	**	*	***
Meso:	Vertical relationships	***	*	*
Macro:	institutional	**	**	**
Form-				
Structural:	Networks	**	**	**
	Bridging structural holes	**	**	***
	New membership	*	**	**
	Ties & glue/lubricant	*	**	**
Cognitive:	Competence/goodwill	**	**	**
Channel-				
Information:	Improve education	**	*	***
Collective action:	Correct government/ social failure	***	**	***
Misc:	Employment stability	**	**	**
	Cohesion:	**	**	**
	Radius of trust/distrust	**	***	**
	Norms of behaviour	**	**	***

Key: no stars = minimal impact, * = some impact, ** = notable impact, *** = potent impact.

A further potent impact of the programme is the way that it is setting a precedent concerning the prioritisation of HIV/AIDS health programmes. Anglo American, a major MNC, is placing such a strong emphasis upon HIV/AIDS prevention and treatment and applying it in a ground-breaking way through its partnership with loveLife. In this way there is increased pressure upon other private sector operators and government agencies to tackle the health crisis in similar ways. In this way norms relating to HIV/AIDS policy are being challenged. Equally, attempts to break down the norm of stigma attached to HIV/AIDS are extremely important at a community level.

Notes

1. See Anglo American (2003a) and loveLife (2005a).
2. *Sources:* Anglo American, 2002a; Anglo American, 2003e; Anglo American, 2005a; Anglo American, 2005c; Anglo American, 2005d; Anglo American, 2005j; Anon, 2005; Mineweb, 2003; Mining Weekly, 2003; Mining Weekly, 2005; Zimele Empowerment Initiative Ltd, 2005a; Zimele Empowerment Initiative Ltd, 2005b.
3. Since 1994 the ANC government have rigorously pursued various policy strategies seeking to promote BEE. In 2004 the Broad-based Empowerment Act was passed (DTI, 2004). The ambitions of this Act are far-reaching and are supported by the BEE Commission set up in 2001. Certain sectors are required to comply with the terms of the Act, whereas other sectors are expected to develop their own charters for transformation. Various targets have been set by which the success of the BEE strategy can be assessed. These include: black individuals, businesses and collective enterprises should hold at least 25% of the shares of companies listed on the JSE; at least 30% of private sector procurement should be to black-owned companies, including SMEs and collective enterprises; at least 40% of senior and executive management in private sector companies (with more than 50 employees) should be black. Furthermore, the government have used various forms of leverage to encourage energy and mining sector companies to accelerate implementation of BEE.
4. *Sources*: Anglo American, 2002b; Farmer Support Group, 2005.
5. See *Economist* (2003).
6. The Henry J. Kaiser Family Foundation is a US-based non-profit, private body focussing on major health care issues (Kaiser Family Foundation, 2006a, b). The Foundation conducts policy research targeted at end users including policymakers, the media, the health care community and the general public. In addition, specific programmes are supported. The Foundation has been operating in South Africa for two decades seeking to assist in the development of a more equitable health system, focussing particularly on women, children and youth. Recent work has focussed on identifying effective ways of controlling the AIDS epidemic.

The Global Fund to Fight AIDS, TB and Malaria is a partnership between governments, civil society, the private sector and affected communities (The Global Fund, 2006a, b).

Operating as a private foundation the Fund, which was launched in January 2002, seeks to attract and disburse resources to fight the scourge of three of the world's most devastating diseases. The Fund is an independent organisation governed by an international set of stakeholders drawn from NGOs, governmental representatives, the private sector and recipient groups.

7   On September 7th 2004 an article by Tony Trahar, CEO of Anglo American plc, was published in the South African newspaper Business Day. In this article Trahar stated: 'I think the South African political-risk issue is starting to diminish – although I am not saying it has gone'. This sentiment aligned to Anglo American's decision to re-locate their main stock market listing to London prompted President Mbeki to produce a letter in response Mbeki, T. (2004). 'This brings us back to the issue of the disjuncture between our political and business leadership mentioned in the government 10-Year Review. Both the ANC and the government would not know what political risk Mr. Trahar is talking about. What is this risk that has started to diminish, but has not gone? Is this the risk that persuaded Anglo American that it should list and re-domicile in London, while speaking to us only about the size of capital markets?' (Mbeki, T., 2004).

References

AMVESCAP (2005), *Anglo American Plc*. Available at: www.check-sure.com/ftse_100_companies/anglo_american.htm. Accessed 11/05/2005.

Anglo American (2002a), *Black Economic Empowerment Report 2002*. Available at: http://www.angloamerican.co.uk/social/bee.asp. Accessed 01/07/2005.

Anglo American (2002b), *'Mondi Forests: Richmond Business Unit, Mondi SEAT Report'*, unpublished internal document.

Anglo American (2003a), *'Anglo American announces new community HIV/AIDS initiative in partnership with loveLife'*, press release, 6th October 2003.

Anglo American (2003b), *The Chairman's Fund Review*. Available at: http://www.angloamerican.co.uk/social/downloads/Chairmans%20Fund%20Review%202003.pdf. Accessed 11/05/2005.

Anglo American (2003c), *'SEAT – Overview'*, Anglo American internal document.

Anglo American (2003d), *'SEAT Toolbox'*, Anglo American, internal document.

Anglo American (2003e), *Zimele: Independence through Enterprise*. Available at: http://www.angloamerican.co.uk/susdev/downloads/ZIMELE.pdf. Accessed 01/07/2005.

Anglo American (2004a), *Anglo American: Report to Society 2003*. Available at: http://kronicle.kiwi.co.uk/documents/programme_directory/percent_club/index.html. Accessed 10/05/2005.

Anglo American (2004b), *Annual Review 2004*, Anglo American Plc.

Anglo American (2004c), *'Minercao Catalao – SEAT Report'*, Anglo American, internal document.

Anglo American (2004c), *Anglo American 2004 Hippo Valley Estates Limited SEAT Report 2004*, http://www.angloamerican.co.uk/static/uploads/HIPPO%20SEAT%20REPORT.pdf.

Anglo American (2004d), *Anglo American plc 2004 New Denmark Colliery, SEAT 2005*, http://www.angloamerican.co.uk/static/uploads/ACSA%20SEAT%20REPORT%2029%20SE%2005.pdf

Anglo American (2005a), *Anglo American plc: Report to Society 2004*, Anglo American Plc.

Anglo American (2005b), *Anglo receives major international responsibility award*. Available at: http://www.angloamerican.co.uk/article/?afw_source_key={142EDCBF-F071-4D28-8512-04D1AE01F7E9}. Accessed 10/05/2005.

Anglo American (2005c), '*Anglo Zimele Showcase of Companies*', Presidential visit July 2005, unpublished report.

Anglo American (2005d), '*Anglo Zimele: Independence through enterprise. Buffalos and Oxpeckers*'.

Anglo American (2005e), *The Chairman's Fund*. Available at: www.angloamerican.co.uk/social/chairfund.asp. Accessed 10/05/2005.

Anglo American (2005f), *Company History*. Available at: www.angloamerican.co.uk/about/comphist.asp. Accessed 09/05/2005.

Anglo American (2005g), *Global Donations Policy*. Available at: http://www.angloamerican.co.uk/article/?afw_source_key=4B1A37EB-E942-41F2-A74C-94F7C01F5BB6. Accessed 22/11/2005.

Anglo American (2005h), *Good Citizenship business principles*. Available at: http://www.angloamerican.co.uk/article/?afw_source_key=50A97184-4473-48DC-93A4-F61106497751. Accessed 22/11/2005.

Anglo American (2005i), *Presentation to Financial Community on Anglo American's Sustainable Development Performance 2004/5*, internal presentation document, May 17th 2005.

Anglo American (2005j), '*Update, Anglo American Transformation and Black Economic Empowerment*', July 2005, newsletter.

Anglo American (2005k), *Anglo American 2005 Mondi Business Paper SCP SEAT Report 2005*, http://www.angloamerican.co.uk/static/uploads/MBP%20SCP%20SEAT%20FINAL.pdf.

Anon (2005), '*Anglo Zimele: Creating Sustainable Businesses*', an independent management review September 2005.

Corporate Watch (2005), *Report Update: The Commission for Africa and Corporate Involvement*. Available at: http://www.corporatewatch.org.uk/?lid=1535. Accessed 24/11/2005.

DTI (2004), *South Africa's Economic Transformation: A Strategy for Broad-Based Black Economic Empowerment*. Available at: http://www.dti.gov.za/bee/complete.pdf. Accessed 31/05/2006.

Economist (2003), *Follow my lead – Companies take practical steps to help Africa's AIDS tragedy*. Available at: www.businessfightsaids.org/site/apps/nl/content2.asp?c=nmK0LaP6E&b=239247&ct=280098. Accessed 26/05/2005.

Economist (2006), 'The Shedding Giant. Why Anglo American is selling some of its parts', *The Economist*, 8 April, pp.72/3.

ERM (2004), *Working with Anglo American to create a global framework*. Available at: www.erm.com/ERM/Updates/people.NSF/(Page_Name_Web)/2004CaseStudies. Accessed 15/07/2005.

Farmer Support Group (2005), *Making Land Work for Rural People*, University of KwaZulu Natal.
Friends of the Earth (2004), *Anglo American Plc: financing the summit, plundering the earth*. Friends of the Earth International Briefing. Available at: www.rio-plus-10.org/en/press/91.php. Accessed 15/07/2005.
Kaiser Family Foundation (2006a), *About the Kaiser Family Foundation*. Available at: www.kff.org/about/index.cfm. Accessed 25/04/2006.
Kaiser Family Foundation (2006b), *South Africa's Health Care Plans and National Health System Development*. Available at: www.kff.org/southafrica/index.cfm. Accessed 25/04/2006.
loveLife (2001), *Hot Prospects, Cold Facts: Portraits of Young South Africa*, Kauffman, Levin and Associates, Johannesburg. Commissioned by the Henry J. Kaiser Family Foundation (USA).
loveLife (2005a), *About Us*. Available at: www.lovelife.org.za/corporate/ about_us/index.html. Accessed 26/05/2005.
loveLife (2005b), *Anglo-American announces new community HIV/AIDS Initiative in partnership with loveLife*. Available at: www.lovelife.org.za/corporate/search/results_final.php?newsarticle=340. Accessed 26/05/2005.
Mbeki, T. (2004), *Letter of the President, 10th September*. Available at: http://www.saembassy.org/Letter%20of%20Question%20that%20demand%20answer.htm. Accessed 09/05/2005.
McIntosh Xaba and Associates (2005), *Directory of Grants, Loans and Funding Sources for South African Municipalities*. Available at: www.mxa.co.za/Grants_Database/Private_Sector/ANGLO_AMERICAN_CHAIRMANS.HTM. Accessed 11/05/2005.
Mineweb (2003), *Anglo's Zimele set for 20% transaction growth*. Available at: www.mineweb.net/events/conferences/2003/bee_survey/70596.htm. Accessed 26/06/2005.
Mining Weekly (2003), *Platinum miner sets empowerment procurement target at R750-million*. Available at: www.miningweekly.co.za/components/print.asp?id=34217. Accessed 26/05/2005.
Mining Weekly (2005), *Resources giant boosts BEE support*. Available at: www.zimele.co.za/about_zimele_o.asp. Accessed 26/05/2005.
Pettifor, A., Rees, H., Kleinschmidt, I., Steffenson, A., MacPhail, C., Hlongwa-Madikizela, L., Vermaak, A. and Padian, D. (2005), 'Young people's sexual health in South Africa: HIV prevalence and sexual behaviours from a nationally representative household survey', *AIDS* Vol.19: pp.1525–1534.
The Global Fund (2006a), *How the Fund works – About the Global Fund to fight Aids, Tuberculosis and Malaria*. Available at: www.theglobalfund.org/en/about/how/. Accessed 25/04/2006.
The Global Fund (2006b), *A Partnership to prevent and Treat AIDS, Tuberculosis and malaria*. Available at: www. theglobalfund.org/en/files/publication/qaen.pdf. Accessed 25/04/2006.
TheTimes100.co.uk (2005), *Anglo American – Working for sustainable development in primary industry*. Available at: www.thetimes100.co.uk/case_study.php?cID=65&ID=173&pID=5. Accessed 15/07/2005.
Zimele Empowerment Initiative Ltd (2005a), *Early Beginnings*. Available at: www.zimele.co.za/about_eb.asp. Accessed 26/05/2005.

Zimele Empowerment Initiative Ltd (2005b), *Philosophy and Business Development Model*. Available at: www.zimele.co.za/about_zimele_p.asp. Accessed 01/07/2005.

9
GlaxoSmithKline and its Corporate Citizenship Programme

A brief corporate biography

GSK's history is based around a series of mergers and acquisitions, dating back to the opening of John K. Smith's drug store in Philadelphia in 1830. Key dates in the firm's history include: the building of the world's first medicine factory by Thomas Beecham in 1859, the opening of the Wellcome Tropical Research Laboratories in 1902 and the registration of Glaxo as a trademark for dried baby milk in 1906 (GSK, 2005i). In 2000 Smithkline Beecham (which had formed in 1989) and Glaxo Wellcome (who had merged in 1995) joined forces to create GSK – one of the world's leading research-based pharmaceutical companies (GSK, 2005k). The firm is headquartered in the UK with operational headquarters based in the US and operations in 118 countries. The firm has two main divisions – pharmaceutical and consumer healthcare. The pharmaceutical division (which generates about 85% of GSK's sales) deals predominantly with vaccines and prescriptions drugs, whilst the consumer healthcare side produces over-the-counter medicines, healthcare products and nutritional drinks. Well-known products include, *Zantac* and *Paxil/Seroxat* (pharmaceuticals) and Macleans toothpaste and Lucozade (consumer healthcare).

The 2004 Annual Review records that GSK's sales were £20.3 billion in 2004 with a pre-tax profit of £6.1 billion (GSK, 2005i). The firm employs 100,000 people, 40% of whom are in sales and marketing. There are 82 manufacturing sites in 37 countries and 24 R&D sites in 11 countries, employing 15,000 people. The firm operates in 160 national markets, the main ones being the USA, Japan, France, Germany and the UK. GSK has a leading edge position in genetics and technologies for drug development. On the pharmaceutical side the firm is a leader in the development of drug products in the following

Table 9.1 Regional data for GSK plc 2004

	USA	Europe	Asia Pacific	Japan	Latin America	Middle East/Africa	Canada	Excluding USA/Europe	Total
Pharmaceutical turnover (£m)	8,425	5,128	1,162	770	581	669	411	3,593	17,146
% of total	49	30	6.5	4.5	3.5	4	2.5	21	
Employees	23,782	44,679	16,109	2,965	5,603	5,134	1,747	31,558	100,014
% of total	24	45	16	3	5.5	5	1.5	31	

Source: http://www.gsk.com/financial/reps04/annual-report-2004.pdf, pp.160–164.

areas; central nervous system, respiratory, anti-infectives and gastro-intestinal/metabolic. The firm markets a number of 'blockbuster drugs' which dominate the market and produce high revenues. Overall, GSK holds second place (to Pfizer) in the world's pharmaceutical market with a 7% share. The company's declared mission is to 'improve the quality of human life by enabling people to do more, feel better and live longer.'

Corporate citizenship – strategy and management

Pharmaceutical and healthcare firms operate within a controversial area of business and there are tensions in the relationship between firms and broader society (Baker, 2003). Firms such as GSK produce socially desirable goods that save and improve lives. Yet, as a profit motivated corporation decisions have to be made that do not necessarily improve or save the most lives. Indeed, 'Big Pharma' (New Internationalist, 2003) has been the subject of much criticism in recent years. Accusations launched specifically against GSK include: hiding research data concerning the safety of *Paxil/Seroxat*; perceived excessive remuneration for the CEO at a time when shareholder value was dropping; underpaying the US Inland Revenue Service; and changing drug names in order to overcharge Medicaid in the US (Weyzig, 2004, p.18). Furthermore, critics have pointed to apparent inconsistencies between the company's stated objectives and its actions. An Action Aid report states, 'GSK publicises its efforts to increase access to essential medicines in poor countries. At the same time, it is an influential member of the Pharmaceutical Research and Manufacturers of America (PhRMA), which lobbies aggressively for World Trade Organization rules and national laws that restrict people's access to low-cost drugs in developing countries' (Action Aid, 2005, p.10). Whilst the firm's financial backing for the US Republican Party might seem to contradict the firm's objective of supporting the provision of healthcare for the underprivileged, especially in light of the Republican Party's staunch opposition to the 1993 Clinton Health Reform programme, which sought to ensure broader access to healthcare across the social spectrum within the USA. Of course, the animal rights lobby also pose challenges for the firm to negotiate. This is particularly the case within the UK where various forms of violent direct action have been taken against those perceived as being stakeholders within the animal experimentation process.

The company's CSR strategy and management indicates that the firm has responded promptly to the various concerns expressed by its internal and external stakeholders. According to the CEO/Chairman's statement in the 2004 Corporate Responsibility Report, 'Corporate Responsibility is not just a job for selected people at GSK it defines the way we do business' (GSK, 2004c). The firm has decided to adopt the term Corporate Responsibility rather than CSR as CR invokes a broader remit incorporating environmental and ethical, as well as, social dimensions. CR is overseen by a dedicated committee consisting of four non-executive Directors who report directly to the Board. In 2003 this Committee met three times. In addition, a small corporate team co-ordinates policy development, reporting and communication with socially responsible investors. In 2003 the company identified ten principles that form the structure of the company's CR programme: *employment practices, human rights, access to medicines, leadership and advocacy, community investment, engagement with stakeholders, standards of ethical conduct, research and innovation, products and customers, caring for the environment* (GSK, 2003). 'Community investment' and 'caring for the environment' are managed as line functions whilst the other principles are embedded within different parts of the organisation. The CR committee focusses upon the risks the company is exposed to, the overall strategy and considers items to be included in reporting. Corporate responsibility is managed within individual business operations and the CR team links with a strong internal network. There are a dozen or so key people (Head of Divisions) and a network of 100–150 people across the firm who deal with specific issues relating to the CR Principles (Interview with member of Corporate Responsibility Committee, July 6th 2005).

According to a 2002 Report (Oxfam et al., 2002) GSK has a more integrated and explicit approach to CSR compared to other firms and is credited with being 'best in class' in terms of transparency. The authors note that GSK has an independent committee that advises the board on corporate responsibility issues and GSK is one of only two companies that have a stated policy on access to medicines. As GSK is the world's leader in the production of drugs to treat the three most critical diseases in the developing world (HIV/AIDS, Malaria and TB), the company has faced considerable pressure to ensure that the relevant medications become more widely available within the regions of need. In response the firm released a document, 'Facing the Challenge' (GSK, 2002; GSK, 2004d), which outlines the company's approach to these issues. This report represents the industry's first comprehensive attempt to address the issue of drug access in the developing world.

Community spending

According to the company's CR Report (GSK, 2005c), GSK's global community investment activities in 2004 were valued at £328 million, equivalent to 5.4% of the company's pre-tax profits. Product donation (£260 million) represented a large proportion of the total donation, whilst cash donations were £48 million, in-kind donations £2 million and the costs of management and delivery were valued at £18 million. The data provided in the Guardian Giving List (see below) gives different statistics as there are variations in methodologies used for producing valuations. GSK's data is calculated using the Committee

Table 9.2 Community investment performance (£m) according to the Annual Giving List

Date of publication of Giving List	Cash donation £m	Staff/ management costs	Gifts in kind	Total donation	% of pre-tax profits	Rank 2004
2005	48.4	17.7	56.8	122.9	2.0	10
2004	79.19	16.57	48.54	144.29	2.3	8
2003	101.76	5.26	25.96	132.99	2.41	9
2002	25.55	3.33	46.45	75.35	1.22	20

Sources:
http://image.guardian.co.uk/sys-files/Society/documents/2004/11/08/giving.pdf
http://image.guardian.co.uk/sys-files/Guardian/documents/2004/04/28/2003amendedtable.pdf
http://society.guardian.co.uk/givinglist/tables/0,10999,848892,00.html
http://image.guardian.co.uk/sys-files/Society/documents/2005/11/28/GivingList_paper_281105.pdf

Table 9.3 Overall community investment by sector

Education	Health	Arts	Environment	Other
37.8%	44.3%	2.1%	2%	13.8%

Source: http://www.gsk.com/corporate_responsibility/cr_report_2004/community_investment.htm, p.72.

to Encourage Corporate Philanthropy system, which values product donations (drugs) at their **wholesale cost** rather than production cost as is required by the LBG.

The health sector is targeted for the highest proportion of donations by GSK. This reflects GSK's main area of expertise and also the fact that drug donations form an important part of the community investment programme. GSK is keen to support healthcare initiatives in cases where provision is otherwise lacking. Educational initiatives consume more than a third of spending. Many health-related education programmes are supported. Otherwise GSK funds a number of projects which aim to further maths and science education in the UK and the USA. Such support indicates the levels of concern that exist within the company about the problems faced by such subjects in schools and the long term recruitment impacts that may be faced by science-based firms such as GSK in the future.

Donations are made by corporate contribution committees at the group level and by local GSK businesses. The group does not have an overall Foundation but small country specific Foundations exist in Canada, Spain, France and USA amongst others. The GSK France Foundation has supported programmes in 12 African countries and Cambodia to improve HIV/AIDS prevention education, training and care. The North Carolina GSK Foundation in the USA is an endowed self-funding organisation, which supports maths, science and health education initiatives.

The *Community Investment* principle states, 'we will support health and education programmes and partnerships in under-served communities around the world'. The 2004 Corporate Responsibility Report (GSK, 2005c) records GSK's community involvement in the following categories of activity:

- *Humanitarian Relief* – essential products (e.g. antibiotics) are donated to help relief efforts in disaster zones. Medicines were donated to support relief efforts in more than 100 countries during 2003. More

than two million doses of vaccines were made available in the first two weeks after the Asian Tsunami and £2 million was donated to relief agencies to support their work (GSK, 2005j).
- *Major Public Health Initiatives in Less Developed Countries (LDCs)* – donations of medical, financial and practical support are made to target major diseases such as lymphatic filariasis, HIV/AIDS and Malaria.
- *Community participation* – a wide range of community level health and education projects are supported. GSK supports over 70 UK-based charities. In 2004 monies were donated to Breakthrough Breast Cancer, Cystic Fibrosis Trust and the Motor Neurone Disease Association.
- *Supporting Education* – a number of projects emphasising the development of science literacy are supported in the UK and the US. The INSPIRE scheme in the UK aims to raise achievement in science by placing post-doctoral researchers into specialist science schools.
- *Employee Involvement* – GSK employees are encouraged to volunteer via specific schemes such as the Days of Caring programme in the US.

During 2005 three GSK community projects received BITC Big Tick awards (GSK, 2005l). Two of these are featured as case studies in this chapter – the LF programme, which was successful in the 'Oracle International Awards' category focussing upon Africa and Barretstown's European programme which was successful in the European Community Engagement category for the second year running. GSK's Science Education Programme gained recognition in the Investing in Education category. Furthermore, GSK was recognised by the Dow Jones Sustainability Index for 2005 indicating that the firm is among the top 10% in its sector in terms of its approach to social and environmental challenges. GSK is also included in the FTSE4Good Index and is included in the Top 100 Global Companies for Sustainability (GSK, 2005b). The company is a member of the LBG, the PerCent Club and the Committee to Encourage Corporate Philanthropy (CECP) in the USA.

Reporting

Whilst both of GSK's predecessor companies reported on environment, health and safety matters, neither had produced a socially oriented report. Following the merger it was agreed that a more explicit emphasis should be placed upon social and ethical issues. In 2003 GSK published its first Corporate Responsibility report, which utilised the newly identified CR principles to provide a guiding structure for the report.

Third-party analysts (Baker, 2003; Weyzig, 2004) state that the report is uneven in its coverage with various issues of interest to external stakeholders being neglected. For example, there is no mention of the results from internal monitoring on compliance with the firm's Code of Conduct for business ethics and marketing codes. Workplace practices outside of the USA are also neglected. Baker (2003) comments that the report was replete with 'warm words' but lacked overall substance. Weyzig (2004) notes that GSK scores highly for transparency about their CSR policy and governance structure but there is much less information available on performance. The 2004 Report made some strides in attempting to address some of the issues raised by critics. Indeed, the report is substantially longer, the Community Investment section, for example, being 13 pages compared to four illustration-packed pages in 2003. These changes reflect the reality that non-financial reporting remains an emerging discipline still very much in its infancy. The 2004 Report (which is only available online) incorporates the previously separately published Environment, Health and Safety report. The latter elements have been externally verified by Environmental Resources Management; however there is no verification of the remainder of the report's contents. The website provides a section illustrating links between the report's content and GRI criteria (GSK, 2005d). These links are to a degree coincidental as GSK does not explicitly utilise GRI criteria, instead preferring only to deploy measurement systems that are of direct use to the business.

Case study 1: Barretstown Gang Camp for children with serious illnesses[1]

Location: Barretstown, County Kildare, Ireland
Duration: Ongoing since 1994

How the programme started

GSK was a founder partner in the scheme. A 'task force' of senior company executives created a community partnerships plan for the whole company in the early 1990s. Children's health was identified as a key focus area. The concept of Barretstown supporting children from across Europe also reflected the firm's regional structure in that it is truly pan-European. Furthermore, the programme was initiated to demonstrate GSK's ethos of enhancing provision for the underserved. In this case mainstream cancer services have tended to neglect the specific needs of children.

Programme outline

Barretstown Gang Camp was established in 1994, modelled on the Paul Newman 'Hole in the Wall' gang camp in the USA. Newman donated $2 million in order to initiate the Ireland-based charity whilst the Irish government donated the castle in which the facility is based. The Barretstown estate features a lake, an arts and crafts centre, a theatre, dining hall, a children's village of 12 houses and a walled garden. A facility has been created whereby children aged 7–17 with cancer and other serious illnesses are able to experience 'summer camp' supported by the provision of first class medical facilities. The programme is offered free of charge including travel, accommodation and medical care. The summer programme offers a ten-day therapeutic experience. Barretstown is premised on the notion of 'serious fun', whereby children are able to participate in Therapeutic Recreation, which supports their treatment by enhancing their self-esteem, confidence and independence. The children take part in a range of activities such as poetry, music and woodwork. Members of staff are known as 'caras' (Irish term meaning friend) and come from all over Europe. There is a ratio of two campers to each cara. The medical centre is staffed by two paediatric oncologists and four paediatric nurses. There is equipment for routine and emergency procedures.

GSK funds are targeted at supporting the European Liaison Network, which enables children to attend Barretstown following a referral from their specialist. The Network raises awareness about the camp amongst doctors, parents and children in 21 countries. More than 110 hospitals across Europe nominate children to participate. The European Liaison Network is an important interface between Barretstown and children's hospitals. The Network provides a framework across 21 countries for raising awareness about the camp among doctors, parents and children, as well as recruiting children to participate. GSK provides the funding for communications materials that have been produced in a range of languages. The Network also identifies and recruits volunteer caras. GSK businesses provide meeting rooms for interviewing volunteers.

In 2005 a three-year plan for funding Barretstown was approved by the GSK European Community Partnerships Contributions Committee. GSK maintain its involvement as it is an integral component of their European programme of supporting children's health. Between 2005 and 2007 some of the objectives GSK and Barretstown will be seeking to achieve include: improving recruitment of children and young people; developing relationships with other children and family organisations in Europe; increase awareness of the efficacy of Barretstown's programmes internationally; increase European medical recruitment; and assess the viability of Barretstown's outreach programmes.

Working with partners

Organisations involved with Barretstown include patient groups and parents' groups. Additionally, Barretstown works with professional associations, e.g. those specialising in paediatric oncology. Specific bodies include: The European Organisation for Rare Diseases, The International Camping Fellowship, The American Camping Association, the Children's Oncology Camping Association, the European Forum for Child Welfare (Barretstown is a founder member), the Children's Rights Alliance, and the Irish Society for the Prevention of Cruelty to Children (ISPCC). Barretstown has worked with the ISPCC to bring in the statutory vetting of adults working with children through a campaign called 'How do we know they are safe?'. Two hundred and fifty thousand signatures were collected through the campaign and the Government is now introducing the statutory vetting system.

Inputs from GSK

By 2002 GSK had provided more than £2.7 million since the launch of Barretstown. In 2004 GSK gave £250,000 to support Barretstown whilst 40 GSK employees acted as volunteers (n.b. the total annual cost of running Barretstown's programmes is approximately £4 million and 600 volunteers are required). GSK's businesses fund children's flights to Ireland. Employees on secondment provide support in various ways, such as acting as interpreters. Senior managers from GSK have served on Barretstown's Board. GSK employees run fundraising projects across Europe. Products were donated to the Medical Centre to a value of £3,500 during the 1990s. Barretstown's 2004 Annual Review notes that GSK is their 'longest-standing and largest single funding partner' (Barretstown, 2005a).

Outcomes for the corporation, its partners and the community

- Barretstown now supports 1,400 seriously ill children and their family members each year. The children who participate are able to benefit from a unique opportunity that enables them to rediscover their self-esteem and confidence. Their quality of life and survival rates are likely to be enhanced as a result. An increasing number of specialists view Barretstown as a core component of treatment for certain patients.
- GSK's approach has provided a corporate partnership model for other potential donors to replicate. Smaller scale programmes involv-

ing hospitals in Hungary, Portugal and Romania have been set up using aspects of the Barretstown model.
- GSK's inputs have leveraged further support, e.g. American Home Products and the Dublin Millennium committee. Senior managers from GSK have helped Barretstown secure additional funding.
- The partnership between GSK and Barretstown is publicised to a wide range of audiences via: the Barretstown website, Barretstown's annual review, volunteer newsletters and feature articles in Serious Fun magazine distributed to 6,000 Barretstown friends, volunteers and supporters. Opportunities to apply for Awards (such as the 'Big Tick') are actively sought. GSK's partnership with Barretstown received a BITC 'Big Tick' in 2004 and 2005.
- GSK has enhanced its reputation among its peers, competitors and philanthropic service providers. Senior managers are able to network with healthcare providers across Europe. Staff morale is raised and new recruits are impressed by GSK's involvement. Furthermore, GSK's volunteers are able to enhance their personal development, especially in terms of developing creativity, team work and diversity awareness.

Evidence of sustainability

Barretstown is clearly highly dependent upon GSK for support. As long as this support is maintained then the Barretstown project will continue to thrive owing to the high levels of need that exist for its services within Europe. The project is important to GSK as enables the firm to meet various strategic objectives. Components of the Barretstown model have been replicated by other agencies.

How the programme is evaluated

Progress reports and scorecards are completed and reviewed by both organisations every six months.

Case study 2: Lymphatic Filariasis (LF) Programme[2]

Location: Global
Duration: Ongoing since 1998

How the programme started

In 1997 the World Health Assembly passed a resolution calling for '…the elimination of lymphatic filariasis as a public health problem…', as it was one of only six diseases that was believed could be eradicated at that time. The institutional infrastructure required to fulfil this ambition was, however, absent. A chain of events was set in motion following a chance discussion at a charity dinner between Smithkline Beecham's CEO, who at the time was seeking inspiration for a significant millennium philanthropic project, and former US President Jimmy Carter. Carter subsequently contacted Bill Foege, an advisor with a track record of high profile interventions in the realms of public health, including polio, river blindness and Guinea Worm. Key trial results indicating the effectiveness of *albendazole* had just been released and Foege saw an opportunity to build on the success of Merck's *Mectizan* donation programme and develop a ground-breaking programme to eliminate Lymphatic Filariasis throughout the developing world. A meeting was held at the Atlanta-based Carter Centre between GSK senior executives, Foege and other health officials. Foege was impressed that senior business people wanted 'to use their influence beyond making a profit to create social capital' (Dean, 2001, p.13). After detailed negotiations the idea of a donation of one of Smithkline Beecham's drugs, *albendazole*, was proposed and agreed upon – 'the largest single act of corporate philanthropy in any industry' according to the Financial Times (quoted in Garnier, 2002, p.5). GSK met with top officials at the WHO in Geneva, leading to the signing of a Memorandum of Understanding on a joint campaign to eliminate LF.

Programme outline

Lymphatic Filariasis (LF) affects more than 120 million people in Asian, African and Latin American countries and more than 1.2 billion people are at risk. It is one of the major causes of permanent disability in these regions. It is estimated that the economic losses resulting from decreased production and lost work days approximate to at least US$1 billion per annum. The disease is transmitted by mosquitoes. Elephantiasis is one of the conditions induced by LF. The disease is disseminated by a microscopic parasitic worm that affects the human lymphatic system. Research conducted in the 1990s revealed that a single dose of *albendazole*,[3] an anti-parasitic drug developed by Smithkline Beecham, taken with either *DEC* or *ivermectin* (*Mectizan*) could be 99% effective in eliminating the microfilaria from the blood of infected individuals thus disrupting the process of transmission. WHO strategists believe that the global disease cycle can be broken within 20 years via concerted drug administration programmes within the infected regions.

GSK was a founder member of the Global Alliance to Eliminate LF (GAELF). In its early stages the Alliance was based around a coalition including the Ministries of Health from LF endemic nations and international organisations such as the Arab Fund for Economic and Social Development, the US Centre for Disease Control and Prevention and DFID. In 1998 GSK (then Smithkline Beecham) announced a long term strategic collaboration with WHO, thus ensuring the strategic and practical success of GAELF. GSK committed to donate *albendazole* at no cost for as long as necessary. GlaxoSmithKline's partnership with WHO has been described by a WHO representative as, 'the key to providing an impetus to the cause of elimination of lymphatic filariasis' (WHO Medical Officer: electronic communication, 9th November 2005).

At a local level the National Ministries of Health of the LF endemic countries develop Plans of Action for the elimination of LF with a strategy planned in line with the epidemiology of LF and the available resources. Applications for drugs are then sent to the regional WHO office for review by a Programme Review Group comprising independent experts appointed by the WHO.

The LF programme was selected for a Big Tick in the BITC's annual awards. The award was attained in the Oracle International Award category which focusses upon Africa and is made in association with the International Business Leaders' Forum and the UK government-sponsored Commission for Africa.

Working with partners

GSK is an active and involved partner in the global elimination programme. With the WHO, GSK helped initiate the formation of the Global Alliance to Eliminate Lymphatic Filariasis (GAELF) – a partnership that now includes the 83 countries affected by LF, working with over 40 international organisations in the public and private sector. GSK is an active member of the Global Alliance Executive Group whose key focus is to help garner advocacy and resources to support the national programmes. In addition, regular meetings are held between GSK and WHO to ensure that forecasting and planning for tablet production and shipping are effective, and to monitor the safety of the medicines used. Partners include: World Bank, UNICEF, Bill and Melinda Gates Foundation, DFID, The Carter Centre, Interchurch Medical Assistance, Lymphatic Filariasis Support Centre at Liverpool School of Tropical Medicine and Health Ministries from the affected nations.

Inputs from GSK

There are three full-time staff dedicated to the LF programme: two based in London and one based in Philadelphia. Their roles are to ensure that the company's promise to help eliminate LF is being met through timely supply of medicines. The team members also work directly with partners and governments by bringing business management discipline to help with coalition-building, resource mobilisation, strategic planning, research, training, and communication initiatives. In addition there are several part-time staff involved in the programme plus the teams engaged in the manufacture of the donated medicine.

Three hundred and fifty million *albendazole* treatments have been provided and more than £5 million in cash grants has been donated to other Alliance partners. In 2004 GSK donated more than 67 million treatments worth £7 million (wholesale valuation) to 34 countries.

In several countries, GSK's local operating companies have directly supported the country programmes by helping produce educational materials such as banners and leaflets to encourage communities to participate in the elimination campaigns. In other countries, involvement has included participation in local fund raising committees, public relations and media support, and assistance with coalition-building.

GSK is fully committed to GAELF and has set no time limits or conditions on its participation. GSK expects to donate more than US$1 billion in terms of medicines (6 billion treatments) and cash donations in the programme's projected 20-year existence. The company's commitment to eliminating LF is a flagship programme within GSK's CR strategy. It represents one of the pharmaceutical industry's largest donation programmes.

Outcomes for the corporation, its partners and the community

- Over 100 million people were covered by the LF programme in 2004. Several countries are nearing completion of five years of annual mass community treatment and the preliminary data on LF elimination look promising, including Egypt where 95% of villages are now estimated as free from LF infection.
- Treatment with *albendazole* has the added benefit of eliminating intestinal parasites such as hookworm, whipworm and roundworm – infections that adversely affect children's growth and cognitive development.
- The programme has provided GSK with an opportunity to build working relationships with a range of partners operating at global, regional, national and local scales.
- The programme establishes GSK's credentials as a good corporate citizen, which is important to various of GSK's internal and external

stakeholders. GSK employees are proud to be part of a company, which sets ambitious socially oriented targets – such as aiming to eliminate a serious disease.
- LF programmes are being increasingly integrated with other community-based health initiatives, such as river blindness, schistosomiasis and malaria. Such integration increases the cost effectiveness of the programme.
- Precedents have been set: global alliances can work and large corporate donations can reap handsome dividends in terms of public health. The identification of suitable institutional arrangements for delivering mass programmes is of immense importance, 'what society is doing now is creating equivalent public health cathedrals, which through diagnostic treatment and surveillance programmes, will improve public health across the board' (Dean, 2001, p.20).

Evidence of sustainability

The GAELF is built upon a dense network of high level organisations committed to achieving the elimination of LF. In this sense the overall programme is highly sustainable as backing and resources have been attained from key agencies. Furthermore, the generation of the Alliance has yielded crucial lessons which are facilitating the development of other forms of alliance to tackle global scale health issues.

How the programme is evaluated

The LF programme is part of GSK's Global Community Partnership department which manages all corporate community initiatives. Progress and impact on LF and other programmes are reported to GSK management and the Corporate Responsibility Committee (composed from GSK's Board of Directors). There have been external evaluations of the programme undertaken by key partners such as DFID and the Bill and Melinda Gates Foundation.

Case study 3: Referral Management Initiative (RMI), Children's Health Fund (CHF)[4]

Location: USA
Duration: Since 1997 (partnership with CHF since 1995)

How the programme started

CHF's first proposal to Smithkline Beecham (SB) was submitted in 1992, but was not funded. In 1994, another proposal was successful, entitled 'Strengthening the National Children's Health Project Network to Meet Health Care Challenges for America's Children.' Thus, the partnership between the two organisations began. The partnership evolved in the ensuing years and in December 1996 it was announced that SB would provide backing for a new CHF programme – the Referral Management Initiative (RMI). The RMI targets disadvantaged children, thus fulfilling GSK's aim to address healthcare privations.

Programme outline

The CHF started in New York in the late 1980s. The fund focusses upon making healthcare available to homeless and other children who do not have access to care. Mobile medical units, which are in effect fully equipped paediatric clinics on wheels, travel to areas of need such as homeless shelters, low-income urban neighbourhoods and remote rural communities. The programme was initiated by a paediatrician, Irwin Redlener, and singer/songwriter Paul Simon. The latter donated the funds needed to kick-start the programme. The programme has been expanded to provide support in several US states. The CHF operates a Corporate Council for America's Children, which brings together leaders from major corporations and government agencies in order to build cooperative alliances. The Council meets in Washington DC with government figures to discuss policy issues affecting the wellbeing of America's children. Organisations represented on the Council include the Democratic and Republican parties, GSK, Wyeth, Bristol Myers Squibb, Merck and Co, Sanofi-aventis and Harpo Productions.

The need for RMI was identified early on by Redlener, the staff of CHF and the New York Children's Health Project (NYCHP) when it was observed that there was a need for subspecialty care among NYCHP children that was five times as high as observed among a general paediatric population. When a referral was made, only about 7% of these patients attended their appointment with the relevant sub-specialist. A range of barriers exist (cultural, geographic, economic) that prevent children in poor communities from accessing appropriate, timely treatment. The majority of subspecialty services needed by these underserved children were for critical medical problems, which have a high impact on social behaviour and school performance as well as health status. In 1997/8 the RMI was implemented to streamline the processes by which children's acute and chronic medical needs are identified, diagnosed and treated. RMI case managers provide assistance ensuring that children attain the care they need, for example by telephoning parents to remind them of appointments, providing transportation, assisting people in finding their way around hospitals and enhancing communication between primary care and specialist providers. The RMI is an integral component of the CHF's 'medical home' model, ensuring that appropriate specialist services are accessed by those in need. The RMI is run through a partnership between CHF and GSK, who are the sole financial supporters of the initiative. GSK's support for the RMI programme is ongoing.

Working with partners

CHF is the main partner. Through the Corporate Council for America's Children GSK work with key political and corporate groups. Medical affiliates of the RMI sites include: The Children's Hospital at Montefiore, Cedars-Sinai Medical Centre and the Department of Paediatrics, University of Texas Southwestern Medical School.

Inputs from GSK

Inputs specific to RMI: In the initial phase of the RMI, CHF and SB established a 'Partnership Committee' to discuss big picture issues of how the programme would proceed, major changes being instituted, and ideas for marketing the concept internally and externally. This committee met bi-monthly until RMI was well-established. Between 1994 and 2003 GSK provided $4.4 million to set up and run the RMI. GSK has made a three-year grant of $2 million to allow the RMI to expand into seven US states.

Inputs specific to CHF: David Stout, GSK's President of Pharmaceuticals is a trustee of CHF's Corporate Council for America's Children. GSK have made a contribution to CHF of US$1 million for a four-year period and provided US$175,000 to fund 'Strengthening the National Children's Health Project Network' to expand CHF's coordinated electronic data collection to improve health care delivery. GSK has contributed US$200,000 to sponsor Icahn House, a New York Children's Health Project clinical site. GSK has been a Trustee of the Corporate Council for America's Children since 1995. GSK's commercial business is complementing work of one of their key customers, United Health Group, by providing a grant to CHF's New York Clinic in support of a family-centred management approach to adult diabetes.

Inputs to both programmes include: GSK staff time, communications expertise, visits by senior staff including CEO. In addition, GSK nominated CHF for the first non-profit award from the Committee to Encourage Corporate Philanthropy. CHF won this award which has helped raise their profile.

Outcomes for the corporation, its partners and the community

- Approximately 75% of the children in the RMI programme are getting specialist care compared to 5% when the initiative began.
- The RMI has been presented as a national model to increase adherence to urgent speciality care. Information about the RMI model and results have been disseminated in professional journals and the media.
- GSK's support enables CHF to extend the range of their provision and further their objectives. CHF also benefits from skill and knowledge transfers provided by support from GSK's employees. GSK's support adds prestige to CHF's activities which can aid in the leverage of funding support from alternative sources.
- Through RMI, CHF has documented for the first time the nature of the increased clinical needs of medically underserved children and the higher rates of referral for specialist care. Such evidence is clearly important if public policy is to be influenced.
- GSK is able to meet its objective of helping to provide for the needs of the underserved and is able to demonstrate its corporate citizenship credentials through its support for an award winning programme.

Evidence of sustainability

The RMI programme has been important in setting precedents in terms of healthcare management and has been influential at a national policy level. Thus, the lessons learned are being disseminated more widely within the US healthcare system. Certainly the programme has been dependent upon GSK's financial inputs; however these have facilitated the leveraging of further funds and the adoption of key ideas by other institutions.

How the programme is evaluated

CHF provides regular reports of progress and outcomes of RMI and the documented success has been a key factor in the continuation of funding. CHF has compiled and analysed data on issues such as compliance and patient profiles. Information on the barriers to healthcare has been presented at many public, government and scientific meetings.

Project-by-project assessment of social capital impacts

In this section we summarise the social capital aspects of each project. We conclude by using the format of Table 4.1 to create a table, which allows a comparison of the social capital elements of each project (see Table 9.4).

Barretstown

The Barretstown project generates several interconnecting forms of potent social capital development. Collectively these focus around the benefits associated with the drawing together of key organisations into cooperative networks. Thus, representatives from the private sector, government, NGOs and key individual champions (such as Paul Newman) are working together to provide the necessary resources and systems to run Barretstown. In the process a network has been created through which highly innovative healthcare projects have been generated. This collective action has corrected a government/social failure. Prior to the setting up of Barretstown such provision for seriously ill children had been severely lacking within Western Europe. The programme has demonstrated the necessity of bringing together representatives from different types of organisation in order to deliver such a ground-breaking project. In so doing a significant structural hole in the network of healthcare provision has been bridged.

Thus, it is within the realms of 'form' that the Barretstown project exhibits its most significant impacts upon social capital building. There are certainly some notable impacts in terms of 'scope' as individuals from different backgrounds are drawn together through the Barretstown network and through its daily operations. The project is also important for building trust at different scales, whether between the public and private sectors and society and, indeed, between different European states. In terms of norms, important precedents are set concerning the ability of the private sector to contribute to broader society and in terms of pan-regional cooperation to achieve social goals.

LF

The LF programme is notable for the fact that it has stimulated a range of potent impacts within all realms of social capital. The pioneering role played by GSK is a particularly interesting aspect of this example. As such the LF programme should be recognised as a best practice case study of social capital development in action. Critical to the programme's success has been the creation of a strong and effective network of organisations operating at global, national and local levels. Diseases of this type can only be tackled effectively through the generation of such complex networks. In effect the creation of the GAELF represents a remarkable example of a case where structural holes within international networks have been bridged, significantly strengthening the overall global healthcare network and bringing in a number of important new members. The development of appropriate social bonds and goodwill has been instrumental in the programme's success as an institutional development exercise. Clearly the programme has established new norms of behaviour, particularly with regard to the key roles that MNCs can play. In the process there have been notable shifts in the ways that pharmaceutical MNCs are viewed from the perspective of public trust. The dividends to the firm are very important in this regard. The programme's very initiation was predicated upon important examples of 'scope' forms of social capital in that the building of links between people and organisations were essential in getting the project off the ground. Vertical relationships have been very important, not least the pre-eminent role played by important global figures such as Jimmy Carter, whose interventions helped to realise the broad ambitions of GSK's CEO.

Table 9.4 GSK case studies – summary assessment of social capital impacts

		Barretstown	LF	RMI
Scope-				
Micro:	Person to person	**	**	**
Meso:	Vertical relationships	*	***	**
Macro:	Institutional	***	***	**
Form-				
Structural:	Networks	***	***	**
	Bridging structural holes	***	***	***
	New membership	**	***	*
	Ties & glue/lubricant	**	***	*
Cognitive:	Competence/goodwill	**	***	**
Channel-				
Information:	Improve education	*	**	*
Collective action:	Correct government/social failure	***	***	***
Misc:	Employment stability		**	
	Cohesion	***	***	***
	Radius of trust/distrust	**	**	*
	Norms of behaviour	**	***	**

N.B.: For the purposes of social capital impact analysis the assessment provided here is based solely upon GSK's contribution to the RMI.

Key: no stars = minimal impact, * = some impact, ** = notable impact, *** = potent impact.

CHF/RMI

The most important aspect of GSK's contribution to the RMI relates to the ways in which the firm have been involved in a project that, on a local scale at least, seeks to correct severe failings within the national healthcare system. In order to do this efforts have been made to bridge structural gaps within healthcare provision networks. There have been important dividends within the firm as the project reinforces GSK's commitment to the principle of providing healthcare for the underserved. Thus, support for the RMI helps to build goodwill with both internal and external stakeholders. Involvement more broadly with the CHF has been important in terms of network development, particularly through the Council for Corporate America, whose links to US political parties are important examples of vertical relationships of scope. Institutional relationships have been enhanced and important channels have been opened up for the dissemination of information that may help re-direct public health policy.

Notes

1 *Sources*: Barretstown, 2005a, b, c, BITC, 2004, Department of Health and Children, 2002, GSK, 2003, 2004a, b, GSK-Barretstown, 2005.
2 *Sources*: Dean, 2001; GAELF, 2004; GAELF, 2005a; GAELF, 2005b; GAELF, 2005c; GSK, 2003; GSK, 2004a; GSK, 2005e; GSK, 2005f; GSK, 2005h; GSK, 2005l; Lymphatic Filariasis Support Center, 2004; Oxfam et al., 2002.
3 Albendalzole (an anti-parasitic medication) was developed in Pennsylvania for the treatment of helminth infections in domestic animals. It was subsequently developed for human use against the major intestinal nematodes.
4 *Sources*: Children's Health Fund, 2005a; Children's Health Fund, 2005b; Children's Health Fund, 2005c; GSK, 2003.

References

Action Aid (2005), *Under the Influence: Exposing undue corporate influence at the World Trade Organisation*. Available at: http://www.actionaid.org.uk/_content/documents/under_the_influence_final.pdf. Accessed 05/05/2006.

Baker, M. (2003), *GlaxoSmithKline – Seeking a cure for public mistrust*. Available at: www.mallenbaker.net/csr/CSRfiles/page.php?_ID=910. Accessed 28/06/2005.

Barretstown (2005a), *2004 Annual Review*. Available at: http://www.barretstown.org/library/Barretstown%20Annual%20Report%2004.pdf. Accessed 08/08/2006.

Barretstown (2005b), *Barretstown Gang: FAQs*. Available at: www.barretstowngc.ie/faqs/. Accessed 08/07/2005.

Barretstown (2005c), *Barretstown Gang: History*. Available at: www.barretstowngc.ie/about/history.html. Accessed 08/07/2005.

BITC (2004), *GlaxoSmithKline – Barretstown, therapeutic recreation for children with serious illnesses*. Available at: www.bitc.org.uk/resources/case_studies/ea_291_gsk.html. Accessed 09/07/2005.

Children's Health Fund (2005a), *Corporate Council for America's Children.* Available at: www.childrenshealthfund.org/whoweare/council.php. Accessed 08/07/2005.
Children's Health Fund (2005b), *Every Child Counts, Every Family Matters – timeline.* Available at: http://www.childrenshealthfund.org/whoweare/timeline.pdf. Accessed 08/07/2005.
Children's Health Fund (2005c), *Referral Management Initiative.* Available at: www.childrenshealthfund.org/whatwe do/rminitiative.php. Accessed 08/07/2005.
Dean, M. (2001), *Lymphatic Filariasis. The Quest to Eliminate a 4000-Year Old Disease*: Hollis Publishing Company. Hollis, New Hampshire.
Department of Health and Children (2002), *Martin announces E1.27m Barretstown Gang Camp Grant.* Available at: www.dohc.ie/press/releases/2002/20020311.html. Accessed 12/07/2005.
GAELF (2004), *'Freeing the World of LF: A Call to Action.'* Report of the Third Meeting of the Global Alliance to Eliminate Lymphatic Filariasis, 23–25 March 2004, Cairo, Egypt.
GAELF (2005a), *The Framework of the Global Alliance to Eliminate LF.* Available at: www.filariasis.org/index.pl?iid=2766&printer_friendly=1. Accessed 27/06/05.
GAELF (2005b), *GSK.* Available at: http://www.filariasis.org/index.pl?id=2767. Accessed 27/06/2005.
GAELF (2005c), *Partnership.* Available at: www.filariasis.org/index.pl?iid= 1847& printer_friendly=1. Accessed 27/06/2005.
Garnier, J. (2002), *Bold Solutions for Global Health Challenges.* Available at: http://www.corporatephilanthropy.org/ncp/pubs/CECPspring2002.pdf. Accessed 22/05/2006.
GSK (2002), *Facing the Challenge.* Available at: http://www.gsk.com/community/downloads/facing_the_challenge.pdf. Accessed 02/12/2005.
GSK (2003), *Corporate Responsibility Report 2003.* Available at: http:// www.gsk.com/financial/reps03/cr_2003.pdf. Accessed 27/05/2005.
GSK (2004a), *80 million people now treated to prevent elephantiasis.* Available at: http://www.gsk.com/ControllerServlet?appId=4&pageId=402&newsid=211. Accessed 27/06/2005.
GSK (2004b), *Corporate Responsibility Report.* Available at: http://www.gsk.com/corporate_responsibility/cr_report_2004/community_investment.htm. Accessed 27/05/2005.
GSK (2004c), *Corporate Responsibility Report: Community Investment.* Available at: http://www.gsk.com/corporate_responsibility/cr_report_2004/community_inv estment.htm. Accessed 27/05/2005.
GSK (2004d), *Facing the Challenge – two years on.* Available at: http://www.gsk.com/community/downloads/FTC-TwoYearsOn.pdf. Accessed 02/12/2005.
GSK (2005a), *Annual Report 2004 New Challenges and New Thinking.* Available at: http://www.gsk.com/financial/reps04/annual-report-2004.pdf. Accessed 30/11/2005.
GSK (2005b), *Corporate Responsibility Overview.* Available at: http://www.gsk.com/corporate_responsibility/index.htm. Accessed 02/12/2005.
GSK (2005c), *Corporate Responsibility Report: Community Investment.* Available at: http://www.gsk.com/corporate_responsibility/cr_report_2004/community_inv estment.htm. Accessed 27/05/2005.

GSK (2005d), *CR Report 2004: GRI Index*. Available at: http://www.gsk.com/corporate_responsibility/cr_report_2004/GRI_index.htm. Accessed 01/12/2005.
GSK (2005e), *FAQs – Lymphatic Filariasis*. Available at: www.gsk.com/filariasis/quanda.htm. Accessed 27/06/2005.
GSK (2005f), *The Global Alliance to Eliminate Lymphatic Filariasis*. Available at: http://www.gsk.com/filariasis/index.htm. Accessed 27/07/2005.
GSK (2005g), *Global Community Partnerships – European programmes*. Available at: www.gsk.com/community/europe.htm. Accessed 08/07/2005.
GSK (2005h), *Global Community Partnerships – UK Corporate Contributions*. Available at: www.gsk.com/community/uk.htm. Accessed 28/06/2005.
GSK (2005i), *GSK Overview*. Available at: www.gsk.com/about/about.htm. Accessed 27/05/2005.
GSK (2005j), *GSK Response to Tsunami Disaster Update*. Available at: www.gsk.com/press_archive/press2005/press_01042005.pdf. Accessed 01/12/2005.
GSK (2005k), *Heritage*. Available at: www.gsk.com/about/background.htm. Accessed 01/12/2005.
GSK (2005l), *Three GSK community programmes win BITC Big Tick awards*. Available at: www.gsk.com/press_archive/press2005/gcp_06172005.htm. Accessed 01/12/2005.
GSK-Barretstown (2005), '*GSK Barretstown Partnership 2005–2007 programme scorecard*', internal document.
Logan, D. and Tuffrey, M. (2000), *Companies in Communities: assessing the impact. Using the London Benchmarking Group model to assess how the community and company benefit from corporate community involvement*, Charities Aid Foundation.
Lymphatic Filariasis Support Center (2004), *Global Program to Eliminate Lymphatic Filariasis. Extending the Benefits*, Emory LF Support Centre, Rollins School of Public Health.
New Internationalist (2003), *Big Pharma: Making a killing*. Available at: www.newint.org/issue362/keynote.htm. Accessed 28/06/2005.
Oxfam, Save the Children and VSO (2002), *Beyond Philanthropy*. Available at: www.savethechildren.org.uk/temp/scuk/cache/cmsattack/622_beyondphil.pdf. Accessed 28/06/2005.
Weyzig, F. (2004), *GlaxoSmithKline company profile*, SOMO (Centre for Research on MNCs).

10
Vodafone Group and its Corporate Citizenship Programme

A brief corporate biography

Vodafone was formed in 1984 as a subsidiary of Racal Electronics plc (Vodafone, 2005a). In 1991 it was demerged from Racal and became an independent company known as Vodafone Group Ltd (Vodafone is an abbreviation of Voice Data Fone). In the 1980s Vodafone became committed to aggressive development by entering into consortia to bid for licences and by identifying opportunities for acquisitions on a global scale. High profile examples include the merger with AirTouch Communications Ltd in 1999 and the acquisition of Mannesmann in 2000, which doubled the size of the Vodafone group. At the end of 1985 the company had 19,000 customers, by 1999 this had risen to ten million and during 2002 the 100 million mark was achieved. Vodafone is now the largest mobile telecommunications company in the world, with operations in Europe, the USA and the Asia Pacific region (Wikipedia, 2006a).[1] Vodafone provides an extensive range of mobile telecommunication services including voice and data communications. As well as 14 controlled networks, Vodafone also has nine associates and 14 partner network agreements (as of 31/12/2004). The company has approximately 180 million customers and 57,000 employees in 26 countries (biz.yahoo.com, 2005; Vodafone Group, 2005a; Wikipedia, 2006b). As of 23rd May 2005 Vodafone had a total market capitalisation of £94 billion, making it the third largest firm in the FTSE100 and the eleventh largest firm in the world. The Group's turnover in 2004/5 was £34 billion (Vodafone Group, 2005a, p.35). The Group's success is predicated upon rapid and effective technological innovation allied to timely strategic responses to market opportunities.

Table 10.1   Regional data for Vodafone plc 2004/5

	UK/Ireland	Southern Europe, Middle East and Africa	Northern Europe	Asia Pacific	Americas
Proportionate customers 2004[1]	15,959,000	40,139,000	40,587,000	19,489,000	17,257,000
% share	12	30	30	14	13
Turnover 2004 £m[2]	5,504	10,073	8,531	7,353	–
% share	17	32	27	23	n/a
Employees[3]	11,397	26,579	13,618	5,610	174
% share	20	46	24	10	0.3
Social Investment 2004/5 £m[4]	8.8	14.0	3.6	5.1	3.1
% share	25	40	10	15	9

Sources:
(1) Vodafone Group plc Annual Report 2004, p.8 ; (2) Annual Report 2004, pp.32–35; (3) Vodafone Group plc Annual Report 2004, p.105; (4) Vodafone Corporate Responsibility Report 2005, p.28.
N.B.
Turnover data for Americas appears as 'zero' as the Americas Region largely comprises the Group's interest in Verizon Wireless, which is accounted using equity accounting and as such is not included in statutory profit and loss accounts data.
Employee data relates to the mobile telecommunications segment of the business. A further 4,352 people are employed in other areas within the business.

Corporate citizenship – strategy and management

In little over a decade mobile communications have grown from being relatively marginal elements of western economies to becoming integral parts of daily life. Services are evolving all the time and product lifecycles are constantly diminishing. The novelty of the technology and its popularity clearly stimulates many issues and concerns in terms of the relationship between the technology, and the firms who produce it, and broader society. Thus, there are 'classic' concerns related to supply chain management and raw material sourcing (see Fauna and Flora International, 2005; Hayes and Burge, 2003 for example) whilst there are a whole raft of other issues emerging related to the environmental and potential health impacts of mobile phone masts and phone usage itself. Vodafone utilise a carefully structured Corporate Responsibility (CR) strategy, which is fully integrated into their operational structures in order to confront these many challenges. According to Vodafone Chief Executive Arun Sarin (Vodafone Group, 2005c), 'CR is a vehicle for achieving prosperity in society *and* in business...when Vodafone talks about CR we mean sustainable development'. Furthermore, '...my vision for CR is that it becomes fully integrated into everything we do...it becomes instinctive. We are some way from that position...'

The Group has recently adopted the expression CR rather than CSR as the former term resonates better with global audiences, whilst reflecting the broad array of responsibilities that the firm embraces. CR is managed within the firm's operational management systems and line managers are charged to deal with CR issues. The Group's CR team tracks issues and measures performance; however the implementation of CR rests with operating companies and group functions. 'Being a responsible business' is one of the Vodafone Group's six medium term strategic goals. CR issues are of strategic importance, therefore the reporting line for CR runs all the way up to the Group Executive Committee (Vodafone Group, 2005d) 'reflecting the strategic importance we (Vodafone) attach to CR' (Vodafone Group plc, 2006, p.8). The Group CR Director reports to the Group Corporate Affairs Director who is the Executive Committee member with responsibility for CR. The Chief Executive of each operating company takes responsibility for implementing Group CR policies. There are also monthly teleconferences and the Group CR Director meets senior executives from the firm's operating companies on a regular basis. Key performance indicators for CR are reported upon quarterly. These include: level of commitment, management of issues and integration. A global CR workshop is held every six months providing opportunities to share experiences and best practice. Furthermore, the firm's business principles underpin Vodafone's approach to CR. These principles cover corporate and individual behaviour and are communicated to employees via induction training, team briefings and operating companies' websites. CR is integral to the daily management of the company across all aspects of the business, including risk management, business planning and product development. The firm's CR strategy is clearly articulated and, structurally at least, is well embedded into the firm's management systems. According to one internal source the company's relative youth has been a positive factor as there are no legacy issues to overcome when implementing CR.

CR considerations are particularly prevalent within the following operational functions: Group Supply Chains, Group Marketing, Employment and Network Rollout. The Company's annual CR reports are structured to cover areas where CR considerations are particularly important. In the 2004/5 report these included:

- Mobile phones, masts and health – a number of concerns relating to public and employee safety exist in relation to mobile phone technologies, including radio frequency emissions from masts and base stations. Vodafone is responding to these concerns through supporting scientific research and by engaging in dialogue with stakeholders.
- Employees – one of the firm's strategic goals is to 'build the best global Vodafone team'. Vodafone's employment policies are consistent with the UN Universal Declaration of Human Rights and the ILO's core conventions. Vodafone conducts an annual survey of employee views, which it uses in order to gauge levels of employee satisfaction and engagement.
- Environment – key environmental issues confronted by Vodafone include high levels of energy usage and network equipment waste. The company is committed to detailed audits of its impacts in these areas and the identification of ways of reducing them. Targets are set for recycling and reductions in energy usage.
- Supply chain – in 2004/5 Vodafone made payments of £23 billion to third parties, of which £12 billion was spent on handsets, network equipment, marketing and IT services. The company sets out the standards expected of its suppliers through its Code of Ethical Purchasing (CEP). During 2004/5 Vodafone has made progress in three areas: CR is a key part of supplier performance management, CEP is incorporated into supplier contracts and 25 global and 47 local suppliers have completed self-assessments.
- Social investment – this aspect is explored in more detail below.

Social investment

The group operates a social investment policy which applies across the Vodafone Group (Vodafone Group, 2005f). According to the policy social investment should be:

- At the heart of the business
- Global in scope, local in focus
- More than just financial contributions
- Based if possible on Vodafone's areas of expertise
- Engaging for its employees, who should benefit from the opportunity to become involved in their local communities
- Furthermore, Vodafone aims to help bridge the digital divide by reaching those excluded from the benefits of mobile technology.

Vodafone has decided that Foundations are the main way that it will contribute to local communities and thus has established a 'family of foundations' across its global operations. The Foundations share a common strategy, management approach and focus. The Vodafone Group Foundation has been established to support the network of local national Foundations. According to an internal source there are 'close but appropriate links' between the Group Foundation and the main business and there 'is synergy between the two sides within the confines of the relevant regulations'. The Group Foundation itself responds to international circumstances beyond the markets within which Vodafone operates. Nineteen foundations now exist and there are plans to initiate four more, thereby ensuring that there will be a Foundation in all but two of the 25 markets where Vodafone has operating companies or associates. According to Lord Broers, Chairman of the Board of Trustees of the Vodafone Group Foundation, the company's utilisation of Foundations as the primary mechanism for channelling funding to projects is 'unique amongst multi-nationals'. The Foundation structure enables funding to be targeted at both global and local projects, which address social, economic and environmental needs. It is believed that country-based foundations are the most appropriate mechanism for responding quickly to local needs. There is an active network in operation between the different foundations and the Group. The Group provides a lot of support including toolkits to help local foundations make grant applications. Utilisation of the core technological and entrepreneurial skills of the workforce is an integral component of many projects. The Group aims to provide a common approach to social investment in the following areas: conservation, education, young people, disaster relief and the environment. As Table 10.3 below illustrates the largest proportion of funds are directed towards young people reflecting the fact that young people are the firm's main market. Other areas receiving support tend to have some form of technological dimension.

Table 10.2 below illustrates the social investment donations made by the firm in the last four years. These figures do not reflect the totality of giving for the group as a whole as the Giving List data only refers to Vodafone UK's activities. During 2004/5 the Vodafone Group and its Foundations donated a total of £34.6 million (9% of which was compulsory under the terms of national licence agreements in Spain and Portugal)[2] directly to social projects, representing an increase of 50% over the £23 million donated during 2003/4. These sums comprise cash donations, the value of donated products and services, employee

Table 10.2 Community investment performance (£m) according to the Annual Giving List

	Cash donation £m	Staff/ management costs	Gifts in kind	Total donation	% of pre-tax profits	Rank
2005	7.65	0.53	0.11	8.29	0.5	56
2004	9.90	0.57	0.04	10.51	n/a	n/a
2003	11.02	0.36	0.25	11.63	n/a	n/a
2002	5.70			5.70	0.81	33

N.B.: Figures refer to Vodafone in the UK, except for 2002 which refers to Vodafone Group. In 2003 and 2004 Vodafone made a loss therefore they cannot be ranked.

Sources:
http://image.guardian.co.uk/sys-files/Society/documents/2005/11/28/GivingList_paper_281105.pdf
http://image.guardian.co.uk/sys-files/Guardian/documents/2004/04/28/2003amendedtable.pdf
http://image.guardian.co.uk/sys-files/Society/documents/2004/11/08/giving2.pdf
http://image.guardian.co.uk/sys-files/Society/documents/2005/11/28/GivingList_paper_281105.pdf

Table 10.3 Overall community investment by sector 2003/4

Young people	Health	Disasters	Teaching and technology	Environment	Other
32%	14%	3%	25%	8%	18%

Source: Vodafone Corporate Social Responsibility Report 2003/04, p.19.

volunteering, donations of redundant IT equipment and the costs of running the Foundations. Since 2001 Vodafone's Foundations have invested more than £60 million in social investments around the world. The strategic direction of the Foundations is now being shifted such that investments are increasingly focussing upon fewer, larger and longer term partnerships in order to pursue shared interests. Furthermore, Vodafone is focussing increasing attention upon developing technologies with wider benefits for society. The commercial value of some of these may be negligible, however the social benefits may be considerable (Vodafone, 2005c). In 2004 a Social Products and Enterprise Team was set up in order to investigate the development of technologies such as Textphones for deaf people and the Speaking Phone for blind people. In addition, the team is involved in developing systems that can facilitate improved access to credit in developing societies. Vodafone diverts part of its annual social investment funds directly to the Social Products and Enterprise team.

An interesting facet of Vodafone's strategic outlook is the recognition that, 'the next billion mobile users live in developing countries' (Vodafone Group, 2005c) and that there must be a symbiotic relationship between mobile market growth and economic development in the global South. On the one hand mobile products and services can contribute to socio-economic development and socio-economic development will create more market opportunities. Thus, Vodafone's '…interest in the developing world is not borne out of a philanthropic drive to "do good" but a recognition of the commercial reality' (CEO's introduction to 2004/5 CR Report) (Vodafone, 2005b). As Jonathan Porritt observes in an introductory article in the 2004/5 CR Report, 'in a world where 3 billion people are still living in chronic poverty, the positive opportunities for a company like Vodafone for generating prosperity and building social capital are enormous. How can mobile networks become catalysts in delivering lasting solutions to public health problems, climate change and access to education?' Vodafone has supported research examining the impacts of mobile technology upon societies in developing countries (Vodafone, 2005b) and as our case studies illustrate significant steps are being taken by the firm to enhance the potential benefits.

Vodafone has been recognised by the Dow Jones Sustainability Index indicating that the firm are strong performers within their sector in terms of their approach to social and environmental challenges. Vodafone is also included in the FTSE4Good series and their status as a firm with strong sustainability credentials is indicated by the fact that Vodafone shares are the largest single holding in Jupiter Asset Management Ltd's Environmental Income Fund (Jupiter Asset Management Ltd, 2005). The company is a member of the LBG. Vodafone was ranked 83rd in the 2003 Corporate Responsibility Index (for comparison UK competitor MMO2 were ranked 32nd) and was ranked third amongst global firms for putting responsible practice at the heart of their business in the 2005 AccountAbility ratings (AccountAbility.org.uk, 2005).

Reporting

Vodafone has produced a CR report for each of the last five years (until 2004/5 these were entitled CSR Reports). A consultation with stakeholders helps to identify key issues that are used as the basis for the report (Vodafone Group, 2005e). The CR section of the website provides further information on policy, case studies and environment, employment and community issues. Envoy, a web-based data collection system, is used to collect information on environmental impact and community controls. The Group collects data twice a year, although local management in some operating companies may do so more frequently. Group guidelines are set for data collection and reporting. Senior executives are required to sign off local reports. Deloitte and Touche provide assurance for the Group with regard to data collection and reporting processes. Several of the operating companies published local reports at a national scale. In 2003/4 reports were produced for Germany, New Zealand, Spain and the UK. The Group applies GRI reporting guidelines, using the specific telecommunications protocols published by GRI in July 2003. The LBG model is utilised for measuring social contributions and the Group's management framework for CSR has been benchmarked by the consultancy group CSRnetwork. In 2005 the Group Foundation produced its own report detailing the Group's Social Investment activities (Vodafone Group Foundation, 2005b).

Case study 1: Vodacom Community Phone Shops[3]

Location: South Africa
Duration: Since 1994

How the programme started

The Vodacom Group is the largest of the three cellular operators (the others being MTN and Cell C) in South Africa with in excess of 8 million subscribers. Vodafone has recently increased their stake in the company to 50% following a $2.4 billion investment plan, which represents the second largest foreign direct-investment since the end of apartheid. Vodacom was originally granted a Network Cellular licence in September 1993 by the de Klerk administration. In 1994 the newly elected post-apartheid government led by Nelson Mandela reviewed the terms of the licence and decided that Vodacom should be required to provide affordable mobile technology in underserved areas such as urban townships and rural regions. Specifically the company were required to provide 22,000 public phones over a five-year period (to 30th June 1999).

Programme outline

Inadequate access to telecommunications was one of the many legacies of apartheid. For example, the former homeland region of the Transkei in the Eastern Cape possessed only 19,000 telephones serving a population of 4 million. The advent of mobile technology in the mid-1990s offered an opportunity to massively extend national communication networks. However, the costs were prohibitive for individuals within disadvantaged communities. Hence the government was keen to encourage the private sector to identify systems for improving provision in disadvantaged areas. Vodacom responded to the regulatory demand by creating a Community Service Programme whose delivery team had a budget of R5 million (US$778,731). Research was carried out within communities in order to identify the best way forward in terms of providing the phone service. It was decided that access to phones could best be provided via phone shop franchises. In this way individuals within disadvantaged communities could be empowered as entrepreneurs whilst Vodacom's management responsibilities were reduced. One of the initial challenges was to identify an appropriate physical structure for the shops especially bearing in mind the reality that security is a significant concern in the townships where the vast majority of phone shops would be located. Vodacom's team decided to utilise refurbished shipping containers as these are relatively cheap, sturdy and can be secured relatively easily. Each container is six meters long and is internally fitted out with a service counter at one end and a series of phone stalls along the walls. The phones resemble landline phones but are connected to the cellular network. The containers are painted 'Vodacom green' and have signage and promotional materials added to the décor. Each container costs R30,000 (US$4,675)[4] to purchase and modify. Prospective entrepreneurs need to be able to make an initial investment of R26,000 (US$4,052) to cover the cost of equipment for five phone lines and the cost of transporting the container to their location. Vodacom provides the containers free of charge.

Vodacom has tended to target individuals amongst their subscribers who were already acting in an entrepreneurial manner by renting out their own phone to friends and neighbours. Vodacom offers a certain level of training to the selected entrepreneurs during the set-up and early operational phases of each business. Vodacom has developed a partnership with a company, 'Running Business Today', who assist by providing appropriate training to owners. A quarterly newsletter 'Ringers' is sent out to shop owners in order to share ideas and information. During 2003 more than 90 million minutes per month of call time were delivered through the phone network, generating revenues of US $129.5 million. Vodacom is paid two-thirds of the total revenue with the remainder (approximately $12,000 per annum per shop) representing the shop owners' income. Vodacom's earnings enable the firm to recover overheads. The terms of the licence agreement do not allow the firm to profit from the venture. Vodacom succeeded in meeting the regulatory requirements three months ahead of schedule. Their main competitor at the time, MTN, followed a different delivery model and failed to meet their target. They subsequently replicated the Vodacom model. By mid-2003 30,000 phones were accessible through the programme.

As demand for franchises exceeds Vodacom's capacity to support them there is potential to further expand the phone shop network. New services such as fax and data sharing are being introduced and Vodacom have applied for a government licence to provide internet access through the phone shop network. Consideration is being given to replicating the model within Vodacom's other African markets.

Working with partners

Running Business Today is a partner.

Inputs from Vodacom

Vodacom has created a Community Service Programme team with an initial budget of R5 million (US$778,731). Vodacom sources, modifies and maintains the shop premises shipping containers at a cost of R30,000 (US$4675). Vodacom provides the entrepreneurs with initial training and support and circulate a quarterly newsletter.

Outcomes for the corporation, its partners and the community

- By mid-2003 1,800 entrepreneurs owned over 4,400 phone shops of which 3,500 utilised shipping containers and the rest either operated from store fronts or owner-supplied kiosks. Many entrepreneurs own small chains of phone shops. For example, one businessman manages seven shops employing 28 people within the Cape Town township of Langa.
- Whilst muggings are an all too common threat at individual phone boxes the containers provide a secure environment from which to make calls. Many people are able to make regular phone calls for the first time in their life. People are able to spend relatively small amounts of money on each occasion rather than incurring the full cost of purchasing a phone card. Thus, people can purchase precisely the amount they can afford at a given point in time.

- Families are able to stay in contact (especially with migrant workers) and also manage family affairs more effectively. Phones are used to pay bills and to access services such as doctors and utility providers. Delivery drivers use the phones to maintain contact with managers and to report any problems that they encounter.
- Approximately 20,000 jobs have been created through the programme so far. Multiplier effects are notable as informal businesses are generated around the phone shops. Overall the programme enables the development of a range of professional skills and networks in various ways. The net benefit for local economies and thus social welfare can be considerable.
- The entrepreneurs learn transferable business skills and become part of the formal tax paying economy.
- The programme has demonstrated an effective *modus operandi* for government-business relations. In this case the government has set quantifiable, ambitious but attainable social objectives which business can fulfil utilising its innovative and management capacities.
- Vodacom is building a distribution channel for its services and generating traffic through its cellular infrastructure. The shops increase familiarity with the Vodacom brand and sales of handsets and services increase as people become familiar with the benefits of Vodacom's cellular technology. Thus, by investing in disadvantaged communities Vodacom is investing in its future customer base. As individuals become wealthier they are likely to invest in a personal phone.

Evidence of sustainability

The programme demonstrates good characteristics in terms of sustainability. Firstly, the programme has been ongoing for several years, it has exceeded its original targets and there is still demand for further expansion. Secondly, the majority of individual phone shop businesses are not only surviving but are thriving. Thirdly, the programme is being replicated by other providers in South Africa and Vodacom is considering roll-out within other markets.

How the programme is evaluated

The programme has been evaluated by a research team based at University of North Carolina's Kenan-Flagler Business School (Goodman, 2003) resulting in a report published by the World Resources Institute. Internal reviews are performed to ensure that the programme is attaining its objectives.

Case study 2: Opportunity International (OI) – Provision of Personal Digital Assistants for Loan Officers[5]

Location: Albania and Romania
Duration: March 2003–June 2004

How the programme started

OI submitted an application to the Vodafone Foundation.

Programme outline

OI, the UK's largest microfinance agency, is a faith-based organisation that is affiliated to a global network providing microfinance services (small loans, deposit and insurance services) to people in poverty. OI operates in 25 countries helping 400,000 people. In 2002 OI made over 500,000 loans to the value of £81.7 million. The bureaucratic nature of microfinance administration is a major obstacle to the extension of such schemes. However, the rapid evolution of information and communication technologies offers a significant opportunity to reduce operational costs and extend the availability of microfinance. The Vodafone Group Foundation has offered support to OI's operations in Romania and Albania by donating monies that have enabled loan officers and support staff to be provided with Personal Digital Assistants (PDAs) that link in with overall Management Information Systems. Thus, data such as (client information, applications and loan calculations) can be processed much more speedily than has been the case hitherto. Operating costs are significantly reduced and more loans can be expedited. Once the impacts of this pilot project's have been fully assessed the technology can be extended to other partners around the world.

Twenty-five loan officers have been equipped with PDAs during the pilot phase of the project. The PDAs are programmed to link in with Management Information Systems (MIS). It is envisaged that the technology will help OI become a virtually 'paperless' organisation. The implementation of the new technology is radically altering the organisation's *modus operandi*. Customer relationship management is streamlined as loan officers have total access to client information including loan history. Updates to a client's file can be made on the spot, rather than on a paper form, which would have to be typed up in the office. The loan application process is streamlined and repeat customers can have the new application processed immediately. Loan repayment calculations can be swiftly performed on the PDA allowing loan officers to provide clients with detailed and accurate information. Cash transactions can be tracked more thoroughly as the use of portable printers enables receipts to be given to clients, whilst electronic records are retained within the system. Thus, the potential for fraud is greatly reduced.

The majority of the grant from Vodafone has been used as a one-off payment for the programming needed to adapt the PDAs to OI's operating system. Disseminating the system to other partners will be relatively easy once the initial programming has been completed. It is envisaged that spreading the system across OI's entire network could lead to 76,000 additional families benefiting from micro-finance opportunities. OI plans to takes the project forward by using PDA enablement for their Common Impact Mainstreaming System (CIMS), which maintains data on client satisfaction, impact and retention. Such information is essential management data informing future practice. PDA automation will enable significant time and paper savings to be made. The Vodafone grant has enabled OI to purchase additional hardware that can be utilised alongside the PDAs. These include portable keyboards, portable printers and voice recording software. The benefits of each of these pieces of hardware will be assessed so that the most useful elements can be included within the eventual rollout of the system across the network.

Thus, the pilot project has the potential to not only transform the operation of OI's network but also to stimulate benefits for the broader global microfinance industry. OI has strategic partnerships with World Vision and other NGOs who may benefit from the technology in the future. OI is also a signatory to the Micro Credit Summit. It is envisaged that the PDA technology could become the future industry standard.

Working with partners

OI is the principal partner. It, in turn, works with country partners such as Opportunity Microcredit Romania Ltd (OMRO) and Partneri Shqiptar ne Mikrokredi (PSHM) in Albania. In total OI works with 42 local partners in Africa, Asia, Latin America and Eastern Europe.

Inputs from Vodafone

The Vodafone Foundation granted £102,361 to fund the delivery of the pilot project. These monies were disbursed as follows: £54,924 for labour costs, including technical services consultants, technical project management and partner training; capital equipment costs £15,724; equipment maintenance costs £4,179; travel expenses £16,694; and administration and monitoring £10,300. Plans to take the project forward into a second phase have been held up as Vodafone froze future funding plans during 2005 whilst a strategic review of the Foundation's funding strategy was undertaken.

Outcomes for the corporation, its partners and the community

- Significant efficiency gains result from the streamlining of the data management system. OI estimates that overall savings of 55 hours per loan officer per month can be achieved. For example, loan application processing times can be reduced by 40%, loan monitoring times by 70% and client file preparation times by 50%. Additional savings can be made in the following areas: 30 hours per month for head office staff as data collected in the field no longer needs to be re-entered by branch staff; telephone costs are reduced as loan officers no longer need to phone the office several times a day and paper usage is reduced by 20–50% as transactions are processed electronically rather than by fax.
- The time saved can be re-invested into value added activities such as direct marketing, client selection and delinquency management. The number of loans disbursed in Albania and Romania could increase by about 20% benefiting 600 clients in the first year.
- These savings are enabling more loans to be disbursed and thus levels of local economic activity are increasing and household poverty levels are decreasing.
- The project is enabling both local micro-finance partners to improve their financial sustainability. This will enable them to access more commercial funds and thus expand their activities.
- The project, and Vodafone's contribution to it, has been publicised in several outlets including OI's Annual report, a Virtual Conference on E-Banking for the Poor, OI's Global Conference and via a five minute segment in the BBC World programme 'Earth Report'.

Evidence of sustainability

Initial indications suggest that the technology piloted in this project has the potential to be rolled out across OI's global network and indeed across the networks of similar providers. The cost savings thus engendered are important in enabling OI to operate more efficiently, thus increasing the organisation's own sustainability.

How the programme is evaluated

The project is monitored by OI and reports are made to the Vodafone Foundation as and when required. A final report was submitted in

January 2005. PSHM is performing an activity-based costing exercise to analyse the time and cost differences resulting from the introduction of the PDA system in the Albanian component of the pilot. The data gained through this exercise will form the basis of a project evaluation, which may be made available for public dissemination as a review article.

Case study 3: Supporting Télécoms Sans Frontières (TSF) after the 2004 Tsunami[6]

Location: Sri Lanka and Indonesia
Duration: Post-January 2005

How the programme started

Vodafone made a spontaneous decision to provide funds for TSF in the immediate aftermath of the 2004 Asian Tsunami. The Vodafone Group Foundation have been partners of TSF since 2003, providing financial support for TSF's emergency missions and long term cooperation programmes.

Programme outline

France-based NGO TSF, which was launched in 1998, provides a rapid response to disaster zones in which established communication systems have been damaged or may even have been lacking in the first place. TSF aims to reach affected areas within 24–48 hours of a disaster striking and set up an emergency technical centre with satellite phone lines and high speed internet connections. Such Internet 'cafes' can be set up within minutes of arrival. Relief organisations make use of the services available as do hospitals and survivors of disasters who are desperate for a means to contact their families, often providing a huge psychological uplift for survivors. TSF is rapidly expanding the breadth of its remit. On the one hand it is setting up permanent logistics bases in regions regularly affected by disasters, such as Central and South America. On the other hand, TSF is initiating projects that bring long-term developmental benefits to areas being rebuilt in the aftermath of a disaster. Delivering such ambitious programmes clearly requires considerable resources much of which are provided by major companies including Cable and Wireless, Inmarsat, Alcatel, France Telecom, AT&T, Ericsson and Carrefour. Support usually takes the form of financial donations. However, technical support is a necessary component as well. Various firms, including Vodafone, provide PR support by arranging media interviews and TV pieces.

Following the Asian Tsunami on 26th December 2004, the Vodafone Group Foundation announced a £1 million package to support the humanitarian rescue operation: £650,000 was granted to the Disasters Emergency Committee, £250,000 to the International Federation of Red Cross and Red Crescent Societies and £100,000 to TSF and MapAction (an NGO which specialises in the production of dynamic maps in disaster zones). These funds enabled TSF to guarantee better and longer service to victims and develop sustainable projects in Sri Lanka. Vodafone provided public relations support by organising a TV crew to be sent to Sri Lanka to witness TSF's work in refugee camps.

Working with partners

Vodafone works directly with TSF. At the time of writing this partnership is limited to the provision of resources.

Outcomes for the corporation, its partners and the community

It should be noted that Vodafone is one of a number of commercial organisations that provided funding to support TSF's relief efforts. The outcomes referred to here refer to the overall impacts of TSF's work on this occasion.

- TSF records that it succeeded in directly supporting 10,779 families and 249 rescue teams and NGOs in Sri Lanka and Indonesia. Telecoms centres were set up in Banda Aceh and Meulabah in Indonesia. Internet connections, email, phone and fax were all made available.
- After four months of humanitarian phoning operations in Sri Lanka in 117 of the 262 relief camps TSF began to provide post emergency support in the realms of education and economic development. Computer and Internet programmes have been started in Matarra and a study initiated into the logistics involved in developing GSM satellite and Internet facilities for fishing and agricultural cooperatives. Families dispersed in different relief camps were able to be reunited.
- Individuals were provided with psychological support through the opportunity to call family and friends. The phones provided people with opportunities to access desperately needed money, including support from expatriates.
- The communication network helped to establish the geographical distribution of affected areas and individual victims.
- NGOs and rescue teams were able to communicate effectively between their headquarters and their teams in the field. In addition,

rescue coordination was improved on the ground and information, reports and medicine lists were exchanged between different agencies thus improving the efficiency of the overall relief operation.
- Vodafone directly supported activities that have raised TSF's profile including arranging TV segments and providing publicity via press releases and on the Vodafone website.
- Vodafone has also gained positive publicity thus building trust in its corporate brand, which plays well with both internal and external stakeholders. Thus, the firm has been able to affirm their 'passion for the world around us'.

Inputs from Vodafone

The financial donation received from Vodafone was an important contribution to the delivery of this relief effort helping to pay for flights, local transport, accommodation, subsistence and communications. Negotiations are underway in 2006 between TSF and Vodafone with regard to the development of a more sophisticated partnership in the future. Matters being discussed include the sharing of human and technological resources. TSF likes to include partner staff in its emergency response teams; however the need to depart at a moment's notice is a stumbling block which TSF is considering how best to overcome.

Evidence of sustainability

Direct measurement of sustainability is not appropriate in this case as Vodafone's input was a one-off grant directed towards the delivery of operational activities in a disaster zone. However, Vodafone's efforts to reinforce and raise the profile of TSF will certainly support the latter in building their international reputation. Furthermore, this venture may facilitate further, more involved, collaborative work between the two organisations.

How the programme is evaluated

TSF produced a summary evaluation of their post-Tsunami efforts.

Project-by-project assessment of social capital impacts

In this section we summarise the social capital aspects of each project. We conclude by using the format of Table 4.1 to create a table, which allows a comparison of the social capital elements of each project (see Table 10.4).

Community phone shops

The community phone shops programme is notable for the range and depth of social capital impacts that it has generated. It can be argued that the programme's most significant achievement has been to correct a market failure (or perhaps it can be argued a government failure due to the telecoms industry's historic status as a nationalised industry); such a failure existed in the form of the inadequate distribution of telecommunications within South Africa. The development of the community phone shop network has revolutionised telecommunications access for hundreds of thousands, if not millions, of South Africans. This process has facilitated the extension and deepening of micro-level networks between individuals and families. Such network development is essential for building social cohesion. The beneficial structural effects are immense at a community level. On the one hand social ties are able to evolve rapidly, whilst entrepreneurial networks are also developing apace. Previously a lack of access to affordable communications had stymied small-scale business development within township communities. Not only do the phone shops themselves support individual entrepreneurs but they also provide a means for others to develop their business activities. This is important in promoting employment stability in areas where unemployment is an immense social challenge. Thus, business networks have been transformed. There is evidence of important vertical relationships of scope between Vodacom and the entrepreneurs running the phone shops. There are also important impacts within the firm as the programme is clearly inducing significant social dividends and thus it is clear to the firm's internal stakeholders that the company is making a positive contribution to transformation in the 'new' South Africa. Perhaps most importantly of all, the programme is an excellent example of a case where government have succeeded in harnessing the talents of the private sector for the greater good of society.

Opportunity International (OI)

Vodafone's contribution has been important in this case as they have allowed OI to experiment with new technologies. Through the process of technological experimentation OI has been able to increase the efficacy of their existing work and thus extend their services to more clients. Thus, Vodafone's inputs are particularly important in facilitating the expansion of OI's work. Through this work significant social capital impacts are observable, particularly in terms of correcting failures in the area of credit provision amongst poorer members of communities. Neither the government nor market-oriented organisations have been able to successfully fill this void, therefore OI's contribution has been pivotal in meeting unmet demand within society. Thus, there have been significant achievements in terms of bridging structural holes through the provision of essential support for locally based micro-credit organisations. Support networks operating via Vodafone, OI and locally based organisations can be conceptualised as an example of vertical relationships of scope, which ultimately draw in individuals within impoverished communities. There are clear impacts upon employment stability, which in turn facilitates greater social cohesion. Micro-credit schemes are important as they promote positive business norms such as the formalisation of economic activity and encourage people to respect laws and protocols. In this way trust is built and positive norms of behaviour are promoted.

TSF

In evaluating the social capital impact of TSF we distinguish between the project itself, (which we label the 'indirect' impact) and the social capital created by Vodafone's involvement (which we label the 'direct' impact). We do this, because unlike for all of the other projects we look at in chapters 7–10, this project is 'merely' a financial donation. The direct social capital impacts of Vodafone's involvement with TSF are relatively limited as Vodafone are just one of a number of significant funders who support TSF's work following the Asian Tsunami. However, there were some important direct social capital outcomes from Vodafone's contribution. Vodafone was able to provide TSF with important publicity and positive public relations exposure. Such support and endorsement from a leading technology company is vital in building up TSF's own reputation and image. Equally, there have been important social capital dividends within Vodafone in terms of building the firm's reputation as an outward looking company that makes significant contributions to society. Trust and goodwill are generated with both internal and external stakeholders in this way. TSF's own work which is supported by the Vodafone grant has a number of significant social capital impacts. Most importantly perhaps is the way that TSF is able to offer an essential service for disaster victims, a service that other major global and national institutions have failed to facilitate or provide. TSF has thus taken a significant place within the matrix of organisations and institutions involved in disaster relief. TSF's work is essential in re-building networks of people following disasters as well as smoothing the operation of relief networks. There are

Table 10.4 Vodafone case studies – summary assessment of social capital impacts

		Community phones	Opportunity International	TSF Direct	TSF Indirect
Scope-					
Micro:	Person to person	***	**		**
Meso:	Vertical relationships	**	**		*
Macro:	Institutional	*	*		**
Form-					
Structural:	Networks	***	*	*	**
	Bridging structural holes	*	***		***
	New membership	***	**	**	**
	Ties & glue/lubricant	**	**	*	**
Cognitive:	Competence/goodwill	***	**	**	***
Channel-					
Information:	Improve education	*	**		**
Collective action:	Correct government/ social failure	***	***	*	***
Misc:	Employment stability	**	***		*
	Cohesion:	**	**		**
	Radius of trust/distrust	**	*	*	**
	Norms of behaviour	**	**	*	**

Key: no stars = minimal impact, * = some impact, ** = notable impact, *** = potent impact.

crucial impacts here in terms of promoting social cohesion and in ensuring that communications enable networks of trust to be sustained and promoted.

Notes

1. Vodafone is the largest company in terms of turnover. However, China mobile has more proportionate subscribers. Wikipedia (2006a), *List of mobile network operators*. Available at: http://en.wikipedia.org/wiki/Largest_mobile_phone_companies. Accessed 11/05/2006.
2. Vodafone subsidiaries were required by the terms of their licences to establish Foundations in these markets. A Foundation was created in Spain in 1994, which contributed £3,299,522 during 2003/4. The Vodafone Portugal Foundation was created in 2002 and contributed £218,894 during 2003/4 (Vodafone Group Foundation, 2005b, p.4).
3. *Sources*: digitaldividend, 2004; Goodman, 2003; Hamilton, 2002; Reck and wood, 2003; Vodafone, 2005c; World Business Council for Sustainable Development, 2004; Reuters (South Africa), 2006.

4 Currency conversation rate of US$1.00 to R6.416 as of 16th May 2006.
5 *Sources*: Opportunity International, 2003; Opportunity International, 2004; Opportunity International,2005a; Opportunity International, 2005b; Vodafone Group, 2005c.
6 *Sources*: Agence de Presse, 2005; AT&T, 2004; Judge, 2005; Reid, 2005; Telecoms Sans Frontieres, 2005; Vodafone Group Foundation, 2005b.

References

AccountAbility.org.uk (2005), *The Accountability Rating 2005*. Available at: http://www.accountabilityrating.com. Accessed 12/12/2005.

Agence de Presse (2005), *untitled*. Available at: http://www.tsfi.org/revuedepresse/anglais/e_afp.pdf. Accessed 27/07/2005.

AT&T (2004), *AT&T supports Telecoms Sans Frontieres*. Available at: www.business.att.com/emea/tsf/. Accessed 30/09/2005.

biz.yahoo.com (2005), *Vodafone Group Plc Company Profile*. Available at: http://biz.yahoo.com/ic/47/47982.html. Accessed 27/07/2005.

digitaldividend (2004), *Vodacom Community Phone Shops*. Available at: www.digitaldividend.org/pubs/pubs_02_vodacom_intvw.htm. Accessed 29/09/2005.

Fauna and Flora International (2005), *Corporate Partnerships*. Available at: http://www.fauna-flora.org/partners/corporate.html. Accessed 12/12/2005.

Goodman, J. (2003), 'Linking mobile phone ownership and use to social capital in rural South Africa and Tanzania', Vodafone Policy Series, Number 3, March 2005.

Hamilton, R. (2002), *Community Phones Connect SA townships*. Available at: http://newsvote.bbc.co.uk/mpapps/pagetools/print/news.bbc.co.uk/1/hi/technology/3246732.stm. Accessed 28/09/2005.

Hayes, K. and Burge, R. (2003), 'Coltan Mining in the Democratic Republic of Congo: How tantulum-using industries can commit to the reconstruction of the DRC', Flora and Fauna International.

Judge, E. (2005), *Telecom charity forges links for tsunami victims*. Available at: http://www.tsfi.org/revuedepresse/anglais/e_times.pdf. Accessed 28/07/2005.

Jupiter Asset Management Ltd (2005), 'Socially Responsible Investment Bulletin', no 35, winter 2005.

Opportunity International (2003), 'Proposal to the Vodafone Foundation', March 2003.

Opportunity International (2004), 'Project Update', report to the Vodafone Group Foundation Trustees Meeting 22nd April 2004.

Opportunity International (2005a), *Albania*. Available at: http://www.opportunity.org.uk/our-clients-albania.htm. Accessed 05/08/2005.

Opportunity International (2005b), '*PDA Empowerment for Loan Officers in Albania and Romania with the Vodafone Group Foundation*', January 2005 Final Report.

Reck, J. and Wood, B. (2003), *What works: Vodacom's Community Services Phone Shop*, World Resources Institute.

Reid, D. (2005), *Telecoms sans Frontieres*. Available at: http://www.bbcworld.com/content/clickonline_archive_05_2005.asp?pageid=666&co_pageid=3. Accessed 30/09/2005.

Reuters (South Africa) (2006), *S. Africa competition body OKs Vodafone/Vodacom deal*. Available at: http://www.tralac.org/scripts/content.php?id=4430. Accessed 25/04/2006.

Telecoms Sans Frontieres (2005), *'TSF's Tsunami Operation Results 6 months later'*, TSF evaluation brief.
Vodafone (2005a), *History*. Available at: http://www.vodafone.com/section_article/ 0,3035,CATEGORY_ID%253D30102%2526LANGUAGE_ID%253D0%2526CO NTENT_ID%253D230692,00.html. Accessed 20/10/2005.
Vodafone (2005b), *Key findings of SIM research. Mobiles are used and owned differently in developing countries from the developed world*. Available at: http:// www.vodafone.com/article/0,3029,CATEGORY_ID%253D3040302%2526LAN GUAGE_ID%253D0%2526CONTENT_ID%253D266250,00.html?, Accessed 12/12/2005.
Vodafone (2005c), *Products with High Social Value*. Available at: http:// www.vodafone.com/section_article/0,3035,CATEGORY_ID%253D30406%252 6LANGUAGE_ID%253D0%2526CONTENT_ID%253D265546,00.html. Accessed 12/12/2005.
Vodafone Group (2004a), *Approach to CSR*. Available at: http://www.vodafone.com/ section_article/0,3035,CATEGORY_ID%253D30403%2526LANGUAGE_ID%2 53D0%2526CONTENT_ID%253D232456,00.html. Accessed 26/07/2005.
Vodafone Group (2004b), *Message from Arun Sarin, Chief Executive*. Available at: http://www.vodafone.com/section_article/0,3035,CATEGORY_ID%253D3040 1%2526LANGUAGE_ID%253D0%2526CONTENT_ID%253D232436,00.html. Accessed 26/07/2005.
Vodafone Group (2004c), *Our Role in Society*. Available at: http://www. vodafone.com/section_article/0,3035,CATEGORY_ID%253D30402%2526LAN GUAGE_ID%253D0%2526CONTENT_ID%253D232446,00.html. Accessed 26/07/2005.
Vodafone Group (2004d), *Reporting*. Available at: http://www.vodafone.com/ section_article/0,3035,CATEGORY_ID%253D3040301%2526LANGUAGE_ID %253D0%2526CONTENT_ID%253D232466,00.html. Accessed 26/07/2005.
Vodafone Group (2004e), *Social Investment*. Available at: http://www.voda-fone.com/section_article/0,3035,CATEGORY_ID%253D30404%2526LAN-GUAGE_ID%253D0%2526CONTENT_ID%253D232546,00.html. Accessed 25/07/2005.
Vodafone Group (2004f), *Corporate Social Responsibility Report 2003–04*. http://www.vodafone.com/assets/files/en/CSR_Report_2003-04_VF GROUP_20050802.pdf. Available at: Assessed 05/07/05.
Vodafone Group (2005a), *Annual Report*. Available at: http://www.vodafone.com/ assets/files/en/VOD_annual_report_2005_3.pdf. Accessed 05/12/2005.
Vodafone Group (2005b), *Case Study: Community mobile phones increase access to telecommunications in South Africa*. Available at: http://www.vodafone.com/ article/0,3029,CATEGORY_ID%3D207%26DOPRINT%3D1%26LANGUAGE_I D%3D0%26CONTENT_ID%3D233470,00.html. Accessed 27/07/2005.
Vodafone Group (2005c), *Corporate Responsibility Report 2004–5*. Available at: http://www.vodafone.com/assets/files/en/group_cr_report_2004_05.pdf. Accessed 26/07/2005.
Vodafone Group (2005d), *Managing CR*. Available at: http://www.vodafone.com/ section_article/0,3035,CATEGORY_ID%253D30401%2526LANGUAGE_ID%2 53D0%2526CONTENT_ID%253D265256,00.html. Accessed 05/12/2005.
Vodafone Group (2005e), *Reporting*. Available at: http://www.vodafone.com/ section_article/0,3035,CATEGORY_ID%253D3040105%2526LANGUAGE_ID %253D0%2526CONTENT_ID%253D265306,00.html. Accessed 20/08/2005.

Vodafone Group (2005f), *Vodafone Group Social Investment Policy*. Available at: http://www.vodafone.com/article/0,3029,CATEGORY_ID%253D3040107%2526LANGUAGE_ID%253D0%2526CONTENT_ID%253D266236,00.html?, Accessed 21/08/2005.

Vodafone Group Foundation (2005a), *Emergency Communications in areas struck by disaster*. Available at: www.vodafonefoundation.org/2.1html(projects/item8.xml). Accessed 27/07/2005.

Vodafone Group Foundation (2005b), *Vodafone Foundation Yearbook*. Available at: http://www.vodafonefoundation.org/assets/downloads/Foundationsyearbook.pdf. Accessed 25/07/2005.

Vodafone Group plc (2006), *We said we have we will. Vodafone Group Plc Corporate Responsibility Report for the 2006 year*. Newbury, UK: Vodafone Group plc.

Wikipedia (2006a), *List of mobile network operators*. Available at: http://en.wikipedia.org/wiki/Largest_mobile_phone_companies. Accessed 11/05/2006.

Wikipedia (2006b), *Vodafone Group, plc*. Available at:. Accessed 11/05/2006.

World Business Council for Sustainable Development (2004), *Vodacom: Extending telecom services to South Africa's poor*. Available at: www.wbcsd.org/web/publications/case/vodafone_full_case_final_web.pdf. Accessed 29/09/2005.

11
What Makes for Good Corporate Citizenship Projects and Programmes?

Introduction

This chapter attempts to draw some lessons from the case studies of the preceding four chapters. Using our social capital analysis we compare projects between and across the different companies. The beauty of the social capital approach is that projects in different countries and of different types can be compared.

We begin by a discussion of the distinctive features of just four projects drawn from each of the four case study companies. Two of the projects can be thought of as very successful in building social capital, while the other two are less successful. These projects illustrate the particular ways in which companies can create social capital through their corporate citizenship (CC) activity and also how limited the external social capital impact of such activity might be, even in projects self-selected by the companies to represent their most successful (for them) projects.

We go on to develop a general comparative framework that allows all the case study projects to be compared. We use the theoretical concepts of social capital outlined in chapter 4 and applied in chapters 7–10 to develop a pragmatic representation of the social capital impact of CC projects. This allows us to see at a glance the key metrics of social capital impact for each project.

The 13 projects can be divided into three types. First, some represent company participation in an activity that exists independently of the company (e.g. Diageo's involvement with Tomorrow's People). Second, others represent attempts by the company to solve a business problem by use of a community project (e.g. RBU involved implementation of Anglo American's SEAT methodology). Third, another group represent company developed responses to general external pressure to reduce the negative social capital impact of their industry (e.g. Projeto Bartender in Brazil focussed on encouraging socially responsible drinking). For each type we discuss how they can have a high positive social capital impact and what the problems in achieving high social capital impact are.

Finally, we discuss lessons for corporate citizenship programmes for building social capital highlighting themes that are common to all of the cases. We suggest how companies should choose social capital building projects and how they can take a professional approach to implementing their corporate citizenship projects.

Comparing corporate citizenship projects

We begin by looking at Diageo's Earthwatch tie-up, Anglo American's Anglo Zimele, Vodafone's Télécoms Sans Frontières (TSF) and the

Table 11.1 A comparison of the social capital impact of four projects

		Earthwatch *Diageo*	Anglo Zimele *Anglo American*	TSF *Vodafone*	LF *GSK*
Scope-					
Micro:	Person to person	**	**		**
Meso:	Vertical relationships	*	***		***
Macro:	Institutional	*	**		***
Form-					
Structural:	Networks	**	**	*	***
	Bridging structural holes	*	**		***
	New membership	*	*	**	***
	Ties & glue/lubricant	**	*	*	***
Cognitive:	Competence/goodwill	***	**	**	***
Channel-					
Information:	Improve education		**		**
Collective action:	Correct government/ social failure		***	*	***
Misc:	Employment stability		**		**
	Cohesion:	**	**		***
	Radius of trust/distrust	*	**	*	**
	Norms of behaviour	**	**	*	***

Key: no stars = minimal impact, * = some impact, ** = notable impact, *** = potent impact.

Lymphatic Flariasis (LF) programme of GSK. The summary scoring of the social capital impact, based on the summary tables in chapters 7–10, from each of the projects is given in Table 11.1.

It is important to remember that we would expect that company selected projects such as these would score highly. It is therefore interesting to note that the TSF project scores poorly at least in terms of its direct impact: this is because the project simply received cash from Vodafone with little company follow-up or involvement. In that sense Vodafone's involvement was peripheral to facilitating the social capital built by the project. Such involvement involves little by way of multiplier effect or corporate innovation in social capital creation. This may be indicative of many CC projects which are designed to leave little lasting impact on local communities.[1] The contrast with GSK's involvement with the LF project is striking. GSK's involvement was crucial both in terms of its original innovation of the drug and its innovative involvement in the vaccination programme. GSK's inputs delivered a significant multiplier effect to international efforts to eliminate the disease. Clearly this was a landmark social capital project involving a multinational and was of a very significant size. The contrast between the near blank scope, form and channel boxes of TSF and near full ones of LF is striking.

It is also informative to compare the Earthwatch and Anglo Zimele pairing of projects. Earthwatch was a project not focussed on the society around Diageo *per se*. The training involvement of the champions with the Earthwatch NGO was not the benefit to society of the project. The major benefit was within Diageo in terms of building internal social capital and improving the local environment in and around Diageo facilities. This provides a contrast with Anglo Zimele. This project was enacted to correct societal failures to deliver economic benefits to the Black community as part of the South African government's Black Economic Empowerment (BEE) initiative. This project did bring benefits to the firm but it was motivated by external societal demands. Hence it scores three stars under Collective Action against none for Earthwatch. Anglo Zimele was also excellent in building vertical relationships between company purchasing officers and small and medium sized BEE suppliers. However Earthwatch achieves a weaker score on vertical relationships because of the limited extent that Local Action Plans (where these were developed) involved such relationships.

What is clear from this indicative comparison of four projects is that some projects score better than others on some of the social capital dimensions, but also that some can offer comprehensive social capital impacts against others that are very narrow in their impact. Some of this may be to do with money: LF is an expensive project. It may be that some companies find it easier to deliver a few high profile projects well rather than make a range of donations that yield little or no additional value as a result of company involvement (which has partly been Vodafone's strategy). However, the size of the financial commitment is not the only factor. Projects can deliver significant benefits to society at little or no cost to the company. Anglo Zimele offers a great example of this. These sorts of projects may involve some up front business risk, arising from the initial investment that may not pay off. However companies are well placed to take such risks especially if they involve projects close to their own business and hence have similar (familiar) risks.

How social capital building by corporate citizenship projects works

In this section we take the categories of social capital that we have been using in our case studies and convert them into a pragmatic form that allows the social capital impact of the projects to be compared more fully.

The pragmatic model we develop here attempts to combine and extend some of the facets of those mentioned in Table 11.1 in order to tease out what allows a project to make a significant contribution to social capital. We begin by focussing in on the network aspects of the social capital, as these seem to be crucial to the improved relational quality that is the essence of any social capital building activity. Trust and norms are subsumed into our characterisation of the networks supported by company projects. This is because they are part of what allows a network to add to the stock of a society's social capital in a meaningful way. Such a characterisation begins with defining what sort of network is being set up by the project in question. We look at how the network works (network vitality), its scope in a social capital sense (partners) and its geographic extent. We describe these elements as the *existence of networks*. We then examine the *functioning of networks* – namely, the bridging role of the firm (in the Burt, 2001, sense), the firm's contribution, the network learning and the sustainability of the project. We then conclude by looking at the ultimate *outputs of networks* for society and for the company. The outputs for society are based on the extent to which they contribute to Millennium Development Goals. These would seem to be appropriate for analysing multinational company projects most of which are in developing countries. We examine each of these elements in turn:

Existence of networks

Network vitality

For each project we would want evidence that social networks are being created or supported. Socially beneficial social networks are open, flexible, and creative and invite others to participate. They also contribute to wider consensus rather than being interest group-based. The relationships have to have an element of reciprocity or they are not networks at all. Weak links and an absence of distrust characterise the best networks. loveLife would be a good example of a project that is part of an open network, whereas Earthwatch, because it is an internally focussed project, is part of an exclusive network.

Partners

This refers to the diversity of the network in terms of the kind of participants. A diverse corporate network will involve public sector and civil society participants as well as those from the private sector. A wide range of active participants from different backgrounds is a consequence and a cause of an open and non-exclusive network. The unwillingness of multinational corporations to participate in networks led by locals from host countries is the consequence of a lack of trust or trustworthiness. Barretstown and Youth Business Initiative (YBI) are good examples of effective, diverse networks. Barretstown involves networking European health professionals and the local organising committee, while YBI involves networking governments, NGOs and the private sector around the world.

Geographic scope

The scope can also be international, involving actors at a worldwide level and across national borders or national where the actors, for a particular project, are principally from within one country. Some projects can involve a hybrid of national and international scope, for instance where the activities are predominately national but there is significant involvement with others outside the country. Some projects are local, but actually only two of our 13 projects are local (RBU and Projeto Bartender). What we have observed is that successful projects often go national, or involve national partners. Indeed it is the nature of the multinational that it can provide opportunities for the replication of successful local projects and that it, unlike small local firms, can interact with international and national partners easily.

Functioning of networks

Boundary crossing

This concerns enabling something to happen which would not otherwise happen because of boundaries or barriers or lack of contact. This would incorporate bridging structural holes. It represents an exceptional contribution that would probably not have been achieved without the association between actors. Multinationals are well placed to provide bridging of structural holes in networks, with their international, national and local operations. Projects that provide links between local people and global institutions may be a particular contribution of multinationals. GSK's LF project does this strongly. Anglo Zimele provides the closing of structural holes between the haves and have-nots in post-apartheid South Africa.

Contribution

This concerns the corporate input of capabilities into the network, which could involve money, sharing of business skills, knowledge and attitudes. Clearly the more specific these are and tailored to the problem in hand the more valuable they are. Thus projects which combine money and focussed thinking time of company staff are more likely to be innovative and involve multiplier effects compared to simply giving money. The ingenuity of the SEAT approach developed through the RBU project is striking while Vodafone's mere financial involvement in TSF limits the social capital impact. Indeed projects which only involve financial contributions would seem to be a missed opportunity, particularly where the projects have the potential to be significant within a company's portfolio of CC projects.

Learning

This concerns the understanding gathered from the project that can be used in other situations. This could include an understanding that feeds into other projects or a greater awareness in the company. Here we are looking for a demonstration effect. It may be that the real value of corporate citizenship projects is in their innovative approach to social capital development. This is where second round multiplier effects are to be found, i.e. where the company or others take the lessons from the first project and implements them elsewhere. The RBU SEAT model has this property within Anglo American, while Anglo Zimele and LF have yielded important lessons for the South African government and the World Health Organization (WHO) respectively.

Sustainability

This concerns whether the project is sustainable in the long term. The natural test of sustainability is what might happen if the company substantially reduced their level of support over time. We have in mind a steady withdrawal, not a sudden one that would probably challenge any set of relationships. A project that involved a commitment to give until a problem is solved would be sustainable because there is a defined end point and associated commitment. A low sustainability project is one that has no apparent end except collapse should the principal donor withdraw. Lack of sustainability is a measure, therefore, of dependence. Anglo Zimele and LF have sustainability for different reasons. Anglo Zimele has a working business model that is being replicated outside of Anglo American. LF is sustainable due to the very public commitment of GSK to complete the project over a long time frame. However some of the other projects exhibit either long-term dependency or vulnerability to the short-term nature of funding. Tomorrow's People is in the first group while the Earthwatch project exhibits the latter.

Table 11.2 maps the scope, structure and channel elements of social capital in Table 11.1 into the elements of Existence of Networks and Functioning of Networks just described.

Outputs of networks

Outputs for society

Multinationals are in a position to deliver projects in many countries across the world. They have choices of where to locate their projects and what issues to address. They are in a position to work with local, national and international partners. All of the projects that our four case study companies selected were ones that meet (albeit indirectly in some cases) major developmental goals. This suggests that the ultimate benefits to society could be classified using recognised development criteria. The UN's Millennium Development Goals (MDGs) offer a recognised way of categorising the impact of each project on society. These set global targets for improvement in the World's development record to be met by 2015. The Millennium Development Goals Report 2006 (UN, 2006) reviews progress towards these targets and provides metrics of success. We classify each of our projects according to which of the MDGs they would help to improve. In doing so we focus on the primary goal(s) that they address. Box 11.1 reports the eight Goals and the targets they incorporate.

Table 11.2 Reconciling the pragmatic model and the theoretical basis of social capital

	Network vitality	Partners	Geographic extent	Boundary crossing	Contribution – provision of skills, knowledge and attitudes	Learning from the project	Sustainability
Scope		Micro, meso and macro	Micro, meso and macro			Meso-vertical relationship	
Form	Weak ties, lubricant/ glue, new membership			Bridging structural holes	Competence Trust		Competence and Goodwill Trust
Channel	Trust, reduced radius of distrust				Information/ Education	Information/ Education	Employment Stability/ Norms/ Collective Action

Box 11.1 The UN Millennium Development Goals and Associated Targets

Goal 1: Eradicate extreme poverty and hunger
Target: Halve, between 1990 and 2015, the proportion of people whose income is less than $1 a day

Target: Halve, between 1990 and 2015, the proportion of people who suffer from hunger

Goal 2: Achieve universal primary education
Target: Ensure that, by 2015, children everywhere, boys and girls alike, will be able to complete a full course of primary schooling

Goal 3: Promote gender equality and empower women
Target: Eliminate gender disparity in primary and secondary education, preferably by 2005, and in all levels of education no later than 2015

Goal 4: Reduce child mortality
Target: Reduce by two-thirds, between 1990 and 2015, the under-five mortality rate

Goal 5: Improve maternal health
Target: Reduce by three quarters, between 1990 and 2015, the maternal mortality ratio

Goal 6: Combat HIV/AIDS, malaria and other diseases
Target: Have halted by 2015 and begun to reverse the spread of HIV/AIDS

Target: Have halted by 2015 and begun to reverse the incidence of malaria and other major diseases

Goal 7: Ensure environmental sustainability
Target: Integrate the principles of sustainable development into country policies and programmes and reverse the loss of environmental resources

Target: Halve, by 2015, the proportion of people without sustainable access to safe drinking water and basic sanitation

> **Box 11.1 – *continued***
>
> *Target*: By 2020, to have a significant improvement in the lives of at least 100 million slum dwellers
>
> **Goal 8: Create a global partnership for development**
> *Target*: Address the special needs of the least developed countries, landlocked countries and small island developing States
>
> Target: Develop further an open, rule-based, predictable, non-discriminatory trading and financial system
>
> *Target*: Deal comprehensively with developing countries' debt
>
> *Target*: In cooperation with developing countries, develop and implement strategies for decent and productive work for youth
>
> *Target*: In cooperation with pharmaceutical companies, provide access to affordable essential drugs in developing countries
>
> *Target*: In cooperation with the private sector, make available the benefits of new technologies, especially information and communications
>
> (*Source*: UN (2006), Millennium Development Goals Report, New York: United Nations.)

Several of the case study projects in chapters 7 to 10 are directly targeted on meeting the MDGs. The LF project clearly addresses Goals 6 and 8, while the loveLife initiative also addresses Goal 6. It is interesting that none of the selected projects address Goal 4 and none can really said to address Goal 2. Clearly a limitation of multinational projects is that they will tend to be focussed on some of the goals and are unlikely to address others. Our classification of projects draws on a World Business Council for Sustainable Development report (WBCSD, 2005) that classifies 45 projects according to MDGs.

Outputs for the company

There may be many reasons why companies benefit from community engagement. In some cases there are direct business benefits, though these rarely justify the initial cost or they would not strictly be classifiable as corporate citizenship projects. All the projects we have looked at in our case study companies received some support from the audited CSR budget according to guidelines on what can be counted as CSR expenditure. To the extent that projects bring advertisable benefits they are financed partially from advertising budgets. However none of our projects are the primary focus of the advertising of the company. The main output for the company lies in being seen to respond to external influence to do CC projects.

The role of influence is explored in Jones and Pollitt (2002). CC projects provided a variety of ways in which companies can respond to pressure to justify their 'licence to operate' from society. First, projects allow the company to engage constructively in public debates about ethical issues raised by business activity. There clearly is a lot of mistrust of multinationals, much of it based on a misunderstanding about the value of business to society and a lack of appreciation of both the limits to and the capabilities of multinationals in solving developmental problems. Engagement helps improve understanding on both sides. Second, related to the first point, projects increase company sensitivity to public concerns. Earthwatch may be seen as a project of this type as it exposes company employees to environmentalists' concerns. As Jones and Pollitt (2002) point out it is very important for companies to anticipate ethical issues that might affect their ability to do business and be capable of responding to them. The alternative is to always be lagging behind the public mood. Anglo American's leadership on the AIDS debate in South Africa is a good example of a company not waiting to be pushed into action on business ethics but acting pre-emptively.

Examples of the sorts of ethically related concerns that companies are addressing via their engagement strategies include:

Defensive sensitivity

Some firms are national targets of public criticism because of their part in social problems. Alcoholic drinks firms such as Diageo are clearly vulnerable to this because of the problems of anti-social misuse of their products. Mining firms, such as Anglo America in South Africa are associated, in the public mind, as beneficiaries of the apartheid system.

Society dependence

This applies to companies in highly regulated sectors that depend on the public sector for approval or right to operate. There could be potential damage to society and there is the potential for expensive sector specific regulation or taxation. Mining, pharmaceutical and alcoholic drinks firms are clearly in this category.

Public goods

These might be called 'good outcome' industries where society (especially a small developing country) would be better off if the price were lower and the quantity supplied were higher, i.e. the public might be better off if the operation of the price mechanism was limited or legal protection against copying was reduced. Clearly pharmaceutical firms in developing countries are vulnerable to this sort of pressure to reduce prices. WTO rules might make such actions by developing countries against multinationals difficult but very public battles between poor countries and lawyers of rich multinationals does not make for good publicity around the world (such as happened over AIDS drugs in South Africa).[2]

Local operating sensitivities

Multinationals are powerful players nationally and internationally and find it easy to gain political support at this level. However their local operations are vulnerable to local action, especially where this involves the very poor with little to lose. RBU exhibits this well. Often multinationals are forced to respond because of very local sensitivities as much as to global concerns.

Attracting the best professional staff

When the company employs highly educated, high quality managers and professionals there is a strong motive to be the kind of organisation that these people wish to work for. This applies especially when the managers are mobile and can get jobs elsewhere.

Vulnerability to consumer pressure

Consumers are increasingly sensitive to the behaviour of multinationals. Shell's problems in Nigeria in 1995 lead to declining petrol sales in Germany. Among our companies, Vodafone has a valuable consumer brand in a competitive market. Being seen to be good members of the community rather than bad ones is very important in protecting the company from consumer activism.

Summarising our projects

We draw the Existence of Networks, Functioning of Networks and Output of Networks elements of each our 13 projects together in Table 11.3.

It is the final two columns of Table 11.3 that contain the information on outputs that are worthy of comment.

Table 11.3 Classification of community engagement projects

	Network vitality	Partners	Geographic Crossing	Boundary Crossing	Contribution	Learning	Sustainability	Output for society (MDG Goal)	Output for company
Tomorrow's People Diageo	Open network	Govt, European social fund	National	Gap between government and community	Leadership, human resource and risk management, mentoring	Established worldwide model of best practice in work creation	Crucially dependent on company	Goal 8	Constructive Engagement, Defensive
Youth Business International Diageo	Open network	Huge govt, NGOs, private sector	International	Gap between formal and informal economy	Input of experience from Tomorrow's People, marketing plans, local general manager	A universal model	Broadly organised and sustainable	Goal 1, Goal 8	Constructive Engagement, Defensive
Earthwatch Diageo	Exclusive	One NGO	International	None	Limited	Only learning within the company	Highly dependent on company	Goal 7	Company sensitivity, Attracting staff
Projeto Bartender Diageo	Exclusive	Other private sector	Local exploitation	None	Management skills and basic training	Not significant	Highly dependent on company	Goal 1, Goal 8	Defensive, Societal dependence

Table 11.3 Classification of community engagement projects – *continued*

	Network vitality	Partners	Geographic Crossing	Boundary Crossing	Contribution	Learning	Sustainability	Output for society (MDG Goal)	Output for company
Anglo Zimele Anglo American	Trust, open	Local and national govt	National	Significant	Sharing of business skills, etc	Model transferred internationally	55% recipients no longer dependent	Goal 1, Goal 8	Defensive, Society dependence
RBU Anglo American	Trust, open	Community liaison forums, local NGOs, local community, sub contractors	National	Provided skills, opportunities, resources which would not have been available	Training, marketing, entrepreneurial skills, information	Endorsed company SEAT process, model for community collaboration	Lasting network of people working together	Goal 1	Business case, local operating sensitivities
loveLife Anglo American	Trust, open	Public sector, civil society	National with international links	Significant access	Business skills, management systems, advice	Mechanisms for delivering public health	Well established and not entirely dependent on co	Goal 6	Business case
Barretstown GSK	Significant open network	Dublin committee, medical bodies	International	A huge gap	Senior management, and fundraising	A model of healthcare transferred within Europe	Getting alternative funding	Goal 8	Constructive Engagement

Table 11.3 Classification of community engagement projects – *continued*

	Network vitality	Partners	Geographic Crossing	Boundary Crossing	Contribution	Learning	Sustainability	Output for society (MDG Goal)	Output for company
LF GSK	Significant, open network	Network of public, civil and private	International	Substantial hole which can only be filled by drug company	Dedicated staff, strategic plans, etc	Model for other interventions	Will continue until disease is contained or eliminated	Goal 6	Defensive, Public goods, Attracting staff
RMI GSK	Part of very significant, open network	Network with many companies, gov't agencies and NGOs	National	Very high, overcoming barriers which prevent children from poor communities getting healthcare	Huge through senior staff, transfer of staff, and communications	Develop means of identifying needs of medically underserved children to guide public programmes	Despite large subsidy from company, the network would survive without GSK	Goal 8	Defensive, Societal dependence
Community phone shops Vodafone	Not really a network	No	National	Big need to overcome digital divide	Finance, Technology	Developed model which could be applied elsewhere	Highly dependent on Vodafone's continuing support	Goal 1, Goal 8	Society dependence, public goods
Opportunity International Vodafone	Limited network	With an NGO	National	Facilitating	Technology, service consultants, project managers	Established as a great idea. It may be exploited commercially	Not highly dependent on company support	Goal 1, Goal 8	Constructive Engagement
TSF Vodafone	Hardly a network	With an NGO	National across borders	Essential help	Largely money	None particularly	Dependent on company support	Goal 1, Goal 8	Constructive Engagement

319

It is clear that most of the projects fall under the general MDG Goal 8, which specifically talks about partnerships and hence is directly linked to our social capital approach. Interestingly a surprising number do touch on Goal 1, which addresses extreme poverty. However Goals 2, 3 and 4 are not addressed by any of these projects. Although some companies do have projects that address these goals (see WBCSD, 2005), they are not common.[3] Indeed it is interesting to point out that some of them may be unlikely to be met by MNC projects because of the lack of proximity of the multinationals to the problem. Thus multinationals often focus their education projects on older children about to enter the labour market rather than on primary school-age children.

In terms of company outputs, we choose to highlight the more interesting outputs from the projects. Arguably all the projects from the same company have similar outputs in that they are part of a package of projects aimed at company level objectives. However it is interesting that while this may be true of new projects, projects from the past may have reflected concerns of an earlier era. Thus Diageo has the Tomorrow's People project which represented a desire for constructive community engagement begun in the 1980s before current concerns about anti-social drinking, while a newer project such as Earthwatch is a response to internal pressure to make local employees feel valued within an expanded global company and hence meets concerns about staff morale.

Understanding how projects build social capital effectively

In this section we discuss what makes a successful business involvement in a community project. Looking at our 13 case study projects we can identify three types of project with very different characteristics. First, there is a group of projects which are discrete from the business and which deliver high profile results. Tomorrow's People and LF might be very good examples of this. Second, there is a set of projects which are a response to a specific operational relationship problem, but which do build social capital. The RBU and the Anglo Zimele projects are good examples here. Third, there is another group of projects that respond to specific relational problems that are not strictly operational. The Projeto Bartender (responding to societal concerns about responsible drinking) and Earthwatch projects (responding to the need to build internal social capital within the firm) are examples. Of course, the distinction between these three types of project is sometimes blurred. The

LF project does respond to relational problems that GSK has with society as regards its focus on first world diseases, but we do not view this as its primary motivation or characteristic.

Distinguishing between the three different categories of project allows us to discuss what makes for high social capital building by companies via a project of this category, the limitations of company involvement in such projects and the nature of the successful company management of such projects. We end this section with a comparison of the three categories of projects in Table 11.4.

Category 1: Discrete projects with high profile results

loveLife, RMI, LF, Barretstown, Tomorrow's People, YBI are examples of projects that have a life of their own and have a high degree of sustainability. They score highly in our comparative measures of social capital. They address well-known social problems, produce results and are models of successful partnerships for meeting social problems (MDG 8). Other projects such as TSF and OI are less successful examples of discrete projects.

What makes for a successful project of this type?

Partnership. These projects involve strong relationships with diverse partners. All of the successful projects either involved the creation of a new NGO or working with existing host country NGOs. They often enjoy significant host government support or international agency involvement.

Significant company contribution. All these projects involve significant contributions of company management skills, technical knowledge (or product donation) and money. In all cases company contributions have been at least initially crucial to the success of the project. The exact nature of the crucial contribution might vary (in LF it is product donation, while for Tomorrow's People it was money and the initial set up idea).

Sustained commitment. In all of these projects company involvement has been over a prolonged period since the beginning of the initiative. This has facilitated relationship building and created a pro-development community of partners. LF is the supreme example of this with a long-term commitment in place from GSK, but Diageo has been committed to Tomorrow's People for more than 20 years.

Independent management. The actual project delivery is independently managed from the company and is outside the company's immediate operations. This is a sign of project sustainability and the fact that company involvement has built independent social capital capacity. As in most businesses independent management is likely to be more focussed and efficient over the long term, than the in-house management by a company of a non-core activity.

Narrow scope. Related to the previous point, each of these projects is limited in its development scope. This is a particularly important feature of those projects that were directly initiated by businesses: LF, Tomorrow's People and YBI. These projects addressed a specific problem in a particular way and were given the resources they needed to make an impact.

What are the limitations on company involvement in this type of project?

Unreliability of partners. Working with partners outside the organisation exposes the firm and NGOs to potentially unreliable partners. loveLife illustrates the vulnerability for companies of working with edgy high profile NGOs who may themselves offend public opinion. Opportunity International (OI) illustrates the problems that NGOs have in investing in relationships with companies that may not be sustained. Such risks need to be managed via widening the group of partners (so that the conduct of an individual partner places the project at less risk), choosing less risky partners via careful monitoring or improving the capacity of partners, and being prepared to withdraw at short notice should the risks become too high.

Dependency. Although projects may have a separate identity they may be highly dependent on the company, e.g. Tomorrow's People. This is a problem because the company may want to withdraw due to the separateness it now has from a project that has matured but there may be continuing financial dependency. Unlike LF, which is dependent on GSK but also publicly associated with it, Tomorrow's People is dependent but not publicly associated with Diageo. Diageo might like to withdraw but finds it difficult to do so for fear of negative publicity. Avoiding such dependency is difficult but must involve diversifying the project's sources of funding as its scope widens.

Highly philanthropic. These projects are highly philanthropic in nature because of their separateness from business operations and the scale of the financial commitment involved. Although there are benefits to company involvement these are difficult to quantify and may become less cost effective (in terms of the optimal use of the CC budget) over time. This makes them vulnerable to changes in the company's policy towards philanthropy. In particular if a company decides to adopt a more strategic approach to their choice of projects or profits fall, genuinely philanthropic projects are vulnerable to change. In these circumstances, independent ventures are vulnerable to being cut off at short notice, particularly if they are not well established. The partnership with OI would seem to have been stalled by Vodafone's reappraisal of its giving at a time of worsening business performance.

The nature of successful management of these projects

It is striking that many of these projects have identifiable origins with known sponsors who made the initial commitment. LF for instance was a millennium project of the CEO; Tomorrow's People was a response of the CEO to inner city riots. This created project champions and meant that the resources were available. Senior managers continue to be involved on the boards of these projects.

Category 2: Projects responding to a specific operational business relationship problem

RBU application of the SEAT approach, Community phone shops and Anglo Zimele are examples of projects that have made the company operations more sensitive to the needs of the community and environment. They have been initiated (or in Anglo Zimele's case extended) to respond to specific operational problems. In the RBU case this was the breakdown of relations with the local community which had led to damage to company property; with Community phone shops it was the need to reach out to poor customers as part of Vodacom's licence condition; with Anglo Zimele it was the need to meet objectives for the business under government Black Economic Empowerment policy. They may be visionary in terms of going beyond what the company needed to do, but they are still very close to the operations, and clearly built social capital very close to the business operations of the firms. This is not to say that these projects were any less effective in building social capital than the projects under Category 1 above. The fact that they were close to the business and yielded direct benefits to the company may make them examples of social capital projects which could be undertaken only by business.

What makes for a successful project of this type?

As with projects in Category 1, significant company contribution and narrow scope are important in the success of these projects. However partnerships can be less diverse and more strategic as the project is near to the business operations. NGO involvement can be more focussed (as in RBU) and may not be necessary (as in Anglo Zimele). Indeed social capital may be being built as a result of giving outsiders' access to the normal business relations of the firm (e.g. via guarantees to suppliers or banks). The company contribution may take the form of employee time rather than direct cost (RBU in particular). In contrast to Category 1 these projects were not especially philanthropic or independently managed. However we might add a new success feature of these projects:

Built in sustainability. The long-term social capital impact of such projects crucially depends on whether they are internally and externally sustainable. All of our highlighted projects did have a path to sustainability built into them. The unique business contribution is to provide the initial resources to build social capital that can be independently sustained. RBU demonstrated the value of community relations around all Anglo operations and facilitated the roll out of the SEAT approach. Anglo Zimele demonstrated the value of venture capital for BEE start-ups. Community phone shops pioneered a new business model for small-scale phone service entrepreneurs in poor areas. What made these projects so worthwhile is that they facilitated sustainable businesses and pioneered new models of social capital building projects that could be rolled out at low cost elsewhere.

What are the limitations on company involvement in this type of project?

Temptation to focus on profit. These are development projects that do affect company profitability. There may be a pressure to operate the projects in a way that reduces the social capital benefit and gives too much priority to profit. Clearly a company venture capital fund may be less focussed on helping the poorest out of poverty than a government backed scheme and this may be a developmental weakness.

Gap between rhetoric and reality. There is a tendency to claim that such projects are more 'socially responsible' or 'philanthropic' than is really deserved. Such projects may just be good business. All three of our featured projects have very identifiable business benefits, yet they are featured prominently in CSR reports. The fact that they (or something like them) were required by government policy or had little or no net cost to the company is not highlighted in CSR reports. Indeed it is not clear whether these have much part in the calculation of a company's community contributions.

The nature of successful management of these projects

In contrast to the major independent projects, these business improvements operate at a local level and have to be embraced by local management. Vision from the centre may be important but delivery relies crucially on the buy-in of local managers. This is obvious in the case of the RBU project (which was a response to local management problems) and very important for the Anglo Zimele project (which relies on allowing access to the local Anglo American supply chain). Leadership from the top of the company may be important in encouraging local managers to implement projects effectively and to suggest new initiatives.

Category 3: Projects which respond to specific relational problems that are not strictly operational

Projeto Bartender and Earthwatch are examples of this type of project. The character of these projects is that they are neither truly self-standing as philanthropic projects, nor are they part of the operations. Projeto Bartender is a response to the issue of reducing alcohol abuse and societal damage caused by the alcoholic drinks industry. Such concern may increase public pressure against the industry and the risks of government action. The project is clearly not discrete from the business as in the Category 1 projects, nor does it address an operational problem in the business as in Category 2 projects because the bartenders work for Diageo's clients rather than with Diageo. The Earthwatch project is also not discrete from the business nor does it address a specific operational problem. This project is largely focussed within the business and is aimed at building corporate identity and indirectly improving the environmental impact of the business. Because these projects lack the focussed development rationale of Category 1 projects or the business rationale of Category 2 projects they are in some ways the most problematic and difficult to get right.

What makes for a successful project of this type?

This type of project shares characteristics with Category 1 and 2 projects. Partnerships are important as the company is operating outside its normal business. Company inputs can be significant and are certainly crucial to success. The Earthwatch project clearly relies on support from an NGO whereas Projeto Bartender relies on support from customer companies. However neither of these projects could exist without company input as they are motivated by a desire to respond to relational problems that the company has. The projects do not need sustained commitment or built-in sustainability beyond their usefulness to the firm and do not require independent management. However this limits their likely long-term impact on social capital building in society. We might however note a particular feature of these projects:

Creativity. These projects can demonstrate some creativity in the course of the company's attempt to address non-operational relational problems. This may be because they remain close to the business but are not driven by operational priorities. Thus they may offer scope for experimentation. The demonstration effect may be of benefit to other companies and more widely. Projeto Bartender is a good example of this as it has led to better training of other firm's employees while meeting MDG 1 and reaching the attention of government ministers.

What are the limitations on company involvement in this type of project?

Introverted nature. There seems to be a danger that the project turns in on itself. The Earthwatch project is not really a project about the environment but an exercise in building corporate identity. The lack of follow through in terms of Local Action Plans indicates that generating social capital useful to wider society is not the focus of the project. The connection with the Earthwatch NGO is not a genuine partnership for development (MDG 8) but a service relationship where the company purchases training from the NGO. Overtime the payoffs from this sort of project may become increasingly focussed on meeting the company's business objectives directly.

Lack of vision. As these projects can lack a clear development or business rationale they may prove difficult to sustain and develop. It is not clear where the Earthwatch project is going and it is clear that there is a lack of follow through on Local Action Plans. Without a clear rationale the project may struggle to deliver measurable benefits and be open to being reviewed by senior management and hence lack sustainability.

The nature of successful management of these projects

Successful management of these projects means avoiding the problems noted above. This means that clear development or business goals should be set, so that the project can be classed in Category 1 or Category 2 (or both). It is only then that the project will be encouraged to reach its full potential. For instance with Projeto Bartender, this would be as a development project of the Tomorrow's People/YBI type; with Earthwatch this would be as a mechanism for delivering local

Table 11.4 Summary of success factors and limitations of main project categories

Type of project	Success factors	Limitations
Category 1 Discreet projects with high profile results	Partnership Significant company contribution Sustained commitment Independent management Narrow scope	Unreliability of partners Dependency Highly philanthropic
Category 2 Projects responding to a specific operational business relationship problem	Significant company contribution Narrow scope Built in sustainability	Temptation to focus on profit Gap between rhetoric and reality
Category 3 Projects which respond to specific relational problems that are not strictly operational	Partnership Significant company contribution Creativity	Introverted nature Lack of vision

environmental improvements rather than as a corporate identity building exercise. Without clearly defined goals in category one or two the programme will degenerate into meeting departmental objectives such as increasing the quality of service of the product in outlets to the benefit of sales and marketing, or improving human resources by allowing staff to feel good. Both of these may be best met by policies outside the corporate citizenship activity.

How to design a corporate citizenship programme

Our discussion so far has focussed on individual CC projects. In this section we consider the wider issues involved in running a corporate citizenship programme made up of a set of community engagement projects. We frame our discussion around five themes: the nature of the industry the firm is in, the importance of reputation building, the observation of due management process, the importance of appropriate partners and the benchmark of project added value.

The strategic nature of the industry in the choice of social capital projects

Corporate citizenship projects need to be consistent with the strategic issues facing the firm due to the industry it operates in. Companies are doing projects in order to build reputation, therefore being seen to be responsive to societal concerns raised by industry operations is an essential part of this. The nature of the company's political environment, regulation and other sensitivities could be captured as follows:

Character of the host country. South Africa is a key example of a country that requires companies to support development and to some extent be seen to undo some of the problems of the past. It is important that companies are sensitive to political and social concerns. Thus supporting the Ballet in Cape Town should be seen as less of a priority than promoting Millennium Development Goals.

Industry operating conditions. The best projects we have looked at are often addressing issues related to the wider social impact of industry operations. RBU and loveLife are projects of resource extraction companies aimed at community building in the face of the disruptive effect of multinational operations on traditional communities. RMI and LF are addressing issues of health equality raised by large pharmaceutical companies. CC programmes need to assess project choice in relation to the impact that the industry has on the community.

Regulation factors. Many industries are highly regulated and face the threat of tighter regulation. Companies need to pay attention to the regulatory environment in which they operate as they design CC programmes. CC projects may be a way of anticipating future legislation (as with Local Action Plans) or delivering on meeting current legislative targets (e.g. Anglo Zimele). All of our chosen case study companies are in industries where increased regulation is a real threat.

Campaigning NGOs and opinion leaders. Multinationals are the target of high profile attacks from NGOs. Their visibility makes them vulnerable to investigation and criticism. MNCs must be in the business of using their CC programmes to address the actual and potential concerns of such opinion formers. The campaigns of today will be the public policy of tomorrow (see Jones and Pollitt, 2002). Programmes such as LF very much demonstrate a visionary response to longer-term trends in the NGO and opinion leader pressure on MNCs. Indeed it is interesting that the idea emerged from a conversation with one such global opinion leader.

The importance of networking for reputation building

It is easy to be sceptical about the benefits of networking and there appears to be an element of greenwash about much corporate citizenship activity. However we should not underplay the importance of corporate networking for the company and for society. Well-connected companies are more responsive to societal needs and in turn more appreciated by the societies in which they operate. It is important for companies to realise that the overall shape of their corporate citizenship programmes is important.

Companies need to have regard to what their corporate citizenship programme says about their company. Does it reach out to local people, governments, NGOs and international agencies? Does it reflect legitimate political agendas, such as the MDGs? If it simply panders to the company's business interests and does not involve high quality external partners it will not build a reputation for serious engagement with building social capital. Companies like Anglo American have worked hard to think about the shape and content of their CC programme and enjoy an improved reputation because of it.

Due management process

Corporate citizenship programmes should not be accidents of history or built on the whim of the chief executive. Of course there is a role for serendipity, as in the LF project, but this be should within an overall programme that makes sense and where initially useful ideas are properly assessed. Much of Vodafone's CC activity seems to have been conducted without careful consideration of the overall shape of its programme. Due process would involve:

Proper approval process. This would involve professional assessment and honing, followed by presentation to the Board of Directors for approval. Original suggestions could still be from the chief executive but these would need to be assessed objectively.

Review of major projects. This would include detailed impact analysis of the cost effectiveness of the company's contribution in terms of meeting objectives. Due attention should be given to the geographical spread, MDG focus and level of networking of the overall portfolio of projects. Objectives could be primarily developmental, but proper assessment is necessary to ensure value for money.

Consideration of overall programme shape. All four of our case study companies had a small number of high profile and expensive projects as well as a larger number of smaller projects. Careful thought needs to be given to the size distribution of the portfolio of projects. It seems reasonable to suggest that the very best projects require a level of resources and executive support which means that, within each firm, such projects can only be very few in number. Companies may also be poorly placed (given the size and competence of their CSR departments) to monitor large numbers of small projects.

Spreading of learning. CC projects are supposedly about the company contributing to wider society. The company has an obligation to spread the lessons for others from its own experience. As one of the biggest benefits of CC programmes is learning from innovative projects, a systematic process for learning the lessons and disseminating them is important.

Exploitation through public relations. It is right and proper that firms get the credit from successful CC programmes. This has a double benefit: it promotes good practice and it increases the incentive on the company to keep investing in social capital building activities by reinforcing the enlightened self-interest in doing so. Such information produces public goods of improved attitudes to the company within and without the organisation.

Among our companies, Anglo American stands out as following such due process (much of it via SEAT), whereas Diageo and Vodafone have a more mixed record on following through on each of these elements of good practice.

The importance of appropriate partners

Social capital is a community concept and cannot be built by companies in isolation. A key feature of all of the major social capital building projects is that they have involved effective partnerships with external organisations. For projects on a global scale this has involved international agencies (LF with WHO), for national projects it has involved national bodies (such as Tomorrow's People with UK government agencies) and for local projects local organisations (such as RBU with the NGO Farmer Support Group).

Multinationals need to give thought to the overall shape of their partnership strategy. It would seem odd if multinationals did not participate in global initiatives but also if they ignored national and local institutions in delivering projects. It is important that companies reflect a balance in their partnerships. An impressive feature of GSK's CC portfolio is the combination of large multinational projects with much more localised projects.

This balanced approach represents part of the potential for vertical networking of multinationals and offers opportunities for information sharing and bridging of structural holes that are unique to multinationals. Thus an idea generated in a local project in South Africa can potentially be globalised quickly if the multinational concerned is part of the appropriate global network of interested international organisations and like-minded multinationals. YBI is a good example of such an idea that has been globalised.

The benchmark of project added value

CC programmes can produce innovation and development multiplier effects. Unless they can be demonstrated to do this there is a serious question about their rationale. Clearly companies could decentralise their community engagement activity by simply giving money to NGOs with no further corporate involvement. This would be cost effective in terms of minimising management time. This provides a benchmark for each project that appears within a corporate citizenship portfolio. Companies should be able to demonstrate that company involvement has added value beyond a straightforward donation.

This benchmark of project added value is important because it relates directly to a standard critique of CSR that says that firms should concentrate on maximising profit and that government should address social objectives. This doctrine was originally advanced by Milton Friedman (1970) but has recently been promoted by those who attack current trends in CSR as bad for economic development. Henderson (2004, p.17) suggests that '[CSR's] general adoption, whether from social pressures or legal requirements, would do more harm than good. The case against CSR is not that it would necessarily be bad for profits, but that whatever its effects on enterprise profitability in particular cases, it would make people worse off in general.' This view is extreme but it does highlight the need for company CSR programmes to demonstrate that they are adding value above giving the resources directly to shareholders or charity.

Company projects should involve some non-financial input that can be demonstrated to add value to the project (in terms of innovation or increasing project effectiveness). Most of the 13 projects we have discussed do demonstrate this property. Successful projects in Category 1 and 2 seem to do this with ease. It is not clear that the OI or the TSF projects really demonstrated added value from company involvement. Whilst the specific contexts of these particular projects[4] might explain this lack of company involvement, it is all too clear that many projects receiving MNC funding lack a clear focus and hence have little rationale within a CC portfolio.

Notes

1. In fairness however, disaster relief projects, due to their nature, may not be designed with long term impacts in mind. There may be specific short term needs to be met and in those terms they may be very successful.
2. See Ofeibea Quist-Arcton, 'South Africa: Drugs' Giants Drop Case Against South Africa', *allAfrica.com*, April 19, 2001 at www.allAfrica.com.
3. Only two of the featured projects in the WBCSD report are recorded as addressing MDG 2 directly. However one is a housing project and the other does not improve access to primary education, which is the substance of MDG 2 (see WBCSD, 2005, pp.26–27 and 40–41).
4. It is clearly the case that firms may wish to start a relationship with an NGO with a simple donation and that this might be a prelude to the development of a deeper collaboration. However none of our four case study firms articulated this as their strategy.

References

Burt, R.S. (2001), 'Structural Holes versus Network Closure as Social Capital', In N. Lin, K. Cook and R.S. Burt (eds), *Social Capital Theory and Research*, New York: Adeline De Gruyter, pp.31–36.

Friedman, M. (1970), 'The Social Responsibility of Business is to Increase its Profits', *New York Times,* 13 September 1970.

Henderson, D. (2004), *The Role of Business in the Modern World*, London: IEA.

Jones, I.W. and Pollitt, M.G. (2002) (eds), *Understanding How Issues in Business Ethics Develop*, Basingstoke: Palgrave.

UN (2006), *The Millennium Development Goals Report 2006*, New York: United Nations.

WBCSD (2005), *Business for Development: Business solutions in support of the Millennium Development Goals*, Geneva: World Business Council for Sustainable Development.

12
Learning the Lessons: What Directions should Corporate Citizenship Programmes Take in the Future?

Conclusions

This book has addressed the issues relating to multinationals and the communities in which they operate. The purpose of the book is to assess how it is that multinationals can be more effective in contributing to economic and social development, particularly in developing countries, via their corporate citizenship (CC) programmes.

We outlined our approach in the first four chapters. The next six chapters presented and analysed first empirical and then case study evidence from our research into corporate citizenship. At the end of the empirical chapters and in the preceding chapter we drew conclusions from these two strands of our research.

This chapter seeks to draw together the lessons from the whole of the book and suggest future directions for the development of CC programmes. We begin by putting our analysis in the context of the issues which communities face.

Understanding the aspirations of communities

It is useful to distinguish between the development agenda being placed on multinationals and the agenda itself. Development aspirations of communities are a fact of life and form the context within which multinationals operate. Communities in developing countries and rich country pressure for third world development will continue to expect MNCs to be involved in community development. The likelihood is that such pressure will continue to grow and become more intense. Such pressures for development goals to be met will exist whether or not multinationals take account of them. This book makes clear that in responding to these pressures MNCs must make strategic choices: about whether or not get involved in community development and, once involved, which projects to pursue.

Thus it is useful to reflect on what the world agenda is for communities and how it is developing. The model of Jones and Pollitt (2002) on how issues in business ethics develop applies. This model identifies three stages in the development of a business ethics issue. The first of these stages – awareness – involved public debate, which put an issue on the public agenda. This involved a political process of exchange of views, of lobbying, of targeting others, especially via undermining the leaders of the opposite viewpoint. An example of this might be NGOs picking on high reputation multinationals such as Shell. Our discussion in Chapter 3 has underlined the many influencers who are involved at the awareness stage. These would include multilateral agencies, national government, non-governmental organisations and 'busybody' consultants. In this context we might note the increasing intensity of advocacy by NGOs. Save the Children, Oxfam and Christian Aid have increasingly redirected resources towards advocacy and have particularly targeted multinationals. Disasters or events can reinforce trends or start new directions for the public debate with cases involving multinationals being particularly newsworthy (Shell in Nigeria, Union Carbide in Bhopal, etc). Increasingly the development agenda has been internationalised via the Millennium Development Goals, the focus on Africa and concerns about global security and environmental issues. This exposes MNCs to further political pressure. The media bringing events and opinions into the living room is another influencing factor, as well as international communication, such as email and international travel. Putting all this together, one reaches the conclusion that concern for community issues has been rising and will continue to do so. It is also part of a decidedly international agenda and any player who is international – like a significant multinational or NGO – has to think internationally if it addresses the issue.

It is important to recognise that the focus of the development agenda switches over time as well as following a rising trend. In an earlier period, the focus was on the environment. During the period of this research global poverty and sub-Saharan African development in particular have moved up the agenda. The anecdotal evidence collected during the case studies suggests that the environment is likely to move up the agenda again.

There are many and varied examples of the changing intensity and direction of social interest. One could mention the interest in poverty in the G8 meeting of 2005. There has been the explosion in interest in 'fair trade' and widespread concern about AIDS/HIV.

The multinational enterprise response

Against this background the multinational has a choice whether to respond to the community agenda. Multinationals have to recognise that 'no man is an island'. They are corporate citizens. Strategic interest would suggest that MNCs should choose to respond to the community agenda. This is a rational response to the pressures that they are under to be involved in building local communities from all the initial stage influencers. Doing corporate citizenship projects can help companies to manage their corporate reputation risk. This is important if they are to reduce community distrust, stand up to NGO scrutiny and also mitigate the likelihood of business ethics scandals and reduce the damage from them if they do occur. Multinationals will continue to be at the forefront of the process of globalisation. Thus they can expect that as the beneficiaries of globalisation that they will be expected to provide some compensation for the disappointments of globalisation by way of dividends for the local communities in which they operate.

Our point is that given the broad debate about how communities should promote development, then multinationals as members of that community have to make a strategic choice about corporate citizenship projects. Doing nothing is a strategic choice. Doing projects at the whim of the CEO, which do not address pressing local development needs, is a strategic choice. Making that or any other decision by default or without reflection is un-businesslike.

The MNC response to community pressure will be governed by a set of objectives. Some of these will be pragmatic like reputation-building by Intel in Costa Rica (see chapter 4). For others (such as Guinness in Dublin) it will be a matter of principle about the role of companies in their communities. Further research might be able to tease out whether different objectives make a difference to the nature and effectiveness of community engagements. Our observation is that the clarity of objectives is very important in maximising the benefit to the company of corporate citizenship projects. However differing objectives will influence the social capital building potential of projects.

Another strategic consideration for multinationals is the global integrity of their corporate citizenship programmes. We have observed that in our samples from Poland and Mexico engagements by EU and US multinationals respectively were not that easy to explain. Furthermore, our case studies did not give us a sense that companies had thought strategically about the rationale for the global distribution of their projects. Companies need to strategically decide the global shape of their corporate citizenship programme rather than let it arise by accident. Part of this is to think as carefully about corporate citizenship decisions as they would about decisions of equivalent importance or expenditure in their core business.

The foregoing observations illustrate the value of thinking about the multinational response to the community development agenda as part of their citizenship, rather than their responsibility. Responsibility implies guilt or duty whereas citizenship allows choice. A good corporate citizen might simply choose to pay their taxes and obey the law having decided that there is no useful role for it to play in supporting community citizenship projects. However the poor corporate citizen ignores the needs of its local communities for corporate citizenship projects and spends its Corporate Social Responsibility (CSR) budget un-strategically on lesser priorities for the community.

Value of our focus on social capital

Focus on benefits rather than expenditure

The use of social capital concepts to analyse CC projects has placed the focus on the impact of projects and the evaluation of benefits. Traditionally CC activity is accounted for as a cost. The comparative measures of activity in the US and the UK (e.g. the UK LBG) are in terms of cost and the essential issue is whether the cost is being reasonably and comparably estimated. It is interesting to observe that production cost valuation of pharmaceuticals is explicitly not a measure of the benefit of the pharmaceuticals to society. Hence the US use of wholesale price, rather than production cost, may be a better measure of societal benefit.

The orientation of this work is therefore in terms of contribution to the community and is output oriented. That is inherent in the use of the social capital concept. In our approach the benefits matter and the costs are not considered. This gives an entirely different focus to measurement. CC expenditure matters but it is not sufficient. It is about what is done with that expenditure.

Makes progress towards a universal standard of measure

Social capital provides a proven model of viewing the world that is used by academics and development practitioners. Although there are varying descriptions of social capital, the approach in this study demonstrates its use value in the area of analysing corporate citizenship projects.

The success of the social capital analysis and the universality of its basic approach suggests that it should provide the basis for external reporting of company activities.

We believe that some development is still required before standardised social capital measures could be used to evaluate and compare projects. It seems likely that simplified metrics, condensing the tables used in chapters 7–10, would be required. However simplification risks losing the intellectual coherence of the social capital concepts summarised in the tables. Any project output measure based on benefits would be ex-post and therefore there would be a delay between initiation and reporting. There is a danger that the measurement of benefits is more subjective than the measurement of expenditure inputs as the elements are less easy to define or measure, though a robust theoretical model such as social capital suggests concrete ways forward for measurement (such as numbers of people involved in any social network).

Focus on external relationships

Social capital with its emphasis on reciprocal relationships and building trust underscores the value of working with others. It presents non-involvement as lacking in value and thus highlights the weakness of support that is hands off. It underscores the value of involvement and demonstrates the multiplier effect of a multinational getting engaged in a project, sharing its expertise, and also achieving things that would be difficult or impossible for other actors working alone. MNCs are also excellent at bridging vertical structural holes in society. This also increases the durability of the projects as effective relationships can last longer than the initial expenditure of resources and exchange of skills. The relationships and the knowledge and goodwill they generate can leave an enduring imprint.

Focus on the detail of projects and networks of relationships

As noted in chapter 2 there are studies that look at the correlations between CSR activity (or corporate donations or corporate giving) and selected characteristics such as performance and nature of industry. This study has the value of collecting detail about the programmes themselves thus making it possible to relate macro relationships with the micro features of practice. This provides evidence that has compelling concreteness and provides significant real patterns. Social capital concepts have allowed us to do this for individual projects and at the country level. Analysing corporate giving activity at these levels is simply not possible in a systematic way.

General observations on our results

We have seen some excellent examples of corporate citizenship programmes and these have been analysed in considerable detail in chapters 7–10. There are several which are strategic. Anglo American shows a self-consciously strategic interest in projects in South Africa. The empirical results in chapters 5 and 6 also showed up some more general strategic effects. The observation of a positive industry effect on the social capital building activity of companies in the mining and extraction industries reflects strategic choices. The result that newer companies are more engaged in Mexico also seems to reflect the strategic needs of MNCs to become established and accepted within a host community.

In the spirit of an 'end of term report' we pick out some of the failings and areas for improvement in the area of corporate citizenship, based on our analysis:

- *General lack of engagement in some countries.* We have seen from the empirical analysis that a large number of multinationals do not participate in international corporate citizenship. The US companies in Mexico were significant in the low proportion of companies involved in international initiatives. We have noted that in the case of US companies in particular, there is a strong tendency to be home country focussed.
- *Lack of clear CC project strategy.* The empirical analysis also reveals the difficulty in explaining the size of CC programmes in relation to key variables. The implication of this is that many companies do not see their CC programme as strategic. There would appear to be little or no attempt to relate Corporate Citizenship to where the business is. There is also little connection between CC and where employees, suppliers or customers are. By implication, in these companies there is no attempt to use CC in a way that stimulates and interacts with the business.
- *Apparent corporate cynicism about CC.* The empirical separation between CC and the business leads to the reflection that for some companies there is a cynicism about CC. CC is approved as a lump sum by the main board. The aim is to spend a significant proportion of profits to stand out in the ratings. A specialist in the field, who may be extremely professional, is appointed to 'run the show' and senior management can get on with the business. The emphasis on expenditure would appear to be a symptom of this hands-off approach.

- *Making CC more strategic is possible, but difficult.* We have observed companies struggling with making CC more strategic but instead making CC less of an investment and more of a support to business generation. For instance with Diageo and Vodafone, board level questioning about the return from projects and the underlying strategy appears to have resulted in good initiatives not being followed through (Opportunity International) and an attempt to derive short term commercial gain from projects by strengthening the involvement of operating departments such as marketing in CC (as at Diageo). The vision of CC thus becomes subordinated to immediate business objectives. Whereas, with GSK and Anglo, we have seen outstanding projects being undertaken which have a strategic impact on the business and on people's perception of the business.
- *Inconsistency of internal monitoring and external reporting.* Our case study research revealed that, for at least one of our companies, while they were very conscious of public relations and image building for their brands and were also aware of pressures on the reputation of their industry, they were unsystematic in collecting data about their CC projects and publishing them on the website. While there were good operational reasons for this – a shortage of CC staff resources – this did mean that the head office was not fully appraised of the extent of CC activity worldwide.

Recommendations about best practice CC for multinationals

It has been our privilege, as part of this research, to discuss corporate citizenship with some of the leading exponents amongst multinationals as well as to carry out a significant study of conduct in this area. There are some excellent examples of good practice in community engagement. Anglo American has taken leadership in Africa and in the Mining and Resources Sector. There are excellent examples of collective action, e.g. the Extractive Industries Transparency Initiative and the Ethical Trading Initiative. There are encouraging new initiatives such as Business Action for Africa which brings together 330 companies from 36 countries 'united in the belief that business should be an active partner with governments, donor institutions and other parts of civil society in supporting sustainable development in Africa.'[1] Corporate foundations responsible for company approaches to development have done significant thinking on the role of the private sector in solving development problems. The Shell Foundation for instance has produced a detailed policy document entitled 'Enterprise Solutions to Poverty – Opportunities and Challenges for the International

Development Community and Big Business'[2] recording experience from the Foundation's programmes and suggesting new ways to thinking about business role in poverty reduction.

The principal recommendation from our study is that multinationals have to become *strategic* in the deployment of corporate citizenship. This means:

- *Having clear objectives* for their engagement in the community, recognising that non-engagement is a logical option. This means recognising the basic drivers in terms of reputation building, influencing regulators and those granting permissions and influencing the community who may have power to limit operation. Although philanthropy is intended to be free from direct interest, the company should be clear about its own enlightened self-interest in its CC programme.
- *Deriving a vision and strategy* for this engagement. This strategy should be international and recognise the location of action as being a key element. It should relate to industry and company specific issues. It should recognise the probability of influence by major influencers such as advocacy NGOs, government, and even events. Multinationals need to have and be able to articulate a clear corporate citizenship strategy. This should include a discussion of the way that projects are selected and the rationale for their distribution between types and across countries.
- *Building membership of international and national networks* for the benefit of the community. There may be an element of cynicism in the attraction to senior executives of membership of such networks (i.e. meeting royalty, pop stars, etc). However the focus has to be on being there to seize opportunities or to facilitate connections for the benefit of the community.
- *Monitoring and assessment of the impact* of corporate citizenship projects needs to be significantly improved. Companies need to apply the same quality standards to their reporting and assessment of CC projects that they apply in their main business.
- *Embracing flagship projects*. The research has suggested the kind of projects which make a contribution and have a positive impact on reputation. The 'flagship' projects (such as Anglo Zimele and LF) have been shown to be very important.
- *Being extremely cautious about simplistic approaches to community citizenship*. A 'CSR prize winning mentality' or a 'claim whatever you can' approach adds to scepticism and distrust amongst a growing

audience of well informed observers and advocates. 'Greenwash' or its equivalent is a serious charge for a CC policy that consumes 1% of taxable profits and needs to be countered with socially significant CC projects.
- *Reconciling global policy and local ownership.* MNCs need to address the dilemma of the need for a global CC policy and the need to encourage local action and engagement. We have encouraged CC practitioners to take an overall strategic view whilst being active throughout the world. Taking the decision-making to the local operators, for instance in the way that Vodafone is doing by creating several local trusts, would mirror that approach. How that decentralisation is brought together strategically is probably organisation specific.
- *Anticipating commercial exploitation to the benefit of the community and to business.* Being profitable is sustainable in a way that philanthropy cannot be. Certain CC projects may actually be highly risky business investments which can only be justified in terms of their current and potential social capital payoffs, rather than on a business case alone. However if they do turn out to be financially successful this ensures sustainability. The Vodafone community phone shops and Anglo Zimele projects illustrate this. Projects with this potential for commercial sustainability are to be encouraged and to be fully exploited (via replication or outsourcing) when financially successful.
- *Prioritising knowledge transfer and internationalisation of CC projects.* A major benefit from successful CC projects undertaken by multinationals is the lessons that can be learned elsewhere. Lessons can be used by other members of MNC networks and/or by other parts of the multinational itself. MNCs need to be encouraged to exploit the potential for replication that successful CC models may have.

Social capital as a tool of evaluation and reporting

We have discussed the increasing global advocacy for community development and the increasing concern for development within communities. We have argued that multinationals are logically free to decide whether to have a CC policy but are operating in an environment where they are targeted by advocates.

In this situation, the model of the ethical issue life cycle (see Figure 1.1) would seem to apply. The community will feel entitled to know what companies are doing, whether they are being strategic and what priorities they are giving to community projects. The demand in the first instance will be for reporting in a coherent and comparable way about community projects and philanthropic giving.

We noted in the introduction recent moves along the ethical issue life cycle in environmental standards, health and safety and treatment of third world suppliers. It is as yet unclear what will be required for CC, which is still in voluntary best practice/voluntary group response stage. There is pressure for information which is readily available and in a form which is understood and allows comparison and evaluation. It would seem that a reporting system will emerge in accordance with the ethical issue life cycle, with companies developing reporting systems and for these to become standardised and embedded by regulatory approval.

The success of social capital, demonstrated by this research, as a measure which is outward looking for the firm and resonates with the practice and thinking of other stakeholders, suggests that the reporting standard should be based on this model. The actual use may be subject to simplification and adaptation, and this is no bad thing so long as the principal theoretical insights are captured.

We have hinted that the current emphasis on the reporting of CC expenditure is insufficient and potentially counter productive because as we have suggested, it is introspective and not concerned with results. Costs, as in accounting, provide hard facts which please accountants but may not enlighten others. A requirement to state a corporate policy on corporate social investment would have a powerful demonstration effect. This effect would be similar to earlier requirements to declare executive remuneration and corporate governance policies.[3] The currently abandoned Operating and Financial Report requirements of the UK Company Law Review would have included a statement on CSR policy.[4] As we have seen in earlier chapters initiatives to develop measures for multinationals (such as the GRI) have not gone far enough The challenge for multinationals is to lead the way in best practice reporting by devising, perhaps with other interest groups, standardised reporting that is outward looking and geared to performance. Our view is that community citizenship will become recognised as possessing increasing strategic importance and as an area where greater investment is needed. Shareholders and financial markets will therefore demand much better information to ensure the multinational is using its corporate citizenship budget to influence its operating environment in ways that alter the reward risk ratio of their investment, and add value above what investors could do with the money if it were distributed as profits.

The role of wider society in CC projects and programmes

The elegance of this work has been to examine company activity in relation to all other actors in society. The emphasis has been on partnership and complementary roles. We have seen that organisations working together can produce stunning results. Together with other actors in society MNCs have allowed social bridges to be crossed and structural holes in social relations to be filled.

Advocacy and pressure have had a significant impact too. Large pharmaceutical companies would not give large quantities of product away if the public did not care about their actions. Multinationals would not have addressed youth employment problems if not approached by politicians. Many of the South African-based firms have worked wonders with CC projects under public pressure and legislation on black economic empowerment and poverty reduction. NGOs have played their part revealing bad practice, spreading good practice, collaborating with companies and making MNCs accountable in their corporate citizenship.

This criticism and collaboration needs to be sustained in order to drive performance forward. Multinationals need to be pressed to be outward looking especially when company performance is in decline or there are grounds for self satisfaction. In one sense, there will always be more that a multinational can do, either because there is a specific capability or because there is no money elsewhere.

On the other hand, other members of society have to recognise that multinationals are not all competent nor sources of unlimited wealth. They need to be left to get on with their business. There is a key danger that governments and society will expect too much from MNCs' CC programmes and seek to ask them to take on social objectives which cannot be funded by government. As business leaders never tire in pointing out companies cannot be expected to be responsible for social (as opposed to economic) goals. The public, governments and NGOs should recognise this. As corporate citizenship becomes more sophisticated and government recognise the budget limitations on multinationals, it may be that governments could explore collaborative mechanisms for encouraging and guiding corporate philanthropy and engagement at the local level.

Our study suggests the following roles for wider society in shaping CC:

- Government and international agency pressure for CC should be targeted on areas close to the business competence of private companies. Targeted product donation (particularly of pharmaceuticals and technological equipment) and support for entrepreneurship and workplace skills and local environmental clean up are good examples of areas where there is a track record of successful multinational involvement. Governments and international agencies have a legitimate role in setting wider developmental priorities and inviting MNC support for them. Furthermore, government should explore options for using opportunities, such as the granting of mobile phone licences, to engage with the creative dynamism of the private sector when attempting to solve socio-economic problems.
- NGOs have a key role in promoting good practice by highlighting successful NGO-company collaborations. NGOs need to adopt a partnership approach to multinationals where this is the most beneficial to local communities. NGOs need to balance this role with accurately exposing misleading or wrong statements on CC in company reports or activity on the ground. This policing role of multinationals continues to be an important agent of change in CC policy.
- NGOs need to be responsible in their use of information and publicity. Just as we have recommended that 'over presenting' information to an increasingly knowledgeable audience is a dangerous tactic for companies. Excessive exaggeration on limited evidence can undermine the NGO strategically. It diminishes its right to be heard. It also loses the goodwill of other members of the network. It increases suspicion and reduces trust, which as the social capital approach shows is critical to deriving creative solutions to complex social problems.
- Wider society needs to recognise both the strength and the limitations of multinational CC programmes. They should not restrict their capacity to innovate solutions to developmental problems by overly prescriptive CC requirements. They should have realistic expectations about multinational CC programmes in terms of size and focus. Company projects are best focussed on projects where innovation, multiplier and sustainability effects are likely to be highest and this makes particular MNCs more effective in meeting some MDGs rather than others.
- Public pressure has a legitimate role in shaping the direction of CC effort. Pressure needs to be applied to companies to remind them of

their strategic interest in redirecting their giving overseas (this is particularly true of US companies) in line with their distribution of profits, revenue and employees. This is because for multinationals there is considerable untapped potential for promoting international development. There is also scope for bringing to the attention of companies the projects most valued by society and where their participation can offer most benefit.
- Regulatory pressure, such as via stock market listing rules, for more consistent reporting of CC activity, given that it is for social benefit, should be increased. Corporate governance has improved significantly through improved reporting requirements and transparency. A requirement to report on corporate citizenship expenditure and to include a statement on corporate citizenship policy in company annual reports would be consistent with earlier developments in corporate governance. Shareholders should be encouraged to develop their own understanding of what CC does for them and engage in a dialogue with the company. Ultimately CC spends their dividend. Companies need their owners to have a constructive and informed view of what they the owners will support and encourage.

Overall, company CC programmes should not been seen simply as a source of charitable funds. Pure corporate philanthropy will always be limited. Companies that give strategically to corporate development projects with high social capital payoffs are doing more good than companies that simply make charitable donations. We have demonstrated that companies can use their CC projects to successfully build valuable social capital. However successful and well governed core businesses will continue to be the most important contribution that companies can make to social development goals.

Notes

1 Mark Moody-Stuart (2005), Business Action for Africa Conference 5th–6th July 2005, – Conference Statement, p.1. See www.BusinessActionforAfrica.org
2 See Shell Foundation (2006).
3 See Jones and Pollitt (2002, chapter 2) for a discussion of the evolution of corporate governance in the UK during the 1990s.
4 See Parkinson (2002).

References

Jones, I.W. and Pollitt, M.G. (eds) (2002), *Understanding How Issues in Business Ethics Develop*, Basingstoke: Palgrave.

Moody-Stuart, M. (2002), 'Reading the Business Ethics Radar: Lessons from Shell', in I.W. Jones and M.G. Pollitt (eds), *Understanding How Issues in Business Ethics Develop*, Basingstoke: Palgrave, pp.157–164.

Parkinson, J. (2002), 'Inclusive Company Law', in J. de Lacy (ed.), *The Reform of Company Law in the UK*, London: Cavendish.

Shell Foundation (2006), *Enterprise Solutions to Poverty*, http://www.shellfoundation.org/download/pdfs/SF_Exec_Summary_Enterprise_Solutions_to_Poverty.pdf. Accessed 10/05/2005.

Index

Accor, 23, 219, 220
AccountAbility, 26, 50, 51, 288
Action Aid, 59, 261–2
Action on Smoking, see Christian Aid, 58
Agence de Presse, 302n
Alcatel, 296
Alcohol Education, 204
Alexander, M., 70
Altman, Dr. Drew, 248
Altron Group, 122n
Amnesty International UK, 59, 65, 84n
AMVESCAP, 227, 228
Anglo American, 4, 17n, 23, 27, 55, 122n, 227, 228, 229, 230, 231, 233, 235, 237, 238, 244, 252
    Anglo Chairman's Fund, 233–5
    focus areas, 234
    Anglo Zimele Empowerment Initiative Ltd, 238–43, 251–2
    corporate biography, 227–8
    corporate citizenship, strategy and management, 229–30
    CSI spending, 231–3
    Hippo Valley Estates (HVE) Ltd, 236–7
    HIV/AIDS Community Partnership, 15, 247–51, 253–5
    Mondi Business Paper (MBP) SCP, 237–8
    New Denmark Colliery, 237
    reporting, 230–1
    Richmond Business Unit (RBU), 243–7, 252–3
    SEAT methodology, 235–6
Anglo Base Metals, 228, 249
Anglo Coal, 228
Anglo Khula Mining Fund, 239
Anglo Platinum, 228
Anglo Zimele Empowerment Initiative Ltd, 238, 306
    and Bambanani, 242
    evaluation, 243
    evidence of sustainability, 243
    inputs from Anglo American, 240–1
    outline, 238–40
    social capital aspects, 251–2
    startup, 238
    summary, 319
    working with partners, 240
AngloGold, 228, 247
Anon, 221, 255n
Anti-Retroviral Treatment (ART), 248, 249, 250
Arango, M., 72
AT&T, 296, 302n
Austin, J., 37
Australia, 77, 101, 216, 218, 228

Baileys, 199
Bain and Co., 37
Baker, M., 81, 82, 83, 261, 266
Bambanani, 242
Banai, M., 113
Barbecue Restaurant, 219, 220
Barretstown Gang Camp, 266–9, 306
    evaluation, 269
    evidence of sustainability, 269
    inputs from GSK, 268
    outcomes, 268–9
    outline, 267–8
    social capital aspects, 277
    startup, 266
    summary, 319
    working with partners, 268
Baue, W., 46n, 68, 79
Baum, S., 121n
BBC News, 79
Bedzir, V., 114
Bek, D., 7
Bells, 199
benchmarking, 53, 73, 78
    of project added value, 331
Bendell, J., 24

Biernot-Fawkes, D., *see* Siegfried, J.J.
Big Pharma, 261
biz.yahoo.com, 282n
Black Economic Empowerment (BEE), 116, 117, 231, 252, 255n
Black Gold Products Charcoal project, 245
Blowfield, M., 120
bottom-up social capital, 175–6
boundary crossing, 310
Bowles, S., 119, 122n
BP, 23, 55, 72, 111, 194
Brammer, S., 16n, 17n, 32, 33, 46n
Brazil, 14, 25, 218, 221, 306
British East India Company, 110, 122n
British South Africa Company, 110, 122n
Broers, L., 286
BT Group Ltd, 23, 55
Buchholtz, A.K., 32, 33
 see also Saiia, D.H., 33
Buckley, P., 109
Buerkle, K., 103, 179, 198n
Buffett, S., 37
Bullen, P., 101
Burge, R., 283
Burger King, 199
Burt, R.S., 95, 100, 308
Business Action for Africa, 66, 339
Business Action on Education, 53
Business in the Community (BITC), 39, 40, 52–4, 78, 79, 80, 202, 233, 265, 269, 271, 279n
 guidelines, 39
business-led organisations
 BITC, *see* Business in the Community
 IBLF, *see* International Business Leaders Forum
Business Partners for Development (BPD), 24–5
Business Trust, 233
Business Week, 36–7, 38, 42, 44

Cable and Wireless, 296
Campbell, C., 118
Campbell, D., 16n, 17n, 33
Campbell, K.E., 101
Captain Morgan, 199
Cares, 53
Carpenter, J.P., 121n
Carrefour, 296
Carroll, A.B., *see* Saiia, D.H.
Carter, J., 270, 278
Carter, M.R., 118
Casson, M., 109, 115
Cause-Related Marketing Campaign, 53
channel, of social capital, 12, 40, 94, 100, 109, 312
China, 95, 212, 301n
Chloupkova, J., 113
Christian Aid, 58, 65
 see also Amnesty International UK
Clay, J. 17n
Cohen, D., 17n, 106, 131
Coleman, J., 93, 120n
Collier, P., 98, 100
commitment, 204, 222, 311, 321
Committee to Encourage Corporate Philanthropy (CECP), 34–5
community development, 10, 111, 112, 230, 333–4
community engagements, 197
 in Poland, 174
 in South Africa and Mexico, 129
community phone shops, 15, 299, 324
Community Service Programme, 290, 291
competence trust, 97, 99
Conley, J., 60, 83
Conlin, M., *see* Hempel, J., 46n
consultancies, 51
 AccountAbility, 26, 50, 51, 288
 Corporate Citizenship Company (CCC), 52, 76, 77, 203, 206
consumer pressure, vulnerability of, 316
contribution, 3, 6, 7, 10, 28, 29, 30, 33, 40, 67, 109, 112, 119, 223, 231, 253, 299, 300, 310, 321, 323, 324, 325, 333, 345
Copebras, 228
'core competency movement', 37
corphilanthropy.org, 46n

corporate citizenship (CC)
  projects/programmes, 2–4, 30, 200–2, 305
  of Anglo American, 227
  Anglo Zimele Empowerment Initiative Ltd, 238
  appearance, 9
  Barretstown Gang Camp, 266–9, 277
  comparison, 306–8
  contribution, to development, 10
  corporate giving
    in UK, 38–42, 42–5
    in USA, 34–8, 42–5
  corporate philanthropy trends, 32–4
  and corporations, 25–32
  designing methodology, 327–32
  of Diageo, 199
  Diageo-Earthwatch Champions Programme, 213–16
  due management process, 329–30
  evolution, 8
  firms' involvement in, 30–2
  future directions, 333–45
  of GlaxoSmithKline, 260
  global instruments, 20–5
  with high profile results, 321–3
  HIV/AIDS Community Partnership, 15, 247–51, 253–5
  key players in, 49
  lessons drawn, 9–10
  Lymphatic Filariasis (LF) programme, 269–73, 277–8
  multinationals
    best practice for, 339–41
    observations on, 338–9
    response, 335–6
  operation business relationship problem, responding to, 223–5
  Opportunity International (OI), 293–6, 299–300
  principal actors, 8
  Projecto Bartender, 218–21
  Referral Management Initiative (RMI)/Children's Health Fund (CHF), 273–6, 279
  relational problem, responding to, 325

  Richmond Business Unit (RBU), 243
  role of wider society in, 343–5
  and social capital, 1, 4–5, 8–9, 98–100, 308, 336–7
  in community projects, 320–7
  networks existence, 309
  networks functioning, 310–11
  networks outputs, 311–16
  as tool of evaluation and reporting, 341–3
  with strategic issues, 328
  summary, 316–20
  Télécoms Sans Frontières (TSF), after 2004 Tsunami, 296–8, 300–1
  Tomorrow's People, 206–9
    in UK, 63–8
  understanding, 5–8
    aspirations of communities, 333–5
    in USA, 60–3
  Vodacom Community Phone Shops, 289–92, 299
    of Vodafone Group plc, 282
  Youth Business Initiative (YBI), 210–13
  see also individual entries
Corporate Citizenship Company (CCC), 52, 76, 77, 203, 206
Corporate Community Investment, 53–4
Corporate Council for America's Children, 274, 275
Corporate Environmental Research Group (CERG), 214
corporate financial performance (CFP), 107
corporate giving, 2, 129
  in UK, 1
    comparison with US corporate giving, 42–5
    PerCent Standard, 38–42
  in USA, 1–2
    Business Week survey, 36–7
    CECP, 34–5
    comparison with UK corporate giving, 42–5
    foundations and individual donations, 37–8
  see also philanthropy

Corporate Responsibility Coalition (CORE), 59–60
Corporate Responsibility Index (CRI)
  comments on, 80–1
  methodology, 78–80
Corporate Social Investment (CSI), 70, 107, 230, 231
corporate social responsibility (CSR), 1, 3, 26–7
  rapidly evolving institutional matrix, 49
Corporate Watch, 58–9, 230
Costa Rica, 216
creativity, 326
CSR Academy, 54
CSR.gov.uk, 84n
CSRwire.com, 55
Cuerva, 199

Daniele, P., 221
Danielson, A., 105
Danone child malnutrition initiative, 178–9
Dasgupta, P., 5, 93, 120n
De Beers Investments,, 65, 227, 228, 238
Dean, M., 270, 273, 279
Decuir-Viruez, L., 114, 122n
defensive sensitivity, 315
Denny, K., 121n
Department of Health and Children, 279n
Department of International Development (DFID), 17n, 65, 66, 245
dependency, 322
Development Gateway, in Poland, 176–7
Diageo, 3, 4, 7, 27–8, 29, 199, 200, 203, 204, 205, 209, 213, 218, 221
  community spending, 201, 202–4
  corporate biography, 199
  corporate citizenship, strategy and management, 200–2
  Diageo 2004, regional data for, 200
  Diageo-Earthwatch Champions Programme, 213–16, 223, 318
  evaluation, 206
  Foundation, 205, 213, 215, 220
  initiating projects, 204–5
  Local Action Plans (LAP), 217–18
  Projecto Bartender, 218–21, 223–4, 318
  reporting, 206
  Tomorrow's People, 206–9, 222, 318
  Youth Business Initiative (YBI), 210–13, 222–3, 318
Diageo Brazil, 221
Diageo-Earthwatch Champions Programme, see Earthwatch
digitaldividend, 301n
'DNA of business', 30, 31, 252
Dow Jones Sustainability Index, 288
Draft Boundary Protocol, 230
Department of Trade and Industry (DTI), 64, 65, 255n
due management process, 329–30
Dunfee, T.W., see Hess, D.
Durlauf, S.N., 104, 121n
Dutch firms, 191

Earthwatch, 14, 205, 213–16, 218, 306–8
  evaluation, 216
  evidence of sustainability, 216
  inputs from Diageo, 215
  outcomes, 216
  outline, 214–15
  social capital aspects, 223
  startup, 213
  summary, 318
  working with partners, 215
Easterly, W., 121n
Economist, The, 69, 71, 72, 73, 228, 255n
Emmett, T., 117
endorsement, 62–3
Enron, 91
Envelope Drop, 104, 105
Environmental Resources Management (ERM), 235
Ericsson, 296
Ethical Corporation, 55
ethical investment indices, 55–60
  Action Aid, 59

Index

advocacy groups, 57
  Christian Aid, 58
  Corporate Responsibility Coalition (CORE), 59–60
  Corporate Watch, 58–9
  FTSE4Good Index series, 56–7
  Oxfam, 57–8
ethical issue life cycle, 6, 342
Ethical Trading Initiative (ETI), 6, 65, 66
European Liaison Network, 267
European Union, 26, 73, 113
  EU MNC focus groupings, 180
  EU multinationals, in Poland, 192–5
Extractive Industries Transparency Initiative (EITI), 66, 233

facilitation, 63, 114
Fafchamps, M., 108
Farmer Support Group (FSG), 243, 245, 255n
Fauna and Flora International, 283
Faust, K., 121n
Fernandez-Young, A., 49, 84n
Fig, D., 17n, 117
Finlay, A., 84n
firms
  involvement, in project, 30
  and social capital, 105–9, 112–13
  UK firms in South Africa, 145–53, 167–8
  US firms in Mexico, 153–66, 168–70
Foege, B., 270
Foreign Corrupt Practices Act, 110
Forestry Stewardship Council (FSC) certification, 243, 245
form, of social capital, 12, 94, 95, 99, 253, 277, 312
foundations and individual donations, 37–8
Fox, J., 115
Foyer Federation, 209
France Telecom, 296
Frank, S., 37–8
Freeman, L.C., 138
French firms, 191
Friedman, M., 107, 331
Friends of the Earth, 65, 230

see also Christian Aid, 58; Amnesty International UK
Frynas, J.G., 111, 112, 120n
FTSE4Good Indices, 56–7, 143, 181, 265
FTSE4Good.com, 56
Fuchs, S., 175
Fukuyama, F., 93, 97, 120n, 176
Fullemploy, 209
Fulton, K., 17n

game theory, 96
Gard, L., *see* Hempel, J., 37
Garnier, J., 270
Gates, B., 37
Gates, M., 37
Gates Foundation, 38
geographic scope, 15, 309
German firms, 191
Gershman, J., 115
Getting London Working, 207
Ghosal, S., 106, 110
Gibbon, G., 49
Gintis, H., 119
Giving List, 39, 42, 76, 203, 231
givingstandard.com, 46n
Glaesar, E.L., 98, 100, 104
GlaxoSmithKline (GSK)
  Barretstown Gang Camp, 266–9, 277, 306, 319
  community spending, 263–5
  corporate biography, 260–1
  corporate citizenship, strategy and management, 261–3
  Lymphatic Filariasis (LF) programme, 269–73, 277–8, 306, 320
  principles, 262
  Referral Management Initiative (RMI)/Children's Health Fund (CHF), 273–6, 279, 320
  reporting, 265–6
Global Alliance to Eliminate LF (GAELF), 270–1, 272, 273, 279n
Global Compact
  benefits, 23
  objectives, 22
  principles, 22–3
  progress, 23–4

Global Fund, 256n
Global Partnership for Youth Development, 25
Global Reporting Initiative (GRI), 81–4, 230
  evaluation, 82–4
Global Road Safety Partnership (GRSP), 25
Global Value Chain critique, 111
globalisation, 20, 22, 90, 110, 111, 335
  corporation's role, 91
Globescan Inc., 120n
Goodman, J., 292, 301n
Goodyear, 113
government, 61, 67, 70, 72, 90, 116, 116, 188, 209, 253, 344
Government Accountability Office (GAO), 61–2
Grand Metropolitan, 199
Grandmet, 201, 207
Granovetter, M.S., 95, 100
'greenwash', 2
Grootaert, C., 17n, 94, 96, 99, 122n, 135–6, 140, 171n
group membership, 102
Guinness, 199, 201
Guinness UDV, 220, 221
Guista, M.D., 115
Guseva, A., 103, 179, 198n
Gwynne, R., 71

Haddad, L., 116, 121n, 134–5
Hall, P.A., 103, 121n
Hamilton, R., 301n
Harvey, O., see Sherif, M.
Hayes, K., 283
Healy, K., 115
Helliwell, J., 121n
Helper, S., 97, 99, 120n
Hempel, J., 37, 46n
Henderson, D., 331
Henley, J.S., 90
Hertz, N., 90
Hess, D., 153
high-profile results, projects with
  limitations, 322–3
  success factors, 321–2
Hilb, M., 109

Hilton, S., 49
Hippo Valley Estates (HVE) Ltd, 236–7
HIV/AIDS Community Partnership, 15, 247–51, 253–5
  evaluation, 247
  evidence of sustainability, 250–1
  inputs from Anglo American, 249–50
  outcomes, 250
  outline, 247–9
  social capital aspects, 253–5
  startup, 247
  summary, 319
Hjollund, L., 121n
Hlongwa-Madikizela, L., see Pettifor, A.
Hockey, V., 122n
Hoffer, T.B., 93
Holm, H.J., 105
Holyoke, T.T., 121n
Hood, W., see Sherif, M.

INCLUDE, 209
India, 23, 211, 212
individual giving, 37–8
information services
  Ethical Corporation, 55
  MallenBaker.net, 55
  SRI World Group Inc., 54–5
Inglehart, R., 91
InKindDirect, 39
Inmarsat, 296
InstitutionalShareholder.com, 55
Intel, 109
International Business Leaders Forum (IBLF), 54, 210, 213
introverted nature, 326
investments, 71
  ethical investment indices, 65–6
  in social capital, 96, 98
Isham, J., 97

J&B, 199
Jansen, P., 37
Jemicz, M., 114
Jenkins, R., 17n, 84n, 122n
Johannesburg, 227, 229
Johannesburg Securities Exchange, 84n

Johannesburg Stock Market Listing, 145, 152
Johnnie Walker, 199, 212
Jones, H., 31
Jones, I.W., 5–6, 7, 17n, 50, 120n, 130, 315, 328, 334, 345n
Judge, E., 302n
Jupiter Asset Management Ltd, 288

Kaiser Family Foundation, 255n
Kay, C., 71
Keefer, P., 5, 17n, 101, 102, 121n, 133, 142
Keep Walking Fund, 210
Kenan Consensus, 60
Kent, T., 78, 79, 80
Kenya, 216
Key Performance Indicators (KPIs), 237
key players, in corporate citizenship debate, 49
 business-led organisations, 52–4
 consultancies, 51–2
 corporate citizenship
  in UK, 63–8
  in USA, 60–3
 corporate community involvement, 73
 ethical investment indices, 55–60
 information services, 54–5
 institutional matrix, 50
 social and economic contexts, to MNC activity, 69
  in Mexico, 71–2
  in Poland, 72–3
  in South Africa, 69–70
Klein, N., 90
Kleinschmidt, I., see Pettifor, A.
Knack, S., 5, 17n, 101, 102, 121n, 133, 142
Knowledge Resource Group (KRG), 25
Kostova, T., 109
KPMG, 230–1
Kreps, D., 120n
Krishna, A., 102
Krzyszkowski, J., 175
KwaZulu-Natal Income Dynamics Survey (KIDS), 135

La Porta, R.F., 105
lack of vision, 326
Lafarge, 23
Laibson, D., 98, 100
 see also Glaesar, E.L., 104
Lall, S., 114
Latin America, 212
LBG model, see London Benchmarking Group model
learning, 107, 310, 333
Levine, R., 121n
Lin, N., 95, 96, 100
Litvin, D., 110, 111
Local Action Plans (LAP), 214, 216, 217–18
 outcomes, 218
 outline, 217
 selection, 217–18
Local Citizens, 204
local operating sensitivities, 316
Logan, D., 108
London Benchmarking Group (LBG) model, 73, 74, 75–8, 203
 methodology, 76–8
Lopez-de-Silanes, F., see La Porta, R.F.
loveLife, see HIV/AIDS Community Partnership
Lund-Thomson, P., 116–17
Lymphatic Filariasis (LF) programme, 15, 306
 evaluation, 273
 evidence of sustainability, 273
 inputs from GSK, 271–2
 outcomes, 272–3
 outline, 270–1
 social capital aspects, 277–8
 startup, 269–70
 summary, 320
 working with partners, 271
Lymphatic Filariasis Support Center, 271, 279n

McElroy, K.M., see Siegfried, J.J.
MacPhail, C., see Pettifor, A.
Majola, S., 242
maketradefair.com, 58
MallenBaker.net, 55
Maluccio, J.A., 102, 116, 118, 121n, 132, 134–5

management, 321–2, 323, 325
mandatory response, 6
Mandela, N., 205, 298
Mann, A., 37
Margolis, J.D., 107, 122n
Marsden, P.V., 101
May, J., 116, 134–5
Mbeki, T., 231n, 241, 256n
Mbigi, L., 116
McIntosh Xaba and Associates, 233
McQuaid, R.W., 122n
Metzger, M.   16n, 17n
Mexico, 71–2, 174, 194, 197, 211, 212
 crime rates, 115
 cultural differences, 114
 multinationals and community
  engagement, 129
 social capital, 114–15
 US firms in, 153–66, 168–70
 volunteerism, 115
Mezias, J.M., 110
Milgrom, P., see Kreps, D.
Millennium Development Goals
  (MDG), 2, 10, 241
Millington, A., 16n, 17n, 32, 46n
 see also Brammer, S., 33
mine working, 241–2
Mineweb, 255n
Mining Weekly, 255n
Minnesota principles, 143
Minten, B., 108
MNC, 1
 analysis, impediments to, 130–1
 limitations, in community development, 112
 in Poland, 174
  norm index, 188–9
  patterns, 185–8
  significance and types, 182–5
 response, to community agendas,
  335–6
 and social capital, 90, 109
 in South Africa and Mexico, 129
 suitable measures, 138
Mondi, 118
Mondi Business Paper (MBP), 237
Mondi Packaging, 228
Moody-Stuart, M., 345n
Moon, J., see Fernandez-Young, A.

Moore, G., 16n, 17n
Morris, M., 171n
Mosakowski, E., 110
Moyer, L., 36, 45
Mubangizi, B.C., 118
multinationals, see MNC
Murgasova, Z., 73
Mzandume, Z., 118

NACE codes, 182, 183, 184
Narayan, D., 102, 121n, 133–4
narrow scope, 322, 323
National Contact Points (NCP), 21–2
Natural Resources, 24–5
Nell, E.L., 122n
Nestle, 23, 56
NETPOL, 192
network, 93, 97
 existence
  geographic scope, 309
  partners, 309
  vitality, 309
 functioning, 310–11
  boundary crossing, 310
  contribution, 310
  learning, 310
  sustainability, 311
 membership, 103
 outputs, 311–16
  attracting best professionals
   for company, 314–15
  consumer pressure, vulnerability
   to, 316
  defensive sensitivity, 315
  local operating sensitivities, 316
  public goods, 316
  for society, 311–14
  society dependence, 315
  for reputation building, 329
network engagement scores, econometric analysis of, 141
 UK multinationals in South Africa,
  167–8
 US multinationals in Mexico,
  168–70
network map score, 12–13
network mapping, 138–40
 in Poland, 180–1
 results, 182

Index 355

New Denmark Colliery, 237
New Economics Foundation, 206, 209
New Internationalist, 281
New Steps, 207
Newell, P., 112
Newman, Paul, 267
NGO FSG, 253
NGOs, 344
Nigeria, 111, 112
Nike, 23
Nilsson, E., 106
Nokia, 23
norm indexing, 140–4
  in Poland, 181–2, 188–9
    constituent criteria, 181
    results, 182
norm score, 13, 129
North American Free Trade
    Agreement, 114
Nyland, C.M., 7, 130
NYSE Magazine, 199

O-groups, 92, 120n
OECD, 20, 21–2, 46n
  Anti-bribery Convention, 6
  guidelines for multinationals, 91, 21–2
Offe, C., 175
Ogilvie, S., 120n
Olson, M., 120n
On-Trade clients, 220
Onyx, J., 101
operational business relationship
    problem, projects responding
    to, 323
  limitations, 324–5
  success factors, 323–4
Oppenheimer, Sir Ernest, 227, 229
opportunism, 96–7
Opportunity International (OI), 15
  evaluation, 295–6
  evidence of sustainability, 295
  inputs from Vodafone, 294–5
  outcomes, 295
  outline, 293–4
  social capital aspects, 298–300
  startup, 293
  summary, 320
  working with partners, 294

Organisation for Economic
    Co-operation and
    Development, see OECD
Orlitzky, M., 107
Oxfam, 57–8, 58, 262, 279n
Oxfam International, 58
Oxfam.co.uk, 57
Oxfam.org.uk, 58
Oxford Economic Forecasting, 75, 206, 207, 209

P-groups, 92
Padian, D., see Pettifor, A.
Padlam, M., 94, 100
Paras, P., 115
Parkinson, J., 345n
partnerships, 63, 309, 321, 324, 325, 330–1
Pavelin, S., see Brammer, S., 33
Peek, S., 118
PerCent Club, 74
Pernod Ricard, 199
Personalismo, 114
Pettifor, A., 251
Pfizer, 23
philanthropy, 29, 32–4, 36, 72, 236, 322, 340, 345
  CECP, 34–5
  see also corporate giving
Piazza-Georgi, B., 102
Pillsbury, 199
Poland, 72–3, 174
  assistance-needed areas, 176
  bottom-up social capital, 175–6
  Danone child malnutrition
    initiative, 178–9
  Development Gateway, 176–7
  EU multinationals, 192–5
  health, 187
  at international level, 187, 191
  at local level, 187
  MNC engagements
    norm index, 188–90
    patterns, 185–8
    significance and types, 182–5
  at national level, 187, 190
  network mapping, 180–1
  results on, 182

Poland – *continued*
  norm indexing, 181–2
  results on, 182
  number of projects, 176, 195
  social capital, 113–14, 175
  and South Africa and Mexico, comparison, 187–8
  top-down social capital, 175
Polek, D., *see* Hempel, J.
politics.co.uk, 66
Pollard, D., 114
Pollitt, M.G., 5–6, 7, 17n, 50, 120n, 130, 315, 328, 346, 345n
Porritt, J., 288
Portes, A., 93, 131
Powell, C., 60
PriceWaterhouseCoopers, 46n
Prince's Trust, 213
Principal Compound Analysis (PCA), 100–1
Pritchett, L., 102, 121n, 133–4
Pro Natura, 112
ProbusBNW, 202, 205, 206
profitability, 324
Project Advisory Committee, 212
Project for Statistics on Living Standards, 135
Projeto Bartender, 14, 218–21
  evaluation, 221
  evidence of sustainability, 221
  inputs from Diageo, 220
  outcomes, 220
  outline, 219
  social capital aspects, 223–4
  startup, 218
  summary, 318
  working with partners, 219–20
Prusak, L., 17n, 106, 131
public goods, 316
public pressure, 345
Putnam, R.D., 4, 5, 17n, 92, 93, 94, 96, 97, 100, 120n, 121n, 136–7

Reck, J., 301n
Redlener, Irwin, 274
Rees, H., *see* Pettifor, A.
Referral Management Initiative (RMI)/Children's Health Fund (CHF), 273–6
  evaluation, 276
  evidence of sustainability, 276
  inputs from GSK, 275
  outcomes, 276
  outline, 274–5
  social capital aspects, 279
  startup, 273–4
  summary, 320
  working with partners, 275
regulatory pressure, 345
Reid, D., 302n
Reinke, J., 117
Reisel, W.D., 113
relational problem, projects responding to
  limitations, 326–7
  success factors, 325–6
reputation building, 329
rhetoric and reality gap, 324
Richmond Business Unit (RBU), 15, 243
  evaluation, 247
  evidence of sustainability, 247
  inputs from Mondi, 246–7
  outline, 243–6
  social capital aspects, 252–3
  startup, 243
  summary, 319
  working with partners, 246
Roberts, J., *see* Kreps, D.
Robey, J.S., 114, 122n
Rodmell, G., 17n
Rogovsky, N., *see* Hess, D.
Rose, R., 131, 132–3, 171n
Roth, K., 109
Rotstein, F., 109
Running Business Today, 290
Rutherford, M.A., *see* Buchholtz, A.K.
Rynes, S.L., *see* Orlitzky, M.

Sabatini, F., 121n
Sacerdote, B., 98, 100
Saiia, D.H., 33
Sarin, Arun, 283
Sato, M., 97, 99, 120n
Save the Children, 334
  see also Oxfam, 58, 262, 279n
Scheinkman, J.A., *see* Glaesar, E.L., 104

Index 357

Schlumberger, 141–2
Schlumberger Excellence in
    Educational Development, see
    SEED
Schmidt, F.L., see Orlitzky, M.
Schuller, T., 120n
scope, of social capital, 12, 94, 99,
    253, 278, 312
Seagram spirits, 199
SEAT
    adoption, 236
    aims, 235
    Hippo Valley Estates (HVE) Ltd,
        236–7
    implementation, 235
    Mondi Business Paper (MBP), 237
    New Denmark Colliery, 237
    partnership development, 236
    Richmond Business Unit (RBU),
        243
    stages, 235
'secondary' social capital, 176
SEED, 141–2
SENAC (Servicio Nacional de
    Aprendizaje Comercial), 219
Senac Brazil, 221
Serageldin, I., 96
Sethi, R., 97
Shell, 111, 112, 194, 228
Shell Foundation, 339, 345n
Sherif, C., see Sherif, M.
Sherif, M., 121n
Shleifer, A., see La Porta, R.F.
Shumulyar, 114
Shutte, A., 122n
Siegfried, J.J., 46n
Simon, P., 274
Skytyvkar, 228
Slack, R., 17n, 33
Smirnoff, 199
social capital, 1, 4, 8–9, 90, 92–6, 106
    benefits versus expenditure, 336
    channel, 12, 40, 94, 100, 109, 312
    cognitive forms, 99
    company investment, 96
    and Corporate Citizenship projects,
        4–5, 98–100
    economists, 97
    for economic development, 96–8

    external relationships, 337
    and firms, 105–9
    form, 12, 94, 95, 99, 253, 277, 312
    Game Theory, 96–7
    indirect effects, 96
    investment, 97–8
    measures, 100–5, 131
        of Grootaert, 135–6
        of Knack and Keefer, 133
        of MHM, 134–5
        of Narayan and Pritchett, 133–4
        of Putnam, 136–7
        of Rose, 132–3
    in Mexico, 114–15
    and multinationals, 109–13
    in Poland, 113–14, 175
    projects and networks of
        relationships, 337
    scope, 12, 94, 99, 253, 278, 312
    in South Africa, 115–19
    structural forms, 99–100
    as tool of evaluation and reporting,
        341–3
    universal standard of measure,
        336–7
Social Capital and Poverty Survey,
    133
Social Capital Index (SCI), 136, 137
social norms, 92, 93, 97, 102
Social Products and Enterprise Team,
    287–8
social relations, 95
SocialFunds.com, 55
Socially Responsible Investment, 55–6
society dependence, 315
Solidarity, 175
Somanathan, E., 97
South Africa, 69–70, 115–19, 174,
    197, 227, 233, 238
    AIDS awareness in, 116, 118
    Black Economic Empowerment
        (BEE), 116
    community development in, 112
    environmental racism, 118
    multinationals and community
        engagement, 129
    social capital, 115–19
    UK multinationals in, 145–53,
        167–8

SouthAfrica.Info, 70
Soutter, C.L., *see* Glaesar, E.L., 104
SRI World Group Inc., 54–5
Stachowicz, J., 113
Statoil, 112
Steffenson, A., *see* Pettifor, A.
Stimson, R., 121n
Stopford, J.M., 90
Stout, D., 275
Strange, S., 90
strategic nature, of industry, 328
Sturrock and Robson, 242
Stutterheim Local Economic
    Development Initiative, 117
Sunday Times, 78, 79
sustainability, 209, 213, 216, 221,
    243, 247, 250, 269, 273, 276,
    292, 295, 298, 311, 324,
    326
Svendsen, G.L.H., Chloupkova, J.
Svendsen, G.T., 121n
    see also Chloupkova, J.
Sweden firms, 191
Switzerland, 227

Tanqueray, 199
Tanzer, J., *see* Hempel, J.
Tarmac plc, 228
Télécoms Sans Frontières (TSF), after
    2004 Tsunami, 306
  evaluation, 298
  evidence of sustainability, 298
  inputs from Vodafone, 298
  outcomes, 297–8
  outline, 296–7
  social capital aspects, 300–1
  startup, 296
  summary, 320
  working with partners, 297
TheTimes100.co.uk, 235
Tolbert, C.M., 105
Tomorrow's People, 14, 201 202, 205,
    206–9, 219, 220
  evaluation, 209
  evidence of sustainability, 209
  inputs from Diageo, 208
  outcomes, 208–9
  outline, 206–7
  social capital aspects, 222

startup, 206
summary, 318
working with partners, 207–8
top-down social capital, 175
Trahar, T., 256n
trust, 92, 93, 96, 97, 102, 104, 113
Trust Game, 104, 104–5
trustworthiness, 97, 104
Tsai, W., 106, 110
Tshikululu Social Investments (TSI),
    235
Tuffrey, M., 108

ubuntu, 116
UK, 1, 228
  corporate citizenship in, 63–8
UK firms, 191, 195
  in South Africa
    network engagement scores,
      econometric analysis of,
      167–8
    survey findings, 145–53
UN, 17n, 311, 314
UNCTAD, 2–3, 17n
UNEP DTIE, 81
unglobalcompact.org, 46n
Unilever, 3
unreliability of partners, 322
US firms in Mexico, 153–66, 168–70
  network engagement scores,
    econometric analysis of,
    168–70
  survey findings, 153–66
USA, 1
  corporate citizenship in, 60–3
Utting, P., 24

Van Bastelear, T., 17n, 94, 99, 122n
Van Deth, J.W., 103
Van Gelecun, Y., 121n
Vermaak, A., *see* Pettifor, A.
Vishny, R., *see* La Porta, R.F.
Vivendi, 199
Vodacom Community Phone Shops
  evaluation, 292
  evidence of sustainability, 292
  inputs from Vodacom, 291
  outcomes, 291–2
  outline, 290–1

social capital aspects, 298
startup, 289
summary, 320
working with partners, 291
Vodafone Group, 15
corporate biography, 282–3
corporate citizenship, strategy and management, 283–5
Opportunity International (OI), 293–6
social aspects, 299–300
reporting, 288–9
social investment, 285–8
Télécoms Sans Frontières (TSF) supports, after 2004 Tsunami, 296–8
social aspects, 300–1
Vodacom community phone shops, 289–92
social aspects, 299
Volkswagen, 71
voluntary best practice, 6
voluntary group response, 6
voluntary initiatives, 93
volunteerism, 115
Volvo AB, 23
VSO, see Oxfam, 58, 262, 279n

Waldstrom, C., 120n
Walesa, Lech, 175
Wallace, C., 114
Wallace, J., 218
Walsh, J.P., 107, 122n
Walsh, P., 210
Walukiewicz, S., 113
Ward, H., 30
Wasserman, S., 121n
Water and Sanitation, 25
Water of Life, 204, 213, 217
Waterlow Directory of Multinationals, 144
WBCSD, 314, 320, 332n
wealth, 102
Weedon, C., 16n
Western, J., 121n
Westlund, H., 106

Westpac Banking Corporation, 23
Weyzig, F., 261, 266
White, B., *see* Sherif, M.
Wikipedia, 69, 70, 71, 72, 73, 282, 301n
Williams, C., 60, 83
Wilson, R., *see* Kreps, D.
Wod, B., 301n
Woolcock, M., 4, 94, 130–1
Working it Out, 207, 209
World Bank, 73
World Business Council for Sustainable Development (WBCSD), 17n, 241, 301n
World Economic Forum, 26, 90, 120n
World Health Assembly, 269
World Summit on Sustainable Development, 229
World Values Survey (WVS), 101, 103, 133
World Vision, 294
Worldcom, 91

Young, R., *see* Fernandez-Young, A.
Youth Business, 213
Youth Business Initiative (YBI), 210–13
evaluation, 213
evidence of sustainability, 213
inputs from Diageo, 211
outcomes, 211–13
outline, 210–11
social capital aspects, 222–3
startup, 210
summary, 318
working with partners, 211
Youth Business International, 14
Youth Development Bonds (YDBs), 212
Youth Employment Network (YEN), 210, 212
youth initiatives, 187

Zadek, S., 26, 46n, 106–7, 110, 122n
Zaheer, S., 110
Zimele, *see* Anglo Zimele Empowerment Initiative Ltd
Zinkin, J., 90